INDUSTRIAL RELATIONS RESEARCH ASSOCIATION SERIES

Industrial Relations Research in the 1970s: Review and Appraisal

AUTHORS

THOMAS A. BAROCCI
JEANNE M. BRETT
LEE DYER
ROBERT J. FLANAGAN
JONATHAN GROSSMAN
TOVE HELLAND HAMMER
HERVEY A. JURIS
THOMAS A. KOCHAN
DANIEL J. B. MITCHELL
OLIVIA S. MITCHELL
WILLIAM T. MOYE
MYRON J. ROOMKIN
DONALD P. SCHWAB
JAMES G. SCOVILLE

EDITORIAL BOARD

First Edition

Library of Congress Catalog Card Number 82-082857

Price $15.00

INDUSTRIAL RELATIONS RESEARCH ASSOCIATION SERIES

PROCEEDINGS OF THE ANNUAL MEETING (Spring Publication)

PROCEEDINGS OF THE SPRING MEETING (Fall Publication)

Annual Research Volume (Fall Publication)
(MEMBERSHIP DIRECTORY every sixth year in lieu of research volume)

IRRA NEWSLETTER (Quarterly)

INDUSTRIAL RELATIONS RESEARCH ASSOCIATION
7226 Social Science Building, University of Wisconsin
Madison, WI 53706 U.S.A. Telephone 608/262-2762

Pantagraph Printing, 217 W. Jefferson, Bloomington, IL 61701

CONTENTS

Preface

It has been approximately ten years since an IRRA volume was devoted to a review of research in the various components of the field. It was fitting, therefore, for the Executive Board to choose this as the theme for the 1982 volume. Any such review must be selective rather than exhaustive and must choose an approach that is geared to the needs of the research community. Our approach was to ask active contributors to research in the 1970s to review critically and appraise industrial relations research conducted in their areas and to draw implications for the directions that future work might take. The authors were not asked to provide a comprehensive catalog of all topics, authors, and works published in their areas during this period. Rather they were encouraged to stress the major developments in theory, research methodology, and applications of research findings in public policy or private practice. Ample space was allocated to the bibliographies found at the end of each chapter since we believe that these can be helpful to students and veteran researchers alike.

We wish to thank our fellow authors for agreeing to undertake, and for completing in fine fashion, the awesome task of taking stock of the field. We also wish to thank Barbara Dennis for once again performing her invaluable function for the IRRA of shaping a pile of documents into a final manuscript and seeing the whole works through to publication.

THE EDITORS

CHAPTER 1

A Review of International and Comparative Research in the 1970s*

JAMES G. SCOVILLE
University of Minnesota

I. Introduction

The purpose of this chapter is to review the breadth, depth, and general strength of international and comparative research conducted in North America during the 1970s, with an occasional look at work being done elsewhere. This purpose, laid down by the editors of this volume, stands in some contrast to the purpose apparently behind the last such review. In the 1971 research volume, John Crispo reviewed all industrial relations research on Canada and Western Europe, by whomever done (Crispo 1971). What developments may account for this change of focus?

Let me suggest that the editors chose this new vantage point to underscore the serious problems they perceive in the stature of international/comparative research as a subfield of our profession capable of attracting new, young scholars. For instance, at the Denver IRRA meetings in 1980, there was a star-studded panel on international developments which attracted a crowd of perhaps 100 people: only two of these people (as far as I could see) were under the age of 40. Also, I have been told by numerous assistant professors that they simply cannot enter the international field as the payoff is too uncertain and too far down the road. Such indicators could suggest that the new vantage point will help to emphasize the hard times upon which this area has fallen.

* The support of the Industrial Relations Center and the School of Management, University of Minnesota, is gratefully acknowledged. This support provided the services of two indefatigable research assistants, Kirsten Ingerson and Rhonda Kriss, who developed the bibliographic materials from which this essay was written. Without their help, this task would have been beyond the realm of feasibility. I am also indebted to Oliver Clarke, Walter Galenson, O. J. Scoville, Koji Taira, Morris Weisz, and John Windmuller for thoughtful comments on earlier drafts.

II. Trends and Cycles in International/Comparative Research, 1960–1980

The tables and figure that follow show the quantity of international and comparative research published in the three North American scholarly periodicals with the greatest prestige and the broadest scope of inquiry in the industrial relations field, and which are likely to reflect the shifting focal concerns of the field: *Industrial and Labor Relations Review, Industrial Relations,* and the *Proceedings of the Industrial Relations Research Association.* It is to be noted that the data apply to three conceptually distinct kinds of publication: those which are international in nature (a study of the Soviet wage system), those which are comparative (efficacy and costs of disputes settlement procedures in France, Germany, and the U.S.), and those which are international to a U.S. reader but domestic to a Canadian writer or reader. This latter group of writings, including the few U.S.-Canadian comparative studies, are separated out from the rest of the material for reasons that will shortly become clear.

A word about classification of the journal materials, as carried out by the author and his assistants, is in order. While it was usually pretty obvious that an article is "international" in nature, because it dealt with a particular issue or problem in a specified country, tougher cases do crop up with respect to "comparative" material. Clearly, a single footnote referring to Otto von Bismarck does not make an article on the U.S. social security system into a piece of comparative research. Generally speaking, articles needed to have something on the order of half their content devoted to international comparisons for us to class them as comparative. The hardest cases could be exemplified by a number of the articles in early issues of *Industrial Relations* (the May 1962 issue, for example), in which relatively few explicit comparative references might be made, but where the whole article was cast in a thoroughly comparative mold.[1]

Table 1 shows the number of pages in each publication, year-by-year, devoted to articles, research notes, communications, pres-

[1] In the particular case of the May 1962 issue, a very conservative approach was followed: None of the articles was classed as comparative. Thus the trends and cycles in the data are possibly understated, but are certainly not a result of overly liberal classification in the early years of *Industrial Relations.*

TABLE 1

Pages Published in Core Industrial Relations Periodicals

	ILRR			Industrial Rels.			IRRA			All Three			Percentages	
	Canada-Related	Intl/Comp.	Total	Canada-Related	Intl/Comp.	Total	Canada-Related	Intl/Comp.	Total	Canada-Related	Intl/Comp.	Total	Intl/Comp. All	Except Canada-Related
1960	0	123	431	—	—	—	0	47	297	0	170	738	23.4	23.4
1961	0	124	412	0	62	136	0	0	425	0	186	973	19.1	19.1
1962	0	89	402	0	44	344	4	64	345	4	196	1091	18.0	17.7
1963	0	82	442	0	138	414	0	42	268	0	262	1124	23.3	23.3
1964	0	100	436	0	49	365	0	121	307	0	270	1108	24.4	24.4
1965	0	47	413	0	134	401	0	0	354	0	181	1168	15.5	15.5
1966	0	51	396	0	45	352	0	49	375	0	145	1123	12.9	12.9
1967	0	46	441	0	122	323	0	46	394	0	214	1158	18.5	18.5
1968	0	64	411	0	58	300	0	22	392	0	144	1103	13.1	13.1
1969	13	108	413	0	35	283	0	60	343	13	203	1039	19.5	18.3
1970	8	64	384	16	128	478	0	9	383	33	201	1245	16.1	13.5
1971	0	47	442	0	51	361	0	38	417	0	136	1220	11.1	11.1
1972	28	90	355	14	78	421	112	133	454	154	301	1230	24.5	12.0
1973	16	75	371	0	147	353	0	19	284	16	241	1008	23.9	22.3
1974	0	86	453	0	66	334	7	33	365	7	185	1152	16.1	15.5
1975	0	120	377	21	113	374	9	41	281	30	274	1039	26.4	23.5
1976	11	27	368	18	22	359	32	61	355	61	110	1082	10.2	4.5
1977	20	48	375	6	46	365	9	68	450	35	162	1190	13.6	10.7
1978	0	0	358	18	59	368	8	8	335	26	67	1061	6.3	3.9
1979	19	37	387	17	134	363	8	44	373	43	215	1123	19.1	15.3
1980	0	16	412	76	99	372	0	28	338	76	143	1122	12.7	6.0
1981	21	52	419	0	52	347	8(e)	32(e)	348(e)	29(e)	136(e)	1114(e)	12.2(e)	9.6(e)

(e) Based on average number of pages in IRRA Proceedings in previous three years and the number of international papers (4, of which 1 is Canada-related) in proportion to the 43 papers listed in the program for December 1981 IRRA meetings.

idential addresses, and the like (excluding book reviews, reports of meetings, etc.). Also shown are the number of pages given over to international and comparative topics and, of that total, the number of pages covering Canada, either by itself or in a comparative fashion. Proportions of space given to international/comparative, with and without the contributions on Canada, are also shown; these proportions are also depicted in Figure 1, which makes more obvious the trends and cycles in the level of activity.

Focusing our attention on the Figure, let us consider the situation at the beginning of the period under consideration. The last years of the 1950s were a period of highly significant international and comparative research activity, perhaps exemplified best by that enormous enterprise, the Four Horsemen's Inter-University Study (Kerr et al. 1960).[2] As can be seen from the Figure, this boom continued into the 1960s, and then encountered a general down-trend. In all, the following periods seem to stand out from the Figure:

Period	*International/ Comparative Pages*	*Total Pages*	*Percent*
1. Boom, 1960–1964	1094	5074	21.6
2. Recession, 1965–1972	1525	9286	16.4
3. Revival, 1973–1976	700	3199	21.9
4. Depression, 1976–1978	399	3333	10.2
5. Revival (?), 1979–	494(e)	3359(e)	14.7(e)

(e) Partially estimated, see Table 1.

Breaking up the data into these five periods underscores the rather sad shape of the international/comparative field in recent years, if levels of publication in the core journals can be taken as any sort of index.[3] Recent levels of activity in the field are less than half what they used to be, although there is perhaps some evidence of a revival of interest as the 1980s begin. Maybe the assistant professors cited earlier who saw no payoff to interna-

[2] See Dunlop et al. (1975) for a listing of the research output of the Study.

[3] These figures may overstate the real decline, as the *Comparative Labor Law Journal* was founded in the seventies, publishing some materials which could have gone into the three publications surveyed.

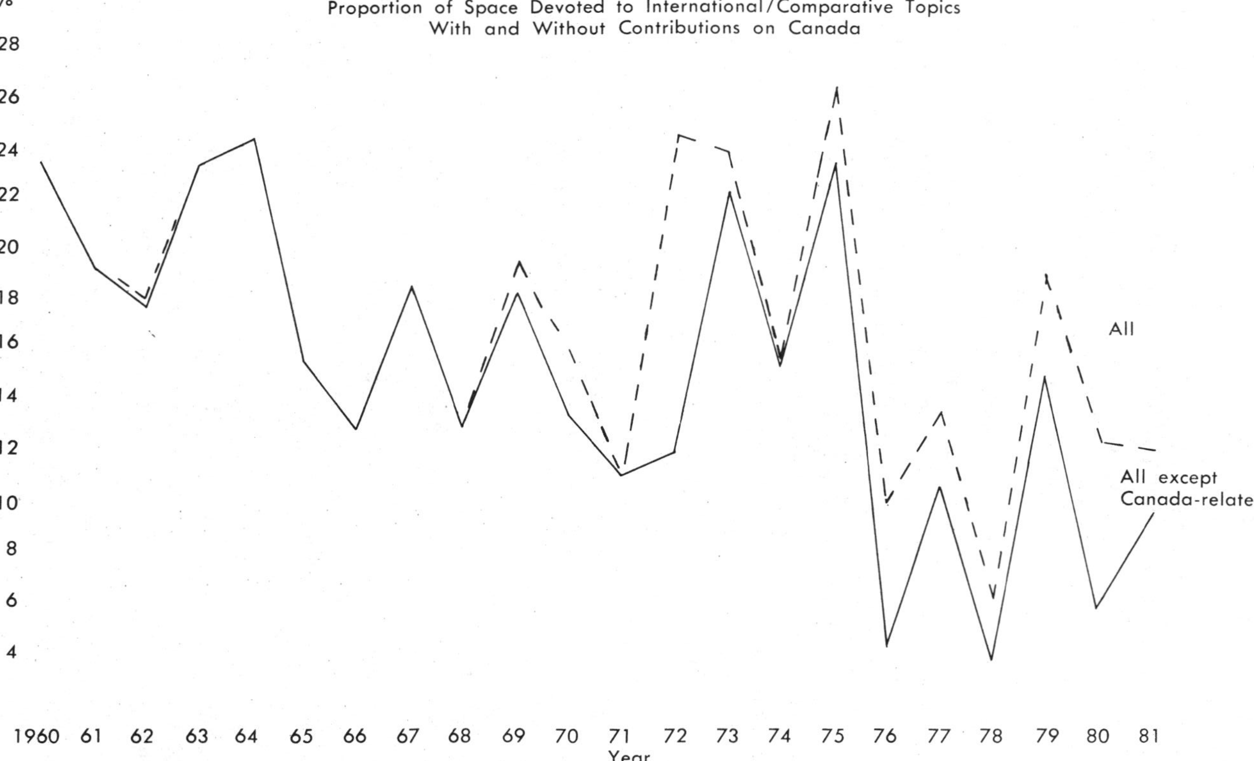
%
Proportion of Space Devoted to International/Comparative Topics
With and Without Contributions on Canada
28
26
24
22
20
18
16
14
12
10
8
6
4
All
All except
Canada-related
1960 61 62 63 64 65 66 67 68 69 70 71 72 73 74 75 76 77 78 79 80 81
Year

tional/comparative work had some basis in fact for this contention.

For those who collect trivia or minutiae, the breakdown also reveals the curiosity that the first great slump in activity on the international front is coterminous with the Vietnam War; this is perhaps the most astounding discovery since sunspot theories!

Some idea of the dynamics of these trends and cycles can be obtained by looking at the data for each publication separately for each of the subperiods. Such an examination reveals interesting differences in the paths of the various publications. International/comparative interest at the IRRA meetings collapsed at the end of the early sixties boom and never recovered. Interest in the subject at Ithaca may possibly have died at the end of the mid-1970s revival. Only the Berkeley journal seems as strongly committed to international/comparative as it was at its inception.

Perhaps the most startling piece of data in Table 1 is the recency of the appearance of publications on Canada. I was really not prepared for the fact that only 17 pages on Canadian industrial relations appeared in all three publications in the entire decade of the sixties. By contrast, 112 pages on Canada appeared in the 1972 IRRA Proceedings alone (one does observe that those meetings were held in Toronto). Our Canadian colleagues appear —along with their subject matter—to be getting more and more integrated into our journals, professional association, and professional life.[4]

In spite of the generally healthy improvement in treatment of subjects Canadian, it remains true that growth here has by no means offset declines in international/comparative research on the rest of the world. To what factors might the trend be attributed? A very large number of possibilities exist for the culprit's role, and here are some of the ones that figure prominently in my thinking. First, the fact that the field has seemed to be dominated by a group of "grand old men" may both have restricted entry by young people and be generating a falling-off of apparent productivity as this group ages and either retires or publishes more books and

[4] The virtual absence of writing about our northern neighbor during the sixties is still the case today with respect to our neighbor to the south. I have not done separate tabulations, but the number of pieces on Mexico during the past two decades is less than a handful. Some offset to this neglect in the journals is offered by Meyers (1979).

fewer journal pieces. Second, the virtual extinction of any foreign language capability among graduate students and young scholars in the industrial relations field and its related disciplines must reduce the capacity to do basic research, at least somewhat, and may reduce interest in different societies and cultures as well. Third, the rise in the commitment to quantitative methods in research and the use of such research as a test for promotion and tenure in "quality" departments may mean that problems of working in other countries with poorer data, better hidden data, or just plain different data keep young people out of the field. A fourth, more benign, explanation might suggest that the size and importance of domestic issues and research problems (for example, discrimination, illegal immigrants, women's labor force participation) have grown relative to those of international/comparative topics, whose greatest importance may well have been perceived to be part of the now generally discredited search for a "general theory of industrial relations." However one comes out on evaluation of the various factors, it is clear that there is no shortage of strong candidates for villain of the piece.

III. A Review of Research for Various Areas of Industrial Relations

In this section of the chapter, we will review some of the key research in terms of the issues and problems addressed, and perhaps conclusions reached, in half a dozen major areas of comparative industrial relations research during the decade. The review focuses on the areas of (1) industrial conflict, (2) the theory of the labor movement, (3) workers' participation, (4) the role of labor in economic development, (5) some seven subareas of labor markets, and (6) the growth of multinational organizations of capital and labor. Such a layout of the work adds to the traditional concerns with comparative labor movements and labor relations the related problems in areas of labor economics, such as incomes policy, discrimination, or wage differentials. Thus, this review seeks to parallel in its content a very broad, but still loosely integrated, stream of research.

Industrial Conflict

It is arguable that the most important comparative contribution to the industrial conflict literature during the decade was Shorter and Tilly (1974). For many, its significance comes in reminding us of the differences in forms, purposes, and meanings of the various types of social conflict, for indeed in France (and elsewhere) the strike is not simply a method of industrial conflict. Shorter and Tilly's unfinished agenda thus included a full survey of acts of civil commotion as well as strikes. However, when considering only strikes, they reminded us that strikes differ between countries in their "shapes": typical size, length, and frequency. This has been a course of further fruitful research in itself. Two major lines of argument emerged from Shorter and Tilly's meticulous digging into the French strike record. First, they noted the changing shapes of the strike in France and linked this to changes in the organizations and institutions of the economy and the labor market. Second, they advanced the argument that French strikes were primarily to be explained by political factors. Their view on this—"Workers, when they strike, are merely extending into the streets their normal processes of political participation" (Shorter and Tilly 1974)—is similar to that of Sellier (1973) where the efficacy of political actions is also stressed. Both Shorter and Tilly and Sellier focus on how this came to be the "normal process" in France.

Perhaps Shorter and Tilly's greatest contribution, though, was to stand in contrast to the work of Hibbs (1976), who subjected their strike shapes to econometric analysis, which yielded interesting results but entirely suppressed the qualitative differences among nations.

In connection with the discussion of differences in the meaning and role of strikes in various societies, I would award the Grand Prize for the decade's best title to Michael Shalev for "Lies, Damn Lies, and Strike Statistics," the only contribution by a U.S.-based scholar (at that time) to Crouch and Pizzorno (1978). His discussion of the subject stressed technical problems of measurement, reliability, and intranational (as well as international) comparability. It is a useful and sobering review although, given the title of his essay, readers might be ill-prepared for his conclusion that these data can be quite useful, even in comparative analysis.

An exploration of the reasons for the differences in underlying political, social, and industrial relations structures and processes which affect the purposes and level of strikes is found in Kassalow

(1977). His task is to explain the apparent paradox that industrial conflict is so much higher in the U.S., where the labor movement fundamentally accepts the social and economic order of things, than in Europe where labor has traditionally rejected "capitalism." Kassalow identifies a number of "purely industrial relations factors"—bargaining structure, employers' view of unions, the more direct role of the state—in tending to lower levels of conflict in Europe.

Shorter and Tilly, along with a great deal of the foreign literature (for example, Dubois 1976), insisted to American scholars that industrial conflict could embrace a wider variety of forms of action than just the strike—that not only sabotage, but absenteeism, quits, self-injury, and so on might well constitute ways of expressing your "voice" to the boss (using Freeman's (1976) adaptation of Hirschman). One treatment of this subject, including the suggestion that there may be (technologically based) trade-offs between forms of conflict, is found in Levine and Taira (1977). One interesting result of the recognition of nonstrike forms of conflict is to discredit the standard picture of harmony in Japanese industrial relations: Japan stands at about the middle of the league in their broad international comparisons of levels of total conflict.

Perhaps from an awareness of data deficiencies, or perhaps from other causes, few authors have followed the lead of Hibbs in estimating formal equations for the dimensions of strikes emphasized by Shorter and Tilly. Hibbs's work stressed the importance of economic (labor market, price, etc.) variables and political variables in explaining movements of strike activity in the postwar period in a pooled sample of western industrial countries. One of the problems with this analysis, however, is that the coefficients on some of his variables (such as the proportion of socialist cabinet members) as well as the specific country intercept terms are themselves partly influenced by political factors. This makes generalizations outside of the specific political context of each country quite difficult. Other quantitative studies were not so ambitious: Vanderkamp (1970) looked only at a time-loss measure; Sapsford (1975) looked at frequency. Both studies supported the influences of economic variables on measures of industrial conflict.

Two studies did look at all three of the Shorter-Tilly dimensions. Walsh (1975) fitted equations to the Canadian data which gave some limited support to the influence of economic variables on the dimensions of strike activity although the meaning of the results, for example, for strike duration in relation to profits seems unclear or subject to alternative explanation. In passing, it should be noted that both the Hibbs and the Walsh studies are single equation models; in a world where both employers' and workers' bargaining powers are changing in response to conditions, simultaneous models would no doubt be more appropriate.

While most comparative strike research has been limited to nations in advanced stages of development, Scoville (1979) applied a largely economic model to strike activity in five mostly less-developed countries of Southeast Asia. The central focus of the model was on shifts in the state of the labor market on workers' and employers' positions and, hence, on changes in the three Shorter-Tilly dimensions of strike activity. The use of the four possible changes in the state of the labor market (dominant demand increase, . . . , dominant supply decrease) is probably the key input to modeling industrial conflict. The results showed that frequency was procyclical, duration countercyclical; size was treated as exogenous.[5]

The foregoing discussion has focused on the meaning and shape of conflict, and on the emerging empirical study of its determinants. Although this seems to be the area of the hottest current development, it should not be forgotten that major contributions were made in other, more conventional areas of comparative research such as studies of conflict and the law (Aaron and Wedderburn 1972) or of conflict resolution (Aaron, 1971, 1979).

In the coming decade, I would expect research on all these topics to continue. The sociologists and economists will continue to explore the meaning and econometrics, respectively, of the strike. Meanwhile, policy-oriented scholars will be looking abroad for new wrinkles in dispute resolution and the shaping and controlling of conflict through law.

---

[5] We note in passing the subsequent speculative follow-up, this time with no data at all, but perhaps the worst title of the decade; see Scoville, "Crucial Factors in the Evolution of Industrial Relations: The Choice of Development Models and the Potentials for Bargaining and Conflict," IIRA Vth Congress, September 1979.

The Theory of the Labor Movement

Cart-before-the-horse or not, the end of a discussion of industrial conflict serves as a good way to begin a review of the decade's developments on a broad stream of topics which comprise the major parts of the theory of the labor movement. What is the labor movement all about? Who are the principal "actors," and what are the relationships between them? As Shalev and Shorter and Tilly pointed out, we have to obtain some understanding of these issues before we know what strike behavior, above all, is really about.

North American scholars addressed themselves to these issues in a variety of ways. There were a number of excellent studies of specific national experiences, for example, Weimar Germany (Braunthal 1978), the U.S.S.R. (Kahan and Ruble 1979), or Dubcek's Czechoslovakia (Windmuller 1975), and an analysis of the appropriate form of union organization most likely to be able to influence national economic policy (Barbash 1972). All these are important building blocks for our understanding of how industrial relations systems are shaped and how they evolve. However, I wish to focus in this section on some more general discussions of what has happened or is happening to the goals and methods of labor, and why.

We can recall Kerr et al.'s (1960)[6] comparison of their fundamental assumption about industrial conflict in contrast with the Marxian notions of class conflict. They spoke of the inevitable conflict between the managed and the managers in a setting of industrial employment. Hence, conflict was not a result of the social system, in particular the arrangements for the private ownership of the means of production that we loosely call capitalism; conflict of the same sort would appear under a socialist, communist, or almost any social-industrial system save one founded on the purest altruism. One can think, for example, of workers at a textile factory in Minneapolis, Minsk, Beijing or Zagreb being sent home at the start of their shift due to an accident at the local

[6] The only major conflict between the author and the editors has been over references to Kerr, Dunlop, Harbison, and Myers as "the Four Horsemen." The editors assure me that whole generations of students of industrial relations have arisen who have never heard the term applied to these scholars. With regret, I concede this may be true; I must, however, take this occasion to note the passing of the expression from usage.

power plant which forced their employer to shut down. The issue—how much pay do I get for showing up?—will have to be faced in each instance, and the way it is faced will have a great deal to do with the continuing relationship between the workers and their employers. "The industrial relations system everywhere has its managers, its managed and a pattern of interaction between them" (Kerr et al. 1960).

Such a formulation constitutes the starting point for one of the decade's major reviews of the progress of industrial relations systems and of the labor movements that are part of them. Dunlop and Galenson (1978) must, in spite of the fact that four-fifths of the chapters are by foreign scholars, be regarded as part of the American literature; certainly the tone of Dunlop's introduction fits into that tradition. Dunlop quotes Kerr et al.'s dictum on the managers and the managed, and then concludes (in words that would comfort all Perlmanites): "Everywhere, collective bargaining . . . has become an established institution. . . ." This is modified by recognition that, in the words of Sidney and Beatrice Webb, "The method of legal enactment is an increasing alternative to the method of collective bargaining" (Dunlop and Galenson 1978). The factors behind these developments in the five major industrial democracies (U.S., U.K., F.R.G., France, and Japan) are then explored in the balance of the book. Chapter-by-chapter, data on hours of work, wages, labor force participation, conflict, and so on are marshalled to support the book's opening conclusion: "A reader of this volume must conclude that the twentieth century is likely to be known as the century of the *worker* or of the *employee* in advanced democratic societies. Unprecedented improvements in the living standards, social status, economic security, political power, and influence of industrial workers have occurred in this century" (Dunlop and Galenson 1978).

The role of economic conditions, and in particular the unprecedented burst of productivity that has been the hallmark and legacy of the Industrial Revolution, are stressed in these analyses. Such economic conditions, with special reference to the long-run state of the market, along with the social and political status of the working classes, are among the key variables stressed in work by Sturmthal (1972) and Sturmthal and Scoville (1973). I shall leave it to the reader to determine whether "certainly international comparative methodology should vastly improve as a result of this [latter] provocative volume" (Levine 1977), or whether the book merely proves that "ethnocentrism dies hard" (Blum 1976). Sturmthal and Scoville also stressed the rather narrow range of circumstances in which "free collective bargaining" can exist, thus paralleling the Dunlopian conclusion about the various forms of "legal enactment," including, in their case, wage-price policy along with more traditional policies.

The Dunlop-Galenson volume focused on the twentieth century explicitly; Sturmthal and Scoville contributors picked the long haul or the short, according to the topic, country, or period they wished to study. Recent developments were the focus of Barkin (1975). This edited collection reflected a concern with the perceived upsurge of industrial conflict and radical rhetoric in the period under study. Once again, a major variable in the analysis centers on aspects of the labor market: younger workers altering the demography of the supply side, technological change reducing the content and security of the job on the demand side. The result is dissatisfaction with "capitalism" and sometimes with the unions, although this dissatisfaction appeared to the editor to have been transitory.

The class-oriented analysts were not without their entries in the lists, although the two strongest volumes are almost 100 percent of foreign manufacture. Korpi (1978) maintains that private ownership of the means of production sets up the class lines in a capitalist society and provides the basis for conflict groupings. Therefore, it is the 44-year reign of the Social Democrats as a class-based party that is important to the working class, and not so much the powerful LO-SAF bargaining arrangements that we often tend to study. It is, however, cross-class issues that seem to Korpi to make the swing that determines whether labor will hold political power.

The other key study has already been referred to: Crouch and Pizzorno's two-volume edited work on the "resurgence of class conflict since 1968." Their collection was stimulated by the assumption that "institutionalized conflict" was in trouble at both plant and national levels of industrial relations (Crouch and Pizzorno 1978). Volume I thus focused largely on local, "spontaneous" activity, while Volume II was centered on national or other aggregates. Basing his arguments on a theory of "political exchange," Pizzorno perhaps summarized the whole thrust of the study: "Through the analyses carried out in the various papers of our two volumes, it is possible to see how the differences in form and content of conflict and in the policy of unions and governments are a function of the degree of control of new entries to the political market and of the degree of dispersion of power within the system of the representation of labor" (Crouch and Pizzorno 1978).

I mentioned the Korpi and Crouch-Pizzorno studies in such detail because they make up for a substantive gap in the American literature. Nothing as good has appeared from strictly American authors. So much for the theory of the labor movements in developed countries.

A second principal area of study relating to labor and economic development focused on the role of the labor movement in policy formulation and implementation with respect to the development process. Here again the pile of cards culled from the book reviews in North American industrial relations journals is relatively thin, and a fair number of cards relate to reviews of works by foreign scholars—for example, the works of Ananaba (1979) and Damachi (1974) on various African countries, which (although published in the U.S.) are clearly foreign contributions to the debate. A few titles do come to mind, though, relating to unions and development: Bates (1971), Schlagheck (1977), and from a rather confining viewpoint, Spalding (1977). In general, this literature leaves me pessimistic about the emergence of widespread bargaining institutions in the developing areas, and unsure in many cases how "real" labor's political participation is.

When we turn from the issues of labor in developing societies to more general considerations about the theory of the labor movement, we see at least two key areas of evolution that have significant impacts on the direction, orientation, and activity of the labor movement. The first area focuses on the changing relationships between what Europeans call the "industrial arm of the labor movement" and the "political arm," that is, loosely speaking, between the trade unions and the political party or parties. In recent years, this evolution would appear to have been dominated by shifts in the strategies of popular appeal adopted by the parties.

The second major influential area of evolution that will affect the nature and interests of the labor movement comes from changes in the structure of employment and, hence, in the balance among the various occupational and industrial groups which are organized into trade unions.

Both of these subjects have attracted a fair amount of attention in American industrial relations research, at least judging from occasional outbursts of interest. The first area of union-party relations, for example, has its "literature" dominated by a single big wave: a two-part symposium in the *Industrial and Labor Relations Review* in the middle of the decade (Windmuller, ed., 1974–1975). This symposium features articles on Sweden (Nils Elvander), Norway (Penny Gill Martin), Britain (Lewis Minkin), Germany (Richard Willey) in October 1974, and on Belgium (Val Lorwin), France (Jean-Daniel Reynaud), Switzerland (Jürg Siegenthaler), and Italy (Peter Weitz) in January 1975. On the whole, the impression one gets from these generally first-class country papers includes the following general trends: a trend toward greater separation between the two arms of the labor movement, often accompanied by explicit moves on the part of the political arm to divest itself of its "cloth cap image" (in the case of the British Labour Party) or to become a popular as opposed to a working-class party (as with the German Social Democrats). There are moves toward unification of competing trade union organizations (as in Italy and the Netherlands in years more recent than the symposium) or on the party side (off and on in France). Weinberg (1978) also notes the weakening ideological divisions as part of the response to multinational corporations. Galenson (1977) observed the moves by Scandinavian labor parties and unions away from some of their social goals and toward greater private consumption and lower taxes. There were some moves, in response to the emerging spirit of East-West detente, toward trade union contacts of a truly pan-European nature (Windmuller 1976a, 1976b), although a visit to the U.K. by the general secretary of the Soviet Union Federation produced an uproarious reaction to his previous background in police work! What is quite striking in all of this, as John Windmuller noted in his introduction to Part II of the Symposium, "is the relatively greater importance of the unions than the parties as initiators of social and economic reform ideas. This is something of a reversal of historic roles" (Windmuller, ed., 1974–1975). Against a backdrop of less laboristically-oriented parties and generally less politically-oriented unions, the industrial and occupational diversity of the trade union movement provides such occasional "niches" as exist for proponents of greater industrial and economic democracy (as in Sweden), perhaps of unilateral disarmament (in Britain), and so on.

A couple of handfuls of other studies during the decade have focused on exceptions to the apparent trend toward depoliticization and a reduced role for ideology. Kassalow's (1971) article on the CFDT traces the evolution of French Christian trade unionism into a group at the center of militant, left-wing political and trade union activity. On this side of the Atlantic, Boivin (1976) examined the politicization of Canadian trade unions. The authors stress two very different factors which seem to be the key to the divergent situations: in France, the CFDT was dominated by youthful members whose radicalism was fueled by the surprisingly moderate leadership of other confederations (especially in the CGT) during the strike wave of May 1968; in Canada, it is above all the much enlarged role of the state and the importance of centers of economic power outside the country which makes politicization "inevitable" by posing problems that collective bargaining cannot handle.

As indicated earlier, one of the factors that alters the "meaning" of the labor movement stems from changes in the groups that make up the target population for trade union membership. During the past decade, there were substantial shifts in this base in the U.S., which saw erosion of traditional areas of strength and the appearance of organization and, subsequently, of collective bargaining in new industries and occupations—for example, teaching and other public-sector employments. There was also a shift away from traditional manufacturing employment toward the service sectors, but the novelty of bargaining in services and the upsurge of strike activity was not so apparent. Thus (perhaps) it is that North American scholars noticed the first trend abroad, while ignoring the second; at any rate, such a conclusion could be supported by the pattern of writings in this subsector of the comparative field.

Early in the decade these parallels were discovered, not surprisingly in our neighbor to the north, and often by Canadian scholars. Thus, the 1972 IRRA Proceedings contained papers by Goldenberg (1972) on disputes settlement in the Canadian public sector, and articles by Kleingartner (1972) and Lebel (1972) on collective bargaining by professionals. Somewhat in the same vein is Thompson's (1975) paper to a later IRRA meeting on bargaining in Canadian universities. In all of this, the "comparative" Canadian literature is paralleling research on similar U.S. problems, raising similar concerns, and often coming to highly similar conclusions, modified by the Canadian context, of course. Thus, concerns with impasse procedures, preservation of essential services, and so on are typical problem areas.

Outside of Canada, the focus has been most heavily (if one can speak so of a generally light showing of interest) on public-sector labor relations as well. A survey of the literature shows two articles (Meyers 1973 and Keller 1978) and an edited volume (Rehmus 1975) containing (largely foreign) contributions to this subject at the Third Congress of the International Industrial Relations Association. Beyond this, we find two additional articles on new areas of unionism in the white-collar and managerial areas (Adams 1974, Gospel 1978). Given the hotness of the interest in all these subjects (except perhaps the last) in the U.S., the lack of interest by North Americans in developments overseas is quite remarkable.

In closing this section, I should note one prominent issue regarding the theory of the labor movement in late twentieth century "capitalism" that has not received much play in the American industrial relations literature, at least in the mainstream being reviewed. A good deal of discussion in the British literature, for example, is related to the possible emergence of the "corporate state." In such a state, the leaders of the labor movement have come to terms with the employer/capitalist side, and with the state which recognizes the need to share power with major interest groups, to the end that the concerns at the shop level and of individual workers—especially political or class issues—are not being advanced or dealt with. While this viewpoint does possibly seem a trifle "British" in its orientation and posing of the issues, it is clear that the U.S. literature on the subject consists only of Thomson's (1979) review of the topic. It is also probably true that this sort of pluralistic decision-making is needed for workable policies to be adopted in various areas of national industrial relations policy (for example, in the areas of basic labor legislation or wage-price policies), a point long argued in the U.S. by John Dunlop.[7]

In a general retrospect of the decade's research on the theory of the labor movement, it seems to me that we have moved ahead a good bit. The idea of a "mature labor movement" as typifying the U.S. rather than Europe appears to have been put on the back of the shelf. The mechanical elites of Kerr et al. (1960) have been replaced with more detailed analyses. Such models will certainly be of more value than elites in understanding the evolving role and structure of labor movements during the coming years of sharp economic and demographic shifts.

Workers' Participation

In some sense this subject is a hybrid of the two topics just discussed—conflict and the theory of the labor movement. It is an index of the concern with the topic variously called "workers' participation," "industrial democracy," etc., that the decade both opened and closed with a symposium on the subject in *Industrial Relations* (Strauss, ed., 1970 and 1979), with at least one other major collection on a wide range of countries (Windmuller, ed., 1977).

Over the period the principal objects of concern were (1) historical and descriptive accounts of participation in individual countries, (2) evaluations of the effects of the various experiments on the welfare of workers, and (3) comparisons of the participation gained in various schemes of industrial democracy with that coming from U.S.-style collective bargaining. These concerns seem broadly similar to those characterizing the literature of the sixties. Moreover, although the general "economic orientation" with regard (for example) to the evaluation of the benefits of participation does seem to have moderated, the more micro tools of industrial psychology have not yet made a major impact on the mainstream industrial relations literature on workers' participation. The major exceptions to this statement are the Industrial Democracy in Europe project (IDE 1979) and the reports on the Norwegian

[7] See Dunlop's "samizdat" publication, the November 12, 1975, memo on regulation which has been widely circulated among the academic industrial relations community.

Volvo experiments. These studies are discussed in the Brett and Hammer chapter of this volume and, therefore, will not be repeated here.

The studies of individual country experiences need not be listed, but a few words about them are in order. First, the kinds of participation arrangements which the field apparently finds of interest are confined to only part of the range of possible forms of participation. Profit-sharing as a form of participation seems to be of most limited interest, although worker stock-ownership plans are not so lightly regarded. The 1960s' interest in works councils seems to have been replaced with two general lines of interest: one of primary academic interest as relates to the "capitalist" countries and the other related to experiments in some form of market socialism. The first line of inquiry draws on the rich complexity of the German system of codetermination, with its varieties of forms and scopes of participation over various issues and subjects (Hartmann 1970), looking at its application in other countries (Emery and Thorsrud 1970, Westenholz 1979), and perhaps toward the likely adoption of some parts of the German system in any forthcoming Community Company law.

The second line of work has generated further intensive study of the Yugoslav model of self-management. In terms of number of studies, it is clear that Yugoslavia wins the race hands down, but the Yugoslav experiment has also permitted a good deal of more micro-level data to be examined as the age of that experiment rises. As with many of the other experiments in industrial democracy, there is usually conceded to be a gap between theory and practice (Bertsch and Obradovic 1979) and by no means is participation evenly spread across the workforce (nor would we have expected it to be) (Rus 1970, Obradovic 1975).

The evaluations of the worker participation schemes which accompany individual country or comparative studies tend to indicate that the fruits are generally modest (Rosenstein and Strauss 1970). Although there is evidence that the organization itself has substantial impact on the kind and amount of participation (Nightingale 1979, IDE 1979), the bulk of the evidence suggests, as the DIO group found in its study, that workers have very little control on any topic (DIO 1979). Such a finding is reassuring to American scholars, who spend a good deal of time comparing systems of industrial democracy with American collective bargaining, and perhaps to American workers, who generally seem to find European systems less efficacious than their own (Schrank 1979). Derber's (1970) conclusion that the strongest aspects of experiments in industrial democracy are in the areas of bargaining, rather than integration, probably remains true today. Certainly, notable recent developments in Europe might support such a conclusion—for example, the debate in Wolfsburg before the Volkswagen decision to locate a new plant in Pennsylvania, the reversal of the famous "clause 32" in Sweden to give the workers' view primacy regarding "grievances" on the shop floor, the increase of board-member strength to (almost) parity in large enterprises in Germany.

Nevertheless, to interpret European experiments in worker participation and industrial democracy solely in terms of their involvement in or promotion of "bargaining" is surely to miss a good deal of the point. At the base of much of the European work is a theory of society that rejects the idea that mere ownership per se gives one a right to control: that workers have rights in the enterprise which stem from the fact of working there, with legitimacy equal to if different from that stemming from the ownership of capital. Such a presumption is certainly coming to be one of the central features of what Clarke (1980) has called the general "European model" of industrial relations.

Nor does the "bargaining" point of view appear to cover another case, one where labor has not yet rejected capital's "innate" right to control in the workplace: Japan. The roles of workers, employers, and unions in the Japanese context of tradition, modernization, and change are considered by Cole (1979). In this situation, the integration and productivity orientation of such participatory mechanisms as "quality control circles" do seem to be paramount. Perhaps that is why they appear so attractive to a range of nonunion American managements. Be that as it may, the bargaining motif does not seem strong; a different paradigm seems necessary.

What the two preceding paragraphs suggest is the need for American scholars to recast some of their thinking in order to see schemes and systems of worker participation clearly in the light of the theory of the roles of capital and management which typify the societies under study, especially as embraced by the political and economic arms of the labor movement. This observation applies equally, I think, to the broad surveyors of industrial relations systems and to the more micro organizational behavior researchers.

The Role of Labor in Economic Development

This subject has two principal subcomponents, each of which has been the object of some scrutiny by the American industrial relations profession. The first component relates to the importance of labor as a factor of production and as a means of distributing income in the process of development; the second theme focuses on the role and functions of the labor movement, with particular emphasis on its participation in the process of growth and change, and has already been given brief mention.

The first subject has been a world-wide concern throughout the 1970s—indeed one might say that the topic was firmly launched by the ILO director-general's proclamation of the Employment Decade in 1966. One might further argue that focused concern with the subject came to a peak in 1976 with the Special Tripartite conference at ILO on employment and basic needs (ILO 1976). Naturally, the U.S. scholarly community participated in this lengthy discussion (for example, Ginzberg 1971, Harbison 1973), although it is interesting that the participation was not notably through the medium of American industrial relations journals. Instead the contributions were through other academic journals (in economics, for example), in the international journals (such as the *International Labour Review*), and in the mission reports of special problem-oriented task forces sent out by the various international organizations (such as the ILO, World Bank, Inter-American Development Bank, and so on).

It may be fruitful to ask why this should have been so. When the various international and development assistance agencies were generally groping throughout the decade toward each one's specific formulation of a rather general conception of a "basic needs" development philosophy, why did this topic not intrude upon the American industrial relations journals?

The simple answer, I think, is that the problem was not perceived as one having to do with industrial relations issues; instead, it was a concern of development economics or of labor economics. In general, there has been very little study of industrial relations issues in developing countries by American scholars, and the decade under discussion was no exception. As will be detailed below, there was substantial study of other issues in developing nations, but not much on industrial relations seems to have appeared. A couple of exceptions can be indicated: Gerdes (1971) and Scoville (1973). This is ironic, for there were certainly a large number of challenging issues centering on items ranging from race relations in South Africa to the success of moral incentives in China and elsewhere.

Of course, the basic needs debate didn't hit the U.S. economics journals either. What *was* the rage of the decade was the continuing development of various two-sector models of the labor market, building and elaborating on earlier works by Lewis, Ranis and Fei, and Todaro. These models are simple, attractive, and occasionally seem to be quantifiable; they are especially seductive when they seem quantifiable in terms that seem to have a common-sense, policy-relevant meaning. Here, for example, I refer to Fields (1979), which is concerned with the equity implications of promoting the "modern" versus the "traditional" sector, based on stereotyping assumptions about incomes in the two sectors.

It is in response to the two-sector modelers that the American industrial relations/labor economics researchers have expended a great deal of effort which should, eventually, have a commensurate reward. This research ran parallel with (and in many cases was part of) the field work associated with the development of "basic needs" philosophies. In the various ILO and other employment missions, and in other ways, a great deal of basic labor market research was done in developing countries—often by American scholars. These studies revealed the richness and complexity of the labor markets of developing countries, challenged the assumptions and myths of the simplest labor market modelings, and illustrated the need to know more about the specific functioning of various labor markets. Indeed, the best review of this whole literature will suggest that the two-sector models were not only fairly poor models, but were also positively injurious to analysis, by causing researchers to force their observations into a preconceived intellectual mold (Kannappan mimeo, n.d.). This is a strong charge, but one for which there is some evidence: For example, Kannapan refers to the "inhibiting framework" of "preconceived dualism" as undermining the otherwise excellent work of Joshi and Joshi (1976). This example of a beautifully simple model as a straitjacket on our thinking about what we see should be a caution to us.

Labor Markets

During the 1970s, there was a considerable outpouring of theoretical writing about the labor market in the United States: devotees of the various schools of thought pushed their particular analyses as a means of understanding labor market developments in the U.S. Thus we had writings on behalf of the Thurow school of "job competition," from the various schools of human capitalists, and from the diverse groups favoring radical, segmented, dual, core-periphery, etc. interpretations of the labor market. While one may be permitted some reservations about how much some parts of this flow of words contribute to our understanding, it is nonetheless a rich mosaic. This picture is, perhaps unfortunately, less rich and diverse when one looks at comparative and international work on the theory of the labor market.

As has been suggested earlier, a good deal of the international work, especially on developing areas, has been dominated by a particular, largely nonradical version of dual labor market theory, descended from earlier works by Sir Arthur Lewis, Ranis and Fei, and Todaro. Much of the rest of the literature has been descriptive, occasionally theoretical, attempts to look at the workings of particular labor markets in ways that overcome the simplifying limitations of dualistic theorizing. The human capital school has been a great deal less represented than it has been in work on domestic issues.

Almost by definition, very little *pure* theorizing takes place in an international or comparative framework, since almost all studies will focus on a specific country or countries. Occasional papers have been more sweeping, by trying to develop a more general model for a particular class of countries: examples would be Doeringer's (1974) attempt to apply his version of labor market dualism to the industrialized market economies of Europe and Japan, Scoville's (1976) simple diagrammatics for urban labor markets in LDCs, or the article by Fields (1979) referred to earlier.

Studies of Particular Labor Markets: General. The fairly general studies of labor markets in various countries in the industrial relations literature have three major focuses: developed countries, Japan, and the LDCs. In all these areas, the work is rather thinly spread over the decade. In the area of labor markets in developed countries, the literature seems to cover the U.K. and Canada only, with only two really general studies: Smyth and Lowe's (1970) inquiry into the existence of a labor market "vestibule" in which British unemployment is concentrated, and Smith's (1976) study of the influence of U.S. wage changes on those in Canada. Two of the other British studies focus on that country's 1964 Industrial Training Act (Malm 1972, Hughes 1973), while the last is Jensen's (1971) study of recent developments in dock work in London. The final study of a specific labor market in a developed Western economy was Lightman's (1975) examination of the sources of supply to Canada's nonconscript military; this was, of course, a subject of considerable public interest in the U.S. during this decade.

At the present time there exists a substantial amount of interest in the Japanese success story, not least among American industrial relations practitioners who would like to figure out how they did it, and apply those techniques here. The current interest was anticipated in the relatively large amount of work on Japan by academics during the 1970s. It is less than clear, however, whether the work that has been done has been able to dispel the rather facile stereotypings that exist regarding Japanese industrial relations. Nevertheless, a quick summary of the key works can be offered. At the beginning of the decade, we have two major volumes: Evans's (1971), which compares the whole system of industrial relations in labor market perspective, and Cole's (1971) observations from a participant-observer position. One thrust of these works, along with Cole's (1972) subsequent article on facts and fantasies in our thinking about Japan and his 1979 book, has been that Japanese industrial relations can be understood in comparative fashion, which is to say that they can be understood in many of the same terms as other nations' systems. The unique and incomprehensible quality is removed from the subject. A similar approach is taken by Stoikov (1973) who found that interfirm differences in labor force quality explained most of the size of the firm wage differentials in Japan (a finding similar to that by Weiss (1966) for the U.S.), and by Marsh and Mannari (1973) who concluded that a modern pay system based on work performed or job classification is replacing and will supplant the older traditional system based on seniority. If there is something magical about the Japanese style of industrial relations, clearly these works have not captured it.

A variety of studies focused on labor markets in developing countries. Some of these studies had a very strong theoretical focus—here I have in mind two particular studies by Kannappan (1975) of the Sudan and Scoville (1974) of Afghanistan. Kannappan's major bones to pick were with the dualists and with the ILO-ish anti-labor-market mentality; he stresses the efficacy of labor markets in the Sudan as allocators of vast amounts of labor, especially in agriculture. Scoville was concerned with the formal development of a model of interaction between earnings structures in the emerging modern sector and the pre-existing traditional sector—in essence, to remove the necessity for institutionalist or interventionist explanations for the high level of urban wages. By way of contrast, one should read, for example, Gregory's (1975) study of the role of institutions in the labor markets of LDCs.

A number of less formally theoretical pieces were also published, many of them in the volume of studies edited by Kannappan (1977). Among the essays in that volume which are of particular interest, one should note those by Taira (1976) and Levine (1976) which focus on internal labor markets and the processes of external labor market segmentation. One should also note in passing that the Kannappan volume represents part of the work of an unusual international scholarly enterprise—a group of scholars and researchers from several developed countries and a large number of developing countries who pursued topics on urban labor markets in a collaborative fashion throughout the decade of the 1970s.

Two other specific studies of particular types of LDC labor markets should also be mentioned. Both are by Canadians and come from rather untraditional sources for industrial relations research. McGee and Yeung (1977) focused on hawkers and peddlers in their book; Smith (1978), writing for the Center for Transportation Studies, University of British Columbia, focused on periodic and itinerant markets. Both are of interest to the serious student. One attempt to pull together a large number of specific market studies was made by the present author (Scoville 1976) in the mid-1970s and presented to the IIRA Congress in 1976; this is also a good reference to the work of many foreign scholars, as is Sinclair (1978).

Studies of Particular Labor Markets: Specific. In addition to the fairly general studies of the national or urban labor market phenomena of both developed and developing countries, there are a number of fairly clear-cut, specific submarkets that also received attention during the 1970s.

1. *The female labor market and women's wages.* In this area, the international/comparative studies seem to fall into two clear groups. The first is a set of studies focusing on the importance of "occupational segregation" and other deviations from equal opportunity by sex. The general conclusion of studies by Cook (1975), Cooney (1978) and Izraeli and Gaier (1979) has been to underscore the importance of occupational segregation in determination of the level of women's wages and, hence, of the overall degree of sexual earnings inequality. The other principal strand of inquiry has focused on the claim advanced in various international forums by speakers and writers from the socialist countries that these capitalistic ills have been solved in the course of the Soviet experience. Studies by K. and R. Bartol (1975), Sacks (1976), and Lapidus (1975) have looked at this range of issues and have generally found the successes of the Soviets in eliminating sexual inequality to be overstated by their proponents: in general, many of the same problems remain. Marjorie Galenson's (1973) multicountry comparisons also devote a good deal of discussion to the case of the Soviet Union, even though the moral of her story is—perhaps no surprise—that nowhere have women achieved full equality with men in the labor market. In assessing this piece of the industrial relations literature during the decade, it is perhaps surprising that it is as thin as it is, given the vociferous debate on all aspects of women's equality and/or liberation which raged throughout the 1970s, and moreover that the

focuses of concern are so narrow. For better or worse, the industrial relations academic community does not seem to have been very far out in front in analysis of what seems to be a burning issue of the day: comparable worth considered in its labor market, industrial relations, and labor relations contexts.

2. *Skill differentials.* In spite of the rather extensive debate in the early to mid-1970s on the role and emergence of skill differentials in the United States, there seems to have been rather little done in an international or comparative perspective. The only study involving an American author which appeared in the three leading journals is of some interest, however, as it was part of the general effort by labor market students to put the workings of LDC labor markets into proper focus. In the work by Pastore, Haller, and Gomez-Buendia (1975), an effort was made to assess the degree to which the kinds of labor market variables which explain wage differentials in developed countries could be applied to an LDC: they conclude that such variables operate in the Brazilian case to a significant degree.

3. *Migration and guest workers.* This topic has two subfocuses, only one of which has attracted much of a literature during the decade. The first topic would be the massive labor migration into and among the Common Market countries. In spite of the extensive work in Europe on various aspects of this topic—living conditions, racism, export of human capital for doubtful return home to an LDC, xenophobia, cash flows, etc.—by all manner of European social scientists, and in spite of the general attractiveness to American economists and industrial relations scholars of the stereotyped "exportable unemployment" in the Common Market, only one piece on guest workers has been found, and that one comes four months into the new decade of the 1980s. However, reference should be made to the work of Martin and Miller (1980), especially as they seek to combat the notion of exportable unemployment which has gotten attached to the loose thinking on European labor mobility that persists in this country.

Closer to home, however, the end of the 1970s saw an upsurge in writing on illegal, unsanctioned, and uncontrollable immigration, especially on the enormous flow of Mexican and other Hispanic workers into the U.S. The issue was picked up first through a symposium at the 1974 IRRA meetings, where two lines of analysis emerged. While it seems that everyone conceded the strength of the supply-side "push" forces on generating a high level of willingness to emigrate from Mexico and other nations, the differences of opinion arise on the nature of the "pull" forces. In the 1974 symposium and subsequently, Fogel (1974, 1978, 1980) has taken a position that seems to stress the ad hoc nature of recruitment for Mexican labor ("to provide elastic increments to labor supply in secondary markets") and to suggest that the recruitment process may also have a "decruitment" and deportation phase as well (they "have been courted . . . in periods of labor shortage, but . . . dealt with as unwanted aliens when the shortage disappeared") (Fogel 1974). At the same symposium and later, Piore (1974, 1979) has advanced the more sweeping hypothesis that the new immigration is a "manifestation of the basic process through which industrial societies man the positions at the bottom of their social structures" (Piore 1974). These differences in emphasis are also accompanied by fairly sharp differences in policy recommendations, including the degree to which one thinks it possible or desirable to try to control the problem by *really* controlling the border and the amount of onus to be placed upon employers who are, in either analysis, part of the problem.

4. *The hard-to-employ.* A handful of articles or books have examined the two major ways of making the unemployed more employable: training programs and relocation assistance (Schnitzer 1970, Reubens 1970, Dupre, Cameron, McKechnie, and Rotenberg 1973, Roomkin 1974). What is most interesting is that all these materials antedate the mid- to late-1970s push in U.S. employment policy. The passage and subsequent expansion of the Comprehensive Employment and Training Act appears either to have absorbed all the available time of people who write about training and relocation issues, or to have killed all interest in the overseas experiments.[8] Once again, a major U.S. policy program in the industrial relations area seems to have been undertaken (and conducted for half a decade or more) with a lack of comparative insights into its operation and evaluation.

5. *Wage determination: incomes policies and industrial rela-*

[8] Dan Mitchell suggests an alternative view—that rising European unemployment in the late 1970s dried up interest in the subject. Even so, commentary would seem to have been warranted.

tions. With the U.S. imposing a series of wage-price policy variants at the beginning of the decade, it is perhaps hardly surprising that there was a flow of writings appraising the nature, outcomes, and industrial relations implications of such policies overseas. It is perhaps somewhat surprising that the flow of publications is relatively modest, given the importance of the inflationary problem and the number of foreign experiments which could have been analyzed. It is also true that a very high percentage of the contributions to the "American" literature were in fact written by foreign scholars.

Two general overview volumes presented a multicountry treatment of the various processes of inflation and the policies adopted by the nations involved, and some attempt was made to assess the successes of those policies. The general conclusion that one might draw from the Ulman-Flanagan (1971) and Galenson (1973) volumes is that inflation is a considerably more complex process than might have been suggested by the simple Phillips curve tradeoffs of the mid-1960s. Policies themselves must be more complex than the "simple and straightforward" policies called for in Jimmy Carter's 1976 literature or the policies of the Reagan Administration (at least if one assumes some other arguments in the social objective function besides the rate of inflation).

Several case studies brought out the industrial relations implications and complications associated with incomes policies. Thomson's (1971) study in the U.K. emphasized the importance of being able to implement the policy at the local—that is, actual wage-determining—level, on the one hand reminding us of the very important lessons taught by the Donovan Commission in the mid-1960s about the relevance of the *real* system of industrial relations, and on the other hand giving American readers some of the same lessons which Clegg (1971) drew (above all from a picture of the U.S. situation) for his British readers. Hunter's (1975) study of British incomes policy at the beginning of the decade underscores the point made in the preceding paragraph, by stressing the damage inflicted on the government's policy through attempts to pursue other, notably expansionary, policies. Finally, Mitchell's (1972) appraisal of the French experience suggests the kind of detailed planning and intervention that went into an incomes-income distribution-economic growth plan, suggesting that the industrial relations implications of such policies may be substantially greater than any impacts they may have on inflation.

All in all, given the amounts of effort and political stature that went into attempts to come up with a workable, acceptable, and effective wage-price policy in the first half of this decade, and the amount of policy rhetoric and debate, this does not represent a very large amount of scholarly inquiry into the design and appraisal of incomes policies abroad. No clearer example could be offered of the lack of willingness to learn from others' experiments, a situation which Kochan (1980), in his Department of Labor research agenda for the 1980s, proposed to meliorate, if not entirely to remedy.

6. *Wage determination in centrally planned economies.* The rather slim literature in this area really seems to have one basic theme: how can and should the old-fashioned Soviet model of wage-fixing be modified to take account of labor market realities and to promote productivity and efficient labor utilization? For the Soviet Union itself, we have Brown's (1970) survey of the problems arising in the labor market (problems rather familiar from our Western experience), Kirsch's (1972) appraisal of the centralizing reforms of the mid-1950s which attempted to achieve a number of goals including a more equal wage distribution, and finally Adam's (1973) account of the decentralizing reform of 1965, its failure, and the eventual recentralizing aftermath. Two Hungarian sociologists, Héthy and Makó, have contributed to our understanding of these reform processes in their country, stressing (perhaps surprisingly) the need for resolution of socioeconomic conflicts at the workplace (Héthy and Makó 1971) and later emphasizing the managerial incentive problems inherent in the reformed wage and profit allocation schemes (Héthy and Makó 1973). Howe's (1973) book provides a detailed investigation of the Chinese evolution away from the Soviet wage system, toward a more flexible and "human" wage policy. The upshot of these studies, in my view, is to remind the planners and social designers of the constraints on their freedom imposed, in the case of wage policy, by the forces of the labor market and the need for wages (and other forms of compensation) to motivate desired forms of behavior, including good management.

The Growth of Multinational Organizations of Capital and Labor

Some years ago, in a review of a book in this area, I wrote of a colleague who had told me that he had come to find the whole subject of multinationals boring. Judging by the amount of work in recent years, it would seem that this may have become the judgment of the profession. The topic seems to break down into four subareas, each of which deserves brief comment.

The Labor Market and Industrial Relations Impacts of the MNC. The more spectacular literature on this subject is not really to be found in the industrial relations field, for its focus will be on the buying and selling of politicians, manipulation of tax rules and transfer pricing arrangements, and so on. Good, gray industrial relations scholars leave the juicy details of IT&T in Chile, United Fruit in the banana republics, and so on, to others. Instead, we have discussions of the varying labor market impacts (at home and abroad), exemplified by the Hawkins and Jedel (1975) essay which differentiated between various types of workers and various circumstances under which the international investment takes place. The reader's understanding of the impacts on the home labor market, and steps which have been taken to modify them, would be further expanded by reviewing Mitchell's (1976) volume, with its heavy emphasis on adjustment assistance.

The Prospects for Control of the MNC Through Collective Bargaining. In this area, the literature seems fairly unanimous: whether from a detailed look at particular industries (Northrup and Rowan 1976, Enckell 1977) or from more general perspectives (Kujawa 1975, Banks and Stieber 1977, Flanagan and Weber 1974) the history of recent years does not suggest a strong trend toward international collective bargaining as a means of control over the activities of the MNCs. The differences in national industrial relations systems (which roles are performed by which actors) and the sovereignty of the nation-state seem to be the key influences. Thus, even though two of the three customary issues behind the growth of industry-wide union control are present on the international plane, the barriers, as enumerated most succinctly by Ulman (1975), are strong enough to present what is an otherwise logical development from taking place. Hence, at this point international information-exchange, occasional pledges of solidarity, and even more occasional refusals to work overtime, etc., mark the high-water point of international union power. I would expect, as did some authors—for example, McCullough (1977), that the growth toward political unity of the EEC (and above all the passage of a Community European Company law) will produce more effective international unionism there. Indeed, the international "day of action" against unemployment (April 5, 1978), which ranged from a three-hour general strike in Greece to short demonstrations in other countries and allegedly involved 40 million workers throughout Europe, might be the initial sign of growing unity.

Failing Control by Unions, the Role of Codes of Conduct. If collective bargaining with individual MNCs cannot keep them under control, then it presumably must be done through legislation. Indeed, legislation may be necessary as there may well be odious aspects of MNCs' behavior which might just conceivably not be objects of social-minded control by unionists from more developed countries (for example, dumping industrial wastes or nuclear waste in the Third World). National legislation, despite the ambitious efforts of the Swedes to impose home country behavior on their companies' operations overseas, will be less than effective, one may presume. Hence, the need for international codes of conduct to control the MNCs. As such codes were adopted by the OECD and ILO only toward the latter part of the decade, little literature has appeared to assess them; the latest word is the rather pessimistic evaluation of Windmuller and Baderschneider (1977). In general, the employers and governments of the developed nations, where the powerful trade unions are, will tend to prefer weaker controls; the governments of LDCs will have their prolabor penchants offset by a strong need for jobs and other fruits of foreign investment.

With the mention of the ILO in the context of codes of conduct, it may not be inappropriate to indicate what, if any, writing took place in the industrial relations field relating to the U.S. decision to leave that organization in 1977, and then to return in 1979. The answer is quite simple: there was a panel on the ILO at the 1974 IRRA meetings (with, most appropriately to the topic, one neutral, one employer, and one trade unionist). If one reads the session carefully, one gets the following impression: the employer found the organization to be worse than useless, with a "bleak" prospect for improvement (Smith 1974); the unionist was more positive, stressing achievement in areas of technical assistance and industry-specific work, while noting the aberrations in the human rights area (Seidman 1974); the academic neutral generally found the organization to be a good thing on balance, argued that U.S. participation had been just as political as anybody else's, and generally concluded that our setbacks and problems were insufficient reason to quit the organization (Windmuller 1974). It is quite possible that Windmuller (the neutral) was right, but it remains clear that the ILO had very few friends by the mid-1970s who could draw that kind of balance, and it had many actual or potentially mobilizable enemies in the ranks of labor and management, as well as academia. There was additional consultation about the withdrawal and the rejoining between the government and the academic world, but in neither case was our balanced, equivocating approach determining, insofar as I could tell.

Other Aspects of the International Role of American Labor. Aside from the ILO affair, U.S. labor continued to play a role overseas, in both developing and developed nations. We have noted earlier the impacts of detente and the reactions of European and American labor movements (Windmuller 1976b). There were also a couple of more general studies of the activities of U.S. labor abroad by Taft (1973) and Godson (1976). Godson concluded that a "non-governmental organization based in one country can influence developments in other countries"—but apparently (as in the case of the AFL) most effectively by using government money. The importance of government money is documented by Taft, who shows that 28 of the 31 million dollars spent by the American Institute for Free Labor Development during the 1960s came from AID. I am eagerly awaiting the next chapter of this story, surveying the sources of our "solidarity" with the Polish workers in the early 1980s.

IV. Overview

In general, the bulk of the international-comparative research done in the past decade seems to fall into these six broad areas, subdivided as necessary into specific problems or topics: industrial conflict, the theory of the labor movement, workers' participation, the role of labor in economic development, studies of labor markets, and the growth of multinational organizations of capital and labor. Loosely speaking, it seems that these six major focuses have also been among the most important practical areas in which new problems, new policy challenges, and new political thrusts have emerged. In that sense, one would have to say that the industrial relations research has been "relevant," that is, it has been addressed to the appropriate areas of concern.

However, there are a number of reasons why one would not want to go too far with that conclusion, for the conclusion by no means does justice to what has been said in the preceding pages. As one looks back through those pages, how often have statements like the following been made?

- the literature in this area is surprisingly thin,
- foreign authors' work is mentioned as examples of work not done by North Americans,
- the lack of interest in this topic is remarkable,
- and so on . . . .

Quite frequently indeed, is the answer. In part this must stem from the general decline in the amount of international-comparative work noted in Section II. In part it stems from the intensity of concern with a subject on the domestic scene (for example, public-sector collective bargaining) carrying over into international research, while subjects of great interest overseas may have less than proportionate attraction for North American students (for example, workers' participation). This kind of tendency is hardly unpredictable, given the nature of academic inquiry and the sources of funds for research, but we should keep it in mind lest we sink unknowingly into a provincialism wherein our local problems determine our objects of inquiry and crowd out more general studies.

Moreover, there seem to be at least a couple of very important subjects on which little, if anything, was done during the decade.[9] I will say a few words about each.

[9] Here I refer to things that do not appear in the discussion above because they have not been done, as opposed to matters not discussed because they fall outside the ambit of the operational definition of industrial relations adopted for this review. In the latter class would fall studies of managerial

1. The first major deficiency revolves around what I perceive as the historically central role of comparative studies in the formulation of big ideas and analytical frameworks in the industrial relations field. While one might quibble as to whether Selig Perlman's work was primarily comparative or simply historical, it is clear that he built his theory of what a mature trade union movement would and should do upon the study of other national experiences which had led to deviations from the proper path. More recently, Kerr et al.'s study, culminating in the broad generalizations of *Industrialism and Industrial Man* (as reconsidered), sought to pull synthesis and a general framework from a large number of comparative works. As occurred at the 1976 IRRA meetings, one can ask tough questions about that work, including whether their funding was cost-effective, especially in terms of opportunity costs of other research supported and the subsequent impacts on availability of research support for international and comparative studies (questions asked by Cochrane 1976, 1979). Yet as probing as Cochrane's questions were in 1976, and no matter how many of his respondents quoted Neil Chamberlain's review (which concluded that the analytical framework was that of 19th century German historicism) with approval, Kassalow's (1976) remarks at the same IRRA session still have a good deal of merit. The tenor of Kassalow's comments I take to be the following: It's really too early to evaluate the effects of the Inter-University Study, but—even though one may suspect that their analysis was *so* general that one can predict very little that is concrete—they were after something very important: "a theory in the grand manner, embracing no less than the process of industrialization and with it the evolution of industrial relations, virtually as a universal phenomenon." To suggest, as does Cochrane, that one test of the value of the broader work is that it seems to have lost out to the

---

values, a great deal of detailed labor and social history, labor law, and so on. The operational definition of the international and comparative subfield of industrial relations is thus rather close to that employed in the first IRRA volume on the subject, *International Labor* (New York: Harper & Row, 1967), edited by Sol Barkin, William Dymond, Everett Kassalow, Frederic Meyers, and Charles Myers. Alternatively, one can consider the field as delimited by the three journals I have selected for analysis in Section II, while leaving to one side the more heavily organization theory and industrial psychology materials that would be found (for example) in the *Academy of Management Journal* or the *Journal of Applied Psychology.*

Chicago Paradigm, seems improper—one would hardly confuse the objects of inquiry of broad-gauge industrial relations, neo-institutionalist scholars with the concerns of the human capitalists.

But, among labor economists human capital does seem to be where the action is. One might, I suppose, say something similar about "hot" fields of inquiry in the other disciplines that often supply scholars to the industrial relations field. As a result, the moves toward the "integrating theory" that Dunlop called for in the introduction to *Industrial Relations Systems* have been very limited. Some small efforts in that direction were part of the volume that Sturmthal and I edited, but even there we focused on only part of the problem (principally, the objectives, strategy, and nature of the labor movement), thereby leaving a great deal to one side. I had hoped that the appearance of a fuller report by Cochrane (1979) would stimulate a debate which may, in turn, lead to some concern during the 1980s with the Big Ideas of industrial relations; however, this final report seems to have appeared with little notice.

2. The second major concern that I have is related to the first (which deals with integration of our knowledge): namely, in what way is our comparative knowledge to be applied? It is an article of faith that "industrial relations systems cannot ______ [pick an adverb that indicates whether you want it to be or not in the particular case] be imported." The whole question of what and how we learn from foreign experience is tied in with our "systematic" understanding of how things work in the broadest sense. What can we learn from the nationwide use of a system of job evaluation in the Netherlands after World War II which might be relevant to concerns with comparable worth? What can we apply, if anything, from the Japanese systems of consensual management or the German systems of codetermination to improve labor-management relations in the U.S.? Most critically, how do we even go about thinking about these things?

Let me indicate why I find this a compelling area for research, for the reason has to do with one stream of writing which I fully expected to find in the materials from the 1970s, but found not a trace. (Indeed, in the first outline I prepared for the editors, I indicated that it would be a major area of inquiry.) As is well known, the British passed an Industrial Relations Act in 1971 which rapidly failed to achieve any of its major objectives. As is also well known, that Act contained numerous attempts to implant or graft American ideas and practices (enforceable contracts, unfair industrial practices, etc.); those attempts were in part the product of direct Anglo-American scholarly interaction. What went wrong, not only with the Act, but above all in the thinking and perceptions that underlay it? It seems to me that we have a great deal to learn about and from this experience. One article by Engleman and Thomson (1974) explored the failings of the Act, but did not grapple with the underlying issues of transferability of industrial relations practices, and how one evaluates the degree of transferability ex ante. A research undertaking in that area might well comprise the first major effort of the 1980s to integrate our knowledge and in that same process identify more clearly the factors and forces that determine the applicability of our international and comparative studies.

With this challenge, I lay down the Olympic pen, with hopes that its next wielder will have a more prosperous international and comparative decade to review.

References

Aaron, Benjamin. *Labor Courts and Grievance Settlement in Western Europe.* Berkeley: University of California Press, 1971.

———. "The Administration of Justice in Labor Law." *Comparative Labor Law* 3 (November 1979): pp. 3–30.

Aaron, Benjamin, and K. W. Wedderburn. *Industrial Conflict: A Comparative Legal Survey.* London: Longmans, 1972.

Adam, Jan. "The Incentive System in the USSR: The Abortive Reform of 1965." *Industrial and Labor Relations Review* 27 (October 1973): pp. 84–92.

Adams, Roy J. "White Collar Union Growth: The Case of Sweden." *Industrial Relations* 13 (May 1974): pp. 164–76.

Ananaba, Wogu. *The Trade Union Movement in Africa: Promise and Performance.* New York: St. Martin's Press, 1979.

Banks, Robert F., and Jack Stieber, eds. *Multinationals, Unions, and Labor Relations in Industrial Countries.* Ithaca: New York State School of Industrial and Labor Relations, 1977.

Barbash, Jack, with Kate Barbash. *Trade Unions and National Economic Policy.* Baltimore: John Hopkins Press, 1972.

Barkin, Sol. *Worker Militancy and Its Consequences, 1965–1975.* New York: Praeger, 1975.

Bartol, Kathryn, and Robert A. Bartol. "Women in Managerial and Professional Positions: The United States and the Soviet Union." *Industrial and Labor Relations Review* 28 (July 1975): pp. 524–34.

Bates, Robert H. *Unions, Parties and Political Development: A Study of Mineworkers in Zambia.* New Haven, Conn.: Yale University Press, 1971.

Bertsch, Gary K., and Josip Obradovic. "Participation and Influence in Yugoslav Self-Management." *Industrial Relations* 18 (Fall 1979): pp. 322–29.

Blum, Albert. "Review of Sturmthal and Scoville (1973)." *Industrial and Labor Relations Review* 30 (October 1976): pp. 109–10.

Boivin, Jean. "The Politicization of Canadian Labor Unions: An Inevitable Phenomenon." *Proceedings of the Industrial Relations Research Association, 1976*, pp. 107–15.

Braunthal, Gerard. *Socialist Labor and Politics in Weimar Germany*. Hamden, Conn.: Archon Press, 1978.

Brown, Emily Clark. "Continuity and Change in the Soviet Labor Market." *Industrial and Labor Relations Review* 23 (January 1970): pp. 171–90.

Clarke, Oliver. "The Development of Industrial Relations in European Market Economies." *Proceedings of the Industrial Relations Research Association, 1980*, pp. 167–73.

Clegg, Hugh. *How to Run an Incomes Policy and Why We Made Such a Mess of the Last One*. London: Heinemann Educational, 1971.

Cochrane, James L. "Industrialism and Industrial Man in Retrospect: A Preliminary Analysis." *Proceedings of the Industrial Relations Research Association, 1976*, pp. 274–87.

———. *Industrialism and Industrial Man in Retrospect: A Critical Review of the Ford Foundation's Support for the Inter-University Study of Labor*. New York: Ford Foundation, 1979.

Cole, Robert E. *Japanese Blue Collar: The Changing Tradition*. Berkeley: University of California Press, 1971.

———. "Permanent Employment in Japan: Facts and Fantasies." *Industrial and Labor Relations Review* 26 (October 1972): 615–30.

———. *Work, Mobility and Participation: A Comparative Study of American and Japanese Industry*. Berkeley: University of California Press, 1979.

Cook, Alice H. "Equal Pay: Where Is It?" *Industrial Relations* 14 (May 1975): pp. 158–77.

Cooney, Rosemary Santana. "Changing Patterns of Female Labor Force Participation." *Industrial Relations* 16 (October 1977): pp. 355–62.

———. "A Comparative Study of Work Opportunities for Women." *Industrial Relations* 17 (February 1978): pp. 64–74.

Crispo, John. "Industrial Relations in Western Europe and Canada." In *A Review of Industrial Relations Research*, Vol. II. Madison, Wis.: Industrial Relations Research Association, 1971.

Crouch, Colin, and Alessandro Pizzorno. *The Resurgence of Class Conflict in Western Europe Since 1968*. New York: Holmes and Meier, 1978.

Damachi, Ukandi. *The Role of Trade Unions in the Development Process: With a Case Study of Ghana*. New York: Praeger, 1974.

Derber, Milton. "Cross Currents in Worker Participation." *Industrial Relations* 9 (February 1970): pp. 123–36.

Doeringer, Peter. "Low Paid Workers, Labour Market Dualism, and Industrial Relations Systems." In *Wage Determination*. Paris: OECD, 1974.

DIO. "Participative Decision-Making: A Comparative Study." *Industrial Relations* 18 (Fall 1979): pp. 295–309.

Dubois, P. *Le Sabotage dans l'Industrie*. Paris: Calmann-Levy, 1976.

Dunlop, John T., Frederick H. Harbison, Clark Kerr, and Charles A. Myers. *Industrialism and Industrial Man Reconsidered*. Princeton, N.J.: Inter-university Study of Human Resources in Economic Development, 1975.

Dunlop, John T., and Walter Galenson. *Labor in the Twentieth Century*. New York: Academic Press, 1978.

Dupre, J. Stefan, David M. Cameron, Graeme H. McKechnie, and Theodore B. Rotenberg. *Federalism and Policy Development: The Case of Adult Occupational Training in Ontario*. Buffalo and Toronto: University of Toronto Press, 1973.

Emery, Fred G., and Einar Thorsrud. "Industrial Democracy in Norway." *Industrial Relations* 9 (February 1970): pp. 187–96.

Enckell, Laurent C. "A Trade Union Perspective on Multinational Bargaining." *Proceedings of the Industrial Relations Research Association, 1977,* pp. 90–96.

Engleman, S. R., and A. W. J. Thomson. "Experience Under the British Industrial Relations Act." *Industrial Relations* 13 (May 1974): pp. 130–55.

Evans, Robert Jr. *The Labor Economies of Japan and the United States.* New York: Praeger, 1971.

Fields, Gary. "A Welfare Economic Approach to Growth and Distribution in the Dual Economy." *Quarterly Journal of Economics* 93 (August 1979): pp. 325–54.

Flanagan, Robert J., and Arnold Weber. *Bargaining Without Boundaries: The Multinational Corporation and International Labor Relations.* Chicago: University of Chicago Press, 1974.

Freeman, Richard B. "Individual Mobility and Union Voice in the Labor Market." *American Economic Review* 66 (May 1976): pp. 361–68.

Fogel, Walter. "Mexican Labor in the United States Labor Markets." *Proceedings of the Industrial Relations Research Association, 1974,* pp. 343–49.

———. *Mexican Illegal Alien Workers in the United States.* Los Angeles: Institute of Industrial Relations, University of California, 1978.

———. "United States Immigration Policy and Unsanctioned Migrants." *Industrial and Labor Relations Review* 33 (April 1980): pp. 295–311.

Galenson, Marjorie. *Women and Work: An International Comparison.* Ithaca: New York State School of Industrial and Labor Relations, 1973.

Galenson, Walter, ed. *Incomes Policy: What Can We Learn from Europe?* Ithaca: New York State School of Industrial and Labor Relations, 1973.

Galenson, Walter. "Current Problems of Scandinavian Trade Unionism." In *Scandinavia at the Polls,* by Karl H. Cerny. Washington: American Enterprise Institute for Public Policy Research, 1977.

Gerdes, Victor. "African Provident Funds," *Industrial and Labor Relations Review* 24 (July 1971): pp. 572–87.

Ginzberg, Eli. *Manpower for Development: Perspectives on Five Continents.* New York: Praeger, 1971.

Goldenberg, Shirley. "The Canadian Scene." *Proceedings of the Industrial Relations Research Association, 1972,* pp. 56–63.

Godson, Roy. *American Labor and European Politics: The AFL as a Transnational Force.* New York: Crane, Russak, 1976.

Gospel, Howard. "European Managerial Unionism: An Early Assessment." *Industrial Relations* 17 (October 1978): pp. 360–71.

Gregory, Peter. "The Impact of Institutional Intervention in Industrial Wages in Mexico." *Proceedings of the Industrial Relations Research Association, 1975,* pp. 24–31.

Harbison, Frederick. *Human Resources as the Wealth of Nations.* New York: Oxford University Press, 1973.

Hartmann, Heinz. "Codetermination in West Germany." *Industrial Relations* 9 (February 1970): pp. 137–47.

Hawkins, Robert G., and Michael Jay Jedel. "US Jobs and Foreign Investment." In *International Labor and the Multinational Enterprise,* ed. Duane Kujawa. New York: Praeger, 1975.

Héthy, Lajos, and Csaba Makó. "Obstacles to the Introduction of Efficient Money Incentives in a Hungarian Factory." *Industrial and Labor Relations Review* 24 (July 1971): pp. 541–53.

———. "Incentive Problems in the Centrally Planned Economy of Hungary." *Industrial and Labor Relations Review* 26 (January 1973): pp. 767–77.

Hibbs, Douglas. "Industrial Conflict in Advanced Industrial Societies." *American Political Science Review* 70 (December 1976): pp. 1033–58.

Howe, Christopher. *Wage Patterns and Wage Policy in Modern China, 1919–1972.* New York: Cambridge University Press, 1973.

Hughes, James M. "Britain's Training Act: A Manpower Revolution?" *Industrial Relations* 12 (October 1973): pp. 352–53.

Hunter, Lawrence C. "British Incomes Policy, 1972–1974." *Industrial and Labor Relations Review* 29 (October 1975): pp. 67–84.

IDE. "Participation: Formal Rules, Influence, and Involvement." *Industrial Relations* 18 (Fall 1979): pp. 273–94.

ILO. *Collective Bargaining in Industrialized Market Economies.* Geneva: 1974.

ILO. *Employment, Growth and Basic Needs: A One-World Problem.* Geneva: 1976.

Izraeli, Dafna Nundi, and Kalman Gaier. "Sex and Interoccupational Wage Differences in Israel." *Industrial Relations* 18 (Spring 1979): pp. 227–32.

Jensen, Vernon H. *Decasualization and Modernization of Dock Work in London.* Ithaca: New York State School of Industrial and Labor Relations, 1971.

Joshi, Heather, and Vijay Joshi. *Surplus Labour and the City: A Study of Bombay.* Delhi: Oxford University Press, 1976.

Kahan, Arcadius, and Blair Ruble. *Industrial Labor in the USSR.* New York: Pergamon, 1979.

Kannappan, Subbiah. "The Urban Labor Market in Sudan: Some Implications for Current Theorizing." *Proceedings of the Industrial Relations Research Association, 1975,* pp. 9–16.

———. *Employment Problems and the Urban Labor Market in Developing Nations* (mimeo, n.d.).

Kannappan, Subbiah, ed. *Studies in Urban Labour Market Behavior in Developing Areas.* Geneva: International Institute for Labour Studies, 1977.

Kassalow, Everett M. "The Transformation of Christian Trade Unionism: The Recent Evolution of the French CFDT." *Proceedings of the Industrial Relations Research Association, 1971,* pp. 186–97.

———. "Discussion." *Proceedings of the Industrial Relations Research Association, 1976,* pp. 298–302.

———. "Industrial Conflict and Consensus in the United States and Western Europe: A Comparative Analysis." *Proceedings of the Industrial Relations Research Association, 1977,* pp. 113–22.

Keller, Berndt K. "Public Sector Labor Relations in West Germany." *Industrial Relations* 17 (February 1978): pp. 18–31.

Kerr, Clark, John T. Dunlop, Frederick Harbison, and Charles Myers. *Industrialism and Industrial Man.* Cambridge, Mass.: Harvard University Press, 1960.

Kirsch, L. Joel. *Soviet Wages: Changes in Structure and Administration Since 1956.* Cambridge, Mass.: MIT Press, 1972.

Kleingartner, Archie. "Collective Bargaining by Professionals in Federal Employment in Canada." *Proceedings of the Industrial Relations Research Association, 1972,* pp. 379–86.

Kochan, Thomas A. *Labor Management Relations Research Priorities for the 1980's.* Final Report to the Secretary of Labor. Washington: U.S. Department of Labor, 1980.

Korpi, Walter. *The Working Class in Welfare Capitalism: Work, Unions and Politics in Sweden.* New York: Routledge and Kegan Paul, 1978.

Kujawa, Duane. *International Labor and the Multinational Enterprise.* New York: Praeger, 1975.

Lapidus, Gail Worshofsky. "USSR Women at Work: Changing Patterns." *Industrial Relations* 14 (May 1975): pp. 178–95.

Lebel, Helene. "Collective Bargaining for Professionals under the Public Service Staff Relations Act of Canada." *Proceedings of the Industrial Relations Research Association, 1972,* pp. 387–98.

Levine, Solomon B. "Labour Market Segmentation in the Economic Development of Japan." In Kannappan ed. (1977).

———. "Review of Sturmthal and Scoville (1973)." *Economic Development and Cultural Change* 26 (October 1977): pp. 169–76.

Levine, Solomon B., and Koji Taira. "Interpreting Industrial Conflict: The Case of Japan." *Proceedings of the Industrial Relations Research Association, 1977,* pp. 123–31.

Lightman, Ernie S. "Economics of Supply of Canada's Military Manpower." *Industrial Relations* 14 (May 1975): pp. 209–19.

Malm, F. T. "Britain's Training Act: A Manpower Revolution?" *Industrial Relations* 11 (May 1972): pp. 245–59.

Marsh, Robert M., and Hiroshi Mannari. "Pay and Social Structure in a Japanese Firm." *Industrial Relations* 12 (February 1973): pp. 16–32.

Martin, Philip L., and Mark J. Miller. "Guestworkers: Lessons from Western Europe." *Industrial and Labor Relations Review* 33 (April 1980): pp. 315–30.

McCullough G. B. "Multinational Bargaining: An MNC Perspective." *Proceedings of the Industrial Relations Research Association, 1977,* pp. 97–104.

McGee, T. G., and Y. M. Yeung. *Hawkers in Southeast Asian Cities: Planning for the Bazaar Economy.* Ottawa: International Development Research Center, 1977.

Meyers, Frederic. "Public Employee Unions: The French Experience." *Industrial Relations* 12 (February 1973): pp. 33–50.

———. *Mexican Industrial Relations from the Perspective of the Labor Court.* Berkeley: Institute of Industrial Relations, University of California, 1979.

Mitchell, Daniel J. B. "Incomes Policy and the Labor Market in France." *Industrial and Labor Relations Review* 25 (April 1972): pp. 315–35.

———. *Labor Issues of American International Trade and Investment.* Baltimore: Johns Hopkins University Press, 1976.

Nightingale, Donald V. "The Formally Participative Organization." *Industrial Relations* 18 (Fall 1979): pp. 310–21.

Northrup, Herbert R., and Richard L. Rowan. "Multinational Bargaining Approaches in the Western European Flat Glass Industry." *Industrial and Labor Relations Review* 30 (October 1976): 32–46.

———. *Multinational Collective Bargaining Attempts: The Record, the Cases, and the Prospects.* Philadelphia: Industrial Research Unit, Wharton School, University of Pennsylvania, 1979.

Obradovic, Josip. "Workers' Participation: Who Participates?" *Industrial Relations* 14 (February 1975): pp. 32–44.

Pastore, Jose, Archibald O. Haller, and Hernando Gomez-Buendia. "Wage Differentials in Sao Paolo's Labor Force." *Industrial Relations* 14 (October 1975): pp. 345–57.

Piore, Michael J. "The 'New Immigration' and the Presumptions of Social Policy." *Proceedings of the Industrial Relations Research Association, 1974,* pp. 350–58.

———. *Birds of Passage: Migrant Labor and Industrial Societies.* New York: Cambridge University Press, 1979.

Rehmus, Charles M. *Public Employment Labor Relations: An Overview of Eleven Nations.* Ann Arbor: Institute of Labor and Industrial Relations, University of Michigan–Wayne State University, 1975.

Reubens, Beatrice G. *The Hard to Employ: European Programs.* New York: Columbia University Press, 1970.

Roomkin, Myron. "The Implications of Foreign Training Practices for American Apprenticeship." *Proceedings of the Industrial Relations Research Association, 1974,* pp. 71–79.

Rosenstein, Eliezer, and George Strauss. "Workers Participation: A Critical View." *Industrial Relations* 9 (February 1970): pp. 197–214.

Rus, Veljko. "Influence Structure in Yugoslav Enterprise." *Industrial Relations* 9 (February 1970): pp. 148–60.

Sacks, Michael Paul. *Women's Work in Soviet Russia: Continuity in the Midst of Change.* New York: Praeger, 1976.

Sapsford, D. A. "A Time-Series Analysis of U.K. Industrial Disputes." *Industrial Relations* 14 (May 1975): pp. 242–49.

Schlagheck, James. *The Political, Economic and Labor Climate in Mexico.* Philadelphia: Industrial Research Unit, Wharton School, University of Pennsylvania, 1977.

Schnitzer, Martin. *Regional Unemployment and the Relocation of Workers: The Experience of Western Europe, Canada and the U.S.* New York: Praeger, 1970.

Schrank, Robert. *American Workers Abroad.* Cambridge, Mass.: MIT Press, 1979.

Scoville, James G. "Pre-industrial Industrial Relations: The Case of Afghanistan." In Sturmthal and Scoville, eds. (1973).

———. "Afghan Labor Markets: A Model of Interdependence." *Industrial Relations* 13 (October 1974): pp. 274–87.

———. "Sectoral Interdependence in the Urban Labor Market and Variations in the Social and Economic Environment." In Kannappan, ed. (1977).

———. "The Role and Functioning of the Traditional Industrial Sector: Some Preliminary Evidence." Presented to the IVth IIRA World Congress, Geneva, 1976.

———. "Social Tensions, Labor Market Conditions, and Industrial Conflict," In *Social Tensions and Industrial Relations Arising in the Industrialization Process of Asian Countries.* Tokyo: Japan Institute of Labour, 1979.

Seidman, Bert. "The ILO—Past Accomplishments and Future Prospects." *Proceedings of the Industrial Relations Research Association, 1974,* pp. 94–99.

Sellier, F. "The French Workers' Movement and Political Unionism." In Sturmthal and Scoville, eds. (1973).

Shorter, E., and C. Tilly. *Strikes in France, 1830–1968.* London and New York: Cambridge University Press, 1974.

Sinclair, Stuart W. *Urbanization and Labor Markets in Developing Countries.* New York: St. Martins Press, 1978.

Smith, Charles H. Jr. "ILO—Accomplishments, Prospects, Recommendations: The U.S. Employers' View." *Proceedings of the Industrial Relations Research Association, 1974,* pp. 85–93.

Smith, Douglas A. "Wage Linkages between Canada and the United States." *Industrial and Labor Relations Review* 29 (January 1976): pp. 258–68.

Smith, Robert H. T. *Periodic Markets, Hawkers, and Traders in Africa, Asia and Latin America.* Vancouver: Center for Transportation Studies, 1978.

Smyth, David J., and Peter D. Lowe. "The Vestibule to the Occupational Ladder and Unemployment: Some Econometric Evidence on United Kingdom Structural Unemployment." *Industrial and Labor Relations Review* 23 (July 1970): pp. 561–65.

Soutar, Douglas H. "Co-determination, Industrial Democracy and the Role of Management." *Proceedings of the Industrial Relations Research Association, 1973,* pp. 1–8.

Spalding, Hobart A. Jr. *Organized Labor in Latin America: Historical Studies of Workers in Dependent Societies.* New York: New York University Press, 1977.

Stoikov, Vladimir. "Size of Firm, Worker Earnings and Human Capital: The Case of Japan." *Industrial and Labor Relations Review* 26 (July 1973): pp. 1095–1106.

Strauss, George, ed. "Workers Participation in Management: An International Comparison." *Industrial Relations* 9 (February 1970): pp. 117–214, and 18 (Fall 1979), pp. 247–357.

Sturmthal, Adolf A. *Comparative Labor Movements: Ideological Roots and Institutional Development.* Belmont, Calif.: Wadsworth, 1972.

Sturmthal, Adolf A., and James G. Scoville, eds. *The International Labor Movement in Transition.* Urbana: University of Illinois Press, 1973.

Taft, Philip J. *Defending Freedom: American Labor and Foreign Affairs.* Los Angeles: Nash Publishing, 1973.

Taira, Koji. "Review of Howe (1973)." *Industrial and Labor Relations Review* 28 (January 1975): pp. 316–17.

———. "Internal Labour Markets, Ability Utilization and Economic Growth." In Kannappan, ed. (1977).

Thompson, Mark. "The Development of Collective Bargaining in Canadian Universities." *Proceedings of the Industrial Relations Research Association, 1975,* pp. 257–65.

Thomson, Andrew W. J. "Collective Bargaining Under Incomes Legislation: The Case of Britain's Buses." *Industrial and Labor Relations Review* 24 (April 1971): pp. 389–406.

———. "Trade Unions and the Corporate State in Britain." *Industrial and Labor Relations Review* 33 (October 1979): pp. 36–54.

Ulman, Lloyd. "Multinational Unionism: Incentives, Barriers, and Alternatives." *Industrial Relations* 14 (February 1975): pp. 1–31.

Ulman, Lloyd, and Robert Flanagan. *Wage Restraint: A Study of Incomes Policies in Western Europe.* Berkeley: University of California Press, 1971.

Vanderkamp, John. "Economic Activity and Strikes in Canada." *Industrial Relations* 9 (February 1970): pp. 215–30.

Walsh, William D. "Economic Conditions and Strike Activity in Canada." *Industrial Relations* 14 (February 1975): pp. 45–54.

Weinberg, Paul J. *European Labor and the Multinationals.* New York: Praeger, 1978.

Weiss, L. W. "Concentration and Labor Earnings." *American Economic Review* 56 (March 1966): pp. 96–117.

Westenholz, Ann. "Workers' Participation in Denmark." *Industrial Relations* 18 (Fall 1979): pp. 376–80.

Windmuller, John. "Czechoslovakia and the Communist Union Model." *British Journal of Industrial Relations* 9 (March 1971): pp. 33–54.

———. "U.S. Participation in the ILO: The Political Dimension." *Proceedings of the Industrial Relations Research Association, 1974,* pp. 100–108.

———. "The Authority of National Trade Union Confederations: A Comparative Analysis." In *Union Power and Public Policy,* ed. David Lipsky. Ithaca, N.Y.: Cornell University Press, 1975.

———. "European Regionalism: A New Factor in International Labour." *Industrial Relations Journal* (Summer 1976a), pp. 36–48.

———. "Realignment in the ICFTU: The Impact of Detente." *British Journal of Industrial Relations* 14 (November 1976b): pp. 247–60.

Windmuller, John, ed. "European Labor and Politics: A Symposium." *Industrial and Labor Relations Review* 28 (October 1974): pp. 3–88, and (January 1975): pp. 203–81.

———. "Industrial Democracy in International Perspective." *Annals of the American Academy of Political and Social Science* 431 (May 1977): pp. vii–140.

Windmuller, John P., and Jean A. Baderschneider. "International Guidelines for Industrial Relations: Outlook and Impact." *Proceedings of the Industrial Relations Research Association, 1977,* pp. 81–89.

CHAPTER 2

Wage Determination and Public Policy

ROBERT J. FLANAGAN
Stanford University

DANIEL J. B. MITCHELL
University of California, Los Angeles

More than in any previous period, wage research in the 1970s focused on testing the explanatory power of alternative theories through econometric techniques and the use of novel data files. Section I of this chapter begins with a review of important statistical regularities that economists observed and sought to understand. The causes of wage differentials are considered in Section II, and the special case of public-sector wage setting is examined in Section III. The subject of Section IV is federal programs to put a floor under wages, while efforts to restrain wage increases through incomes policy are discussed in Section V. Finally, in the concluding section, wage "peculiarities"—which institutionalists have long recognized but economists have just begun to analyse—are considered as an important area for future research.

I. Stylized Facts About Wages

Table 1 presents a series of observations about wages which have motivated research in the 1970s. Although the precise figures and results shown depend on the data sets used to prepare the table, the generalizations are "robust." They would be likely to appear regardless of the details of statistical sources.

Education and Age

Panels (1) and (2) illustrate the relationship of age and education with income. The more educated people have higher in-

TABLE 1

Empirical Observations on Income and Wages

Observations	Examples		
1. Incomes of those at the younger and older ends of the age scales are lower than incomes of those in the middle.	Median annual income of year-round full-time workers, 1977 (14–19 years = 100)		
	Age	Males	Females
	14–19	100	100
	20–24	162	133
	25–34	234	169
	35–44	279	165
	45–54	282	162
	55–64	259	157
	65 and older	229	139
2. Incomes of those with more education are higher than incomes of those with less education.	Median annual income of year-round full-time workers, 1977 (0–7 years education = 100)		
	Education	Males	Females
	0–7 years	100	100
	8 years	128	108
	9–11 years	139	122
	12 years	164	146
	13–15 years	172	167
	16 or more years	219	208
3. Males earn more than females.	Median weekly earnings of full-time wage and salary workers, 1980–III		
		16–24 years	25 years and older
	Female/male earnings ratio	80%	62%

TABLE 1—*continued*

Observations	Examples				
4. Whites earn more than blacks.	Median weekly earnings of full-time wage and salary workers, 1980–III				
		Males		Females	
	Black/white earning ratio	75%		91%	
5. Union workers earn more than nonunion workers.	Usual weekly earnings of full-time wage and salary workers, May 1977				
		White males	White females	Nonwhite males	Nonwhite females
	Union/nonunion earnings ratio				
	All occupations	1.06	1.29	1.30	1.34
	Blue-collar	1.32	1.31	1.43	1.38
6. Workers in large firms earn more than workers in small firms.	Annual payroll/employee, 1972 (1–4 employees = 100)				
		Employment size of firm			
	Major industry of firm	1–4 employees	100–249 employees	1000–2400 employees	10,000 or more employees
	All	100	140	151	177
	Minerals	100	116	126	127
	Construction	100	176	182	188
	Manufacturing	100	105	119	148
	Wholesale trade	100	111	114	n.a.
	Retail trade	100	136	128	148
	Selected services	100	110	138	n.a.

TABLE 1—*continued*

Observations	Examples
7. Workers in industries with longer median tenure on the job earn more than workers in industries with shorter tenure.	$AHE = .49 + 3.82 TENURE$ $(3.91)\quad(6.42)$ $\bar{R}^2 = .36$ ( ) = t-statistic AHE = Average hourly earnings in 1978 in dollars $TENURE$ = Median years of tenure as of Jan. 1978 on the job[a]
8. Employees in capital-intensive industries tend to earn more than those in labor intensive industries and have longer tenure on the job.	$AHE = 5.40 + .54K/L$ $(17.24)\quad(2.91)$ $\bar{R}^2 = .23$ ( ) = t-statistic $TENURE = 3.48 + .86K/L$ $(9.74)\quad(4.04)$ $\bar{R}^2 = .38$ ( ) = t-statistic K/L = Capital/labor ratio measured by depreciation per hour worked, 1975
9. Federal civilian employees earn more than private-sector workers; state and local employees earn about the same as private workers.	

	Compensation per full-time equivalent worker, 1978 (private = 100)	Wages and salaries per full-time equivalent workers, 1978 (private = 100)
Federal-civilian	139	140
State and local	101	99

TABLE 1—*continued*

Observations	Examples
10. The impact of unemployment on wage change weakened in the 1970s while the effect of previous inflation increased.	Period of observation: 1954–1969
	$\%W = -.71 + 23.8U^{-1} + .18\%CPI_{-1}$ $\quad \bar{R}^2 = .69 \quad$ DW = 2.35
	$(-.77) \quad (5.48) \quad (1.10)$
	Period of observation: 1970–1980
	$\%W = 2.18 + 16.38U^{-1} + .48\%CPI_{-1}$ $\quad \bar{R}^2 = .46 \quad$ DW = .98
	$(.55) \quad (.95) \quad (2.58)$
	$\%W$ = percent change in nonfarm business compensation per hour
	U^{-1} = inverse of official unemployment rate
	$\%CPI_{-1}$ = percent change in consumer price index lagged one year
	( ) = t-statistic

Sources: Panels (1) and (2), U.S. Bureau of the Census, *A Statistical Portrait of Women in the United States, 1978*, P-23, No. 100 (Washington: U.S. Government Printing Office, 1980), pp. 74–75; Panels (3) and (4), *Daily Labor Report*, November 26, 1980, pp. B1–B17; Panel (5), U.S. Bureau of Labor Statistics, *Earnings and Other Characteristics of Organized Workers, May 1977*, Report 556 (Washington: U.S. Government Printing Office, 1979), pp. 28–31; Panel (6), U.S. Bureau of the Census, *1972 Enterprise Statistics*, ES72–1, Part 1, General Report on Industrial Organizations (Washington: U.S. Government Printing Office, 1977), Table 5; Panels (7) and (8), *AHE* from the U.S. Bureau of Labor Statistics, *Employment and Earnings, United States, 1909–78*, Bull. 1312–11 (Washington, U.S. Government Printing Office, 1979, pp. 5–893, *TENURE* from U.S. Bureau of Labor Statistics, *Job Tenure Declines as Work Force Changes*, Special Labor Force Rep. 235 (Washington: U.S. Government Printing Office, 1980), Tables D and E, *K/L* from *Survey of Current Business* 59 (July 1979), pp. 55, 60; Panel (9), *Survey of Current Business* 59 (July 1979), pp. 54–55; Panel (10), U.S. President, *Economic Report of the President 1981* (Washington: U.S. Government Printing Office, 1981), pp. 264, 276, 293.

[a] Median male and female tenures weighted by proportions of male and female employees.

comes, although the educational gains for males seem greater than those for females. Age, in contrast, seems to increase income to a limit; thereafter further aging is associated with an income decline. Again, the age effect seems more pronounced for men than for women. Obvious questions are posed by these figures. Does education raise worker productivity? Does age reflect changes in "human capital," say, through on-the-job learning and skill depreciation?

Race and Sex

Discrimination in the labor market was a major area of public-policy concern and economic research in the 1970s. Panels (3) and (4) illustrate that in 1980, as in previous years, males on average earned more than females, and whites earned more than blacks (despite a narrowing of racial wage differentials during the decade). Economists wondered how much of the observed sex and race wage differentials could be attributed to discrimination and how much to differences in individual characteristics such as education. To the extent that there was a discriminatory effect, how much did government programs aimed at "equal employment opportunity" alleviate the problem?

Union Status and Firm Size

Although labor economics is no longer synonymous with the study of unions, academic interest in union wage effects increased in the 1970s. Panel (5) indicates that union workers earn more than nonunion workers, even after standardization for length of workweek, race, and sex. Observed differentials seem wider for groups likely to earn relatively low wages—women and nonwhites. Do unions cause wage differentials, or are other explanatory characteristics simply associated with unionization?

Panel (6) shows that firm size is positively associated with wages, in seeming defiance of the "law of one price." Is this a statistical aberration, to be attributed, again, to other factors? Or are there reasons to think that large firms might be motivated to pay "more"?

Turnover and Capital Intensity

According to Panel (7), turnover and wage level are inversely related. Tenure on the job lengthens with the wage level, across a sample of 26 industries. Moreover, Panel (8) suggests that higher wage levels and capital intensity of production are positively correlated. Various hypotheses could be spawned from these observations. Does time on the job develop skills for which employers are willing to pay a premium to retain? Are such desirable characteristics of workers likely to be associated with high levels of physical capital investment?

Public-Private Wage Differentials

Budgetary and industrial relations concerns in the public sector have focused attention on government wage-setting for its own employees. Panel (9) indicates that, at the federal level, employees on average receive higher pay than in the private sector, but that such a differential is not found with regard to other levels of government. These are gross figures. Researchers, looking at public-private wage differentials, wanted to know whether adjustment for characteristics such as occupation would substantially change the gross results.

Wage-Change Determination

Wage change and price change are highly correlated at the aggregate level. As inflation mounted, a substantial research effort was devoted to characterizing macro wage determination. Panel (10) summarizes a prominent finding. For the period from the mid-1950s through the late 1960s, wage equations looked like the old Phillips curve. Unemployment was the main explanatory variable for wage change. In the 1970s, however, inflation seemed to perpetuate itself. Previous inflation seemed an important determinant of wage change, while the significance of the unemployment effect diminished. Recession, the traditional anti-inflation weapon, seemed to lose its anti-inflation punch. As a result, wage-price controls and guidelines were tried, and economists asked two questions: First, empirically, how effective was "incomes policy" as an inflation fighter? Second, theoretically, what factors might account for the refusal of wage-setters to react to unemployment in accordance with classical economic analysis?

II. Wage Structure Research

In a very important sense, the fundamental ideas underlying research into the wage structure during the 1970s were advanced by

Adam Smith some 200 years earlier. In *The Wealth of Nations*, Smith remarked that:

> The whole of the advantages and disadvantages of the different employments of labour and stock must, in the same neighbourhood, be either perfectly equal or continually tending to equality. . . . The five following are the principal circumstances which, so far as I have been able to observe, make up for a small pecuniary gain in some employments, and counter-balance a great one in others: first, the agreeableness or disagreeableness of the employments themselves; secondly, the easiness and cheapness, or the difficulty and experience of learning them; thirdly, the consistency or inconsistency of employment in them; fourthly, the small or great trust which must be reposed in those who exercise them; and fifthly, the probability or improbability of success in them. (Smith 1937, pp. 99–100.)

Smith's concept of equalizing wage differentials between jobs with different employment "costs" (broadly conceived) was at the foundation of most of the major theoretical and empirical advances in wage structure research during the 1970s. Specifically, much of the research into the wage structure centered on conceptual elaborations of Smith's first and third "circumstances," respectively, through the extension of hedonic pricing theory to the analysis of the relationship between wages and employment conditions and through the further development of human capital theory.

Human Capital

Although several economists had previously advanced the proposition that schooling, training, and other labor market decisions should be analyzed in an investment framework, the major theoretical advances did not occur until the 1960s with landmark works by Becker (1967, 1975). Becker's work stressed that rational choices over schooling (and other human capital investments in training, migration, information, and health, for example) involve a comparison of the costs and benefits of an investment by the relevant decision-maker. Human investments typically require both direct costs—for example, tuition and books in the case of formal education—and (usually more importantly) forgone earnings during the period of investment. The return on the investment takes the form of a higher lifetime-earnings stream resulting from increased productivity of an individual associated with the investment.

The human capital formulation of the compensating wage differential idea stressed the importance of lifetime earnings as the central concept in interpreting the wage structure and labor market behavior. As a corollary, the present discounted value of lifetime earnings became the appropriate frame of reference for measuring income inequality. Clearly, current wage rates or annual earnings can be distributed much differently than lifetime earnings. Those who invest in human capital receive more lifetime earnings, but the higher earnings come later in life. In equilibrium, the present discounted value of lifetime earnings of those who invest and those who do not is the same, but in any given year there can be marked earnings differentials between the two groups. On the other hand, an empirical study by Lillard and Willis (1978) found a strong correlation between variations in annual and lifetime earnings.

School and Training Programs

The human capital approach exploited Adam Smith's notion of compensating wage differentials by recognizing that the higher costs associated with higher levels of schooling would have to be offset by higher future earnings in order to induce investments in additional years of schooling. In doing so, it provided a rationalization for the observed positive correlation between earnings and schooling (see Table 1, Panel (1)), although, as will be seen below, this rationalization did not remain unchallenged. Subsequently, extensive exploitation of data on earnings (but not total compensation) and schooling has confirmed that the pecuniary rates of return to schooling are positive, tend to be smaller at higher levels of schooling, compared favorably with investments in physical capital at least until the late 1960s, but can change over time (Hanoch 1967, Freeman 1975). Freeman in particular found a substantial decline in the rate of return to schooling by the mid-1970s.

The human capital view of schooling also provided important insights into the nature of labor market adjustments. Earlier studies of the role of the wage structure in allocating labor among sectors typically rested on statistical correlations of employment changes and wage changes across occupations, industries, or regions over a certain period of time. In general these studies produced rather mixed results concerning the efficacy of the wage structure as an allocational device. One weakness in these studies was their failure to recognize that many of the labor market adjustments posited by competitive labor market theory required substantial human investment costs (for example, in schooling, training, information, and/or migration). Willingness to incur these costs would depend on one's position in the life cycle.

Because the returns to human capital investments consist of a higher earnings stream over the remaining years in the labor force, these investments tend to be concentrated at younger ages when the potential returns will be highest. As a result, the actual mobility of labor between sectors will be concentrated in the younger age cohorts so that the labor market adjustment process may be obscured statistically in analyses using data covering all ages. Where desirable reallocations of labor are tied to schooling investments, the reallocation may not even show up as a labor force flow. Indeed, some of the more important labor force adjustments occur as students make decisions over enrollment specialties before they enter the labor force.

Research during the 1970s demonstrated that changes in relative wages of many professional occupations were a significant influence on the choice of a major or graduate training specialty by individuals currently enrolled in school (Freeman 1971). A significant part of the ultimate labor force response in occupations requiring substantial human capital investments is through the feedback of changing market signals (relative wages, for example) on enrollment choices. As a result, the supply responses in these markets operate with long lags imposed by training times.

A significant body of research during the 1970s challenged both the measurement and interpretation of the relationship between schooling and earnings. The first of these challenges questioned the implicit ceteris paribus assumption underlying many estimates of the rate of return to schooling. If students with better labor market skills are also more successful in school, they will be more likely to remain in school longer than less skilled students. Ability will be spuriously correlated with schooling. Since ability in school is also correlated with productivity in the labor market, studies of the earnings-schooling relationship that do not first control for ability will produce overestimates of the rate of return to schooling.

Two research strategies were used in an effort to estimate the extent of this bias. One set of studies added variables for IQ (consisting of scores from various tests of cognitive ability) directly to regressions of earnings on schooling and other variables (Griliches and Mason 1972, Taubman and Wales 1973). The second strategy exploited data on twins that permitted controls for genetic endowments and the broader family environment (Taubman 1976).

Each of the studies in the first group has distinct limitations. The availability of IQ data limited the studies to nonrandom samples of the labor force from different segments of the skills and earnings distribution. Tests used to measure IQ varied from study to study, information on noncognitive ability (for example, leadership) was not generally available, and there was relatively little consideration of whether the (cognitive) abilities valued by schools are valued by the market. As a group, however, the studies support the view that some of the monetary returns originally attributed to schooling are in fact returns to ability. Moreover, the independent role of ability on earnings may increase with occupational level and/or with age.

Depending on the sample, the results indicate that the returns to schooling may be overstated by 10 to 30 percent when the effects of ability are not taken into account. The twin studies, which control for genetic and family environment influences that go well beyond cognitive ability, indicate that as much as 45 to 65 percent of the simple relationships between schooling and earnings is more properly attributed to factors that are more or less determined before individuals enter the formal education system. The findings also indicate the significant extent to which earnings differentials reflect factors that are beyond the control of the individual.

The second major challenge to the earnings-schooling relationship was theoretical. In the human capital model, the relationship between earnings and schooling arises because education is presumed to increase skills. However, the same empirical relationship could also be rationalized by a process in which the educational system simply identifies more able individuals but does not itself provide an increment to preexisting skills. "Signalling" and "screening" models exploring this alternative interpretation of the earnings-schooling relationship were developed during the 1970s (for example, Spence 1974, Stiglitz 1975).

Signalling models apply to situations in which an employer knows that skill varies among job applicants (that is, the probability distribution of skill is known), but faces high costs of identifying the true productivity of individual applicants. In the absence of direct information on individual productivity, the employer will pay each individual hired the expected marginal revenue product. Under the screening model, if the costs of schooling are inversely related to the level of skill, those individuals who are inherently more skilled will be willing to invest in more schooling to signal their higher ability to employers; the signalling investment would be more costly for the less skilled individuals, and they would be less willing to incur the expense. Given these circumstances, employers would be willing to pay a higher wage to individuals with more schooling. Schooling identifies more able individuals, but does not add to their skills.

The private rate of return to schooling is the same under either the human capital (productivity enhancing) or screening (information providing) interpretation of the underlying process. However, the social return to schooling is quite different. Output increases with schooling in the human capital view of the world, but in a screening process, schooling merely redistributes earnings between individuals with different levels of schooling.

With such fundamental issues at stake, it is surprising that there has been so little effort to explore the relative merit of these two interpretations of the earnings-schooling relationship. It is by no means clear that empirical explorations of earnings-education-ability interactions (discussed above) settle the issue, since the empirical representations of ability in those studies are not obviously the best measure of the skills that matter to employers. In a somewhat different approach, Wise (1975) analyzed the rewards for the performance of college-educated individuals in a large corporation and found that the extreme form of the screening or signalling argument did not hold. Nevertheless, understanding of the relationship between earnings and education would benefit from more research on the screening issue.

Age and Experience

The human capital model also produced important implications concerning the structure of wages by age and, more fundamentally, by experience. While earlier labor economists had frequently stressed the market value of experience, no solid theoretical framework had been developed to explain the tendency for earnings to increase with age until late middle age and then decline (that is, the "inverted U" pattern noted in Panel (1) of Table 1). Research by Jacob Mincer (1970, 1974) began with the assumption that age is often a proxy for experience and explored the wage implications of postschool investments in human capital that are required with labor market experience. Mincer noted that there were two major factors associated with age and experience that influenced the life-cycle pattern of wages. First, following the completion of school or formal training programs, individuals continued to invest in on-the-job training as well as in information and migration. These investments increase individuals' productivity and earnings potential and can account for the initial positive relationship between age or experience and earnings. Since the time horizon that governs returns shortens with age, however, the amount of time allocated to such investments declines with age. Even at lower levels of experience, a diminishing rate of earnings increase is evident. Second, as with physical capital, human capital is subject to depreciation as an individual ages. The depreciation reduces the productivity and, hence, the earnings potential of an individual. Ultimately, the depreciation factor overwhelms the productivity factor, and earnings begin to decrease with age. The distinct peak in the age-earnings data in Panel (1) of Table 1 is therefore explained by the interplay between diminishing postschool human capital and depreciation of an individual's stock of human capital. Mincer's work also showed that experience was a theoretically and statistically more important influence on wages than age. This finding had important implications for the study of wage differentials by sex, as will be seen below.

Human capital analysis of the relationship between earnings, schooling, and experience also provided explanations of the commonly observed tendency for the dispersion of wages among workers in a given age cohort to grow as the cohort ages. The schooling model predicts that the wage differentials for individuals with different educational attainment will increase with age as those with relatively large schooling investments collect the returns on those investments. At the same time, the experience model predicts that for a given level of educational attainment, the dispersion of wages will grow over time as individuals acquire different amounts of postschool investments.

Finally, the work by Mincer provided a stronger theoretical foundation for the earnings function, the primary tool for empirical research on the wage structure during the 1970s. Conceptually, the earnings function is a reduced form that includes as independent variables the various demand and supply factors that influence the wage of an individual. When applied as a multiple regression to data for a sample of individuals, the earnings function yields regression coefficients which describe the marginal contribution of each variable to wages. As part of his work, Mincer derived from human capital theory a specification (in which the dependent variable is the natural logarithm of earnings and human capital investments are expressed in units of time) that became widely used in research on the wage structure.

Search Investments

A second strain of the human capital literature contributed importantly to resolving an apparent conflict between classical formulations of competitive labor market theory and empirical evidence on wages. The competitive theory of the labor market predicts that the equilibrium wage rate for a given occupation in a given labor market area should be uniform across firms for workers of a given quality. However, wage surveys persistently indicate the existence of a dispersion of rates for a given job in a given market. Moreover, older labor market studies consistently found that workers typically do not possess extensive knowledge of alternative pecuniary and nonpecuniary conditions of employment. The theory of information search in labor markets was initially advanced in the 1960s, but was developed extensively in the 1970s (see, for example, Stigler 1962, McCall 1970, and the survey by Lippman and McCall 1976). It successfully resolved this conflict by dropping perhaps the most stringent assumption of the competitive labor market model: perfect information.

Under the investment formulations of labor market search theory, workers compare the cost of another day of search (largely forgone earnings, as in the case of educational investments) with the present value of the expected gain (to the extent that higher wage offers are identified) from that search, over the time that the job will be held. Because there is a cost to acquiring labor market information, search will not be exhaustive, and all wage offers will not be identified. If all offers are not identified, however, there is unlikely to be sufficient mobility from low- to high-wage jobs to eliminate the dispersion of wages in an otherwise competitive market, and the proposition that a competitive labor market equilibrium must yield a single wage rate (for a given skill) is undermined.

In addition to rationalizing wage dispersion, the search branch of human capital theory isolated another individual characteristic with which wages can vary among workers: the personal time horizon. Since one element of the expected return to search activity is the length of time that a job will be held, the theory predicts that individuals with long time horizons will search longer and on average accept jobs with higher wages than will individuals with short time horizons. It also suggests interesting interfirm differences in personnel strategy in competitive markets. Some firms may choose to offer relatively long time horizons, while others (presumably with lower costs associated with turnover) offer lower wages and specialize in workers with relatively short time horizons (Panel (1), Table 1).

Aggregating across individuals, labor market search theory can also contribute to understanding wage differentials between particular demographic groups with systematic differences in the time horizon. For example, if women on average spend a small fraction of their lifetime in the labor force, they may tend to accept lower wages, and some fraction of the observed wage differential by sex therefore reflects the effect of different time horizons on the intensity of search for high-wage positions.

Although many of the theoretical papers on labor market search have indicated important potential empirical and policy implications of the theory, there was very little notable work during the 1970s directed at testing the theory. In particular, the central propositions concerning the structure of wages—the relationships (1) between search costs and the dispersion of wages in a market, and (2) between individual or group differences in time horizon and wage differentials—remain untested.

Compensating Wage Differentials

The human capital approach provided the theoretical and methodological basis for econometric research into the earnings structure and stimulated a large number of empirical studies of individual wage variation. While these studies strongly confirmed the relationships between wages, schooling, age, experience, health, etc., suggested by human capital theory, the statistical results also indicated very considerable residual earnings variation among individuals, even in analyses that adjusted for race, sex, and union status. Clearly, factors other than human capital investments and the more obvious institutional impacts also influenced the earnings structure.

At the same time certain social policy issues focused attention on the relationship between wages and various nonpecuniary aspects of work. Issues of job dissatisfaction, worker-compensation policy, and occupational health and safety all raised questions of whether some of the residual wage variation observed in human capital earnings functions was related to "the agreeableness or disagreeableness of the employments themselves" (Smith 1937, p. 100).

Theoretically, the main approach in developing a behavioral foundation for the equalizing differential idea involved the extension of the theory of hedonic pricing to jobs (Rosen 1974, Thaler and Rosen 1975). Under the hedonic approach, employment contracts are conceptualized as tied sales. Workers are selling labor services and "buying" a package of nonpecuniary employment conditions from employers. Firms jointly produce output and an array of employment conditions, including risk, employment stability, challenge, etc., which are "sold" to workers. In the course of the exchange both the labor services and the employment conditions are "priced."

The key to the resulting job-matching process is the inherent variation in the tastes of workers and the technological possibilities faced by firms. Workers will accept less desirable working conditions only if they receive monetary compensation. But tastes for nonpecuniary conditions (that is, the amount of compensation required to accept less desirable conditions) will vary among workers. At the same time, firms will vary for technological reasons in their ability to produce desirable nonpecuniary conditions of work. Firms that find it prohibitively expensive to improve the work environment will instead offer higher wages than employers who can improve the environment relatively inexpensively. The net result of the variation among firms and workers is a job-matching process in which workers who are least averse to relatively undesirable working conditions (risk, for example) accept jobs with firms that find it most costly to improve conditions, because the wage premium offered by such firms compensates (at least) for the undesirable conditions. Empirically, it is possible to identify the equilibrium schedule of wages and working conditions that is the outcome of the matching process, even though the individual supply and demand schedules for various nonpecuniary working conditions are not observable.

Operating within this general research framework, there were several empirical investigations of the relationship between wages and risk of death or injury (Thaler and Rosen, 1975, Smith 1975 and 1979, Viscusi 1978 and 1979) and various aspects of job content (Duncan 1976, Hamermesh 1978, Brown 1980). These studies provided the strongest support for the theory of compensating differentials. Earnings functions that augment the human capital model with measures of the risk of death associated with an individual's occupation and/or industry consistently show a positive wage premium (averaging 2–6 percent of the average wage of workers in the sample) associated with that risk (Smith 1979).

Estimates of wage-risk tradeoffs have potentially important policy applications. As national regulatory policy moved increasingly in the direction of setting standards for workplace safety, the demand increased for cost-benefit analyses of alternative standards or alternative levels of a given standard. Yet many of the projected benefits of regulatory activity were in the form of reduced risk of death or injury to workers who may have been receiving compensating wage differentials. What is the social value of a reduced risk of death under such circumstances? The cost-benefit standard is willingness to pay, but how does one discover how much members of society are willing to pay to save a life? Interpreted from the perspective of hedonic theory, the earnings-function estimates of risk premium indicate how much an individual will pay for a small reduction in the probability of death. It is straightforward to use this information to estimate the implicit social value of saving a single life.

While there has been consistent empirical support for the existence of a wage premium associated with risk of death, the estimates of the magnitude of the premium (and hence the implicit value of saving a life) have varied substantially. In reviewing the estimates provided by eight studies, for example, Smith (1979) finds that the estimated value of a life (that is, the total amount that workers are willing to pay for a 1/1000 reduction in the risk of death) varies from $.2 million to $3.5 million! The range reflects in part differences in the selection of estimating techniques. Even with methodological uniformity, however, some variation is likely to remain. Nevertheless, even a range of estimates can be a useful base against which the actual costs of regulatory proposals can be contrasted.

Unfortunately, attempts to estimate the effects of injury risk and nonpecuniary job attributes (as opposed to the risk of death) have yielded far less consistent results. Some studies have obtained significant results that are consistent with the theory; others have not turned up the predicted sign or significance on particular nonpecuniary conditions. The relationship between wages and job characteristics may be inherently less systematic, since there may be considerably greater variation among workers in their appraisal of the desirability of particular aspects of job content than in their evaluation of the risk of death. Nevertheless, there are policy issues at stake that would make a more careful estimate of these tradeoffs desirable.

The nature of compensating differentials that emerges in public-sector markets can also have a bearing on the equitable distribution of public services. In an interesting analysis of the labor market for public school teachers, Antos and Rosen (1975) show that the wages of teachers vary with the characteristics of their students, their schools, and the neighborhoods in which they work, as well as with their human capital characteristics. Since the labor market choices by teachers reveal that they prefer to teach smart students at modern schools in stable neighborhoods, simple school finance allocational formulas such as equal expenditure per pupil across districts will not produce equality in real schooling inputs across districts. Poor districts which pay more for teachers will end up with fewer real resources. What is needed is a hedonic index that indicates the labor cost of providing a specific set of inputs in each district.

Wage Differentials by Race and Sex

Some of the largest and most persistent wage differentials in the U.S. labor market are associated with the characteristics of race and sex (see Panels (3) and (4), Table 1). Moreover, these have historically been among the most stable measurements in labor economics. During most of the twentieth century, annual earnings and occupational position of nonwhites relative to whites was low and unchanging with the exception of brief periods of relative gain during wartime labor market conditions. In the 1960s, the differentials began to narrow, particularly between black and white women. In the case of women relative to men, the documentary evidence is even longer. According to the *Bible*: "The Lord spoke to Moses saying '. . . the following scale shall apply; if it is a male from 20 to 30 years of age, the equivalent is fifty shekels of silver by the sanctuary weight; if it is a female, the equivalent is thirty shekels'" (Leviticus 27:1–4). And decade after decade in the twentieth century, the *Census of Population* reports that women earned about 60 percent of the average annual earnings of men.

The apparent persistence of wage differentials by race and sex over time presented a major intellectual puzzle, since the leading economic theory of labor market discrimination (Becker 1971, Arrow 1972) suggested that in general equilibrium, wage differentials attributable to discrimination should not survive. That is, the standard model of employer and employee prejudice against labor market minorities predicts that competition in the labor and/or product markets will erode discriminatory wage differentials. There was thus a significant conflict between the prevailing theory of discrimination and labor market measurements as of the early 1970s. The theory could survive if the measurements were shown to be in error (that is, if factors other than race or sex accounted for the observed earnings differentials between whites and nonwhites or between men and women). But if the measurements survived, a stronger theory was needed.

Most of the research on labor market discrimination during the 1970s addressed the question of measurement error. With the development of large data files with detailed socioeconomic data on individuals and econometric accounting techniques, economists were able to explore the extent to which race and gender, operating independently of factors influencing worker productivity, influenced wages. In most important respects, the exploration was guided more by developments in the human capital literature than by the theory of labor market discrimination, since human capital theory provided both a guide to important sources of wage differences that would exist between groups in a nondiscriminatory labor market (for example, schooling, training, work experience, health status, etc.) and a measurement tool—the earnings function.

Efforts to estimate labor market discrimination proceeded by applying human capital earnings functions, often expanded to include variables controlling for occupation, industry, and region, to very large samples of individuals. The most simple technique was to add a dummy variable for race or sex and interpret the estimated coefficient (if significant) as the "pure" race or sex effect. One drawback of this approach is that by statistically imposing the assumption that the various forms of human capital influence the wages of all groups equally, it provides no information on how the labor market or company personnel systems operate to produce lower wages for blacks and women.

A generally more informative approach is to use econometric accounting techniques to analyze the sources of intergroup wage differences. A gross racial wage differential may be attributable in part to racial differences in the "endowment" or productive characteristics and in part to racial differences in the "value" (in terms of wages) of a particular characteristic. The endowment effects may be separated from the value-effects variable when separate earnings functions are estimated on samples for each race (or sex). In particular, if endowment differences do not provide the entire explanation, the regression coefficients on some variables will differ by race and sex. The overall estimate of the "pure" or net race or sex effect can therefore be traced to racial differences in the returns to different productive attributes (unless the only difference is in the constant term, in which case the two procedures are identical). Unfortunately, virtually all empirical research in this area must use various measures of labor quality as proxies for unobservable marginal products (for a rare exception, see Pascal and Rapping 1972), so that this approach to the measurement of labor market discrimination can never be completely free of ambiguity.

Empirical studies of black-white wage differentials at a point in time have generally found that between half and three-quarters of the overall (or "gross") differential is attributable to racial differences in "endowment" factors—that is, characteristics that are more or less determined before individuals reach the labor market (Blinder 1973, Flanagan 1974, Smith and Welch 1977). The most important of the measured endowment influences on racial wage differences are racial differences in the extent of schooling and the disproportionate concentration of blacks in southern labor markets where wages are lower in general. Less powerful endowment influences include differences in the level of on-the-job training and in health status.

In the 1960s and 1970s, the pure race effect on wages (that is, the residual or "net" wage differential that remains after correcting for racial-endowment differences) was clearly important, if not the dominant source of the gross differential. Moreover, up to 40 percent of the race effect was associated with occupational segregation—the disproportionate concentration of blacks in lower paying jobs. These studies also revealed distinct racial wage variations between age cohorts. As of the 1970s, gross racial wage differentials were smallest for the youngest cohorts of labor force participants and the proportion of the differential attributable to endowment effects was relatively large. Given the nature of the measurement procedures and inherent limitations in the data, the cohort findings present a familiar question in discrimination research: Are the newest black labor force cohorts facing less market discrimination than more experienced black workers—due, perhaps, to government equal employment opportunity efforts—or does measurement error vary across age cohorts?

As noted earlier, the pure race effect on wages is ultimately traceable to racial differences in the wage returns to one or more elements of an individual's endowment. Studies cited earlier indicated that the main factors here were the fact that, relative to whites, blacks earned a lower rate of return on schooling and a lower wage in the South, other things equal. Welch (1973) explored the possibility that the lower returns to schooling might reflect racial differences in school quality rather than market discrimination. Evidence on this point is indirect. By several indicators there have been marked differences in the quality of schooling received by whites and blacks in the United States, but the differences at the primary and secondary level have apparently narrowed over time. Racial differences in rates of return to schooling also narrowed for successive cohorts of black workers during the early 1960s, supporting the school-quality hypothesis. However, subsequent research on racial wage differences in 1960 and 1970 indicated that strong "vintage" effects were only observable for black college graduates, a finding that did not accord well with the more general school-quality interpretation (Smith and Welch 1977).

Empirical studies of male-female differentials were also guided in large measure by key propositions of human capital theory. So long as racial conventions are such that women on average allocate a disproportionate amount of time (relative to men on average) to child-rearing and other home-production activities, their time available for market work will be shorter and more dispersed than men's over the life cycle. Moreover, with a shorter expected work life, women face fewer incentives to pursue school and postschool investments. Consistent with the propositions of human capital theory, the age-earnings profile of women is relatively flat so that male-female wage differentials (for a given level of schooling) increase with age (see Panel (3), Table 1). Some care is necessary in the specification of labor experience for women since periods of labor force withdrawal may be associated with actual depreciation of human capital, as noted earlier. Studies that variously capture discontinuities of work experience empirically by the number of children (Oaxaca 1979), or by specifying periods of labor force withdrawal directly (Mincer and Polachek 1974), confirm the negative impact of interrupted experiences on wages. But even with these amendments, significant wage differentials between men and women remain.

These studies also indicated that the occupational segregation is a more important source of the residual or net wage differential in the case of women than in the case of blacks. Conclusions on the relative role of occupational segregation and unequal pay for equal work rest in part on the scope of the occupational categories used in the empirical analysis. The study of wages in a large professional organization by Malkiel and Malkiel (1973) was particularly revealing in this respect. Their estimate of the overall net male-female wage differential within the organization was similar to estimates from analysis of national data. When they controlled for the job levels to which people were assigned in the organization, however, the unequal pay for equal work component of the net wage differential dropped to 3 percent! Differential job assignment of men and women accounted for virtually all of the unexplained wage difference.

By the end of the 1970s it was clear that the extensive and increasingly sophisticated efforts to measure labor market discrimination had narrowed estimates of the magnitude of wage discrimination, but had not disposed of the original intellectual puzzle. For the most part, observed wage differentials by race and sex could not be completely dismissed as measurement error. But, research directed at amending the theory of labor market discrimination to accommodate the observed persistence of net differentials by race and sex was sparse. The major theoretical contribution was the concept of "statistical" discrimination (Aigner and Cain 1977), which drew on the ideas of the screening literature discussed above. At the root of the statistical discrimination argument is the possibility that when it is extremely costly to become fully informed about an individual's productivity, employers may supplement information on individual characteristics with information on group characteristics. That is, an individual's employment prospects may be helped or hindered by the average productivity characteristics of a group (race or sex) to which (s)he belongs, because it may be cheaper for the employer to use group information than to discover the individual's true productivity. The result is systematic difference in the labor market outcomes by race and sex, even in the absence of prejudice on the part of employers or other employees. Moreover, the difference can persist over time, as is observed in the data.

Union-Nonunion Wage Differentials

Several review articles are available on union wage impacts (Freeman and Medoff 1981, Mitchell 1981 and 1980b, Parsley 1980). Hence, the topic will be covered only briefly here. Panel (5) of Table 1 showed that on a gross basis, union workers earn more than nonunion workers and that this tendency is especially marked for groups who would otherwise be low paid. The gap is much wider for blue-collar workers relative to white-collar. Surprisingly, most single-equation studies find that such results persist even after standardization for employee and employer characteristics.

Some studies indicate that the union-nonunion wage gap is offset by equivalent productivity differentials (Brown and Medoff 1978, Allen 1979). Classical theory suggests that this should be the case for marginal productivity, but that the adjustment needed to accomplish the adaptation—for example, capital substitution—would still represent a net cost to unionized employers. If there is a total offset, one must ask why employers generally oppose unionization when possible (Bernstein 1980). Moreover, widening union-nonunion wage differentials in the 1970s and before seemed to be unraveling by the end of the decade in several major bargaining situations (Mitchell 1980a).

Another development in the 1970s was the application of simultaneous-equation techniques to the estimation of union-nonunion wage differences. Some studies purport to find that the differential is an illusion caused by the propensity of higher-paid workers to unionize in order to obtain union "services." Results of such studies, however, have been ambiguous and contradictory (Ashenfelter and Johnson 1972, Duncan and Leigh 1980, Duncan and Stafford 1980). Nonunion workers apparently believe that unionization *would* raise their wages (Farber and Saks 1980, Kochan 1979).

III. Wage Structure in the Public Sector

In a previous IRRA volume, Mitchell (1979) reviewed the literature on government wage-setting through the mid-1970s. By the late 1970s, the economic environment had changed substantially. Government employment grew more slowly than private-sector employment. The growth in the public unionization rate also slowed.

Table 2 displays a breakdown of three classes of public employees—state workers, local workers, and school district workers (a subcategory of local workers)—by their degree of unionization in 1979, defined as the proportion of full-time workers in bargaining units. The table shows that those with employers characterized by above-average unionization rates tended to have higher wage levels and tended to be located in states with above-average unionization

TABLE 2

Wages, Incomes, and Nonfarm Unionization by Government Unionization Rate

	State Employees		Local Employees		School District Employees	
	Unionization > Mean	Unionization < Mean	Unionization > Mean	Unionization < Mean	Unionization > Mean	Unionization < Mean
State employee wage	$1028	$ 901	—	—	—	—
Local employee wage	—	—	$1020	$ 881	—	—
School district employee wage	—	—	—	—	$ 966	$ 795
Nonfarm unionization rate, 1978[a]	27.6%	17.4%	25.1%	17.0%	23.2%	17.2%
Manufacturing hourly earnings	$5.35	$4.58	$5.18	$4.55	$5.05	$4.44
Per capita income	$6254	$5448	$6278	$5298	$5947	$5115
Annual rate of change, 1975–1979						
State employee wage	6.5%	7.4%	—	—	—	—
Local employee wage	—	—	6.7%	7.1%	—	—
School district employee wage	—	—	—	—	6.9%	7.1%
Manufacturing hourly wage	8.4%	9.0%	8.6%	9.0%	8.6%	9.3%
Per capita income	9.6%	10.6%	10.0%	10.5%	10.5%	10.5%
Number of observations	15	35	22	29	25	20

Note: Figures are simple averages of state figures and apply to 1975 unless otherwise noted. Per capita income and nonfarm unionization refer to entire year. Other figures are as of October.

Sources: U.S. Bureau of the Census, *Labor-Management Relations in State and Local Governments: 1979* (Washington: U.S. Government Printing Office, 1980), Table 4; U.S. Bureau of the Census, *Labor-Management Relations in State and Local Governments: 1975* (Washington: U.S. Government Printing Office, 1977), Table 4; *Employment and Earnings*, various issues; U.S. Bureau of Labor Statistics, *Directory of National Unions and Employee Associations, 1979*, Bull. 2079 (Washington: U.S. Government Printing Office, 1980), Table 18.

[a] Excludes employee associations.

(public and private), higher earnings, and greater per capita incomes.

During the period 1975–1979, however, workers in the more heavily unionized columns tended to receive lower percentage wage increases than other workers. Perhaps this is not surprising since the heavily unionized government workers were located in states experiencing below-average increases in private wages and per capita incomes. But government wages in all categories rose more slowly than private wages and incomes. The political benefits and costs for management to taking a hard line in wage negotiations may have shifted in response to taxpayer pressure. Lack of a "bottom line" in government makes the calculus of taking a strike more a function of public attitudes than of dollar costs of disruption.

The Wage Effect of Government

In the private sector, the standard economic model poses a tradeoff to employers between wage level and turnover for an occupation. A profit-maximizing choice along the tradeoff is assumed to be made. Public employers may also react to turnover (Gunderson 1980, p. 257). But the often intangible output of government and the political process make it difficult to define optimality.

Without knowledge of turnover costs and the tradeoff, economists have usually analyzed public-private wage differentials based on comparable worker characteristics standardized for them through regression analysis. If the results indicate that comparable workers in government would earn more (less) in the private sector, public workers are said to be overpaid (underpaid) (for example, Quinn 1979a).

Apart from the optimal turnover question, there are the usual problems of inability to standardize sufficiently. Employee tastes may vary concerning such job attributes as employment security and risk (Bellante and Link 1981) and working conditions other than pay may vary (Quinn 1979b). Even within a level of government, there may be several pay-setting systems and criteria. For example, members of legislatures and top-level executives in government may have different pay systems than other public workers (Hartman and Weber 1980, McCormick and Tollison 1978). Excessive aggregation in statistical studies can be a problem.

Panel (9) of Table 1 has already shown that average federal

pay (unstandardized) is higher than private pay, but that state and local pay is about equal to the average in the private sector. It is interesting to note that even after such standardization, the same conclusions seem to emerge from comparability studies; federal pay tends to emerge as "too high," while state and local pay is "about right." The similarity between adjusted and unadjusted results parallels the analysis of union wage effects.

Within governments there is another "unionesque" effect. Groups that are low paid in private employment are more likely to emerge as "overpaid" in government. Sharon P. Smith (1977) reports such results for nonwhites and women. Since it is known that sex stereotyping and other trappings of discrimination have a long history in government (Strober and Best 1979), these findings may simply mean that less discrimination (rather than none or reverse) exists in public employment compared with private. Still, government pay practices may reduce overall black-white wage dispersion (D. Alton Smith 1980).

Two suggestions for future research emerge from the experience of the 1970s. First, the impact of the taxpayer revolt needs further quantification. Some empirical research is already taking place in this area (Sharon P. Smith 1981). Second, the analysis of budget restriction should be widened to incorporate pay *structure* effects. In a unique area of government—the military—the costs of tying pay to rank rather than occupation have been documented (Binkin and Kyriakopoulos 1981). Similar rigidities exist for civilian government workers, for example, the police-fire linkage and the tying of teacher pay to tenure and seniority rather than field of specialization. Since such rigidities are found in private employment, public-private comparisons of structural inflexibilities would be useful contributions to knowledge.

Collective Bargaining and Government Wages

Wage differentials associated with unions in the public sector have generally not been found wider than in private employment; indeed, they often are less. Other aspects are also similar to the private union impact. It appears that larger differentials are associated with blue-collar employment than with white-collar, although both groups join unions for economic benefits (Warner, Chisholm, and Munzenrider 1978, Shapiro 1978). In addition, the fringe-benefit effect is disproportionate to the wage impact (Bartel and Lewin 1981, Ichniowski 1980, Becker 1979). As in the private sector, the public union wage impact may accumulate over a period of time rather than occur as a one-shot affair (Ichniowski 1980).

Spillovers of wage settlements have long interested economists studying the private sector. Some evidence has been found of "threat" effects in public employment whereby union wages affect nonunion or one union's settlement affects another (Victor 1979, Becker 1979). So far the studies have been cross-sectional. Research on a time-series basis would also be useful, especially since there may be dynamic elements. For example, in the New York City case, the fiscal crisis is reported to have caused a move from pattern bargaining (a form of spillover) to coalition bargaining (a tighter linkage) (Lewin and McCormick 1981).

One research concern in the private sector that is difficult to address in government is the impact of unions on the cyclical sensitivity of wages. Most bargaining relationships in the public sector have not gone on long enough for an extended time-series analysis to be made. However, there are case studies of particular episodes, and these do suggest that a restrictive fiscal environment does moderate union wage settlements in government (Derber and Wagner 1979, Perry 1979). The New York City example may have had demonstration effects on other cities (Katz 1979a). Potential mobility of the tax base, at least in nonfederal employment, may also impose a kind of market discipline (Courant, Gramlich, and Rubinfeld 1979).

Finally, with unionization often go various forms of impasse procedures such as arbitration and fact-finding. Several studies have sought to determine the wage impact of these union-related processes (Olson 1980, Lipsky and Barocci 1978). As yet this research seems in a preliminary stage. The literature needs both analytical and empirical development.

Union Wages and Resource Allocation

Motivation for resource allocation is more difficult to model in the public sector than in the private sector. Public managers may seek to serve some intangible social welfare goal or to advance the interests of a particular constituency (Borjas 1980). Yet it is still expected that managers will economize on productive inputs that increase in relative cost.

If union wages rise, public managers may reduce employment although the budget impact of the wage increase may not be fully offset (Benecki 1978, Gallagher 1978). They may reallocate funds away from departments whose wages are rising relatively fast (Katz 1979a). They may subcontract work to private suppliers (Hirsch, Rufolo, and Mengle 1981). Strike costs may lead to managerial reorganization (Shannon 1978). Finally, bargaining may lead to changes in the level of productivity and in the nature of services provided (Ehrenberg and Schwartz 1981). But unions may be able to exert political pressure to expand services and counteract substitution effects on jobs (Spizman 1980).

Fringe Benefits in Government

It has been suggested that public management has a short-run horizon and therefore uses deferred benefits as a way of reaching accommodation in collective bargaining (Gunderson 1980). Fringes may also provide a convenient way of differentiating between groups of workers without appearing to do so, since costing the true value of such benefits is complex. In the case of pensions, public employers are not covered by ERISA and can promise future benefits without setting aside full funding.

The wage-fringe mix should reflect both employer and employee preferences. But, as in other aspects of government pay, the optimal mix is hard to assess. Government employers often set wages through surveys that ignore fringes. Recently there has been discussion in the policy literature about the use of total compensation surveys (Hartman 1980, U.S. General Accounting Office 1978, Dickson, Hovey, and Peterson 1980).

A parallel to the comparability literature on government wages exists for fringes. Some studies argue that government fringes are more generous than private due primarily to price escalation of pensions combined with early retirement options. These factors are most important at the federal level and for police and firefighters (Munnell and Connolly 1979). Some question exists about the valuation of underfunded benefits from the employee viewpoint (Ehrenberg and Smith 1979, Ehrenberg 1980, Mumy 1978).

IV. Public Policy on Wage Structure

Government policies pertaining to the labor market inevitably influence wages. Policies toward training and education, unionization, and immigration, for example, all influence some aspect of the wage structure. In addition, some forms of policy, such as minimum wage and prevailing wage legislation, constitute direct government intervention to prevent wages from falling below a minimum level. Recent research on the federal minimum wage is reviewed by Olivia Mitchell in Chapter 4 of this volume. The Davis-Bacon Act, a prevailing wage law passed in 1931, also attracted significant research attention in the 1970s.

The Davis-Bacon Act requires that federal construction contractors pay "prevailing wages" as determined by the U.S. Department of Labor. Passage of the law in 1931 has been variously interpreted as a response to interest-group pressure or to public concern about maintaining wage standards during the Great Depression. Four criticisms have been made of the law: it is charged that (1) the Labor Department tends to select union wage rates to represent the prevailing wage, (2) the law discourages bids from nonunion contractors, (3) the law raises construction prices paid by the federal government by preventing the use of lower-paid nonunion workers, and (4) the law's administrative burdens on the Labor Department, on other government agencies, and on contractors add to federal construction costs (Gould and Bittlingmayer 1980; Goldfarb and Morrall 1978 and 1981; Theiblot 1975; U.S. General Accounting Office 1979; Bourdan and Levitt 1980, Ch. 6; U.S. Department of Housing and Urban Development 1980).

Classical economic analysis does not lend itself to defense of prevailing wage laws. However, one classical defense is that Davis-Bacon prevents the government from exerting monopsony power in the construction marketplace. Another defense is that such laws induce offsetting productivity improvements, thus reducing or eliminating the cost impact (Allen and Reich 1980). The empirical evidence put forward for a productivity offset has been criticized, however (Bourdan and Levitt 1980, p. 84).

In fact, the Labor Department does not always pick a union wage as the prevailing wage, and—even when it does—it sometimes picks out-of-date wages lower than the current union level. However, as long as the nonunion wage that the federal government would have to pay is made a positive function of the union wage, union bargaining power should be strengthened. Demand for union labor in the public and private sectors should be positive functions of the nonunion wage, assuming union and nonunion labor are partial substitutes. Thus, the slope of the demand curve for union labor can be represented by equation (1) (the algebraically-minded reader will quickly note that the terms of equation (1) are partial derivatives):

$$(1)\quad \left(\begin{array}{l}\text{Slope of}\\ \text{demand}\\ \text{curve for}\\ \text{union}\\ \text{labor}\end{array}\right) = \left(\begin{array}{l}\text{Effect of}\\ \text{union wage}\\ \text{on private}\\ \text{demand for}\\ \text{union}\\ \text{labor}\\ \quad (A)\end{array}\right) + \left(\begin{array}{l}\text{Effect of}\\ \text{union wage}\\ \text{on govern-}\\ \text{ment demand}\\ \text{for union}\\ \text{labor}\\ \quad (B)\end{array}\right) + \left[\left(\begin{array}{l}\text{Effect of}\\ \text{nonunion}\\ \text{private wage}\\ \text{on private}\\ \text{demand for}\\ \text{union labor}\\ \quad (C)\end{array}\right)\left(\begin{array}{l}\text{Effect of}\\ \text{union wage}\\ \text{on nonunion}\\ \text{private}\\ \text{wage}\\ \\ \quad (D)\end{array}\right)\right]$$

$$+ \left[\left(\begin{array}{l}\text{Effect of}\\ \text{nonunion}\\ \text{government}\\ \text{wage on}\\ \text{government}\\ \text{demand for}\\ \text{union labor}\\ \quad (E)\end{array}\right)\left(\begin{array}{l}\text{Effect of}\\ \text{union wage}\\ \text{on nonunion}\\ \text{government}\\ \text{wage}\\ \\ \\ \quad (F)\end{array}\right)\right]$$

where $A < 0$, $B < 0$, $C > 0$, $D \overset{?}{\gtrless} 0$, $E > 0$, and $F \overset{?}{\gtrless} 0$.

Although the slope is negative, the less negative it is, the greater will be union bargaining power. $C \times D$ has an ambiguous sign (resulting from offsetting threat and displacement effects) and is not directly influenced by Davis-Bacon. However, Davis-Bacon guarantees that $E \times F$ will be positive (and the slope steeper) if the union wage has any positive influence on the prevailing wage selected ($F > 0$). The likely effect of an increase in the union wage due to the steeper slope is an increase in the average construction wage. Such an impact can be expected unless either the private nonunion wage falls substantially as the union wage rises and/or the weight of the nonunion sector in total employment increases sharply.

While the analytics can suggest a direction of change, the importance of this change is more difficult to specify. Precise estimates of how much construction is covered by Davis-Bacon are hard to find since state and local expenditures which are federally funded may be covered. As a proportion of new construction, public construction put in place accounted for a little over one-fifth in the late 1970s, and exhibited a downward trend. The ratio tended to peak in the late 1960s, a time when construction union wage settlements accelerated relative to others. Government demand for construction, rather than Davis-Bacon per se, may be a more important explanation of wage trends.

It is sometimes argued that nonunion contractors may be reluctant to bid on federal contracts because the shift to Davis-Bacon rates would upset their wage structure. Indeed, even union officials outside the construction industry have complained that their members lose work opportunities to construction union members under Davis-Bacon. A related argument is that nonunion contractors are likely to employ minority workers who are thereby denied jobs. Historically, craft unions were discriminatory in membership practices (Ashenfelter and Godwin 1971). However, affirmative action programs have followed the federal dollar and minority employment has increased (Prier 1979). The minority composition of union and nonunion contractors was not substantially different by the late 1970s (although the situation might vary substantially by locality and type of contractor). Hence, the minority employment case against Davis-Bacon is shaky.

The construction payroll is large enough so that even a small wage impact would produce an impressive dollar effect on costs. However, payrolls account for about 30–40 percent of public construction costs, so the percentage price effect is diluted. Union-nonunion wage differentials in construction appear to be substantial, and inclusion of fringe benefits widens the gap (Litsas 1972). Estimates of dollar savings of abandoning Davis-Bacon or changing its administrative procedures have run into the hundreds of millions of dollars.

While it is unfortunate that there is so much uncertainty about the impact, it seems unlikely that further academic research will resolve the issues. More studies would probably replicate past ambiguities. Hence, if Congress wishes to amend or repeal Davis-Bacon, it probably has as much information on which to act as it can ever hope to get.

V. Incomes Policy

Throughout the 1970s, much of the general concern of economic policy-makers with stagflation was focused on developments in labor markets. There were several reasons for this seemingly elliptical approach to the inflation problem. First, most analyses of price behavior during the 1970s stressed the difference between the "overall" and the "underlying" rates of inflation, where the difference reflects the price movements of "special factors"—most notably, food and energy—whose highly volatile rates of inflation were largely a response to external shocks beyond the reach of macroeconomic policy. For policy purposes, the underlying rate, reflecting the path of industrial prices, received primary attention as it continued to edge up during the 1970s.

Second, econometric analyses of the underlying inflation rate revealed the clear dominance of the cost-markup model of pricing. With a relatively small direct role assigned to product-market demand pressures, the behavior of labor costs became the central element influencing the underlying inflation rate. Finally, the problem of inflationary momentum led to interest in the various explicit and implicit contractual arrangements, discussed subsequently, that create a bias favoring quantity over price adjustments in labor markets.

As a result, there was considerable interest throughout the 1970s in the use of incomes policies to break through the expectations that accounted for the basic momentum of wages. This produced continued interest in research on incomes policies, although the research divided into two distinct branches: research into the effects of past-policy episodes, and research into alternative designs for incomes policy.

One strain of the evaluative research was methodological. During the 1960s, many econometric studies of incomes-policy episodes had simply added a dummy variable that "turned on" during policy periods within otherwise standard money wage and price equations. The coefficient of the dummy variable was interpreted as an estimate of policy impact. Lipsey and Parkin (1970) and Oi (1976) produced forceful critiques of this evaluation methodology by demonstrating why the relatively simple statistical models adopted in most evaluation studies were unlikely to account adequately for the economic impacts of an incomes policy.

There are at least three substantive problems with the dummy variable technique. First, the policy impact is assumed to be uniform throughout the period when the policy was in effect. Second, the statistical procedure assumes that the basic structure of the wage and price determination process—for example, the response of money wages to unemployment or prices—remains unchanged, although even a rudimentary inspection of policy design usually suggests otherwise. (For example, wage guidelines that specify a ceiling on wage increases are normally expected to apply irrespective of the unemployment rate.) Formal statistical tests on data for the United States and the United Kingdom rejected the hypothesis that the structure of the wage-determination processes remained unchanged between policy and nonpolicy periods. Third, it is widely recognized that dummy variables are well-named—they are a measure of ignorance. Any event influencing wages and/or prices that occurs during the policy period, but is not specified in the wage or price equation, will erroneously be attributed to the incomes policy.

The major procedural response to this and other methodological critiques was to adopt a simulation approach whereby the basic wage and price equations are estimated from data for a nonpolicy period, and the coefficients in these equations are used to generate predicted values of wage and price changes during a subsequent policy period. The difference between the actual and predicted values during the policy period are interpreted as the incomes-policy impact. This approach eliminated the first two critiques of the dummy-variable approach, but not the third. Novel nonpolicy influences on wages and prices during the incomes policy period that are not captured in the regression equations will influence the size of the prediction errors.

There was a considerable amount of econometric evaluation of incomes policy impact, with variable attention to the methodological issues that such studies raise, during the 1970s. Probably the main intellectual impact of these studies has been to undermine the view that incomes policies can induce a permanent downward shift in the "Phillips curve." Evidence from Western Europe, where incomes policy had been used more extensively than in the United States, indicated that periods of wage and/or price restraint (1) were relatively brief (one to three years), (2) were characterized by greater wage restraint than price restraint (thereby reducing labor's share of the national income), and (3) were often followed by periods of significant wage acceleration, including, most dramatically, the wage "explosions" experienced by several countries in the late 1960s (Ulman and Flanagan 1971). However, most of the European evidence was derived from evidence in which incomes policies had been imposed on an excess-demand inflation—a situation in which there was no theoretical case for its application in the first place.

Nevertheless, the hope that incomes policy might have a role to play in breaking through inflationary expectations under conditions of excess supply was more or less undermined by evaluations of the impact of the Nixon Administration incomes policy (Phases I–IV) of the early 1970s. Phase I of the policy began in August 1971 with a 90-day wage/price freeze. This was followed immediately by Phase II which established a ceiling of 5.5 percent for wage increases plus an additional .7 percent for fringe benefits. Phase III, intended to be a transition to a period of voluntary restraint, began in January 1973, but culminated in a 60-day freeze (June–August 1973) in reaction to accelerating food and oil prices. The controls were gradually removed during Phase IV, which ran from August 1973 until statutory authority for the program expired in April 1974.

The policy was evaluated in a series of papers by Gordon (1973 and 1977) who applied the simulation methodology to fairly complex wage and price equations. While Gordon's findings varied somewhat in response to revisions in data and estimating equations, his basic results indicated that the policy (1) had no impact on money wage changes, but (2) initially reduced prices below their predicted values by 2–3 percent. In late 1973 and 1974, however, prices increased more rapidly than they would have in the absence of the policy, and by the end of the program the price level equaled or exceeded (depending on the estimate chosen) the price level that was predicted to exist in the absence of controls.

This pattern of impact (and the implied profit squeeze) was the reverse of that observed for most European incomes policy experiments and appeared puzzling to many who observed the effort allocated to enforcing the wage part of the policy. As in Europe, most of the enforcement efforts were directed at the outcomes of the most visible collective bargaining negotiations. Relative to Europe, however, a small proportion of the U.S. labor force is unionized. When the impact of the Nixon program was analyzed separately for union and nonunion wages, however, the data indicated that the policy period was associated with a significant reduction in union wage increases below their predicted value, but nonunion wage increases tended to be higher than predicted (Flanagan 1976). Given the relatively high unemployment of the period, predicted nonunion wage increases, which are more sensitive to market conditions than are union rates, were below the guideline. Actual nonunion increases were almost exactly at the guideline, raising the possibility that it become a sort of norm in the nonunion sector. However, Weber and Mitchell (1978, pp. 373–78) found no evidence of such an effect, based on program and external data.

In a broad sense the failure of incomes policy to achieve other than a transitory impact on money wage or price increases is ultimately tied to limitations on the duration of effective compliance under voluntary programs with limited enforcement mechanisms. (Certain European policy episodes characterized by considerably greater compulsion have also had a rather transitory impact, although these have generally been applied during periods of excess demand.) The compliance incentive provided by general appeals to the national interest is particularly fragile in an economy, such as that of the United States, with comparatively decentralized decision-making over wage determination. In particular, decision-making units that comply with a wage guideline face a risk of real earnings loss if other units do not comply and prices continue to rise.

Considerations such as these led to extensive research activity during the 1970s on the use of the tax system to provide ongoing microeconomic incentives for compliance with the wage or price standards of an incomes policy (for example, Okun and Perry 1978; Okun 1981, pp. 348–53; Seidman 1976; Wallich and Weintraub 1971). The basic idea of the various tax-based incomes policy (TIP) proposals is to create tax rewards or penalties for parties who are in or out of compliance with policy guidelines. Within the general framework, a wide variety of policy designs is possible. In addition to the choice between the penalty or reward approach, a TIP may offer an incentive that varies in size with the extent of compliance or consists of a lump sum payable upon threshold compliance (or noncompliance) with a policy guideline. The strength of the compliance incentive as well as the general administrative complexity varies significantly among the various TIP proposals, but in contrast to the vague rewards or penalties associated with traditional incomes policies, the tax incentives would become a direct element of the compliance calculus by parties subject to the policy.

A further choice is between TIPs that automatically reward (or penalize) compliance (or noncompliance) and TIPs that provide insurance against the basic compliance risk of real earnings loss. The Carter Administration chose the latter approach when it accompanied its program of pay and price standards with a legislative proposal for real-wage insurance late in 1978. This proposal started from the observation that workers complying with a wage guideline have no assurance that other workers will exercise similar restraint. The failure of others to comply is likely to result in price increases that threaten the relative and real earnings position of workers who are in compliance. Under the real-wage insurance proposal, compliance risk would be shifted to the federal government, which would be committed to provide tax credits to workers in compliance with the existing pay standard, if the annual rate of inflation exceeded the government's objectives. The tax credit would in principle equal the difference between the actual and target inflation rates times the annual earnings of the worker, although the Carter Administration proposal placed a ceiling on the payout to each individual. Although the real-wage insurance approach addresses the compliance risk issue more directly than earlier TIP proposals, it offers a rather complex set of compliance incentives in comparison to other TIPS (Flanagan 1979). It can also be quite expensive and difficult to design, a feature that ultimately accounted for congressional disinterest in the proposal during a period of accelerating prices (Mitchell 1980d).

By the end of the 1970s the main effect of research on the impact of incomes policies on wages had been to discourage optimistic assertions that such programs, in the forms adopted in the U.S. and Europe, could achieve a permanent reduction of inflation. The evidence to date suggests that the most that can be expected is a modest shift in the timing of a few percentage points of inflation and that even this effect is not costless. At the same time, the research has been almost uniformly focused on the effect of policy on aggregate wage indices. There has been very limited inquiry into the impact of incomes policies on the distribution of earnings, on fringe benefits, and on the (typically unregulated) nonpecuniary aspects of the employment contract.

VI. The Research Agenda for the Future

Research trends nearly always have antecedents. Thus, the topics of the 1980s will inevitably be extensions of work done in the 1970s. In this section, those elements of the 1970s' literature that are likely to blossom are discussed.

Wage Peculiarities: Implications and Open Questions

During the 1970s, a literature began to develop on "implicit contracting" in the labor market. This literature sought to provide an economic rationale for labor market practices that did not fit neatly into classical economic theory. At the macro level, economists have long puzzled about the rarity of general wage cuts and, indeed, the commonplace observation of aggregate nominal wage increases in the face of recession. The deterioration of the Phillips curve in the 1970s (Table 1, Panel (10)) and the accompanying inflation problem stimulated interest in explaining these macro puzzles. At the micro level are found such nonclassical behaviors as labor hoarding during downturns in demand, layoffs by reverse seniority, situations of "no vacancy," and internal career ladders. These phenomena are inconsistent with a model of the labor market that assumes a "spot" auction process.

Implicit contract theorists have suggested that the employee-employer relationship is better viewed as a "futures" contract than as a spot transaction. The word "implicit" is used because those writing in this field are not examining explicit union agreements. According to the implicit-contract view, even nonunion employees without written contracts may be the beneficiaries of informal commitments from their employers—what Arthur H. Okun (1980) termed the "invisible handshake" to contrast it with Adam Smith's "invisible hand." Implicit contracts indicate to the worker what may be expected from the employer under various future contingencies. These may be contingencies related to the worker (such as future "good" performance or loyalty to the employer) or contingencies relating to future states of the economic health of the firm. Although the contracts are deemed to be implicit, they may shed light on explicit contractual and legal requirements. Union contracts are known to have adopted previous practices when unionization first came on the scene (Feller 1973). The legal restrictions on employers in Western Europe and other countries may reflect extensions into legislation of the "fairness" concepts which arise out of implicit contracts (Aaron 1971). Even American courts are beginning to widen the definitions of employer obligation to nonunion employees, a development that could be viewed as judicial recognition of an implicit bargain (Olsen 1981). As Goldberg (1976, p. 48) notes: ". . . the line between private 'voluntary' agreements and public 'coerced' agreements is not a clear one."

Various motivations for implicit labor market contracts have been put forward. One suggestion has been that employees are more "risk averse" than employers, and that the implicit contract is a form of unemployment insurance or, more generally, insurance against real income fluctuations. The difficulty with this view is that it is unclear why explicit insurance is not provided or why nonunion wage policies are typically not expressed in purchasing-power terms (Bailey 1974, Grossman 1977, Hall and Lilien 1979, Holmstrom 1981, Akerlof and Miyazaki 1980). So far, risk theorists have not fully deduced a contract in which wages are rigid and hours and layoffs are the main means to respond to declining demand. Yet this is the key phenomenon which they seek to explain.

A more promising approach combines costs of transactions and costs of turnover to produce an implicit agreement. Where transactions costs between buyer and seller are high, the nature of their contract is likely to be affected (Cheung 1969). Buyer-seller relationships always operate against a background of uncertainty about future developments. As a result, notions of fair dealing arise which may not always fit neatly into the classical economic framework (Macaulay 1963, Lester 1946). At the time of hiring, the full range of tasks to be required of a worker may not be known (Simon 1951). Rather than haggle with individual employees on a continuous basis, employers may establish uniform (if inflexible) personnel policies dealing with wage determination, promotions, layoffs, etc. (Wachter and Williamson 1978; Williamson, Wachter, and Harris 1975).

Okun's invisible-handshake model depends heavily on turnover costs (Okun 1981). Okun uses an abstraction—the employer is assumed to pay a "toll" at the time of hiring which must be recouped later. The toll could include such items as recruitment, screening, and training costs. In many respects, the Okun view is built on previous research in the 1960s and 1970s by economists who were interested in explaining quit and layoff behavior (Parsons 1972 and 1977, Mortensen 1978, Pencavel 1972, Rosen 1968, Oi 1962). The dual labor market literature, which postulates a primary sector with "Okunesque" features, also appears to have been an influence (Doeringer and Piore 1971). One interpretation of the primary sector of the dual labor market theory is that turnover costs are especially high for employers in that sector.

Given the existence of significant turnover costs, employers have an interest in retaining their workers for sufficiently long periods to recoup the firm's investment of the "toll." They offer employees implicit guarantees about future treatment in good and bad times, about how wages will be determined, and about promotion possibilities and career ladders. Wages premiums may accrue to workers in an effort to discourage quitting. Since all employers cannot pay above-average wages, the result is a wage hierarchy. The observation that firm size, wage level, capital intensity, and low quit rates tend to be associated (Table 1, Panels (6), (7), and (8)), fits nicely into the Okun view.

In the Okun model, firms do not cut wages when demand falls; they average out the business cycle and leave junior employees to experience the brunt of recessions through layoffs. While in a purely classical world, unemployment is "voluntary," laid-off workers and other job-seekers in an Okun labor market may not find work at the "going" wage. Firms do not accept wage-cutting bids of job-seekers when demand falls; they simply post "no help wanted" signs. Workers experience significant costs of unemployment and involuntary turnover and, like employers, have a motive to strengthen the employer-worker linkage. Layoffs and quits are thus inversely related (Burton and Parker 1969). The implicit-contract view suggests a rationale for inflation momentum. If wage-setting is determined on fairness grounds, and if firms average out the business cycle, wages are likely to be set in response to external wage decisions and/or prices. Okun's model, applied to the product market, suggests cost markups as the fair way of price-setting. Thus, the implicit-contracting literature contains a potential explanation of wage-price and wage-wage spirals. Use of some form of direct government intervention to stem inflation—Okun favored the TIP plan discussed in the previous section—is a conclusion that *might* follow from implicit-contract analysis.

There are other possible implications of the implicit-contract view. The union sector can be viewed as situated on a spectrum running from informality to career (nonunion) labor markets to formal written contracts. If the invisible handshake attenuated market pressures on wages of nonunion workers, formal written contracts will make union wages still more insensitive, a position supported by empirical evidence (Pearce 1980, Raisian 1979, Mitchell 1980b). For human capital theory, the implicit-contract approach suggests a blurring of the sharp distinction between general and specific training. If workers and employers are tied together, employers might invest in general training and workers might invest in specific skill acquisitions. The implicit-contract approach, with its emphasis on a worker stake in the employer (and vice versa) could even provide an economic rationale for recent experiments with worker participation in management and gain-sharing.

Some recent debates in macroeconomics may be touched by the implicit-contract approach to the labor market. Rational expectations theorists have been skeptical about the efficacy of demand policy to influence the economy since, they argue, actors in the economic system come to anticipate policy and react to it in advance. The implicit-contract view, by limiting the probable reaction of wages to demand pressures, might provide a reconciliation between older theories and the new propositions, although debate on this issue continues (Barro 1977, Fischer 1977).

While the implicit-contracting view opens an exciting new area of research for economists—and holds promise of bridging the gap between economic theory and institutional observation—it also leaves some questions unanswered. The Okun approach places emphasis on fairness in setting wages and other personnel policies. But defining fairness in any rigorous way is difficult, if not impossible. Almost any behavior might be rationalized as fair in someone's subjective judgment. Since almost any behavior can be so rationalized, there is a tendency to rely heavily on anecdotal tidbits in framing models of wage-setting. Two key issues in wage-setting illustrate this point: expectations and spillover.

An important issue in the analysis of wage-setting is whether forward-looking inflation expectations play a significant role. If they do, incomes policies, guidelines, or simply stern announcements about future economic policy might influence those expectations. If they don't—if wage-setting is based on a backward-looking process of catching up with past inflation—then one might hope to reduce wage settlements by "buying off" wage-setters with tax incentives—that is, Okun's TIP plan. Not surprisingly, Okun (1981, p. 104) asserts that expectations play only a minor role, citing as evidence the fact that he "never heard of an econometric price forecasting exercise in a . . . negotiation."

But, the empirical evidence on forward- vs. backward-looking is ambiguous. A crude index of inflation expectations is the difference between life-of-contract union wage settlements in escalated vs. nonescalated manufacturing contracts. For the period 1971–1980, roughly two-thirds of the variance in this index can be "explained" by regression analysis using as independent variables the three-year past trend in consumer price inflation (a backward-looking measure) *or* the interest rate on long-term Treasury bonds (presumably a forward-looking measure). Despite Okun's assertions, implicit-contract theory does not favor one of these hypotheses over the other. Hence, empirical work in the 1980s will be needed to resolve the issue.

Okun also favored wage limitation and spillover rather than price inflation as a primary influence on wage-setting, although he acknowledged that virtually all union escalator clauses referred to prices rather than wages. Again, the empirical evidence is hazy. Statistical attempts to determine whether union wage settlements spill over to the nonunion sector, or whether nonunion decisions influence union settlements, have produced contradictory results (Flanagan 1976, Johnson 1977, Vroman 1980, Mitchell 1980c). Generally, price and wage inflation are so intercorrelated that distinguishing wage-wage from price-wage influences is extremely difficult. Implicit-contract theory of the Okun type does not favor either view; implicit-contract theory based on risk aversion probably favors the price-wage connection.

The Research Agenda

In the 1980s, wage research can be expected to follow "hot" topics in public policy, as it has in the past. Many of the interests of the 1970s will continue. Deregulation of the labor market under the Reagan Administration in areas such as EEO and OSHA is simply the mirror image of regulation from the research viewpoint. The same techniques can be applied to estimate the effects. Moreover, some regulatory policies are in the hands of the courts. Male/female wage differentials will remain a research target as the courts wrestle with the "comparable worth" issue.

If inflation continues, the role of wage determination in the process will remain an area of important research. And if inflation recedes, the question of whether some shift in the structure of the labor market assisted in the adjustment will certainly be asked. The reaction of union wage-setters to prolonged economic slack beginning in 1979 has captured the interest of journalists; a notable change in bargaining outcomes will also attract academic researchers.

Overall, economists will not lack topics for wage research in the 1980s. The 1970s saw the development of a committed cadre of wage researchers utilizing new data sets, data-processing technology, and statistical techniques. Combined with the willingness of young scholars to use both theoretical and institutional insight, this development holds the promise of future advances in knowledge of wage determination.

References

Aaron, Benjamin, ed. *Labor Courts and Grievance Settlement in Western Europe*. Berkeley: University of California Press, 1971.

Aigner, Dennis J., and Glen G. Cain. "Statistical Theories of Discrimination in Labor Markets." *Industrial and Labor Relations Review* 30 (January 1977): pp. 175–87.

Akerlof, George A., and Hajime Miyazaki. "The Implicit Contract Theory of Unemployment Meets the Wage Bill Argument." *Review of Economic Studies* 47 (January 1980): pp. 321–38.

Allen, Steven G. *Unionized Construction Workers Are More Productive*. Washington: Center to Protect Workers' Rights, 1979.

Allen, Steven G., and David Reich. *Prevailing Wage Laws Are Not Inflationary: A Case Study of Public School Construction Costs*. Washington: Center to Protect Workers' Rights, 1980.

Antos, Joseph R., and Sherwin Rosen. "Discrimination in the Market for Public School Teachers." *Journal of Econometrics* 3 (May 1975): pp. 123–50.

Arrow, Kenneth J. "Models of Job Discrimination." In *Racial Discrimination in Economic Life*, ed. Anthony H. Pascal. Lexington, Mass.: D. C. Heath, 1972.

Ashenfelter, Orley C., and Lamond I. Godwin. "Some Evidence on the Effect of Unionism on the Average Wage of Black Workers Relative to White Workers, 1900–1967." *Proceedings of 24th Annual Meeting, Industrial Relations Research Association.* Madison, Wis.: IRRA, 1971. Pp. 217–24.

Ashenfelter, Orley, and George E. Johnson. "Unionism, Relative Wages, and Labor Quality in U.S. Manufacturing Industries." *International Economic Review* 13 (October 1972): pp. 488–508.

Baily, Martin Neil. "Wages and Employment Under Uncertain Demand." *Review of Economic Studies* 41 (January 1974): pp. 37–50.

Barro, Robert J. "Long-Term Contracting, Sticky Prices, and Monetary Policy." *Journal of Monetary Economics* 3 (July 1977): pp. 305–16.

Bartel, Ann, and David Lewin. "Wages and Unionism in the Public Sector: The Case of Police." *Review of Economics and Statistics* 63 (February 1981): 53–59.

Becker, Brian E. "Union Impact on Wages and Fringe Benefits of Hospital Nonprofessionals." *Quarterly Review of Economics and Business* 19 (Winter 1979): pp. 27–44.

Becker, Gary S. *The Economics of Discrimination,* 2nd ed. Chicago: University of Chicago Press, 1971.

———. *Human Capital and the Personal Distribution of Income,* Woytinsky Lecture No. 1. Ann Arbor: Institute of Public Administration, University of Michigan, 1967.

———. *Human Capital: A Theoretical and Empirical Analysis, with Special Reference to Education,* 2nd ed. New York: Columbia University Press, 1975.

Bellante, Don, and Albert N. Link. "Are Public Sector Workers More Risk Averse Than Private Sector Workers?" *Industrial and Labor Relations Review* 34 (April 1981): pp. 408–12.

Benecki, Stanley. "Municipal Expenditure Levels and Collective Bargaining." *Industrial Relations* 17 (May 1978): pp. 216–30.

Bernstein, Jules. *Union-Busting and the Law: From Benign Neglect to Malignant Growth.* Washington: Center to Protect Workers' Rights, 1980.

Binkin, Martin, and Irene Kyriakopoulos. *Paying the Modern Military.* Washington: Brookings Institution, 1981. Pp. 56–60.

Blinder, Alan S. "Wage Discrimination: Reduced Form and Structural Estimates." *Journal of Human Resources* 8 (Fall 1973): pp. 436–55.

Borjas, George J. "Wage Determination in the Federal Government: The Role of Constituents and Bureaucrats." *Journal of Political Economy* 88 (December 1980): pp. 1110–47.

Bourdon, Clinton C., and Raymond E. Levitt. *Union and Open-Shop Construction.* Lexington, Mass.: D.C. Heath, 1980.

Brown, Charles. "Equalizing Differences in the Labor Market." *Quarterly Journal of Economics* 94 (February 1980): pp. 113–34.

Brown, Charles, and James Medoff. "Trade Unions in the Production Process." *Journal of Political Economy* 86 (June 1978): pp. 335–78.

Burton, John F. Jr., and John E. Parker. "Interindustry Variations in Voluntary Labor Mobility." *Industrial and Labor Relations Review* 22 (January 1969): pp. 199–225.

Cheung, Steven N. S. "Transaction Costs, Risk Aversion, and the Choice of Contractual Arrangements." *Journal of Law and Economics* 12 (April 1969): pp. 23–42.

Courant, Paul N., Edward M. Gramlich, and Daniel L. Rubinfeld. "Public Employee Market Power and the Level of Government Spending." *American Economic Review* 69 (December 1979): pp. 806–17.

Derber, Milton, and Martin Wagner. "Public Sector Bargaining and Budget Making Under Fiscal Adversity." *Industrial and Labor Relations Review* 33 (October 1979): pp. 18–23.

Dickson, Elizabeth, Harold A. Hovey, and George E. Peterson. *Public Employee Compensation: A Twelve City Comparison.* Washington: Urban Institute, 1980.

Doeringer, Peter B., and Michael J. Piore. *Internal Labor Markets and Manpower Analysis.* Lexington, Mass.: D.C. Heath, 1971.

Duncan, Greg J. "Earnings Functions and Nonpecuniary Benefits." *Journal of Human Resources* 11 (Fall 1976): pp. 462–83.

Duncan, Greg J., and Frank P. Stafford. "Do Union Members Receive Compensating Wage Differentials?" *American Economic Review* 70 (June 1980): pp. 355–71.

Duncan, Gregory M., and Duane E. Leigh. "Wage Determination in the Union and Nonunion Sectors: A Sample Selectivity Approach." *Industrial and Labor Relations Review* 34 (October 1980): pp. 24–34.

Ehrenberg, Ronald G. "Retirement System Characteristics and Compensating Wage Differentials in the Public Sector." *Industrial and Labor Relations Review* 33 (July 1980): pp. 470–83.

Ehrenberg, Ronald G., and Joshua L. Schwartz: "The Effect of Unions on Productivity in the Public Sector: The Case of Libraries." Working Paper. Ithaca: New York State School of Industrial and Labor Relations, Cornell University, May 1981.

Ehrenberg, Ronald G., and Robert S. Smith. "Who Pays for Pensions in the State and Local Sector: Workers or Employers?" *Proceedings of the 32nd Annual Meeting, Industrial Relations Research Association.* Madison, Wis.: IRRA, 1979. Pp. 57–63.

Farber, Henry S., and Daniel H. Saks. "Why Workers Want Unions: The Role of Relative Wages and Job Characteristics." *Journal of Political Economy* 88 (April 1980): pp. 349–68.

Feller, David E. "A General Theory of the Collective Bargaining Agreement." *California Law Review* 61 (May 1973): pp. 663–856.

Fischer, Stanley. "Long-Term Contracting, Sticky Prices, and Monetary Policy: A Comment." *Journal of Monetary Economics* 3 (July 1977): pp. 317–23.

Flanagan, Robert J. "Labor Force Experience, Job Turnover, and Racial Wage Differentials." *Review of Economics and Statistics* 56 (November 1974): pp. 521–29.

———. "Real Wage Insurance as a Compliance Incentive." *Eastern Economic Journal* 5 (October 1979): pp. 367–78.

———. "Wage Interdependence in Unionized Labor Markets." *Brookings Papers on Economic Activity* (3:1976): pp. 635–73.

Freeman, Richard B. *The Market for College-Trained Manpower: A Study in the Economics of Career Choice.* Cambridge, Mass.: Harvard University Press, 1971.

———. "Overinvestment in College Training?" *Journal of Human Resources* 10 (Summer 1975): pp. 287–311.

Freeman, Richard B., and James L. Medoff. "The Impact of Collective Bargaining: Illusion or Reality?" In *U.S. Industrial Relations 1950–1980: A Critical Appraisal,* eds. Jack Stieber, Robert B. McKersie, and D. Quinn Mills. Madison, Wis.: Industrial Relations Research Association, 1981. Pp. 47–97.

Gallagher, Daniel G. "Teacher Bargaining and School District Expenditures." *Industrial Relations* 17 (May 1978): pp. 231–37.

Goldberg, Victor P. "Towards an Expanded Economy Theory of Contract." *Journal of Economic Issues* 10 (March 1976): pp. 45–61.

Goldfarb, Robert S., and John F. Morrall III. "Cost Implications of Changing Davis-Bacon Administration." *Policy Analysis* 4 (Fall 1978): pp. 439–53.

———. "The Davis-Bacon Act: An Appraisal of Recent Studies." *Industrial and Labor Relations Review* 34 (January 1981): pp. 191–206.

Gordon, Robert J. "Can the Inflation of the 1970's Be Explained?" *Brookings Papers on Economic Activity* (1:1977): pp. 253–77.

———. "Recent Developments in the Theory of Inflation and Unemployment." *Journal of Monetary Economics* 2 (April 1976): pp. 185–219.

———. "The Response of Wages and Prices to the First Two Years of Controls." *Brookings Papers on Economic Activity* (3:1973): pp. 765–79.

Gould, John P., and George Bittlingmayer. *The Economics of the Davis-Bacon Act.* Washington: American Enterprise Institute for Public Policy Research, 1980.

Griliches, Zvi, and William Mason. "Education, Income and Ability." *Journal of Political Economy* 80 (May/June 1972): pp. S74–102.

Grossman, Herschel I. "Risk Shifting and Reliability in Labor Markets." *Scandinavian Journal of Economics* 79 (2:1977), pp. 187–209.

Gunderson, Morley. "Public Sector Compensation in Canada and the U.S." *Industrial Relations* 19 (Fall 1980): pp. 257–71.

Hall, Robert E., and David M. Lilien. "Effective Wage Bargains Under Uncertain Supply and Demand." *American Economic Review* 69 (December 1979): pp. 868–79.

Hamermesh, Daniel S. "Economic Aspects of Job Satisfaction." In *Essays in Labor Market Analysis,* eds. Orley Ashenfelter and Wallace Oates. New York: Wiley & Sons, 1978.

Hanoch, Giora. "An Economic Analysis of Earnings and Schooling." *Journal of Human Resources* 2 (Summer 1967): pp. 310–29.

Hartman, Robert W. "Retirement for Federal Civil Servants: Down from the Incomparable." *Proceedings of the 33rd Annual Meeting, Industrial Relations Research Association.* Madison, Wis.: IRRA, 1980. Pp. 82-89.

Hartman, Robert T., and Arnold R. Weber, eds. *The Rewards of Public Service: Compensating Top Federal Officials.* Washington: Brookings Institution, 1980.

Hirsch, W. A., A. M. Rufolo, and D. Mengle. "Recent Trends in Municipal Labor Market Research." Working Paper. Los Angeles: Department of Economics, University of California, Los Angeles, 1981.

Holmstrom, Bengt. "Contractual Models of the Labor Market." *American Economic Review* 71 (May 1981): pp. 308–13.

Ichniowski, Casey. "Economic Effects of the Firefighters' Union." *Industrial and Labor Relations Review* 33 (January 1980): pp. 198-211.

Johnson, George E. "The Determination of Wages in the Union and Non-Union Sectors." *British Journal of Industrial Relations* 15 (July 1977): pp. 211–25.

Kahn, Lawrence M. "Union Spillover Effects on Unorganized Labor Markets." *Journal of Human Resources* 15 (Winter 1980): pp. 87–98.

Katz, Harry C. "The Municipal Budgetary Response to Changing Labor Costs: The Case of San Francisco." *Industrial and Labor Relations Review* 32 (July 1979a): pp. 506–19.

———. "Municipal Pay Determination: The Case of San Francisco." *Industrial Relations* 18 (Winter 1979b): pp. 55–56.

Kochan, Thomas A. "How American Workers View Labor Unions." *Monthly Labor Review* 102 (April 1979): pp. 23–31.

Lester, Richard. "Shortcomings of Marginal Analysis for Wage-Employment Problems." *American Economic Review* 36 (March 1946): pp. 63–82.

Lewin, David, and Mary McCormick. "Coalition Bargaining in Municipal Government: The New York City Experience." *Industrial and Labor Relations Review* 34 (January 1981): pp. 175–90.

Lillard, Lee A., and Robert J. Willis. "Dynamic Aspects of Earnings Mobility." *Econometrica* 46 (September 1978): pp. 985–1012.

Lippman, Steven A., and John J. McCall. "The Economics of Job Search: A Survey." *Economic Inquiry* 14 (June and August 1976): pp. 155–89 and 347–68.

Lipsey, Richard G., and Michael J. Parkin. "Incomes Policy: A Reappraisal." *Economica* 37 (1970): pp. 1–31.

Lipsky, David B., and Thomas A. Barocci. "Final-Offer Arbitration and Salaries of Police and Firefighters." *Monthly Labor Review* 101 (July 1978): pp. 34–36.

Litsas, John. "What Subcontractors Pay Construction Workers." *Monthly Labor Review* 95 (September 1972): pp. 57–59.

Macauley, Stewart. "Non-Contractual Relations in Business: A Preliminary Analysis." *American Sociological Review* 28 (February 1963): pp. 55–69.

Malkiel, Burton G., and Judith A. Malkiel. "Male-Female Pay Differentials in Professional Employment." *American Economic Review* 63 (September 1973): pp. 693–705.

McCall, John J. "Economics of Information and Job Search." *Quarterly Journal of Economics* 84 (February 1970): pp. 113–26.

McCormick, Robert E., and Robert D. Tollison. "Legislatures as Unions." *Journal of Political Economy* 86 (February 1978): pp. 63–78.

Mincer, Jacob. "The Distribution of Labor Earnings: A Survey." *Journal of Economic Literature* 8 (March 1970): 1–26.

———. *Schooling, Experience, and Earnings.* New York: National Bureau of Economic Research 1974.

Mincer, Jacob, and Solomon Polachek. "Family Investments in Human Capital: Earnings of Women." *Journal of Political Economy* 82 (March/April 1974): pp. S76–108.

Mitchell, Daniel J. B. "Collective Bargaining and the Economy." In *U.S. Industrial Relations 1950–1980: A Critical Appraisal,* eds. Jack Stieber, Robert B. McKersie, and D. Quinn Mills. Madison, Wis.: Industrial Relations Research Association, 1981. Pp. 1–46.

———. "The Impact of Collective Bargaining on Compensation in the Public Sector." In *Public-Sector Bargaining,* eds. Benjamin Aaron, Joseph R. Grodin, and James L. Stern. IRRA Series. Washington: Bureau of National Affairs, 1979. Pp. 118–49.

———. "Collective Bargaining and Wage Determination in the 1970s." *Proceedings of the 33rd Annual Meeting, Industrial Relations Research Association.* Madison, Wis.: IRRA, 1980a. Pp. 135–42.

———. *Unions, Wages, and Inflation.* Washington: Brookings Institution, 1980b.

———. "Union/Non-Union Wage Spillovers: A Note." *British Journal of Industrial Relations* 18 (November 1980c): pp. 372–76.

———. "The Rise and Fall of Real Wage Insurance." *Industrial Relations* 19 (Fall 1980d): pp. 64–73.

Mortensen, Dale T. "Specific Capital and Labor Turnover." *Bell Journal of Economics* 9 (Autumn 1978): pp. 572–86.

Mumy, Gene E. "The Economics of Local Government Pensions and Pension Funding." *Journal of Political Economy* 86 (June 1978): pp. 517–27.

Munnell, Alicia H., and Ann M. Connolly. "Comparability and Public and Private Compensation: The Issue of Fringe Benefits." *New England Economic Review* (July/August 1979): pp. 27–45.

Oaxaca, Ronald. "Male-Female Wage Differentials in Urban Labor Markets." *International Economic Review* 14 (October 1979): pp. 693–709.

Oi, Walter Y. "Labor as a Quasi-Fixed Factor." *Journal of Political Economy* 70 (December 1962): pp. 538–55.

———. "On Measuring the Impact of Wage-Price Controls: A Critical Appraisal." In *The Economics of Price and Wage Controls,* eds. Karl Brunner and Allan H. Meltzer. Amsterdam: North Holland Publishing Co., 1976.

Okun, Arthur M. "The Invisible Handshake and the Inflationary Process." *Challenge* 22 (January-February 1980): pp. 5–12.

———. *Prices and Quantities: A Macroeconomic Analysis.* Washington: Brookings Institution, 1981.

Okun, Arthur M., and George L. Perry, eds. *Curing Chronic Inflation.* Washington: Brookings Institution, 1978.

Olsen, Theodore A. "Wrongful Discharge Claims Raised by At Will Employees: A New Legal Concern for Employers." *Labor Law Journal* 32 (May 1981): pp. 265–97.

Olson, Craig A. "The Impact of Arbitration on the Wages of Firefighters." *Industrial Relations* 19 (Fall 1980): pp. 325–39.

Parsley, C. J. "Labor Union Effects on Wage Gains: A Survey of Recent Literature." *Journal of Economic Literature* 18 (March 1980): pp. 1–31.

Parsons, Donald O. "Models of Labor Market Turnover: A Theoretical and Empirical Survey." In *Research in Labor Economics*, Vol. 1, ed. Ronald G. Ehrenberg. Greenwich, Conn.: JAI Press, 1977. Pp. 185–223.

———. "Specific Human Capital: An Application to Quit Rates and Layoff Rates." *Journal of Political Economy* 80 (December 1972): pp. 1120–43.

Pascal, Anthony H., and Leonard A. Rapping. "The Economics of Racial Discrimination in Organized Baseball." In *Racial Discrimination in Economic Life*, ed. Anthony H. Pascal. Lexington, Mass.: D.C. Heath, 1972. Pp. 119–56.

Pearce, James E. "Trade Unionism, Implicit Contracting, and the Response to Demand Variation in U.S. Manufacturing." Research Paper No. 8003, Federal Reserve Bank of Dallas, April 1980.

Pencavel, John H. "Wages, Specific Training, and Labor Turnover in U.S. Manufacturing Industries." *International Economic Review* 13 (February 1972): pp. 53–64.

Perry, Charles R. "Teaching Bargaining: The Experience in Nine Systems." *Industrial and Labor Relations Review* 33 (October 1979): pp. 3–17.

Prier, Robert J. "Labor and Material Requirements for Federally Aided Highways." *Monthly Labor Review* 102 (December 1979): pp. 29–34.

Quinn, Joseph F. "Postal Sector Wages." *Industrial Relations* 18 (Winter 1979a): pp. 92–96.

———. "Wage Differentials Among Older Workers in the Public and Private Sectors." *Journal of Human Resources* 14 (Winter 1979b): pp. 41–62.

Raisian, John. "Cyclic Patterns in Weeks and Wages." *Economic Inquiry* 17 (October 1979): pp. 475–95.

Rosen, Sherwin. "Hedonic Prices and Implicit Markets." *Journal of Political Economy* 82 (January/February 1974): pp. 34–55.

———. "Human Capital: A Survey of Empirical Research." In *Research in Labor Economics*, Vol. 1, ed. Ronald G. Ehrenberg. Greenwich, Conn.: JAI Press, 1977. Pp. 3–39.

———. Short-Run Employment Variation on Class-1 Railroads in the U.S., 1947–1963." *Econometrica* 36 (July-October 1968): pp. 511-29.

Seidman, Laurence S. "A Payroll Tax Credit to Restrain Inflation." *National Tax Journal* 29 (December 1976): pp. 398–412.

Shannon, Stephen C. "Work Stoppage in Government: The Postal Strike of 1970." *Monthly Labor Review* 101 (July 1978): pp. 14–22.

Shapiro, David. "Relative Wage Effects of Unions in the Public and Private Sectors." *Industrial and Labor Relations Review* 31 (January 1978): pp. 193–204.

Simon, Herbert A. "A Formal Theory of the Employment Relationship." *Econometrica* 19 (July 1951): pp. 293–305.

Smith, Adam. *An Inquiry into the Nature and Causes of the Wealth of Nations.* New York: Modern Library, 1937 [1776].

Smith, D. Alton. "Government Employment and Black/White Relative Wages." *Journal of Human Resources* 15 (Winter 1980): pp. 77–86.

Smith, James E., and Finis R. Welch. "Black-White Male Wage Ratios: 1960–70." *American Economic Review* 67 (June 1977): pp. 323–38.

Smith, Robert S. "Compensating Wage Differentials and Public Policy: A Review." *Industrial and Labor Relations Review* 32 (April 1979): pp. 339–52.

———. *The Occupational Safety and Health Act: Its Goals and Achievements.* Washington: American Enterprise Institute for Public Policy Research, 1976.

Smith, Sharon P. "Are State and Local Government Workers Overpaid?" Working paper, Federal Reserve Bank of New York, December 1981.

———. *Equal Pay in the Public Sector: Fact or Fantasy?* Princeton, N.J.: Industrial Relations Section, Princeton University, 1977.

Spence, A. Michael. *Market Signalling: Informational Transfers in Hiring and Related Screening Processes.* Cambridge, Mass.: Harvard University Press, 1974.

Spizman, Lawrence M. "Public Employee Unions: A Study in the Economics of Power." *Journal of Labor Research* 1 (Fall 1980): pp. 265–73.

Stigler, George J. "Information in the Labor Market." *Journal of Political Economy* 38 (2:October 1962): pp. 94–104.

Stiglitz, Joseph E. "The Theory of Screening, Education and the Distribution of Income." *American Economic Review* 65 (June 1975): pp. 283–300.

Strober, Myra H., and Laura Best. "The Female/Male Salary Differential in Public Schools: Some Lessons from San Francisco, 1879." *Economic Inquiry* 17 (April 1979): pp. 218–36.

Taubman, Paul. "Earnings, Education, Genetics, and Environment." *Journal of Human Resources* 11 (Fall 1976): pp. 447–61.

Taubman, Paul, and Terence Wales. "Higher Education, Mental Ability, and Screening." *Journal of Political Economy* 81 (January/February 1973): pp. 28–55.

Thaler, Richard, and Sherwin Rosen. "The Value of Saving a Life: Evidence from the Labor Market." In *Household Production and Consumption*, ed. Nester Terleckyj. New York: National Bureau of Economic Research, 1975.

Thieblot, Armand J. Jr. *The Davis-Bacon Act.* Philadelphia: Industrial Research Unit, Wharton School, University of Pennsylvania, 1975.

Ulman, Lloyd, and Robert J. Flanagan. *Wage Restraint: A Study of Incomes Policies in Western Europe.* Berkeley: University of California Press, 1971.

U.S. Department of Housing and Urban Development. *The Davis-Bacon Act: Selected References.* HUD-A-532. Washington: HUD, 1980.

U.S. General Accounting Office. *The Davis-Bacon Act Should Be Repealed.* HRD-79-18. Washington: GAO, 1979.

———. *Federal Compensation Comparability: Need for Congressional Action.* EPCD-78-60. Washington: GAO, 1978.

Victor, Richard B. "Municipal Unions and Wage Patterns." *Proceedings of the 32nd Annual Meeting, Industrial Relations Research Association.* Madison, Wis.: IRRA, 1979. Pp. 294–99.

Viscusi, W. Kip. *Employment Hazards: An Investigation of Market Performance.* Cambridge, Mass.: Harvard University Press, 1979.

———. "Wealth Effects and Earnings Premiums for Job Hazards." *Review of Economics and Statistics* 60 (August 1978): pp. 408–16.

Vroman, Susan. "Union/Non-Union Wage Spillovers." *British Journal of Industrial Relations* 18 (November 1980): pp. 369–71.

Wachter, Michael L., and Oliver E. Williamson. "Obligational Markets and the Mechanics of Inflation." *Bell Journal of Economics* 9 (Autumn 1978): pp. 549–71.

Wallich, Henry C., and Sidney Weintraub. "A Tax-Based Incomes Policy." *Journal of Economic Issues* 5 (June 1971): pp. 1–19.

Warner, Kenneth S., Rupert F. Chisholm, and Robert F. Bunzenrider. "Motives for Unionization Among State Social Service Employees." *Public Personnel Management* 7 (May-June 1978): pp. 181–91.

Weber, Arnold R., and Daniel J. B. Mitchell. *The Pay Board's Progress: Wage Controls in Phase II*. Washington: Brookings Institution, 1978.

Welch, Finis R. "Black-White Differences in Returns to Schooling." *American Economic Review* 63 (December 1973): pp. 893–907.

Williamson, Oliver E., Michael L. Wachter, and Jeffrey E. Harris. "Understanding the Employment Relation: The Analysis of Idiosyncratic Exchange." *Bell Journal of Economics* 6 (Spring 1975): pp. 250–78.

Wise, David. "Academic Achievement and Job Performance." *American Economic Review* 65 (June 1975): pp. 350–66.

CHAPTER 3

Employment and Training Programs in the 1970s: Research Results and Methods*

THOMAS A. BAROCCI
Massachusetts Institute of Technology

Employment and training research and evaluation during the 1970s continued, at an accelerated rate, a trend that had begun in the 1960s toward more inclusive and quantitatively sophisticated efforts. During the earlier decade a consensus had developed that government ought to be involved in correcting labor market imbalances and, therefore, that there should be an active manpower policy. As time passed, this consensus, which had manifested itself in the Economic Opportunity Act, gave way to more skeptical attitudes that emerged from all segments of the political spectrum. Conservatives questioned whether the government should be involved. Liberals questioned the type of involvement. Program dollars became more available or less available as the debate dragged on under several administrations. In the hopes of finding a basis for the resolution of their disagreements, policymakers looked to the research establishment, which was producing increasingly competent studies of employment and training programs, for guidance on whether to alter, discontinue, or extend then current programs.

In some cases the research results were used; in others they were ignored. Currently (late 1981) the employment and training network (primarily CETA) has begun to be dismantled and, as

* Special thanks are offered to William Mates who assisted me in organizing and writing the initial draft of this manuscript. I also would like to thank Ernst Stromsdorfer and Terry Hedrick for their comments on an earlier draft; both aided in correcting errors and provided the needed push to be concise. Finally, Carolanne Foilb and Ruth Fuquen put this chapter into its final form; their contribution far exceeded the chore of typing.

far as this writer can tell, the decision was not based on careful consideration of the results of past research and evaluation; rather, it was justified on the basis of anecdotes and isolated evaluations that happened to conform to campaign promises and the Reagan Administration's political need to balance the budget.

The decisions may have been correct, but they were not based on research on which millions of dollars had been expended during the 1970s. In part, the reason is that there was, and still is, no research consensus on the effects of the programs on either individual participants or society as a whole. The question of whether or not they were a good societal investment has never been answered. Lists of successful programs and participants are easily assembled, as are lists of unsuccessful programs and participants who never found their way out of the poverty cycle. Were the successes and the failures the result of program design, administrative shortcomings, inadequate funding, lack of participant motivation, and/or the economic environment? All, some, or none of the above can be documented by one study or another.

From the point of view of research and evaluation design, huge strides were made, sometimes at the expense of synthesizing efforts to aid in making good policy. Research methods became increasingly sophisticated, as will be detailed later, and the results are as disparate as ever. However, a survey allows a forum for generalizations, and some will be made here. In spite of the methodological battles among the researchers, movement toward a consensus on the efficiency of employment and training programs is building.

Most of the research and evaluation in the employment and training area was and still is funded by the Department of Labor's Employment and Training Administration (ETA) and the Department of Health and Human Services. Within the Labor Department, the Office of Research and Development and the Office of Program Evaluation and Research (both within ETA) were the primary funding agencies. For purposes of simplicity in this review, no differentiation between research and evaluation efforts is offered, as the two branches of inquiry address the same issues: program effects on society and individuals, whether the program should be retained or modified, and whether its funding level and distribution formulas should be altered.

No dollar figure is available on how much was invested in the evaluation of employment and training programs over the decade of the 1970s. The Office of Management and Budget has made estimates on a yearly basis—for example, that $140 million was spent on evaluating all social programs in 1978. Whatever the overall figure, it is substantial and should have had a significant effect on policy.

The purposes of this review are, first, to synthesize the methods and results of employment and training research and, second, to link that research with the policy issues faced during the 1970s. Finally, the prognosis for the field in the 1980s is presented.

First, we need to define our terms. We could, for example, classify employment and training programs (E&Ts) in various ways, but to facilitate comparisons here, they are considered to be in one of the following categories: (1) classroom or institutional training (CT), (2) on-the-job training (OJT), (3) adult work experience (AWE), (4) public service employment (PSE), and (5) youth programs (YPs).

Both CT and OJT can be characterized as skill-training programs since their avowed purpose is to inculcate specific job-related skills. Both have their genesis in the Manpower Development and Training Act (MDTA). The largest single segment of the evaluation literature concentrates on these types of training.

AWE programs attempt to provide the participants with general work experience rather than specific job skills; the aim is to improve their employability.

PSE is an odd form of E&T inasmuch as the programs provide participants with actual jobs rather than training them for some future employment (presumably the "training" in a job-creation program will come from the work itself). Although most PSE programs could be considered employment rather than training programs, they are included here because of their presumed training-like effects (for example, increased long-run earnings due to enhancement of skills through job experience). The major goal of PSE is, of course, short-run earnings for the participants.

Programs designed expressly for youth will be treated separately since, by definition, they have a clientele, and possibly an impact, that is different from those of other types of programs.

Although this study covers a variety of E&Ts, it would be impossible in a survey of this limited scope to include every kind of "training." Of necessity, therefore, formal vocational/technical education programs and apprenticeships are expressly excluded from coverage here.

Thus far no mention has been made of CETA (Comprehensive Employment and Training Act) as a type of E&T, since its main thrust was to decategorize and decentralize the administration of federal E&Ts. As CETA identifies an administrative structure rather than a specific type of training, studies of its impact are evaluations of the difference that program organization, not training, makes. While there have been numerous qualitative studies of the implementation of CETA, there have been few sound quantitative studies of its impact.

Because this review is concerned with evaluating manpower training programs, we need to define what we mean by "program evaluation." Although this may seem elementary, the fact that E&Ts have been "evaluated" for more than 15 years without producing results that could be used with confidence suggests that "program evaluation" is not as simple a concept as it appears to be (see, for example, National Academy of Science 1974, p. 102, and Goldstein 1972, p. 14, on the inclusiveness of past studies of E&Ts).

One can approach this question of defining program evaluation by first stating what it is not. It is not pure research, conducted out of an interest in understanding why programs work as they do (Edwards and Guttentag 1975, Posavec and Cary 1980, p. 10). While such research is important, it is rarely, if ever, the reason why a program evaluation is undertaken. Nor is program evaluation the same as program management, where "management" is taken to mean the making of decisions regarding the allocation of program resources. In fact, confusing program evaluation with program management puts the evaluator (often an external consultant) in the position of making value-laden, political decisions that by right are the province of responsible program managers and legislators (Edwards and Guttentag 1975).

Program evaluation is decision-oriented research—that is, research undertaken to provide the factual support for a forthcoming decision or series of decisions. In Borus's words, "Evaluation is the systematic gathering of information in order to make choices among alternative courses of action" (1979, p. 1). It is a systematic study of the consequences of past decisions; its function is to aid in making future decisions.

One important example of program evaluation's role in decision support is in the funding area. Assuming for the moment that E&Ts are intended to alter income distribution, they may be operated and funded with less than total attention to their monetary payoffs for individuals and for society. It is important that clear benchmarks for expected results be established. If those benchmarks are set by individuals skeptical of program worth, the expectation may be unrealistically high and the political problems of maintaining program funding will be compounded. It is thus important to synthesize past evaluations of E&Ts to set realistic performance expectations. Ideally, these performance standards should include guidelines for program management as well as expected results in terms of increased income and postprogram employment continuity. Efficiency *and* equity considerations must be taken into account. Although various typologies for describing policy evaluation research have been suggested (Borus 1979, Posavec and Cary 1980, Katz 1975), the basic distinction seems to be that between process and outcome evaluation. As Cain and Hollister state,

> There are two broad types of evaluation. The first, which we call "process evaluation," is mainly administrative monitoring. . . . In sum, "process evaluation" addresses the question: Given the existence of the program, is it being run honestly and administered efficiently? A second type of evaluation . . . may be called "outcome evaluation." . . . With this type of evaluation, the whole concept of the program is brought into question. . . . (1969, pp. 120–21)

Another distinction should be made here. A program's built-in management information system may provide a great deal of information that is relevant to program evaluation, but such data must always undergo selection and analysis before they will support conclusions about program outcomes or other values of interest. Thus, the focus of this review is on *formal* program evaluations rather than on the *implicit* evaluations generated by an on-going information system. In line with the foregoing comments on the different types of program evaluation, it would be desirable for such information systems routinely to capture and report information useful for program evaluation, and for formal program evaluations to suggest ways to improve those information systems. But again, such integration is a goal for future evaluation research rather than a reviewable result of past work.

Benefits and Costs

Individual vs. Social Benefits

Defining relevant program outcomes is the necessary first step in evaluation. Outcomes can be positive or negative, direct or indirect, immediate or delayed, intended or unintended. The most fruitful method of selection is to emphasize outcomes that indicate progress toward program goals (Mangum and Walsh 1973, p. 17). Any agreement on program goals, however, is unlikely since goals change as economic and social conditions change. In societal terms, Weisbrod (1969, p. 4) best summarizes this perspective with the goals of allocative efficiency, distributional equity, and economic stability—a combined equity-efficiency goal. Others (Perry et al. 1975, pp. 3–4) define the goals in individual terms, emphasizing that the programs are designed primarily to increase the earning ability of participants. Hamermesh (1971, pp. 6–7) offers still another view, one that combines the societal and individual goals by emphasizing human capital enhancement and the better functioning of labor markets.

Disagreement over goals affects evaluation design. For example, if reducing the unemployment rate were the main goal, the evaluator might simply estimate the impact of E&T expenditures on the national unemployment rate, while paying little or no attention to the gains accruing to individual participants. But if goals centering on human capital enhancement were foremost, no evaluative attention would be directed to labor market questions. Goals do, of course, change over time. MDTA grew out of the Area Redevelopment Act, which emphasized retraining and moving people to alleviate structural unemployment, and it was quite appropriate to define a program goal as a reduction in the unemployment rate in a relevant area. With the Great Society, emphasis shifted to expanding opportunities for disadvantaged individuals, and thus goals were defined more in terms of the labor market experience of disadvantaged individuals (Perry et al. 1975).

The societal and individual benefit distinction would not be important if societal gains (productivity and output) were measured exactly by individual gains (earnings). This equality does not hold since earnings are only one component of total employee compensation; earnings will not equal the worker's marginal product if manpower shortages exist (Hardin 1969, p. 101), and because participants may have to forgo other opportunities to participate, which will reduce the net benefits to individuals and to society. Possibly even more important are the losses and gains due to displacement and vacuum effects. A graduate may find a job at the expense of a previously employed worker, thus reducing the net gain to society while enhancing the graduate's earnings. This is especially true when wages are rigid on the downside (Kiefer 1979, p. 15). Also, a trainee may leave a relatively unskilled position and create a vacancy that might be filled by a new labor force entrant; this "vacuum" effect makes the net gain to society larger than the gains to the individual trainees (Borus 1972, p. 145). Evaluations that fail to take these effects into account may over- or underestimate the benefits of E&Ts (Johnson 1979).

Over time a consensus has emerged (Ashenfelter 1978, Borus 1972, Perry et al. 1975) that was incorporated into the congressional amendments to CETA in 1978 when a phrase was inserted in the Act's goals to state that CETA programs should result in an increase in the earned income of participants. In short, most recent evaluations state that the programs have multiple goals, but then have compressed these goals into a single measure—the change in earnings of the participants.

In the future a preferable approach would be to acknowledge that program benefits depend on the perspective of the evaluator and explicitly to construct estimates of benefits from several perspectives. At a minimum, the perspectives of the participant, the taxpayer, and society should be considered (see Borus 1979). For reference purposes, Table 1 is offered to show the various benefits that would be relevant from each perspective.

A second fundamental distinction exists between pecuniary and nonpecuniary benefits such as job satisfaction and self-esteem. (There are also pecuniary and nonpecuniary social benefits, such

TABLE 1
Benefits of E&T Programs

Benefit	Perspective		
	Trainee	Taxpayer	Society
Output and wages			
In-program output	0	0	+
In-program wages or stipends	+	−	0
Increased postprogram output	0	+	+
Increased postprogram wages	+	−0+	0+
Increased postprogram employment	+	−	0
Reduced costs for other social programs			
Transfer payments	−	+	0
Administrative costs	0	+	+
Taxes			
Increased tax payments	−	+	0
Psychosocial benefits			
Easing entry into the labor force	+	−0+	+
Providing further education	+	−0+	+
Helping the disadvantaged	+	−0+	+
Trainee goodwill	0	+	+
Psychological benefits (self-esteem, sense of security)	+	+	+
Job satisfaction	+	+	+
Improved health	+	+	+
Higher social status	+	0	+
Reduced dependency	+	+	+
Improved family life	+	+	+
Socioeconomic benefits			
Reduced unemployment	+	+	+
Increased employment	+	+	+
More equitable income distribution	+	+0−	+
Increased GNP	0	+	+
More stable prices	+	+	+
Reduced crime	+	+	+
Increased social stability	+	+	+
Reduced discrimination	+	+	+
Better race relations	+	+	+
Better housi g	+	+	+

Note: + = a net benefit. − = a net cost. 0 = neither a benefit nor a cost.

as increased aggregate output and increased social stability.) Virtually all discussions of outcome evaluation admit the potential importance of nonpecuniary factors, and virtually all point out the difficulty of evaluating benefits not measured in dollars. There are various facets of this problem. For one thing, some of the most important nonpecuniary benefits are psychological—for example, increased job satisfaction and a greater sense of personal worth, which are inherently difficult to measure and require the use of psychological tests and subjective interview data. Moreover, while economic benefits can be ranked in terms of their dollar value, noneconomic benefits are difficult to rank (Perry et al. 1975, p. 29; cf. Cain and Hollister 1969, p. 143). It is precisely these nonpecuniary benefits that may have the most important program effects for especially disadvantaged groups (Perry et al. 1975, p. 34).

Short-Run vs. Long-Run Benefits

A distinction should be drawn between short- and long-run benefits—for example, participant earnings three months after program completion and earnings five years later. As Rosen (1975) and other human capital theorists note, annual earnings fluctuate due to random causes, and what is most desirable is some measure of the individual's lifetime earnings curve. Also, if E&Ts are meant to improve the lot of disadvantaged persons permanently, then the life-cycle impact of training on earnings is what the evaluator should estimate. However, what is typically available are data collected shortly after program completion. Evaluation of long-run outcomes raises two conceptually distinct problems: (1) What, if anything, do short-run data tell us about long-run outcomes? (2) How do we weight outcomes occurring at different points in time?

Since only a study that documents a person's entire worklife subsequent to program participation could truly be said to provide evidence on the permanence of training-related benefits in relation to a theoretical standard, *all* of our E&T evaluations are short-run. Hence, the problem of inferring long-run outcomes from short-run data is not one that will vanish. Different studies have used different approaches to this problem. One method is to collect data on various "indicator variables" shortly after program termination; these variables, which include number of terminations, number of placements, number employed three months after termination, etc., are routinely reported in the *Employment and Training Report of the President* and, as Borus notes, they are in common use among CETA prime sponsors for program evaluation. Yet, as Borus discovered, almost none of these indicator variables is significantly correlated with long-run earnings, weeks employed, amount of public assistance or unemployment insurance received, or educational attainment.

The clear implication of the research (Gay and Borus 1980, for example) is that long-run labor market experience must be measured directly rather than inferred from short-run data, and most of the studies that draw conclusions about long-run trends follow this procedure. However, it should be noted that many of the early studies drew *no* conclusions about long-run impact, and some that did merely assumed (incorrectly) that the initial change in earnings would persist over time (Decision Making Information 1971). On the other hand, Parnes and other users of the National Longitudinal Surveys (NLS) have attempted extensive (10-year) follow-up work on the effects of training and other factors on earnings.

The studies that *have* done follow-up work have had varying results, ranging from almost total disappearance of training gains to persistence of substantial benefits five years out. The most frequent finding seems to be that, although the initial advantage of training erodes over time, some advantage persists as long as five years after training. Prescott and Cooley (1972) found an overall decline in the earnings advantage of about 10 percent in the second year after program completion, Farber (1971a) found the five-year average advantage to be 60 percent of the initial impact, and Reid (1976) found the advantage in the fifth year to be about 60 percent for males and 100 percent for females of that in the first year after training. One unanswered question is whether the extent of erosion varies by race or sex: Prescott and Cooley found differences by race, sex, and type of training (CT vs. OJT), and Ashenfelter (1978, p. 56) found erosion of 50 percent after the fifth year for males but no decline in later years for females. Reid found significant erosion for males, slight erosion for black females, and a *widening* of the earnings advantage for white females, while Farber found the earnings gains of minorities and women to be *at least* as long-lasting as those of whites and males. Evidence on the durability of nonpecuniary benefits is nonexistent. Follow-up work with the Continuous Longitudinal Manpower Sample (CLMS) will allow for more definite conclusions on pecuniary benefit durability.

In light of these differing results, we can conclude that inferring long-term benefits from short-run data is unwarranted. We must also conclude that the durability of benefits may vary by race and sex, and possibly by type of training. Therefore, the indicated methodology is to measure long-run impact directly in one or more follow-up studies; presumably, at some point the training effect will appear sufficiently persistent or sufficiently attenuated for us to extrapolate to the rest of the individual's worklife. Of course, if we perceive the goal of manpower training to be the provision of a "quick fix" for low-income individuals, then erosion of the training effect over time would not be of so much concern. Once again, our goals for E&T will determine the kind of durability we demand.

The second major problem in assessing the long-term impact of E&Ts is how to weight benefits that occur at different times. The basic notion, central to modern financial theory, is that a dollar of benefits received now is worth more than a dollar received later, both because individuals are present-oriented and because a dollar received now can be invested. The usual procedure for handling this problem is to discount benefits received in later years by some predetermined discount rate, according to the formula $PV(B_t) = B_t/(1+r)^n$, where the left-hand side is the present value of the benefits received at time t, r is the discount rate, and n is the length of time. Benefits received in different years can thus be reduced to a common metric and added to permit comparison of different programs.

Determination of the appropriate discount rate is a matter of considerable controversy. A high discount rate greatly reduces the value of benefits received far in the future, while a low rate weights them more heavily. Since program costs (see below) are apt to be incurred "up front," with benefits spread out over time, a high discount rate will result in lower estimates of a program's net present value than will a low rate. Many analysts argue for a rate equal to the "market rate" of interest on the grounds that that rate is the best available estimate of how highly society values the future, as well as the best estimate of the opportunity cost of resources withdrawn from private use for public programs. Others maintain that the rates prevailing in market transactions yield underestimates of the social utility of future benefits and, accordingly, urge the use of a rate lower than the market rate of interest. One technique for accommodating this disagreement is to estimate the program's net present value (or benefit-cost ratio) for a range of discount rates, noting the rate at which the program becomes desirable. The reasonableness of *that* rate can then be assessed by the decision-maker.

Few studies address these issues rigorously. Borus (1972), Ashenfelter (1978), and others ignore the time value of money and present earnings gains in future years, with no indication of how a program with a particular earnings pattern may be compared to alternative uses of society's resources. A few studies offer estimates of present value for a range of discount rates (Decision Making Information 1971, p. 7.50). The matter is crucial in a world of limited resources where more programs can be conceived than funded. For example, public housing, national health insurance, manpower training, and enforcement of equal opportunity laws presumably all benefit disadvantaged members of society, but to decide which one (or mix) represents the best use of public funds requires some sort of common metric, such as a net present value or a benefit-cost ratio. Existing studies of E&Ts are severely deficient in this regard.

Costs of E&Ts

The discussion thus far has been couched largely in terms of program benefits. However, the concepts apply equally to program costs. E&Ts, like other social programs, have costs that should be taken into account in assessing program performance. Restatement of the entire preceding discussion in terms of costs is unnecessary; attention will be confined here to a few salient points. Extended discussions of program costs can be found in Borus (1979) and other sources. Like benefits, costs differ according to the perspective being used by the evaluator. The example of stipends received by trainees during training is illustrative; such payments represent a benefit to the trainee, a cost to the taxpayer, and a "wash" (no net benefit or cost) to society as a whole. Table 2 notes the costs that will be relevant from various perspectives.

Evaluation of E&T outcomes rarely, however, attend to costs with the same care devoted to benefits. Many "major" studies do not even include cost data (Decision Making Information 1971).

TABLE 2

Costs of E&T Programs

Cost	Perspective		
	Trainee	Taxpayer	Society
Forgone opportunities during training			
Market output	0	–	–
Earnings	0–	+	0
Nonmarket output	–	0	–
Leisure	–	0	–
Participation costs			
Travel to training site	–	0	–
Out-of-pocket expenses	–	0	–
Program costs			
Instructional salaries	0	–	–
Books and supplies	0	–	–
Physical facilities	0	–	–
Overhead costs	0	–	–
For OJT: supervisory costs	0	–	–
For YPs: lost school time	–	–	–
Administrative costs	0	–	–
Costs of program evaluation, audit, etc.	0	–	–
Governmental costs			
Increased transfer payments during training	+	–	0
Central administration	0	–	–
Reduced tax revenues during training	+	–	0
Psychosocial costs			
Effort needed for training	–	0	–
Feeling of unfairness in those not selected	–	–	–
Increased competition for skilled work	+	–	0
Decreased competition for unskilled work	0	+	0
Separation from family, friends during training	–	0	–
Racial tension after training at sites and in local communities	–	–	–
Heightened expectations that may not be realistic	–	–	–

Note: + = a net benefit. – = a net cost. 0 = neither a benefit nor a cost.

Others take reported program operating costs as given by the agency and add an estimate of forgone participant earnings—for example, Hardin and Borus (1971). Even the studies that use regression methods to estimate program benefits do *not* use the same level of analytical rigor in estimating costs. While this casual approach to cost data is probably good enough for a quick assessment of whether a program "costs more than it's worth," a more thorough study should attempt to gather reliable information on program costs.

Relating Costs and Benefits

In theory, the way to relate costs and benefits is quite simple. Either the present value of program costs may be subtracted from the present value of program benefits to yield an estimate of the program's net present value, or the benefits may be divided by the costs to obtain a benefit-cost ratio. The decision rules are equally simple: if the program's net present value is greater than zero or its benefit-cost ratio is greater than one (the two are equivalent), then the present value of the benefits exceeds the present value of the costs and the program is "worthwhile." If several worthwhile programs are competing for a limited budget, then one undertakes the most worthwhile program first and continues on to the least worthwhile until the budget is exhausted. (In some cases, program "lumpiness" will necessitate taking the programs out of order to maximize utility.)

Simple as it may be, "Few aspects of manpower program evaluation have generated as much conflict and controversy as cost-benefit analysis" (Perry et al. 1975, p. 33). The major criticism is that cost-benefit analysis systematically undervalues or totally neglects benefits (and costs) that are difficult to quantify; in general, these will be benefits or costs that are nonpecuniary and equity-focused rather than pecuniary and efficiency-focused. As Somers has put it, "The cost-benefit calculus is only one piece of evidence in the appraisal process, and it may not be the most significant piece of evidence" (cited in Perry et al. 1975, p. 33).

Most published studies have not undertaken a formal cost-benefit analysis; rather, the usual pattern has been to report the relation between program participation and variables of interest, mainly earnings, wage rates, and labor force participation. A few do compute a benefit-cost ratio—Borus (1972) and the studies reviewed in Hardin (1969). The others provide no equivalent summary statistic that would permit comparison of one program with another or of E&Ts as a group with other uses of societal resources. Given the misuses to which quantification can be put, the strictures against cost-benefit analysis have a point; however, the need for measuring and comparing program impacts so that society's resources can be used in the most productive way is also undeniable. It seems preferable to develop decision analysis to the point where social, nonpecuniary, and long-term benefits and costs can enjoy the same advantages of quantification that are now most applicable to individual, pecuniary, and short-run factors.

Summary

The apparent consensus in the literature can be quickly summarized. The definition of benefits and costs depends on the goals ascribed to particular training programs and on the perspective of the evaluator. While programs have multiple goals, analysts tend to use the change in participant earnings or its components as a proxy for total program benefits, perhaps supplemented by attention to the wage and employment components of earnings. The more recent studies tend to follow up on trainees' later work experience to obtain direct evidence of long-run outcomes, but this follow-up generally does not extend past the fifth year after training. Little attention is paid to nonpecuniary benefits, and societal benefits, as noted, are proxied by individual earnings, which implicitly assumes that displacement and vacuum effects are unimportant.

Program costs, when considered, are typically derived by adding to direct program operating costs some estimate of forgone trainee earnings. Some studies explicitly relate benefits to costs by computing a ratio, but the practice has been less widespread in recent years, leaving assessments of program worth to the implicit judgment of the decision-maker.

Given that the change in participant earnings is to be taken as a measure of program success, the question arises of how best to study that change. The next section of this chapter describes and evaluates the various research designs that have been employed in past evaluations.

Research Design

"Research design" refers to the overall strategy that guides the program evaluation. The evaluation should be designed to provide reliable information about program outcomes—that is, information useful to decision-makers. This may seem obvious, but it is not. As the National Academy of Sciences noted: "Manpower training programs have been in existence a little over a decade, yet . . . little is known about the educational or economic effects of manpower training programs. This is troublesome, especially in light of the fact that about $180 million have been spent over the past ten years in an attempt to evaluate these programs" (1974, p. 1). Mangum and Walsh agreed: "After ten years, there is still no *definitive* evidence one way or the other about MDTA outcomes" (1973, p. 47). Writing at about the same time, Goldstein concluded, "Despite substantial expenditure of public funds for research and evaluation, there is only limited reliable information about the impact of training" (1972, p. 14).

Nor has this deficiency been alleviated during the intervening years, although progress has been made. Writing in 1978, Ashenfelter stated that "it is by now rather widely agreed that very little is reliably known about the actual effects of these programs" (1978, p. 47).

The failure of past evaluations to provide reliable information about program outcomes is due in large measure to inadequate design of evaluation research. In their classic work on research design, Campbell and Stanley (1963) classified research design into three categories: nonexperimental design (often called natural experiments), quasi-experimental designs, and true experiments. The three differ greatly in strategy employed, data requirements, and conclusions that each can support. Of these, the natural experiment is the simplest to initiate but presents the most severe measurement problems. It has been used most widely in outcome evaluations.

Natural Experiments

Although there are many variants on the theme, the essence of the natural experiment is the before-and-after study; the evaluator observes the behavior of the group of interest before and after the occurrence of a "treatment." The basic assumption of this design is that the "before" observation is the earnings level that would have persisted in the absence of training, so that the difference between post- and pretraining earnings is attributed to the program. For example, the Olympus four-cities study used general preprogram labor market trends as a basis for inferring program impact (Olympus Research Corporation 1971, reported by Mangum and Robson 1973).

This research design was the one most widely used in early (pre-CETA) evaluations. Unfortunately, nonexperimental designs have a serious flaw: they cannot tell us whether the earnings gains were due to the training program or to some other factor such as overall economic conditions. Another "threat to internal validity" arises from possible biases in the enrollee group: if, for example, enrollees were more talented than nonenrollees to begin with, we would *expect* their earnings to increase over time. Indeed, given the fact that most people earn more as they grow older, it is hard to conclude anything about program impact from a nonexperimental design such as this. It is probably safe to say that no one today would attempt to evaluate outcomes using what must be regarded as the discredited nonexperimental design.

True Experiments

The polar opposite of the "natural" experiment, in terms of data requirements, difficulty of implementation, and reliability of conclusions, is the true experiment, called by Gilbert et al. the "randomized controlled field trial" (1975, p. 39). That is, out of a sample of persons eligible to enroll, some are assigned *at random* to participate in the program (the "treatment" group) and some are not (the "control" group). Pre- and postprogram earnings, say, are observed and compared. Given this design, and assuming noncontamination of the control group, it is possible to conclude that differences in earnings gains were *caused* by the training program. The strength of this design springs from the fact that random assignment to treatment and control assures that there are no systematic differences between the two groups that would bias the results.

There are several reasons why this design has not been more widely used. First, it requires evaluators to "get in on the ground floor"; once the program is under way, it is usually too late randomly to assign persons to participate or not. It is also necessary that the pool of eligibles be larger than the number of available slots; if the number of slots is larger, then it is morally and politically difficult to deny eligibles the right to enter training. The cost of experimentation and general societal bias against "experimenting on people" are also often cited although, as Gilbert et al. note, true experiments are feasible much more often than we usually, think and, where feasible, they are always to be preferred to non- or quasi-experimental designs (1975). Conlisk further argues that the training context is a well suited to experiment as a social program is likely to be (1979, p. 93).

Quasi-Experiments

On most dimensions of interest—cost, apparent feasibility, complexity, and conclusiveness of results—the quasi-experimental design stands between the natural and the true experiment. Unlike the natural experiment, it uses a comparison group, which increases both its complexity and the strength of its results. Unlike the true experiment, it does not randomly assign individuals to treatment and control, which certainly reduces the conclusiveness of its findings. Yet it has become the generally accepted design for evaluating E&Ts. Because there are numerous ways in which the validity of its results can be compromised, great care must be taken in its execution. There are two main variants of this design: time-series (longitudinal) and comparison-group (cross-sectional), or a combination of time-series and cross-section multiple observations on multiple groups.

Even with time-series data, we do not know what would have occurred in the absence of training. Earnings gains uncovered in studies of this type may actually be due to general societal trends or individual maturation.

Borus and Hamermesh (1978, p. 36) add that the time-series design is not useful unless one has a good predictive model of how the process in question unfolds over time. Of particular importance for our purposes is the fact that the NLS does not collect detailed information on the type of training undergone, so it will not support studies of particular programs. One is driven to the conclusion that while time-series studies may serve as a source of hypotheses concerning training effects and may in some cases resolve ambiguities about the direction of causation, they cannot be used as the main research design in an evaluation of program outcomes.

The comparison-group design, on the other hand, comes closer to the true experiment and has been the design used in most recent studies. The word "comparison" has been used deliberately instead of "control" to call attention to the fact that individuals are not randomly assigned to treatment or no-treatment status in the quasi-experimental design; instead, statistical techniques are used to control for possible biases introduced by differences between nonrandomly selected treatment and no-treatment groups. To the degree that these techniques fail to capture all of those differences, the treatment and comparison groups will be similar but *not necessarily identical,* leaving open the possibility that some factor other than participation in training accounts for observed intergroup differences in, say, earnings. (Technically, this is known as the "missing variable" problem; self-selection bias is one type.)

Such bias has been a major problem with evaluations, according to Stromsdorfer (1980, p. 99). For example, persons applying may be more ambitious than the nonapplicants; in that case we would *expect* their earnings gains to be larger. As Sewell (1971, p. 162) notes, if programs select on the basis of ability, then any change in earnings may simply reflect returns to ability rather than training effects. Perry et al. have noted the possibility of "creaming" in the selection of trainees (1975, p. 151). On the other hand, persons accepted might be *more* disadvantaged than nonacceptees, biasing their earnings gains downward. Gay and Borus (1980) have noted that participants tend to be younger, less educated, and less attached to the labor force, and to have lower pretraining earnings than nonparticipants.

Because of this problem some students of program evaluation have questioned the entire comparison-group design. Campbell and Boruch, for example, call the possibility of selection bias a "fundamental flaw" in the comparison-group design (1975, p. 203); according to them and others, "simple applications of multiple regression, covariance analysis, and matching will usually be inappropriate vehicles for estimating [training] effects" (1975, p. 209).

There have been various defenses of the comparison-group design, however. Gilbert et al. (1975, p. 119), while generally critical of nonrandom comparison groups, state that findings without randomization may be accepted if there is no strong reason to believe that the treatment and comparison groups differ in some unknown ways *and* if there is a strong a priori reason to believe that observed effects are due to the treatment. Cain admits that complete elimination of selection bias is probably impractical (1975, pp. 311-12), but he goes on to suggest a procedure for dealing with it (pp. 314–15). If the trainee and comparison groups differ in mean pretraining earnings, then Cain's procedure is to apply regression coefficients for the comparison group to the mean values of the trainee group's independent variables to obtain an estimate of the bias.

Finally, it should be noted that recent evaluations combine longitudinal and cross-section data to draw on the strengths of each. That is, a series of observations are taken for both trainees and the comparison group, permitting analysis of both gross changes with time series and net changes with comparison groups. This approach in effect unites the work of Parnes and his colleagues with that of Ashenfelter and those who follow his comparison-group approach. Although by its nature the quasi-experimental design can never overcome all theoretical objections, it seems likely that this hybrid approach will allow for the strongest possible research design short of a true experiment. And Mangum and Walsh note (1973, p. 23), the defects of previous studies of E&Ts can only be corrected by evaluations that combine use of a comparison group with long-term longitudinal follow-up.

Seemingly taking the advice offered by Mangum and Walsh (1973), the U.S. Department of Labor's Office of Program Evaluation and Research initiated a large-scale project to collect longitudinal data on CETA enrollees. This data set came to be known as the Continuous Longitudinal Manpower Sample (CLMS) and was begun with the onset of CETA in 1973. The data base collection was, and still is (1981), coordinated by Westat, Inc. (Westat 1979); it provides a longitudinal description of the participants in all major programs sponsored under CETA. This, of course, still leaves the question of what would have happened to the CETA enrollees in the absence of programs. In order to obtain an estimate of the net impact of the program on earnings, a comparison group was needed.

An artificial comparison group was constructed from the Current Population Survey (coupled with earnings data from Social Security records) and was used to contrast the experience of CETA terminees. The matching of the CPS group with the CLMS sample participants involved elaborate disqualification algorithms to best facilitate equality of backgrounds, demographics, and labor force experience of the match group with the CLMS sample (Westat 1981).

Although the Westat research is certainly not without problems, its use of the CLMS represents the most advanced and defensible mechanism for measuring the net impact of the program components on the individual participants. Research regarding the appropriate variables on which to match the CPS and CLMS groups continues, as does work on the elimination of selection bias in the samples (Director 1979).

A Note on Evaluating PSE Programs

Outcome evaluation is especially difficult for PSE programs. To begin with, it is not clear whether such programs are training programs at all, or whether they are better classed as job-creation or counter-cyclical revenue-sharing programs. Palmer cites two different goals for PSE—combatting cyclical and structural unemployment (1978, p. 7); measures of program impact will differ, depending on the goal. Fechter (1977, p. 140) flatly describes PSE programs as job-creation rather than training, and it does seem that these programs are aimed more at stimulating aggregate demand that at skill training (aggregate supply) and more at macroeconomic goals than individual training gains.

Second, it is impossible to ignore the issue of substitution displacement here (Nathan et al. 1978). At its starkest, assume that a local government agency receives funding for 100 PSE positions, but uses all the money to reduce its own wage and salary expenditures. Then the net number of jobs created may be zero even though the gross number is 100, and the job-creation program becomes revenue-sharing (Jerrett and Barocci 1979, Fechter 1977).

Third, the relevance of earnings as a measure of program impact is reduced for PSE since minimum and maximum wages are fixed by law. Perhaps for that reason, most studies of PSE impact have focused on the extent of job-creation under PSE; the change in earnings is typically not used as an impact measure. (See, for example, Wachter's comment that measurement of earnings gains is not appropriate in studies of PSE [1979, p. 286].)

Fourth, perhaps because employment rather than earnings has been the focus of PSE evaluations, new methods have been developed for evaluations of these programs. For example, Jarrett and Barocci (1979) use Markov chain processes to simulate the probable employment experience of age/race/sex cohorts in the absence of PSE; this can be compared to the actual experience of these groups to gauge the extent of displacement and job-creation. Perhaps because PSE has emerged as a major policy thrust (and thus a subject of study) only in the mid- and late 1970s, there is as yet no consensus on how to evaluate these programs; at best, there appears to be agreement that the appropriate methods may differ from those applicable to other E&Ts.

Analytic Methods

This section focuses on the analytic methods used in comparison of the posttraining earnings, wage rates, employment stability, etc., of trainees and "controls." There are two reasons why this is not always so. First, it is impractical to try to match trainees and controls closely enough to eliminate *all* pretraining differences; thus, in most control group studies samples are matched on relatively few variables. Second, matching may introduce regression artifacts (Campbell and Stanley 1963, pp. 10–12), and it increases the probability of Type II errors (Chen 1967).

Because of these problems, one must use more elaborate analytic techniques even with a comparison group design. The two principal ways of measuring treatment effects are analysis of raw or unstandardized change scores and analysis of covariance (multiple regression). As Kenny notes (1975, pp. 346–47), these methods rest on different assumptions and, accordingly, are appropriate in different circumstances. The basic question is how program participants are selected. If they are chosen solely on the basis of *group* characteristics, then analysis of change scores is appropriate, but if selection is based on individual as well as group differences, then analysis of covariance is necessary. Where the basis for selection is not known, presentation of results from both methods is indicated. One assumption common to both methods is that the earnings (or wages or employment) function does not change between the measurement of the pre- and posttraining scores; if it does, neither method will be successful. If the function is stable except for the error variance, it may be possible to correct for this shift in reliability (Kenny 1975, p. 355).

Dependent Variables

Earnings, wage rates, and labor force participation (hours worked, employment stability, incidence of unemployment) have been the major dependent variables in studies of the effects of training. However, these variables have been measured in different ways: by the absolute postprogram level, by the change from the preprogram level, and by the percentage change from the preprogram level. Each appears to have certain advantages. The absolute level of earnings attained after training provides direct evidence of the relevance of training for the reduction of poverty. Similarly, the amount of earnings gain can be related to the cost per trainee to obtain an estimate of the effectiveness of E&Ts relative to other social programs. The percentage change formulation may be most closely related to participants' own perception of what they have gained from training: a doubling of a participant's income may be significant quite apart from the absolute numbers involved. Other dependent variables have included occupational attainment, measured by Duncan's occupational scale (Andrisani 1977) or by the median income in the occupation (Freeman 1974).

Each of these measures of the training effect has its own problems. One general problem is what to use as the base year: when the year preceding training is used as the base, gains from training tend to be overstated. Another general problem, and one not usually addressed, is how to account for inflation, which may push up earnings and wages regardless of training. Suojanen (1977) recognized the problem and suggested the theoretical solution—to deflate posttraining earnings (or wages) by some appropriate price index. Another problem is nonhomogeneity of earnings gains: it may be easier to move from no earnings at all to, say, $3000 than from $2000 to $5000 since the former involves a change from no labor force participation to some, while the latter indicates a move from a low skill level to a higher one (Posavec and Carey 1980, pp. 263–64). The use of the mean change in earnings is also problematic unless we identify the base, since a $100 gain represents 10 percent over a $1000 base but only 2.5 percent over a $4000 base.

It should be pointed out that researchers in this field disagree as to whether earnings is an appropriate dependent variable. Some claim that using annual earnings as the variable will confound market transactions with issues of labor/leisure choice and the more transitory effects of unemployment (Griliches 1977, p. 3). Griliches then argues that the wage rate (per hour or week) is a better measure of returns to schooling; this choice, however, cannot be unilaterally applied when estimating returns to E&Ts since one of their goals relates to lifting people out of poverty by increasing the continuity of employment/yearly income.

Functional Forms

Most of the studies of training impact use a generally linear form; the exceptions are easily noted. Human capital variables—age, education, and experience—and duration of training often have been entered as both quadratic and linear terms to capture possible nonlinear effects—for example, diminishing returns to capital or a U-shaped lifetime earnings curve. Examples include Borus (1978, age and education squared), Flanagan (1974, total training squared), and Borus (1972, age and education squared).

Dependent variables are sometimes entered as log terms, permitting regression coefficients to be interpreted as percentage effects. An example is Andrisani (1977, log of earnings and hourly wage). Rosen (1975, p. 7) cites examples of the use of log terms in human capital studies, but it is not clear that such terms are superior to ordinary linear terms. Also, a number of studies have used interaction terms such as sex × hours worked and education × hours worked (both Borus 1972), race × sex × training status (Westat 1981), education × percent of women in occupation (Ferber and Lowry 1976), and the like to capture the combined effects of the two factors. This procedure represents an alternative to estimating separate equations for difficult demographic groups.

These examples represent only a few of the possible functional forms, and it is difficult to discern firm guidelines in the literature on when to depart from linearity. The linear form is not sacrosanct; if it is used when the phenomenon is in fact nonlinear, the misspecification will introduce bias. One can test for sensitivity to functional form, but while a number of studies do estimate alternate equations, few estimate alternative forms of the same equation (Westat 1981).

Significance Tests

While many of the earlier E&T studies did not report the significance level of their findings, more recent studies tend to indicate which coefficients are significant at the traditional 1 and 5 percent levels. It is striking that many published studies have reported R^2 values substantially less than .5, and in some cases less than .1. For example, Borus (1972) estimated four earnings equations; the highest R^2 value was .12. Given the rarity of R^2 values higher than .3, it is apparent that the earnings equations being used fail to account for the majority of the variance in "outcomes," which is the major shortcoming in a comparison group study that depends for its validity on the ability to specify (and thereby control for) possible sources of selection or other bias.

Another important point should be made: again and again the standard errors of the coefficients, including those on the crucial coefficients of the training variables, are substantial in size. For example, Kiefer's study of MDTA training (1978) reports several 95 percent confidence intervals that include zero—that is, the standard error was at least half as large as the coefficient. It seems essential to report such information, given the relatively small effects that are typically found. Simply to report, say, a $400 training gain significant at the 5 percent level is misleading if the standard error is $250.

Related to the question of significance is the problem of evaluating statistically significant but numerically small training effects. Suppose, to take an extreme case, that the training gain was $50, with a 99.5 percent confidence level and a standard error of 50 cents. Clearly, the training is generating a positive gain, but is a $50 gain worth all the trouble? Kiefer, in both his 1978 and 1979 studies, argues that training programs should be compared to transfer programs since the goal of all such programs is the reduction of poverty; presumably one would compute benefit-cost ratios for training, AFDC, the negative income tax, etc., and choose the program with the highest ratio. (In the case of PSE, one could compare the "training" program to other countercyclical measures; in public works programs, to straight revenue-sharing, etc.). Another question is whether we want a small benefit to many people or a large benefit for a few—that is, how do we assess the variance of training gains? We have as yet no firm answers for these kinds of questions.

Program Effects

Enrollee Characteristics

Prior to presentation of measured effects of the programs, it is useful to present a summary of the characteristics of enrollees in four types of programs—classroom training, adult work experience, OJT, and PSE. As shown in Table 3, there have been several notable changes in the characteristics of enrollees during the two years shown (FY1976 and FY1978).

In general, more disadvantaged clients were enrolled in classroom training and adult work experience than in OJT and PSE during both years. As might be expected, PSE positions were given to the most advantaged enrollees, as measured by family income, enrollee income, labor force experience, and poverty level definitions. This pattern holds in both years.

Comparison of the two years reveals that PSE jobs were offered to more disadvantaged enrollees in FY1978 than in FY1976. The changes in CETA eligibility rules over this period seem to have worked in the direction of targeting positions toward the more disadvantaged.

Classroom or Institutional Training (CT)

Classroom training programs are the ones that have been studied most often. Table 4 displays the results of all 15 comparison group studies that contained data identified as earnings gains of CT trainees, broken down by age and sex. A number of the studies report results that are not statistically significant, while others contain positive or negative outliers. These observations, in conjunction with the wide range of time covered and the fact that some use national samples and some are case studies, preclude inclusion of summary statistics relating to the average gain.

There obviously is great variability in the results, ranging from

TABLE 3

Characteristics of Enrollees in Adult CETA Services FY1976/FY1978
(All Figures Percent of Total)

	Classroom Training		Adult Work Experience		On-the-Job Training		PSE	
Characteristic	FY76	FY78	FY76	FY78	FY76	FY78	FY76	FY78
Female	50	60	48	56	35	36	34	38
Age: < 21	36	40	10	—	33	36	24	23
22–29	40	36	48	49	40	38	43	42
> 30	24	25	42	51	26	26	34	34
Minority	55	50	40	42	38	32	31	39
High school Completor	60	61	64	70	69	69	76	75
Veteran	16	11	20	18	24	21	27	24
Below OMB poverty level	66	74	61	77	52	62	44	73
Family receiving transfer benefits	36	35	26	36	20	18	16	26
Family income < $6000	64	57	64	62	54	45	48	56
Enrollee income < $1000	56	50	48	54	43	35	38	44
Predominant labor force status (12 months pre-CETA)								
Employed (> 90%)	11	10	15	10	16	17	17	8
Unemployed (> 50%)	37	31	34	39	29	24	27	40
Not in labor force (> 50%)	31	30	27	25	27	25	24	22
Residual	22	29	24	27	28	34	32	31

Source: Westat (1981).

a loss of $732 for nonwhite males in Farber study (1971a) of 1968 trainees, to a gain of $1456 for nonwhite females in Kiefer's study (1979). It should be noted that the large losses and small gains that Farber reported can be attributed in part to his methods: he used a comparison group drawn from the Social Security sample and, accordingly, was unable to control for education—possibly a crucial omission. With the exception of Kiefer's work using the OEO/DOL data set, the other studies all report some kind of training gain, generally in the $300–700 range.

It is probably appropriate to characterize these gains as modest, especially in light of the cost of training. As noted earlier, most evaluations do not devote much attention to program costs,

TABLE 4

First-Year Earnings Gains from Classroom Training Programs

Study	White Males	White Females	Nonwhite Males	Nonwhite Females
Main (1968)	409[a]	409[a]	409[a]	409[a]
Farber (1971a)	−48	132	129	211
Farber (1971b)	−676	−368	−732	−364
Hardin/Borus (1971)	557	895	1151	1095
Prescott/Cooley (1972)	719	527	587	624
Sewell (1971)	0	n.a.	429	n.a.
Smith (1971)	416[a]	416[a]	416[a]	416[a]
Reid (1976)[b]	268	571	362	546
Ashenfelter (1978)[c]	121	443	241	455
Kiefer (1978)[e]	−619	n.a.	−342	n.a.
Kiefer (1979)[d, f]	−200	1316	256	1456
Goodfellow (1979)[f]	377*	778	525	737
Cooley et al. (1975)[g]	303	318	303	318
Gay/Borus (1980)[f]	125*	1132	133*	311
Westat (1981)	400	550	200*	500

Note: All figures represent positive gains unless otherwise indicated; if not indicated, gain is from base year (usually year before training) to year after training. Only comparison group studies are included in the table.

* Not statistically significant.

[a] Overall estimate

[b] Five-year average

[c] Base year is 1962; five-year average.

[d] Kiefer's estimate of quarterly gain × 4.

[e] Kiefer's estimate of weekly gain × 50.

[f] Race categories are black and nonblack.

[g] Three-year average; gains not estimated separately by race.

typically taking estimates drawn from program records at face value. For that reason, cost information and benefit-cost ratios are not reported here. However, it seems quite plausible, given the magnitudes of the earnings gains, that costs were at least equal to first-year benefits, which would produce benefit-cost ratios of less than one (or, equivalently, net present values less than zero).

Five comparison group studies provide information on the longevity of CT benefits (see Table 5). Prescott and Cooley (1972) found that benefits in the second posttraining year were 90 percent of those in the first year. Farber (1971a) found that the average earnings gain for the first five posttraining years was 60 percent of the first-year level. Cooley et al. (1975) calculated three-year averages that were *higher* than the first-year level (146 percent

TABLE 5
Projected Earnings Gains

Study	3-Year Average as Percent of Year 1 Level	5-Year Average as Percent of Year 1 Level
Prescott/Cooley (1972)	95% (2-year average)	n.a.
Cooley et al. (1975)	146–163%	n.a.
Farber (1971a)	n.a.	60%
Reid (1976)	Approximately 100%, both sexes	Approx. 100%, women Approx. 70–84%, men
Ashenfelter (1978)	Approximately 100%, both sexes	Approx. 100%, women Approx. 75%, men

for men and 163 percent for women). Reid (1976) and Ashenfelter (1978) also found differences by sex.

Based on these findings, one might expect earnings gains recorded in the first year to persist at least five years out for women, but to decay somewhat for men. To take a single example, suppose a median first-year gain for white females persisted with no decay for five years; at a discount rate of 7 percent, the net present value of that benefit stream would be $1989 (assuming benefits accrue at year's end). Ashenfelter notes that the per-trainee cost for the class of 1964 was about $1800, of which a substantial amount represented transfer payments (subsidies to trainees); since transfers have no *net* social cost, the true cost per trainee is much less than $1800, yielding a benefit-cost ratio in excess of 1.0 and possibly in excess of 2.0. By way of comparison, Hardin (1969, p. 113) summarizes the results of six early studies that computed benefit-cost ratios that ranged from 0 to 17.3, with most well in excess of 2. (Hardin used a 10 percent discount rate and assumed a 10-year benefit stream to standardize the studies.)

In short, the longevity of earnings effects is difficult to document even in the most tightly controlled design. The importance of this measurement depends on whether one believes that programs should inculcate permanent additions to the participant's human capital, or simply allow them to attain a job whereby they can begin an earnings stream with a slope greater than one they would have had in the absence of the program. Finally, it is worth noting that the persistence of earnings gains will depend in great part on the type of position the trainee attains upon completion of training and the characteristics of the attained position in terms of advancement and pay opportunities.

It is also worth noting that nonexperimental studies typically reported much greater training gains than did comparison group studies. For example, the Olympus Research Corporation's study in four cities (1971) reported earning gains greater than $1000 for almost all race/sex/city combinations. And Decision Making Information's study (1971) of a national sample of MDTA trainees reported gains that were lower but still ranged from $400 to $1400 for trainees who were employed both before and after training. For whatever reasons, use of the comparison group method resulted in substantially lower estimates of the gains from training; moreover, with the exception of Farber's studies (1971a), the later evaluations tend to report lower gains than the earlier studies.

There is relatively little information on which to base a decomposition of earnings gains into wage and employment effects. Most early reports of wage effects were based on the Employment and Training Administration's operating statistics which are incomplete and subject to possible bias (exclusion of less successful trainees). Perry et al. (1975) reported that only 15 percent of the records of participants from fiscal 1969 to 1972 contained wage data. Of the early comparison group studies that examined wages, Sewell (1971) and Smith (1971) found gains of about 25 cents per hour. However, Sewell's study was limited to a largely black sample in North Carolina, and Smith's was based on extrapolation over time during a period of rapid economic growth and a tight labor market.

More recent work suggests that wage gains comprise a relatively small part of earnings gains. Goodfellow's study (1979) found hourly wage-rate changes ranging from a loss of 3 cents per hour for nonblack males to a gain of 26 cents per hour for nonblack females. Some of these changes were not statistically significant, however. Cooley et al. (1975) also decomposed earnings gains into wage and employment effects, and while their results are not readily translatable into wage-rate changes, they suggest that the main benefit of training for females was improved skill levels (reflected in higher wage rates), while for males it was reduced unemployment. While these and the earlier studies do not seem to supply sufficient information on which to form a general conclusion, they at least strongly suggest that relatively little of the benefit of CT comes from increased productivity—that is, higher wages.

The opposite side of the coin is the effect of training on labor force participation—that is, the incidence of unemployment and the number of hours worked if employed. Here again the evidence is fragmentary. Main's study (1968) concluded that there was no discernible wage effect and the gains from training were almost entirely attributable to the fact that more of those who completed training were employed; however, it must be pointed out that more completers than controls were high school graduates in the Main study—an obvious source of bias. Nonexperimental studies such as those of Olympus and DMI have also concluded that the largest part of the trainees' earnings gains is due to employment effects. Cooley et al. found that CT increased the probability of employment by four percentage points for men and by three points for women (1975, p. 142). Goodfellow (1979) found that CT significantly increased total hours worked and weeks employed and significantly reduced weeks not in the labor force and weeks unemployed (the latter two for two of the four race-sex groups). Kiefer (1979), however, found numerically large effects only for black female trainees. Thus, while the evidence suggests that training's main effect is to increase labor force participation (and thereby earnings), the studies are not yet sufficiently broad or conclusive to warrant firm conclusions. This aspect is important, however, for if increased trainee employment comes at the expense of other groups in society (that is, if displacement occurs), then the *net* gains to society are far less than those suggested by increased earnings alone.

Information on the noneconomic or social impacts of CT is scant. Studies by Main (1968) and Gurin (1970) show that persons who complete training tend to be more pleased with the program and with their postprogram jobs than are noncompleters, but the use of noncompleters (Gurin) and unemployed relatives and neighbors (Main) as comparison groups introduces obvious sources of selection bias. Cohen's study (1969) found that MDTA training programs had little effect on national unemployment rates, and the Olympus study (1971) found little impact on the supply of labor in occupations with a shortage of skilled labor. However, no rigorous comparison group studies of noneconomic or social benefits have been performed.

In short, it seems reasonable to expect earnings gains of $300–500 from CT, except possibly for white males. Ideally, these figures should be adjusted to real dollars and then compared in terms of percentage changes. Variations in both the type and sophistication of methodology over the time span covered in this review preclude such adjustment; however, the research does not show large "hidden" (noneconomic) benefits, and it is unclear whether the benefits of CT exceed the costs at a reasonable discount rate, especially when the possibility of displacement is taken into account. It is equally unclear whether CT should be assessed solely on the basis of its cost-benefit ratios. There is, however, a clear need for better cost data and more attention to the displacement- and inflation-related issues before a conclusive assessment of CT is offered.

On-the-Job Training (OJT)

Much of what has been said about CT applies also to OJT, as the two types of training are frequently studied together. Table 6 displays the results of past evaluations of OJT, with the same conventions and restrictions as in Table 5. In general, the level of

TABLE 6

First-Year Earnings Gains from On-the-Job Training Programs

Study	White Males	White Females	Nonwhite Males	Nonwhite Females
Farber (1971a)	350	291	551	620
Farber (1971b)	88	104	44	300
Prescott/Cooley (1972)	842	n.a.	755	n.a.
Sewell (1971)	0	756	384	756
Kiefer (1978)[a]	−619	n.a.	−342	n.a.
Cooley et al. (1975)[c]	303	318	303	318
Gay/Borus (1980)[b]	125*	1132	133*	311
Westat (1981)	750	550	1150	1200

Note: All figures represent positive gains unless otherwise indicated; if not indicated, gain is from base year (usually year before training) to year after training. Only comparison group studies are included in the table.

* Not statistically significant.

[a] Kiefer's estimate of weekly gain × 50.

[b] Race categories are black and nonblack.

[c] Three-year average; gains not estimated separately by race.

earnings gains is somewhat lower than that for CT, and again white males seem to gain less than other groups. However, Westat's data (1981) show the greatest gains attained, especially for nonwhites, attributable to OJT programs. Reports of losses from OJT are limited to Kiefer's study (1979). One can hypothesize with some certainty that forgone earnings and possibly program costs are lower for OJT than for CT. There is even less information here on wage and employment components of earnings gains, on noneconomic and social benefits, and on the duration of earnings gains. Thus those questions are left open.

Adult Work Experience (AWE)

Table 7 summarizes the earnings gains reported in past studies of AWE programs. Interestingly, gains are somewhat greater than

TABLE 7

Earnings Gains from Adult Work Experience Programs (One Year)

Study and Program	White Males	White Females	Nonwhite Males	Nonwhite Females
Farber (1971b) (JOBS) (contract)	−90	207	188	747
Farber (1971b) (JOBS) (noncontract)	655	623	692	978
Kiefer (1979) (JOBS)	108	1640	432	728
Goodfellow (1979) (JOBS) (contract)	420*	776	661	463
Gay/Borus (1980) (JOBS)	195*	1011	646	636
Urban Systems (1971) (CEP)	235[a]	235[a]	235[a]	235[a]
Leone et al. (1972) (CEP)[b]	521	187	521	187
Leone et al. (1972) (CEP)[c]	1268	−327	1268	−327
Olympus (1971) (CEP)[d]	300[a]	300[a]	300[a]	300[a]
Westat (1981) (CETA)	450	50	0	300

Note: Gains are from base year (usually year before training) to year after training.

* Not statistically significant.

[a] Overall figure.

[b] Not a comparison group study; gains are for 1969 participants.

[c] Not a comparison group study; gains are for 1970 participants.

[d] Not a comparison group study.

those for either of the skill training programs, although several of the AWE studies did not involve comparison groups. The reason for the apparent superiority of this class of programs may be that many of them are in fact "job development" programs—that is, programs that focus mainly on placing enrollees in job openings. For example, the JOBS program provided placement-type services and incentives for private-sector employers to hire unskilled persons, and it is worth noting that some of the largest gains reported in Table 7 are for this program. Moreover, JOBS was created in 1968, a time when the labor market was tight. The results of past studies thus may not generalize to times of labor market slack.

In general, the studies of JOBS cited in Table 7, as well as nonexperimental studies not cited, show significant earnings gains for all groups except white males. As with other programs for which this result holds, there is no obvious reason for the failure of that single group to benefit as much as the others. The benefits to women and minorities must be interpreted cautiously. Most studies of the program have emphasized the peculiar labor market conditions of the late sixties, and some have concluded that JOBS enrollees could have gotten the jobs they had without the program.

Evidence on the wage and employment components of earnings gains is limited to the studies by Kiefer (1979) and Goodfellow (1979). Goodfellow found statistically significant wage gains (26 cents per hour) only for nonblack males. On the other hand, he found significant effects on total hours worked and weeks employed for three of the four race/sex groups; the group for which the labor force participation gains were not significant was nonblack males. Kiefer found significant effects on labor force participation and the probability of employment only for nonblack females. Goodfellow's results and the general pattern of gains might be explained as follows: if white males as a group had higher preprogram labor force participation than the other three groups and they were more able, then they might reap lower employment gains than the others. However, Kiefer's findings do not offer strong support for that hypothesis.

Evidence on the noneconomic impact of JOBS is limited to a study by Greenleigh Associates (1970) that surveyed the attitudes of JOBS enrollees, who attributed their more adequate incomes, greater self-esteem, and improved family life to program participation.

Data on the economic impact of Comprehensive Employment Program (CEP) is scarce, being limited to four studies: Olympus

(1971), Urban Systems (1971), Leone et al. (1972), and Systems Development Corporation (SCD, 1969). The first three provide data on earnings gains of CEP enrollees and generally indicate substantial gains for males but not for females. However, neither the Olympus nor the Leone studies used comparison groups. The SDC study gathered information on the wage rates obtained by CEP graduates; again, no comparison group was used. SCD's percentile data reveal a general upgrading of wages for both sexes, although the exclusion of those with no work history before or after the program biases the results. It also should be noted that the Urban Systems study was limited to rural CEPs and the Leone study to Philadelphia CEPs. In short, no good evaluation of CEP's economic impact has yet been performed. Evidence on noneconomic impacts is similarly limited and methodologically flawed (see the summary in Perry et al. 1975, pp. 356–59).

Youth Programs (YPs)

Two E&Ts that deal specifically with youth are the Job Corps (JC) and the Neighborhood Youth Corps (NYC). Both have been the subject of several comparison group studies, permitting the formation of some tentative conclusions regarding their impact. One problem, however, should be kept in mind: the mere passage of time can convert a teenager who is not in the labor force to one who is, quite apart from participation in any program. It is hard to construct a control group that will avoid this maturation bias. (Currently, several studies of the impact of the Youth Incentive Entitlement Pilot Program (YIEPP) under CETA, Title IV, as amended in 1978, are being conducted. For a preliminary baseline report, see Barclay et al. (1979).)

It is also apparent that the various studies have obtained markedly different results; at times, even in a single study, earnings gains for the four race/sex groups will vary widely. Overall, however, the pattern seems to indicate that whites of both sexes experienced small gains or large losses relative to comparison groups, while nonwhites of both sexes achieved small losses or large gains. In general, men seem to have done better than women of both races and in both programs.

Part of the explanation of these results may be statistical: the sample sizes in several of the studies were rather small, as evidenced by the unusually high number of statistically insignificant findings (14 of the 40 entries in Table 8 are not statistically significant). Some light is also shed on these results by decomposing earnings changes into components: Kiefer (1979) found that labor force participation declines for the race/sex groups suffering income losses, although he could not explain this result. Goodfellow (1979) found the same decreases in various measures of labor force participation for one or more of the race/sex groups, and he also noted significant losses of transfer payments for some of them.

TABLE 8
Earnings Gains from Youth Programs
(One Year)

Study and Program	White Males	White Females	Nonwhite Males	Nonwhite Females
Cain (1968) (JC)	203[a]	203[a]	203[a]	203[a]
Engleman (1971) (JC)[d]	600	600	635	635
Kiefer (1979) (JC)[b, c]	−764	−1012	960	292
Goodfellow (1979) (JC)[c]	345*	−150*	516*	−71*
Gay/Borus (1980) (JC)[c]	−215*	−1282	148*	−325
Borus (1972) (NYC)	136*[a]	136*[a]	136*[a]	136*[a]
Somers/Stromsdorfer (1970) (NYC)	356[e]	0*	1346[e]	1084[f]
Goodfellow (1979) (NYC)[c]	396*	74*	1282	66*
Kiefer (1979) (NYC)[b]	−844	−592	1336	368
Gay/Borus (1980) (NYC)	−896	−1201	404	1165

Note: All figures represent positive gains unless otherwise indicated.

* Not statistically significant.

[a] Overall estimate.

[b] Kiefer's estimate of quarterly gains × 4.

[c] Race categories are black and nonblack.

[d] Figures for trainees who stayed in the Job Corps 7–12 months; Engleman's estimates were multiplied by 12 to obtain estimates of annual earnings.

[e] After-tax gains.

[f] Before-tax gains (after-tax gains not available).

It may be that program graduates discover that the postprogram employment opportunities available to them are limited and the potential loss of transfer payments large. Acting on a rational calculus, they may drop out of the labor force—temporarily, at least. This would imply some sort of bias in the selection process—for example, those entering these training programs may be doing so as a last effort to find a worthwhile place in the labor force, while controls may have better employment prospects and thus not view training as necessary. On the other hand, the gains for nonwhite males were substantial, so that training may have beneficial effects at least for that group. Ultimately, however, the fact remains that these studies tend to find either a loss (or a gain not significantly different from zero) or a large gain, suggesting that there may be unexplained differences in samples, in selection biases, in program content, or in analytic methods that would explain the wide discrepancies in results.

In light of the comments that youth programs may be better seen as "riot insurance" than as attempts to prepare young people for employment, information on the noneconomic impacts of these programs would be of particular interest. Unfortunately, the available data consist of information on the attitudes of JC and NYC enrollees and graduates; in general, these persons had positive attitudes toward their programs and their chances for success in the labor market (see, for example, Louis Harris and Associates 1967). Robin (1969) and others have concluded that youth programs have a minimal impact on juvenile delinquency, and Walther et al. (1971) came to the same conclusion regarding dropping out of high school. It should be mentioned that the YIEPP program offers a guaranteed job to eligible youth only if they remain in or return to school.

A recent study (Goldberg 1978) is more optimistic: out of 21 measures of noneconomic impact, Job Corpsmen improved, relative to dropouts and no-shows, on eight of them—job-seeking skills, job satisfaction, attitude toward authority, self-esteem, involvement with the criminal justice system, nutrition behavior, family relations, and leisure time. However, benefits were related to the length of time in the program, and the study's authors noted, "Job Corps must make a concerted effort either to screen out those who seem unlikely to survive the first weeks or to strengthen the program so that more enrollees will remain long enough to benefit" (p. 18). Clearly, there was a self-selection bias: evidently completers were different from dropouts and no-shows in some unspecified way, leaving open the possibility that they might have improved without the program.

Public Service Employment (PSE)

As has already been noted, PSE may require different methods of evaluation than other E&Ts; in any event, many of the studies of PSE have used different methods and, as a result, information on the earnings gains of PSE participants is scarce. There are almost no comparison group studies in this area, the major exception being Westat's 1979 study of PEP. That study compared PEP graduates to a matched sample drawn from CPS and Social Security records (Westat 1979). Several different analytic models were employed. As indicated in Table 9, neither the results for white females nor the Model III results were significant; all other findings were significant at the 1 or 5 percent levels. Once again, white males showed lesser gains and experienced greater earnings declines than the other groups. Westat explained this by noting the superior preprogram labor force experience of white males—higher earnings and better work histories (1979, pp. viii–ix).

TABLE 9

Earnings Gains of PEP Graduates

Model and Base Year	White Males	White Females	Other Males	Other Females
II: 1969	307	1127*	552	1678
II: 1970	317	1086	704	1638
III: 1969	−194	373*	144*	870
III: 1970	−181	337*	297*	835

Source: Westat, Inc. (1979), pp. 3-42, Table 3-10.
* Not statistically significant.

Many of the studies of the economic impact of PSE have concentrated on estimating the extent to which the monies provided by the federal government were used as a substitute for local funds, thereby replacing regular employees or paying their salaries with federal funds—the former being the displacement effect, the latter the substitution effect. Among those who examined this issue, there is a great deal of disagreement on method and meaning. One cannot be sure of the extent of fiscal substitution; however, a review of the studies indicates that the rate is at least 10 percent in the first year, and possibly as high as 60 percent. Moreover, it is reasonably certain that the rate of substitution increases with time, as a locality "subsumes" the PSE budget into its regular operating funds and treats it more like general revenue-sharing.

Finally, it is worth noting that the revised regulations, published in 1977, regarding eligibility and pay levels have succeeded in reducing the level of substitution. Although there are dozens of studies of this issue, Bassi and Fechter (1979, as revised) summarize them well and, in addition, make their own conclusions and recommendations.

Summary

Each category of E&Ts contains very different programs, and comparing the categories is even more of an apples and oranges proposition. However, to give some overall sense of the impact of federal employment and training programs (excluding PSE), the median one-year earnings gains are summarized in Table 10.

TABLE 10

Summary Comparison of First-Year Earnings Gains for Non-PSE E&T Programs

Program Type	White Males	White Females	Nonwhite Males	Nonwhite Females
Classroom training (CT)	197	485	333	436
On-the-job training (OJT)	125	318	303	318
Adult work experience (AWE)	360	425	536	507
Youth programs (YPs)	170	−75	576	248
Median	184	372	435	377

Despite the many problems with the data, the general picture is remarkably stable across program categories and race/sex groups. With only one exception (YPs), white males appear to benefit least. For the other groups, AWE seems to be the most beneficial, although the discussion of AWE studies noted possible biases in their results. CT promotes generally larger gains than OJT, and in general YPs are the least beneficial in a strictly economic sense (except for nonwhite males). The range from $303 to $576 includes all medians except four, indicating a general first-year benefit level of about $440. Assuming a five-year life and a 7 percent discount rate, the present value of that benefit level is approximately $1800. This figure, of course, will vary with the discount rate applied to the calculations.

In closing this review of program impacts, three central points must be reiterated. First, given the limitations of the research methods, especially regarding the influence of the overall economy, we may not be able to project these results into the 1980s with any confidence. Persistent inflation, changes in the structure of the labor market, increases in the "natural" unemployment rate, and the emergence of a "postindustrial" economy are of enough significance to change the operation, and thus the expectations, of E&Ts.

Second, assuming that we can satisfactorily project the findings to the next decade, it is still unclear how to evaluate the merit of these programs. What will be the standard of a "successful" program? Is a first-year net earnings increase of $300–600 enough? Part of the answer must come from the utilization of better cost data to enable us to compute benefit-cost ratios or net present values. Another part of the answer must come from comparing the results of E&Ts to those of other social programs and/or to the direct and indirect costs of not funding them at all. In the final analysis, the judgment is a political one than can be aided, but not determined, by the results of research and evaluation.

Finally, assuming that E&Ts pass the economic, equity, and political tests, how can we make them operate better? Estimates of earnings or employment gains for certain demographic groups provide limited help for program managers. In most cases little is known about relating impact data to program content or operation. We lack "production functions," primarily because program goals have never been fully and clearly laid out.

Outcome evaluation can tell us only whether a program is doing well compared to some predetermined benchmarks, but by itself it cannot tell us how to improve programs. Only persons familiar with the day-to-day operations can provide the expertise needed to what in the final analysis may be a very important and necessary series of social programs. In making societal decisions regarding programs, legislators, program operators, and designers must consider short- and longer-run equity as well as impact and efficiency measures.

Summary: The Implosion of the 1970s

Writing in 1971, Garth Mangum emphasized the *explosion* of manpower research that occurred in the 1960s, transforming it from an "obscure field of interest in 1960 to a major area of academic and commercial effort in 1970" (Mangum 1971). In contrast, the research and evaluation done during the 1970s can aptly be described as an *implosion.* The researchers, inside and outside of academia, took the early work, roundly criticized its methodology, convinced the funding sources of its inadequacy in allowing for certainty in recommendations, and proceeded on a new tack. The new approach was inwardly directed and employed the newest and most quantitatively oriented techniques. Using carefully structured samples, longitudinal followup, and statistical analysis packages not previously available, the researchers produced complicated designs and examined the minutiae of resultant data sets.

Research projects aimed exclusively at identification of selection bias in a large data set, for example, may be of use to policymakers, but only in the long run and after multiple iterations as well as critical assessments by academic peers, journal reviewers, public administrators, and, finally, lawmakers. The latter most often are inclined to ask only if the results are reasonably accurate. The structure, intended effects, and, most importantly, funding levels for employment and training programs are the result of historical experience as gauged by carefully structured research efforts *as well as* anecdotal accounts of success and failure. Often the most important dimension is political, and it overrides other considerations. The decision of the Reagan Administration to cut the funding of CETA programs, particularly PSE, was not the result of careful reviews of past program successes; it was the result of political promises to balance the budget *and* a lack of cohesive lobbying strategy on the part of program proponents. The entire elimination of heteroskedasticity in earnings models would not have turned the tide.

All of this is not to say that the research of the last decade is of little practical use; rather, the implication is that the focus of research must return to emphasis on the policy implications of the efforts. Lawmakers, federal and state administrators, research firms, and academics must act in concert, with full realization that all of the risk associated with investments in public employment and training programs will never be removed. Social programs, especially those that are designed to influence long-run earnings and labor market and other experiences, will have participants who do well in the labor market and others who do not. Moreover, the success criteria cannot be narrowly defined by net earnings gain the following year or by placement at completion. Noneconomic and long-run benefits of participation must be considered, as must the ramifications of elimination of the opportunities offered under currently operating programs.

Colleagues who have experience working with both public agencies and private firms have been known to remark that they would rather do a cost-benefit analysis for a private employer. When asked why, the response is quite simply, "They are willing to take risks; inordinate time is not spent looking for biases in the data." It certainly would be imprudent to argue in favor of utilizing bad data, but it is equally if not more imprudent to let very good, but not excellent, data languish as fodder for academic argument rather than offering them, along with coordinated policy prescriptions, to lawmakers and program managers. A major recommendation emerging, after pouring over a seemingly endless series of studies, relates to where attention of the able research establishment should focus. It should be on the assessment of the investment risk associated with public training programs. If the programs must pay off in terms of increased earnings (and taxes paid, transfers not paid, and the like), this aspect must be explicitly addressed. At the same time, the equally important income distributional aspects of employment and training programs must assume a central place in the debate. Even if, at a minimum, the equity comparison must be with the principal alternative—transfer programs—the issue should be front and center. As an illustration, the prose of Zvi Griliches (1977) and his harking back to more classic literature illustrates the dilemma he faced in estimating returns to schooling:

> In a sense, we have circled around our problem and data. We started looking for biases and at first found little. We kept on looking for more and leaned over more until we found ourselves on the other side of the original question. The whole process of such a research venture is perhaps best described by the following conversation between Pooh and Rabbit. (A. A. Milne, *The House at Pooh Corner*)
>
> "How would it be," said Pooh slowly, "if, as soon as we're out of sight of this Pit, we try to find it again?"
>
> "What's the good of that?" said Rabbit.

"Well," said Pooh, "we keep looking for home and not finding it, so I thought that if we looked for this Pit, we'd be sure not to find it, which would be a Good Thing, because then we might find something that we weren't looking for, which might be just what we are looking for, really."

"I don't see much sense in that," said Rabbit.

"No," said Pooh humbly, "there isn't. But there was going to be when I began it. It's just that something happened to it on the way."

The search for bias in our data on employment training programs should not cease, but rather it should be pursued at the same time that we search for better ways to structure and manage employment and training programs. Critiques of the research methods of program evaluation should serve as an input to future evaluation designs, but not as a post hoc condemnation of outcomes of those efforts. Comments on the limitations of studies should be made concurrently with discussion of their strengths.

Research and Evaluation Issues in Search of Consensus

The proper utilization of the longitudinal sample of persons participating in CETA is, in my estimation, the analytical issue of most importance to the research and evaluation establishment. Data are still being collected by Westat, Inc., although analysis has slowed, if not ceased. It would be a much regretted decision to cancel this one-of-a-kind data base. Exploration of the data base for use with comparison groups fashioned from the Current Population Survey and Social Security files is the most fruitful avenue for the econometric research. The problems are well known, but in spite of the econometric issues yet to be resolved, it remains the most comprehensive and usable source of information on the entire employment and training network. There are several ways in which these data can be more effectively utilized: (1) analysis of the longevity of earnings gains, (2) analysis of the usefulness of "placement" rates as an outcome measure, and (3) as a tool for analysis of the influence of the economic environment in which the programs operate, as well as the influence of their management structures on outcomes.

The continuous Longitudinal Manpower Sample (CLMS) was

begun in 1973, coinciding with the launching of the CETA program. Data are now available for one-, two-, and three-year followups of persons who participated in the earlier years, and these data can and should be utilized to answer the longer-run questions on the returns on investment of the programs. Coincident with this research, there is a great need to develop cost data for various programs. Although extremely difficult to make, estimates are needed if the programs are to be subjected to investment/efficiency criteria, as they often are in political and academic forums.

Placement rates used as an outcome measure are subject to a wide variety of reporting and inferential biases. Knowing the percentage of persons leaving any program who are placed in jobs does not tell us about the quality of the positions, or whether the prime sponsor or other placement organization is taking only the most qualified of those who apply for participation, thereby reflecting individual abilities rather than program effectiveness. These and other reasons, mostly related to the Department of Labor's evaluation of prime sponsor performance on the basis of placement rates, makes this measure of program effectiveness suspect. Alternatives must be found. One avenue that might be pursued is to establish a clear definition of what constitutes a person's removal from the poverty cycle, possibly including duration of job-holding after participation, earnings, and degree of reliance on transfer programs. If short-term measures such as placement rates, or even wage rates, are to be used, it must be established that the short-term indicators have a relationship to long-term outcomes that can be categorized and utilized by policy-makers.

In some cases it can be strongly argued that the economic environment—and even the social environment—in a geographic area of program operation can have a significant or even overriding influence on program outcomes. A strong and expanding economy may draw a greater proportion of CETA participants than would a weak economy, regardless of the quality of the programs. Although many studies address this issue, the most valuable source of information, the CLMS, suppresses geo-specific identification of participants. This suppression was agreed upon at the outset of the data collection (to aid in securing prime sponsor cooperation). This decision should be reconsidered, as it is hard to find justification for prime sponsor anonymity in the data base.

Parallel with geo-specific identification, case analyses of the management structure and processes of a sample of prime sponsors should be undertaken. Although there has been some ad hoc work on management systems, none has been linked with a reliable sample of participants and their labor force experience. If the data bases had indicators of management processes as well as location variables, we would be able to respond far more confidently to questions on the determinations of postprogram experiences.

The research establishment has come full circle. The debate of the 1960s concerning whether the U.S. should have an active manpower policy was answered in the affirmative. The 1970s brought the research establishment to the technical issues, often at the expense of losing sight of the larger political and theoretical questions. Now the resources for technical evaluations are drying up quickly; they will not reappear until (if) we reverse policy directions at a later point in this decade or this century. In the interim the research establishment will have to devote time to the broader and important theoretical questions, especially those relating to how internal and external labor markets work—a topic left largely unattended over the entire period of active manpower policy in the U.S.

Over the last decade we have learned a great deal about the proper methods of program evaluation and research design. This knowledge must be constructively combined with the unquestionable knowledge that the effects of social programs cannot be predicted with certainty. Dual goals of efficiency and equity preclude complete reliance on returns to investment in employment and training programs. The substantial portion of the American public who still live in poverty cannot be expected to be pulled out by an expanding business climate, nor will they be able to lift themselves. Public-private cooperation is the key, and the role of researchers and evaluators must be to facilitate that cooperation. This can be done by designing and carrying through useful research with full knowledge of the political realities of the times and realization that certainty before action might well apply solely in the domain of the natural sciences.

References

Adams, Arvil V. "Lessons from the National Longitudinal Surveys: A Commentary." In *Current Issues in the Relationship Between Manpower Research and Policy.* National Commission for Manpower Policy, Special Report No. 7, 1976.

Andrisani, Paul J. "Internal-External Attitudes, Personal Initiative, and the Labor Market Experience of Black and White Men." *Journal of Human Resources* 12 (Summer 1977): pp. 308–28.

Ashenfelter, Orley, C. "Estimating the Effect of Training Programs on Earnings." *Review of Economics and Statistics* 60 (February 1978): pp. 47–57.

Baily, Martin N., and James Tobin. "Macroeconomic Effects of Selective Public Employment on Wage Studies." *Brookings Papers on Economic Activity* 11 (1:1980): pp. 511–39.

Barby, Steven L. *Cost-Benefit Analysis and Manpower Programs.* Lexington, Mass.: D. C. Heath, 1972.

Barclay, Susan, et al. "Schooling and Work Among Youth from Low Income Households: A Baseline Report from the Entitlement Demonstration." Abt Associates, Cambridge, Mass., for the U.S. Department of Labor, Office of Youth Programs, 1979.

Barnow, Burt S. "Theoretical Issues in the Estimation of Production Functions in Manpower Programs." In *Evaluating Manpower Training Programs,* ed. Farrell E. Bloch. Greenwich, Conn.: JAI Press, 1979.

Bassi, Laurie, and Alan Fechter. "The Implications for Fiscal Substitution and Occupational Displacement Under an Expanded CETA Title VI." Technical Analysis Paper 65, U.S. Department of Labor, Office of the Assistant Secretary for Policy, Evaluation, and Research, March 1979.

Becker, Gary S. *Human Capital.* New York: National Bureau of Economic Research, 1964.

Bennett, C. A., and A. A. Lumsdaine, eds. *Evaluation and Experiment: Some Critical Issues in Assessing Social Programs.* New York: Academic Press, 1975.

Blinder, Alan S. "On Dogmatism in Human Capital Theory." *Journal of Human Resources* 11 (Winter 1976): pp. 8–22.

Blinder, Alan S., and Robert M. Solow. "Analytical Foundations of Fiscal Policy." In *The Economics of Public Finance,* ed. A. S. Blinder et al. Washington: Brookings Institution, 1974.

Bloch, Farrell E., ed. *Evaluating Manpower Training Programs.* Greenwich, Conn.: JAI Press, 1979.

Boruch, R. F., and H. W. Reichen, eds. *Social Experimentation: A Method for Planning and Evaluating Social Intervention.* New York: Academic Press, 1979.

Borus, Michael E. *Measuring the Impact of Employment-Related Social Programs: A Primer on the Evaluation of Employment and Training, Vocational Rehabilitation, and Other Job-Oriented Programs.* Kalamazoo, Mich.: W. E. Upjohn Institute for Employment Research, 1979.

———. "Indicators of CETA Performance." *Industrial and Labor Relations Review* 32 (October 1978): pp. 3–14.

Borus, Michael E., ed. *Evaluating the Impact of Manpower Programs.* Lexington, Mass.: D. C. Heath, 1972.

Borus, Michael E., and Daniel Hamermesh. "Study of the Net Employment Effects of Public Service Employment—Econometric Analysis." In *Job Creation Through Public Service Employment, Vol. III,* Report #6. Washington: National Commission for Manpower Policy, 1978.

Brown, Randall S., Marilyn Moon, and Barbara S. Zoloth. "Incorporating Occupational Attainment in Studies of Male-Female Earnings Differentials." *Journal of Human Resources* 15 (Winter 1980): pp. 3–28.

Cain, Glen G. "Benefit/Cost Estimates for Job Corps." Discussion Paper 9-68. Institute for Research on Poverty, University of Wisconsin-Madison, 1968.

———. "Regression and Selected Models to Improve Non-experimental Comparisons." In *Evaluation and Experiment: Some Critical Issues in Assessing Social Programs,* eds. C. A. Bennett and A. A. Lumsdaine. New York: Academic Press, 1975.

———. "The Challenge of Segmented Labor Market Theories to Orthodox Theory: A Survey." *Journal of Economic Literature* 14 (December 1976): pp. 1215–57.

Cain, Glen G., and Robinson G. Hollister. "Evaluating Manpower Programs for the Disadvantaged." In *Cost-Benefit Analysis of Manpower Policies,* eds. Gerald G. Somers and W. D. Wood. Kingston, Ont.: Queen's University, 1969.

Campbell, Donald P., and R. F. Boruch. "Making the Case for Randomized Assignment to Treatments by Considering the Alternatives." In *Evaluation and Experiment: Some Critical Issues in Assessing Social Programs,* eds. C. A. Bennett and A. A. Lumsdaine. New York: Academic Presss, 1975.

———. "Reforms as Experiments." *American Psychologist* 24 (1969): pp. 409–29.

Campbell, Donald P., and J. D. Stanley. "Experimental and Quasi-Experimental Designs for Research on Training." In *Handbook of Research on Training,* ed. N. L. Gage. Chicago: Rand McNally, 1963.

Carliner, Geoffrey. "Returns to Education for Blacks, Anglos, and Five Spanish Groups." *Journal of Human Resources* 11 (Spring 1976): pp. 172–84.

Caro, F. "Evaluation Research: An Overview." In *Readings in Evaluation Research,* ed. F. Caro. New York: Russell Sage Foundation, 1971.

Chen, M. K. "Critical Look at the Matching Technique in Experimentation." *Journal of Experimental Education* 35 (1967): pp. 95–98.

Chow, Gregory J. "Tests of Equality Between Sets of Coefficients in Two Linear Regressions." *Econometrica* 28 (July 1960): pp. 591–605.

Cohen, Malcolm S. "The Direct Effects of Federal Manpower Programs in Reducing Unemployment." *Journal of Human Resources* 4 (Fall 1969): pp. 491–507.

Comprehensive Employment and Training Act of 1973, Statutes at Large, Vol. 87, pp. 839–83, *U.S. Code,* Title 29 (Sec. 801 et seq.).

Comprehensive Employment and Training Act Amendments of 1978, Statutes at Large, Vol. 92, pp. 1909–2021, *U.S. Code,* Title 29 (Sec. 801 et seq.).

Congressional Budget Office. *Temporary Measures to Stimulate Employment: An Evaluation of Some Alternatives.* Washington: U.S. Congressional Budget Office, September 1975.

Conlisk, John. "Choice of Sample Size in Evaluating Manpower Programs." In *Evaluating Manpower Training Programs,* ed. Farrell E. Bloch. Greenwich, Conn.: JAI Press, 1979.

Cook, T. D., and Donald T. Campbell. "The Design and Conduct of Quasi-Experiment and True Experiments in Field Settings." In *Handbook of Industrial and Organizational Psychology,* ed. M. D. Dunnette. Chicago: Rand McNally, 1976.

Cooley, Thomas F., T. S. McQuire, and Edward G. Prescott. *The Impact of Manpower Training on Earnings: An Econometric Analysis.* Washington: U.S. Department of Labor, Employment and Training Administration, Office of Program Evaluation and Research, September 30, 1975.

Decision Making Information. *MDTA Outcomes Study: Final Report.* C.A.L. 778. Washington: U.S. Department of Labor, Manpower Administration, Office of Program Evaluation and Research, 1971.

Director, Steven M. "Underadjustment Bias in the Evaluation of Manpower Training." *Evaluation Quarterly* 3 (May 1979): pp. 190–218.

Duncan, Greg J. "Earnings Functions and Nonpecuniary Benefits." *Journal of Human Resources* 11 (Fall 1976): pp. 462–83.

Eckaus, Richard. *Estimating the Return to Education: A Disaggregated Approach.* Berkeley, Calif.: Carnegie Commission on Higher Education, 1973.

Edwards, W., and M. Guttentag. "Experiments and Evaluations: A Reexamination." In *Evaluation and Experiment: Some Critical Issues in Assessing Social Programs,* eds. C. A. Bennett and A. A. Lumsdaine. New York: Academic Press, 1975.

Engleman, Stephan R. "An Economic Analysis of the Job Corps." Ph.D. dissertation, University of California, Berkeley, 1971.

Farber, David J. "Highlights: Some Findings from a Follow-Up Study of Pre- and Post-Training Earnings History of 215,000 Trainees Participating in Two 1964 and Four 1968 Training Programs." Washington: U.S. Department of Labor, Manpower Administration, Office of Program Evaluation and Research, 1971a.

———. "An Analysis of Changes in Earnings of Participants in Manpower Training Programs." Washington: U.S. Department of Labor, Manpower Administration, Office of Program Evaluation and Research, 1971b.

Fechter, Alan. "Job Creation Through Public Service Employment Program." In *Job Creation: What Works?* ed. Robert Taggart. Salt Lake City, Utah: Olympus, 1977.

Ferber, Marianne A., and Helen M. Lowry. "The Sex Differential in Earnings: A Reappraisal." *Industrial and Labor Relations Review* 29 (April 1976): pp. 377–87.

Finifter, David H. *An Analysis of Two Year Post-Program Earning Paths of CETA Participants Using the Early CLMS Cohorts (January 1975–June 1975 Entry).* Washington: U.S. Department of Labor, Employment and Training Administration, Office of Program Evaluation and Research, December 1980.

Flanagan, Robert J. "Labor Force Experience, Job Turnover, and Racial Wage Differentials." *Review of Economics and Statistics* 56 (November 1974): pp. 521–29.

Freeman, Richard B. "Occupational Training in Proprietary Schools and Technical Institutes." *Review of Economics and Statistics* 56 (August 1974): pp. 310–18.

Friedman, Milton. "A Monetary Theory of Nominal Income." *Journal of Political Economy* 79 (March/April 1971): pp. 323–37.

Garfinkel, Irwin, and John L. Palmer. "Issues, Evidence, and Implications." In *Creating Jobs: Public Employment, Programs and Wage Subsidies,* ed. John L. Palmer. Washington: Brookings Institution, 1978. Pp. 1–42.

Gay, Robert S., and Michael E. Borus. "Validating Performance Indicators for Employment and Training Programs." *Journal of Human Resources* 15 (Winter 1980): pp. 29–48.

Geraci, Vincent J., and C. T. King. "Employment and Training (CETA) Program Performance: Long-Term Earning Effects and Short-Term Indicators." Paper presented at the Allied Social Science Associations Meeting, Denver, September 1980.

Gilbert, J. P., et al. "Assessing Social Innovations: An Empirical Base for Policy." In *Evaluation and Experiment: Some Critical Issues in Assessing Social Programs,* eds. C. A. Bennett and A. A. Lumsdaine. New York: Academic Press, 1975.

Ginzberg, Eli, ed. *Employing the Unemployed.* New York: Basic Books, 1980.

Goldberg, J. F. *The Noneconomic Impact of the Job Corps.* R & D Monograph 64, prepared by Abt Associates for the U.S. Department of Labor, Employment and Training Administration, Office of Program Evaluation and Research, 1978.

Goldstein, J. H. *The Effectiveness of Manpower Training Programs: A Review of Research on the Impact on the Poor.* Washington: U.S. Government Printing Office, 1972.

Goodfellow, G. P. "Estimates of Benefits of Training for Four Manpower Training Programs." In *Evaluating Manpower Training Programs,* ed. Farrell E. Bloch. Greenwich, Conn.: JAI Press, 1979.

Gottman, J. M., and G. V. Glass. "Analysis of Interrupted Time-Series Experiments." In *Single Subject Research: Strategies for Evaluating Change,* ed. T. R. Kratochwill. New York: Academic Press, 1978.

Gramlich, Edward M. "Stimulating the Macro Economy Through State and Local Governments." *American Economic Review* 69 (May 1979): pp. 180–85.

Greenleigh Associates, Inc. "The Job Opportunities in the Business Sector Program: An Evaluation of Impact in Ten SMSAs." Washington: U.S. Department of Labor, Manpower Administration, Office of Program Evaluation and Research, 1970.

Griliches, Zvi. "Estimating Returns to Schooling: Some Econometric Problems." *Econometrica* 45 (January 1977): pp. 1–22.

Gurin, Gerald. *A National Attitude Survey of Trainees in MDTA Institutional Programs.* Ann Arbor: University of Michigan, 1970.

Gwartney, James D., and James E. Long. "The Relative Earnings of Blacks and Other Minorities." *Industrial and Labor Relations Review* 21 (April 1978): pp. 336–46.

Hamermesh, Daniel S. *Economic Aspects of Manpower Training Programs.* Lexington, Mass.: D. C. Heath, 1971.

Hardin, Einar. "Benefit-Cost Analyses of Occupational Training Programs: A Comparison of Recent Studies." In *Cost-Benefit Analysis of Manpower Policies,* eds. Gerald G. Somers and W. D. Wood. Kingston, Ont.: Queen's University, 1969.

Hardin, Einar, and Michael E. Borus. *The Economic Benefits and the Costs of Retraining.* Lexington, Mass.: D. C. Heath, 1971.

Hargrove, E. C. "The Bureaucratic Politics of Evaluation: A Case Study of the Department of Labor." *Public Administration Review* (March/April 1980): pp. 150–59.

Harrison, Bennett. *Education, Training and the Urban Ghetto.* Baltimore: Johns Hopkins University Press, 1972.

Haworth, Joan G., James Gwartney, and Charles Haworth. "Earnings, Productivity, and Changes in Employment Discrimination During the 1960's." *American Economic Review* 65 (March 1975): pp. 158–68.

Heckman, James. "Simultaneous Equations Models with Both Continuous and Discrete Endogenous Variables With and Without Structural Shifts in the Equations." Unpublished, August 1975.

Holton, E. T., and A. A. Lumsdaine. "Field Trial Designs in Gauging the Impact of Fertility Planning Programs." In *Evaluation and Experiment: Some Critical Issues in Assessing Social Programs,* eds. C. A. Bennett and A. A. Lumsdaine. New York: Academic Press, 1975.

Jerrett, Robert, and Thomas A. Barocci. *Public Works, Government Spending and Job Creation.* New York: Praeger, 1979.

Johnson, George E. "The Labor Market Displacement Effect in the Analysis of the Net Effect of Manpower Training Programs." In *Evaluating Manpower Training Programs,* ed. Farrell E. Bloch. Greenwich, Conn.: JAI Press, 1979.

Johnson, George E., and James D. Tomola. "The Fiscal Substitution Effect of Alternative Approaches to Public Service Employment Policy." *Journal of Human Resources* 12 (Winter 1977): pp. 3–26.

Kalachek, Edward, and Fredric Raines. "The Structure of Wage Differences Among Mature Male Workers." *Journal of Human Resources* 11 (Fall 1976): pp. 484–506.

Katz, D. "Feedback in Social Systems: Operational and Systematic Research on Production, Maintenance, Control and Adaptive Functions." In *Evaluation and Experiment: Some Critical Issues in Assessing Social Programs,* eds. S. A. Bennett and A. A. Lumsdaine. New York: Academic Press, 1975.

Kemper, Peter, and Philip Moss. "Economic Efficiency of Public Employment Programs." In *Creating Jobs: Public Programs and the Wage Subsidies,* ed. John L. Palmer. Washington: Brookings Institution, 1978.

Kenny, D. A. "Quasi-Experimental Approach to Assessing Treatment Effects in a Nonequivalent Control Group Design." *Psychological Bulletin* 82 (1975): pp. 345–62.

Kesselman, Jonathan. "Work Relief in the Great Depression." *In Creating Jobs: Public Programs and Wage Subsidies,* ed. John L. Palmer. Washington: Brookings Institution, 1978.

Kiefer, Nicholas M. *The Economic Benefits from Four Employment and Training Programs.* New York: Garland Publishers, 1979.

———. "Federally Subsidized Occupational Training and the Employment and Earnings of Male Trainees." *Journal of Econometrics* 8 (August 1978): pp. 111–25.

Killingsworth, Charles C. "The Role of Public-Service Employment." Proceedings of the 1977 Annual Spring Meeting, Industrial Relations Research Association. *Labor Law Journal* (August 1977): pp. 489–94.

King, Alan G., and Charles B. Knapp. "Race and the Determinants of Lifetime Earnings." *Industrial and Labor Relations Review* 31 (April 1978): pp. 347–55.

King, Randall H. "Some Further Evidence on the Rate of Return to Schooling and the Business Cycle." *Journal of Human Resources* 15 (Spring 1980): pp. 264–72.

Kirk, R. D. *Experimental Design: Procedures for the Behavioral Sciences.* Belmont, Calif.: Brooks/Cole, 1968.

Kohen, Andrew I. "Determinates of Labor Market Success Among Young Men: Race, Ability, Quantity and Quality of Schooling." Columbus: Center for Human Resource Research, Ohio State University, 1973.

Lamond, A. M., and Phyllis A. Wallace, eds. *Women, Minorities and Employment Discrimination.* Lexington, Mass.: D. C. Heath, 1977.

Leone, Richard D., ed. *Employability Development Teams and Federal Manpower Programs: A Critical Assessment of the Philadelphia CEP's Experience.* Philadelphia: School of Business Administration, Temple University, November 1972.

Levitan, Sar A., and Robert Taggart. "Manpower Programs." In *The Promise of Greatness.* Cambridge, Mass.: Harvard University Press, 1976.

Louis Harris and Associates. "A Study of August 1966 Terminations from the Job Corps." *Hearings on the Economic Opportunity Amendments of 1967,* Part I, U.S. Congress, Senate Committee on Labor and Education, 90th Cong., 1st Sess., 1967.

Loury, G. D. "A Dynamic Theory of Racial Income Differences." In *Employability Development Teams and Federal Manpower Programs,* ed. Richard D. Leone. Philadelphia: School of Business Administration, Temple University, 1972.

Main, Earl D. "A Nationwide Evaluation of MDTA Institutional Job Training." *Journal of Human Resources* 3 (Spring 1968): pp. 159–70.

Malkiel, Burton G., and Judith A. Malkiel. "Male-Female Pay Differentials in Professional Employment." *American Economic Review* 63 (September 1973): pp. 693–705.

Mangum, Garth L. *MDTA: Foundation of Federal Manpower Policy.* Baltimore: Johns Hopkins University Press, 1968.

———. *The Emergence of Manpower Policy.* New York: Holt, Rinehart & Winston, 1969.

———. "Manpower Research and Manpower Policy." In *A Review of Industrial Relations Research,* Vol. II. Madison, Wis.: Industrial Relations Research Association, 1971.

Mangum, Garth L., and Thayne T. Robson. *Metropolitan Impact of Manpower Programs: A Four-City Comparison.* Salt Lake City, Utah: Olympus, 1973.

Mangum, Garth L., and Robert Taggart. "CETA Service Components: Results and Reasons." Washington: National Council on Employment Policy, 1981.

Mangum, Garth L., and J. Walsh. *A Decade of Manpower Development and Training.* Salt Lake City, Utah: Olympus, 1973.

Marshall, Ray. "The Economics of Racial Discrimination: A Survey." *Journal of Economic Literature* 12 (September 1974): pp. 849–71.

McCall, R. B. *Fundamental Statistics for Psychology.* New York: Harcourt, Brace, 1975.

Mincer, Jacob. *Schooling, Age and Earnings.* New York: Columbia University Press, 1973.

———. *Schooling, Experience, and Earnings.* New York: National Bureau of Economic Research, 1974.

Mirengoff, William, et al. *The New CETA: Effect of Public Service Programs: Final Report.* Washington: National Academy of Sciences, 1980.

Nathan, R. P., et al. *Job Creating Through Public Service Employment: Vol. II, Monitoring the Public Service Employment Program.* Report prepared by the Brookings Institution for the National Commission for Manpower Policy, March 1978.

National Academy of Education, Task Force on Education and Employment. *Education for Employment: Knowledge for Action.* 1979.

National Academy of Sciences, National Research Council, Assembly of Behavioral and Social Sciences. *Final Report of the Panel on Manpower Training Evaluation.* Washington: Brookings Institution, 1974.

National Commission for Employment Policy. *Sixth Annual Report to the Public Employment Program, Vol. 1.* Prepared for the Office of the Assistant Secretary for Policy, Evaluation and Research, U.S. Department of Labor, 1974.

Nunally, Jason C. "The Study of Change in Evaluation Research: Principles Concerning Measurement, Experimental Design, and Analysis." In *Handbook of Evaluation Research,* Vol. 1, eds. E. L. Struening and M. Guttentag. Beverly Hills, Calif.: Sage, 1975.

Okun, Arthur M. "Conflicting National Goals." In *Jobs for Americans,* ed. Eli Ginzberg. Englewood Cliffs, N.J.: The American Assembly, 1976. Pp. 59–84.

Olympus Research Corporation. "The Total Impact of Manpower Programs: A Four-City Case Study." Report to the U.S. Department of Labor, Manpower Administration, Office of Policy Evaluation and Research, 1971.

O'Neill, Dave M. *The Federal Government and Manpower.* Washington: American Enterprise Institute, 1973.

Palmer, John L. "Evaluating the Economic Stimulus Package from an Employment and Training Perspective." In *Job Creation Through Public Service Employment,* Vol. III, Report No. 6. Washington: National Commission for Manpower Policy, 1978.

Parnes, Herbert S. "The National Longitudinal Surveys: Lessons for Human Resource Policy." In *Current Issues in the Relationship Between Manpower Research and Policy.* Special Report No. 7. Washington, National Commission for Manpower Policy, 1976.

———. "The National Longitudinal Surveys: An Interim Assessment." In *Manpower Research and Labor Economics,* eds. G. Swanson and J. Michaelson. Beverly Hills, Calif.: Sage, 1979.

Parnes, Herbert S., et al. "The National Longitudinal Surveys: Comprehensive Reports." Issued as Manpower Research Monographs Nos. 15, 16, 21, and 24. Available from National Training Information Service (NTIS).

Perry, C. R., et al. *The Impact of Government Manpower Programs in General and on Minorities and Women.* Philadelphia: University of Pennsylvania, 1975.

Pitcher, H. M. "A Sensitivity Analysis to Determine Sample Sizes for Performing Impact Evaluation of the CETA Programs." In *Evaluating Manpower Training Programs,* ed. Farrell E. Bloch. Greenwich, Conn.: JAI Press, 1979.

Posavec, E. J., and R. G. Carey. *Program Evaluation: Methods and Case Studies.* Englewood Cliffs, N.J.: Prentice-Hall, 1980.

Prescott, E. C., and T. F. Cooley. *Evaluating the Impact of MDTA Programs on Earnings Under Varying Labor Market Conditions.* Final Report MEL 73-09. Philadelphia: University of Pennsylvania, 1972.

Reid, Clifford. "Some Evidence of the Effect of Manpower Training Programs on the Black/White Wage Differential." *Journal of Human Resources* 11 (Summer 1976): pp. 402–10.

Robin, G. D. *An Assessment of In-School NYC Projects in Cincinnati and Detroit.* Philadelphia: National Analyst, Inc., 1969.

Rosen, Sherwin. "A Theory of Life Earnings." Discussion Paper 72–25, Department of Economics, University of Rochester, N.Y., 1975.

Schiller, Bradley R. "Welfare: Reforming Our Expectations." *The Public Interest* 62 (Winter 1981): pp. 55–64.

Sewell, David O. *Training the Poor: A Benefit-Cost Analysis of Programs in the United States Antipoverty Program.* Kingston, Ont.: Industrial Relations Center, Queen's University, 1971.

Siegel, S. *Nonparametric Methods for the Behavioral Sciences.* New York: McGraw-Hill, 1956.

Smith, Ralph E. "Analysis of the Efficiency and Equity of Manpower Programs." Ph.D. dissertation, Georgetown University, 1971.

Solow, Robert M. "Employment in Inflationary Times." In *Employing the Unemployed,* ed. Eli Ginzberg. New York: Basic Books, 1980. Pp. 129–41.

Somers, Gerald G., ed. *Retraining the Unemployed.* Madison: University of Wisconsin Press, 1968.

Somers, Gerald G., and W. D. Wood, eds. *Cost-Benefit Analysis of Manpower Policies.* Kingston, Ont.: Queen's University, 1969.

Stafford, Frank P. "A Decision Theoretic Approach to the Evaluation of Training Programs." In *Evaluating Manpower Training Programs,* ed. Farrell E. Bloch. Greenwich, Conn.: JAI Press, 1979.

Stromsdorfer, Ernst W. *Review and Synthesis of Cost-Effectiveness Studies of Vocational and Technical Education.* Columbus, Ohio: ERIC Clearing House on Vocational and Technical Education, 1972.

———. "The Effectiveness of Youth Programs." In *Youth Employment and Public Policy,* eds. Bernard E. Anderson and Isabel V. Sawhill. Englewood Cliffs, N.J.: Prentice-Hall, 1980.

Stromsdorfer, Ernst W., and Gary Goodfellow. "Cost-Effectiveness Analysis of Four Categorical Employment and Training Programs." Unpublished U.S. Department of Labor Report, 1977.

Suojanen, William. "CETA Title I Manpower Programs." Ph.D. dissertation, Sloan School of Management, MIT, August 1977.

Systems Development Corporation. "Impact of the JOBS Program in Nine Cities." Washington: U.S. Department of Labor, Manpower Administration, Office of Program Evaluation and Research, 1969.

Tella, Dorothy, et al. *A Model for Manpower Training Evaluation.* McLean, Va.: Planning Research Corp., 1970.

Tobin, James. "Stabilization Policy Ten Years After." *Brookings Papers on Economic Activity* 11 (1:1980): pp. 19–77.

Ulman, Lloyd. "Manpower Policies and Demand Management." In *Jobs for Americans,* ed. Eli Ginzberg. Englewood Cliffs, N.J.: Prentice-Hall, 1976. Pp. 85–119.

Urban Systems Research and Engineering, Inc. "Impact of Five Rural Concentrated Employment Programs." Washington: U.S. Department of Labor, Manpower Administration, Office of Program Evaluation and Research, 1971.

U.S. Department of Labor, Employment and Training Administration. *Work Experience Perspectives: CETA Program Models.* Washington: U.S. Department of Labor, 1979.

———. *Public Service Employment: CETA Program Models.* Washington: U.S. Department of Labor, 1978.

———. *Classroom Training—The OIC Approach: CETA Program Models.* Washington: U.S. Department of Labor, 1978.

———. *On-the-Job Training: CETA Program Models.* Washington: U.S. Department of Labor, 1978.

———. *CETA Program Status and Financial Summary—Fiscal Year 1980.* Washington: U.S. Department of Labor, 1980.

———. *Summary of Participant Characteristics—Fiscal Year 1980.* Washington: U.S. Department of Labor, 1980.

Wachter, Michael L. "Markov Processes and Public Service Employment: A Comment." In *Evaluating Manpower Training Programs,* ed. Farrell E. Bloch. Research in Labor Economics Supplement 1. Greenwich, Conn.: JAI Press, 1979. Pp. 285–94.

Walther, Regis, et al. "A Study of the Effectiveness of Selected Out-of-School NYC Programs." Washington: Social Research Group, George Washington University, 1971.

Weisbrod, Burton A. "Benefits of Manpower Programs: Theoretical and Methodological Issues." In *Cost-Benefit Analysis of Manpower Polices,* eds. Gerald G. Somers and W. D. Wood. Kingston, Ont.: Queen's University, 1969.

Westat, Inc. *The Net Earnings Impact of Public Employment Programs (PEP).* Washington: U.S. Department of Labor, Employment and Training Administration, Office of Program Evaluation and Research, 1979.

———. *Continuous Longitudinal Manpower Survey, Net Impact Report No. 1: Impact on 1977 Earnings of New Fiscal Year 1976 Enrollees in Selected Program Activities.* Prepared for the U.S. Department of Labor, Employment and Training Administration, Office of Program Evaluation and Research, March 1981.

———. *Continuous Longitudinal Manpower Survey, Follow-Up Report No. 3: (36 Months After Entry) Experiences in the First Two Postprogram Years, with Pre/Post Comparisons for Trainees Who Entered CETA During January–June 1975,* Vol. 1. Descriptive report prepared for the U.S. Department of Labor, Employment and Training Administration, Office of Program Evaluation and Research, January 1981.

Wirtz, Willard, and Harold Goldstein. "Measurement and Analysis of Work Training." *Monthly Labor Review* 98 (September 1975): pp. 19–26.

Zoritsky, Jeffrey, et al. *Program Evaluation at the Local Level: A Systems Approach.* Boston: Department of Manpower Development, Policy and Evaluation Division, Commonwealth of Massachusetts, 1979.

CHAPTER 4

The Labor Market Impact of Federal Regulation: OSHA, ERISA, EEO, and Minimum Wage*

OLIVIA S. MITCHELL
Cornell University

What we have learned about the impact of federal regulation of the workplace in the last decade is evaluated critically in this chapter. Policies selected for special attention are those affecting (1) workplace safety and health, (2) employer-provided pensions, (3) wage minimums, and (4) employment and pay practices with regard to women and minorities. Discussion of each policy is organized in the same way. First, we present a brief overview of the major legislative, administrative, and judicial developments in the policy area that occurred during the 1970s. Next, the theoretical literature is summarized, followed by a discussion of empirical studies of the specific labor market regulation. Finally, for each policy, we ask the question: What have we learned about the effect of the regulatory policy on the level and distribution of social well-being? General observations on all four regulatory programs appear in a final section.

I. Occupational Safety and Health

Until 1970, occupational safety and health standards were not uniform or consistent across the nation's workplaces. In a few industries, federal government supervision was the norm, as with the Mine Safety Act. Some states ran programs varying in scope and impact. For the most part, however, industry-level groups in the private sector developed their own consensus standards for

* Helpful suggestions were provided by Charles Brown, Jennifer Gerner, Alan Gustman, Janet Johnson, Michael Piore, Steve Welch, and the participants in the MIT Industrial Relations Workshop. The author retains responsibility for all conclusions.

job health and safety, and compliance was on a voluntary basis. During the latter half of the 1960s, public policy on workplace safety began to change, in part responding to high and rising injury rates on the job. This concern found a voice in the Occupational Safety and Health (OSH) Act of 1970, and in subsequent judicial and administrative developments in the area.

Policy Overview

The Act's goal was to make the workplace "healthful and safe for working men and women" (Smith 1976, p. 14), imposing on employers the responsibility for insuring that workers were not exposed to hazardous conditions. In addition to this general mandate, employers were instructed to abide by a rather lengthy list of safety and health standards that had been devised by private industry, as well as other federal safety laws such as the Mine Safety Act and the Walsh-Healey Act. Enforcement of the law's general safety and health clause as well as a multitude of individual standards devolved upon Department of Labor inspectors. While inspectors were most frequently allocated to firms in targeted industries, they could also be invited in by employees suspecting violations. Employers found in noncompliance were usually fined, about $25 per violation during the mid-1970s (Smith 1976). Additional administrative agencies were charged with reviewing practice and suggesting changes in policy. These included the Occupational Safety and Health Commission, the National Institute for Occupational Safety and Health, and the National Advisory Commission on Occupational Safety and Health. The OSH Act also indirectly facilitated the formation of union-management committees to deal with occupational and safety matters at the firm and industry level (Kochan, Dyer, and Lipsky 1977).

Various judicial interpretations of the OSH Act influenced the form and substance of the legislation over time.[1] For instance, the Act did not require OSHA inspectors to obtain a search warrant; however in 1978 the Supreme Court ruled that employers could require inspectors to obtain one.[2] Both employers and workers were granted permission to accompany safety inspectors on rounds. An important case in 1977, *Marshall* v. *Daniel Construc-*

[1] Savelson and Wainger (1978) discuss recent legislative developments.

[2] *Marshall* v. *Barlow's Inc.*, 436 U.S. 307 (1978).

tion,[3] produced the ruling that employees would not be allowed to refuse to work even if they feared or suspected dangerous working conditions on the job. The most controversial issue in the safety and health area was only recently reviewed by the Supreme Court: The question was whether economic cost-benefit analysis could be used in evaluating health and safety standards. Several textile firms argued that compliance with the Act's standards would be so expensive as to threaten their economic viability. The defendants argued, and the Court agreed, that the OSH Act did not require a comparison of compliance costs and benefits in determining new standards.[4] The long-term impact of this decision is still unclear, since the Agency's director has argued that OSH standards must still be "the least expensive way of reaching a specific level of protection."[5] The pros and cons of cost-benefit approaches in this context are considered in more detail below.

The Impact of Safety and Health Policy

Most theoretical analysis of safety and health policy applies a neoclassical framework, focusing on how OSH law affects costs and tracing its impact through the economic system. In a world where all employers and workers are competitive and well informed, wages paid in the labor market would reflect workers' evaluations of the risk they face on the job. Different types of employees demand different amounts of on-the-job safety, and employers supply different amounts depending on their own technology and the cost of lowering job risks. The labor market rewards workers willing to take risks with wage premiums depending on the distribution of workers' tastes and employers' technologies (Lucas 1972, Rosen 1974, Thaler and Rosen 1973).

In this neoclassical world, imposing minimum legal standards on workers' physical environment raises employers' costs of hiring labor. Profits are lowered and firms have an incentive to substitute away from labor to capital. Depending on the degree of responsiveness in labor demand and consumption, this process produces a

[3] 229 NLRB No. 24 (1977).

[4] *American Textile Manufacturers Inst.* v. *Donovan*, — U.S. — (July 17, 1981). See the exchange between MacAvoy and Williams in *The New York Times*, for instance.

[5] "Safety Agency to Forgo Cost Benefit Analysis," *The New York Times*, July 13, 1981.

cutback in employment and in overall output. Many neoclassical analysts would therefore view an OSH-type standards approach with some skepticism, since it creates inefficiencies in markets presumed to operated efficiently.

Somewhat less orthodox perceptions of the need for and effect of safety regulations have also evolved during the past decade. Analysts with these views believe that workers are exposed to too much risk because the costs of making jobs safer appear too high. This is explained by workers' and/or firms' imperfect information—they do not have the technical and medical capabilities required to monitor and alter the work environment. As yet, there exists no careful study of the way in which workers obtain, process, and act on information pertaining to workplace safety and health. Bacow (1980) suggests that most workers have difficulty monitoring compliance with OSH standards. Complementary evidence from Kochan (1980) finds that union workers appear to obtain higher risk premiums than do their nonunion counterparts. On the other hand, Smith (1979b) and Viscusi (1979) find no significant effect of unionism on injury rates. Thus, the evidence suggests that large organizations like unions may improve workers' perceptions of risk on the job, but perhaps cannot significantly lower those risks. There is at least fragmentary evidence indicating that there are scale economies for firms in the production of job safety and safety information; Gordon (cited in Smith 1974) suggests that large firms are more able to implement standards for this very reason. Oi (1974) along with Cooke and Gautchi (1981) also find that injury rates are lower in large firms, which is consistent with the view that firms may experience scale economies in injury reduction.

Whether or not these studies judge OSHA favorably in terms of improving the functioning of the labor market depends on whether information problems or scale economies are more important. OSH-type standards imposed by the government benefit workers most if they are unable to determine desirable safety levels on their own. On the other hand, legally required safety equipment and job redesign may be costly and, in fact, be more expensive than fully informed workers would be willing to incur in changing their own working conditions.

Another group of studies has inquired into whether the labor market responds *enough* to information about workplace hazards.

The evidence here is mixed. Viscusi (1979) concludes that workers are often poorly informed about workplace hazards and adapt slowly by quitting their jobs as they learn about the risks involved. Smith (1979a) reviews the literature on wage premiums for higher risks of death on the job and concludes that riskier jobs do pay more, though injury rate differences across industries do not appear to be reflected in wage premiums. Smith (1974) also examined firm behavior, focusing on the relationship between workplace injuries and risk premiums that firms pay their workers. He concludes that "employers do seem to be responsive in their safety efforts to the cost of injuries" (p. 741) and will react to economic incentives by making the workplace safer. However, this responsiveness is not large; he estimates that it would take a per-injury penalty of $1600 to $3000 (in 1974 dollars) to lower the injury rate 10 percent. This was about 100 times as large as the average OSHA penalty at the time. All three types of studies would suggest that OSH regulation was a necessary though probably not a sufficient policy to improve working conditions.

Differences in theoretical frameworks have generated different empirical approaches for evaluating the impact of OSH law. Some authors provide fascinating descriptive analyses of the medical, technical, practical, and bureaucratic difficulties encountered during OSHA's first year. Ashford (1976) has an extensive review of problems encountered in medical research and the difficulties of converting these medical/technical finds into OSH standards. He also provides an interesting overview of the bureaucratic obstacles encountered in developing new standards, complemented by Mendeloff's (1979) review of vinyl chloride and mechanical press standards.

Other new initiatives in the safety area are the focus of authors interested in union-management negotiations over changes in workplace health and safety practice. Bacow (1980), for instance, reviews the quite different approaches to worker safety of the United Auto Workers, United Steelworkers, and the United Association of Plumbers and Pipefitters. Kochan, Dyer, and Lipsky (1977) study the relationships between a single union (Machinists), the perceptions of the workers represented by this union, and management's perception of safety and health issues. These case studies provide a wealth of information about the ways in which particular unions and companies interact in altering workplace safety and health, and they will serve as models for institutional researchers in the future.

In addition to these more descriptive evaluations of OSHA, a few more quantitative studies are also available. Unfortunately, these studies are plagued by almost insurmountable data problems. Perhaps the single most serious problem deterring good quality research in this area is that no good data exist on workers' exposure to risk.[6] Thus, there is no way to determine the relationship between the number of workers affected by workplace illness or injury and the total number actually at risk on their jobs. A second problem with workplace safety data is that statistics collected prior to the passage of the OSH Act are incompatible with post-OSH Act statistics. Analysts therefore cannot determine the effect of OSHA directly[7] by examining trends in injuries or illness over time, and instead must focus on differences in workplace hazards as reflected in post-OSHA data alone. This may lead to underestimates of the effect of OSHA, since one would suspect that inspections would have some spillover effects even on firms not directly subject to inspection.

A third drawback of workplace safety data is that the reporting requirements are better for injuries and very poor on occupational illness (Ashford 1976). Thus, policy evaluations have been restricted almost exclusively to the analysis of work injuries, and virtually nothing is known about the long-run effect of OSH on occupational illness. Other analysts have criticized available data for still another reason: "assessment of small risks requires immense amounts of data" in order to be certain that changes in injury rates are indeed permanent and not due to measurement error (Rosen 1981, p. 242). Efforts to reduce measurement error in data have led analysts to examine industry-level statistics, yet such aggregation obscures a great deal of variation across firms in an industry (Oi 1974).[8]

Another serious drawback of quantitative data in this area is

[6] Rosen (1981) states this even more forcefully.

[7] Mendeloff (1979) examined trends by analyzing changes in injuries over time, rather than injury levels, but assumed that the underlying mechanisms generating injuries did not change structurally over time.

[8] Certain target industries were selected for concentrated government attention, though Oi (1974) points out that several industries *not* targeted had higher injury rates in 1970.

attributable to the problem of defining and measuring the policy variable of interest. Some analysts focus on industry-wide probabilities of OSHA inspection or citations.[9] However, the likelihood of inspection is distributed unevenly across firms, implying that the impact of OSH policy on individual firms is not well measured by industry-level data. Other analysts have focused on plant-level data, representing the effect of OSHA policy by timing of inspections, whether or not there was an OSHA inspection in a given year, or the number of citations over time (Smith 1979b, Cook and Gautchi 1981). No study has yet determined which is the most useful and sensible measure of the policy variable, and more work needs to be done in this area.

With these caveats in mind, let us turn to the evidence. Most empirical studies use injury rates as the dependent variable and relate them to measures of OSHA policy. Mendeloff (1979) uses time-series information. Focusing on national injury rates, he concludes that injury patterns after the passage of the Act did not differ significantly from the overall injury rate that would have been predicted in the absence of OSHA. His further analyses with state-level statistics are almost as inconclusive. Smith (1974) looked at cross-sectional injury rate statistics for 3-digit industrial groupings, and rejects the hypothesis that the Target Industries program reduced injury rates significantly. Viscusi (1979) also uses industry-level data, but follows the same industries over a period of four years; the policy variables he includes are the industry-specific OSHA inspection rate and the proposed OSHA penalty for noncompliance. Again, no significant effect of the government policy was detected.

Because of the drawbacks noted earlier in national and industry-level aggregate data, a few analysts have looked at injuries at the plant level. An early study by DiPietro (cited in Mendeloff 1979) reports firms' injury rates in 1973 as a function of whether or not firms were inspected in the previous year. Firm size and changes in employment were also controlled. Overall, results from this study reiterate the evidence generated by aggregate analyses—OSHA inspection apparently had no statistically significant effect on firm-level injury rates. That author suggested that the null finding might be attributable to the fact that inspections were

[9] Bacow (1980) had a succinct review of these studies.

often targeted at firms with exceptionally poor injury records; in other words, the inspection variable was probably endogenous and thus biased toward zero. A more recent study by Smith (1979b) controls for this potential problem by focusing on a subsample of plants, all of which had been inspected in either 1973 or 1974. In order to measure the effect of inspection, he differentiated between plants which were inspected early in the year, and others which were not visited until the winter months. He postulates that firms visited earlier would have a longer period over which to correct workplace hazards and thus should have experienced lower injury rates than the plants visited later. Interestingly, the evidence indicates that days lost due to injury were significantly reduced by early inspection in 1973, but not in 1974. Various explanations for the lack of consistency are suggested, the most plausible being that firms inspected in the latter year were more likely to be "problem cases" as compared to the plants visited earlier in the program. Overall, the author concluded that injuries were reduced from 5 to 16 percent with additional inspections. A third study of plant-level data (Cooke and Gautchi 1981), investigated changes in days lost due to injury over the period 1970 to 1976. These authors found that an increase in the total number of OSHA citations over the same period reduced days lost due to injury by a (statistically significant) .3 to .5 days per worker in large plants. No effect was discerned in small workplaces, however.

Clearly much more work remains to be done in this area. To reiterate Rosen (1981), the dependent variable should measure which workers are at risk rather than the very crude measures usually used. The endogenicity of inspections at the firm level must also be analyzed in more detail, ideally within the context of a model which takes into account the role of unions and management in enforcing the law. Better ways of modelling the implementation of OSHA policy must be devised, to better reflect the likelihood of apprehension, the likelihood that OSHA inspectors will actually perceive violations, the probable size of penalties if apprehended, and the role of follow-up investigations. On the basis of empirical work in the 1970s, it is suggested that the estimated effect of an increase in OSHA inspections on workplace injuries ranges between zero and about 15 percent, where the lower end of the range is characteristic of empirical studies using aggregate data and the higher estimates are produced by plant-level studies. More empirical studies of behavior at the individual firm level in the future will probably produce estimates of the impact of OSHA at the higher end of this range.

Effects of OSHA Policy on Levels of Well-Being

Has national policy on occupational safety and health had any significant impact on the level and distribution of well-being? This is one of the most interesting of all the research questions in the occupational safety and health area, and yet also the most overlooked.[10] There are, of course, many methods of devising answers to the question. One approach has been to use cost-benefit analysis as an intermediate step in guiding decision-making (Oi 1974). However, others (Chown 1980, Wood 1974) argue that cost-benefit places a price on illnesses and injuries, and "the worker must not be viewed simply as an economic entity." Regardless of whether cost-benefit is the only criterion that should be used, or whether instead it should be one of many, no one in the health and safety area has yet developed a list of the costs and benefits of OSHA and their distribution across the workforce. In addition, no one has asked whether other policies, such as those which impose more safety responsibilities on workers directly, might be more cost effective and/or equitable than the current standards-setting approach.

Conclusion

This review of what we know about job safety and health policy has revealed some strengths and many weaknesses. No one has inquired into the impact of OSH policy on employment and wages. The best available firm-level evidence indicates that current practice has a small negative effect on workplace injuries No one has examined the impact of OSH policy on occupational illness, and this area should receive highest research priority in the next decade. The evidence suggests that workers are not well acquainted with workplace hazards, though they do learn over time. Better ways of making available such information should

[10] Mendeloff (1979) suggests that male, blue-collar, and union employees were perhaps the groups most benefited by OSHA policy, but confirmation of this surmise awaits further research.

be found. Employer responses to OSHA regulations and practice also require more attention. Freedman's (1981) piece may serve as a guide to the various organizational and legal issues in this area. While the socially desirable level and distribution of risk on the job has not been established, existing cost-benefit methodology is probably too narrow in scope to measure completely the effects of workplace risk. On the other hand, more attention must be devoted to understanding the costs and benefits of safety and health policy. A prerequisite to more useful research is better information on who is actually exposed to what kind of risks. Labor, management, and the federal government should join to produce and analyze these sorely needed data.

II. Pension Income Security: ERISA

Private pensions today cover roughly half of the workforce and provide an average of $3000 to retirees receiving a pension (President's Commission on Pension Policy 1981). Pensions grew in importance as a source of retirement income mainly since World War II,[11] spurred by tax deferral of employer contributions to company plans, National Labor Relations Board rulings that pensions were appropriate topics of collective bargaining, and the Taft-Hartley Act which provided the framework for private multi-employer pension plans. The Welfare and Pension Plan Disclosure Act (WPPD) of 1958 was an early attempt to organize data collection on the nation's patchwork of retirement and other employer-provided welfare plans.

During the late 1960s and early 1970s, reports began to surface in the press about companies who reneged on or were unable to keep promises to pay retirement benefits. In addition, concern over workers' difficulties in vesting was expressed in several congressional hearings.[12] This discussion prompted passage of the Employee Retirement Income Security Act (ERISA) of 1974; its purpose was "to reduce the risk of workers not receiving adequate pension benefits, despite long-term participation in a firm's pension plan, by establishing funding standards, reporting requirements,

[11] See Ture and Fields (1979) and Greenough and King (1976) for a history of private pension development in the United States.

[12] Ture and Fields (1979) cite several committee findings and statements of concern.

and regulations on information that must be provided to participants and minimum vesting rules" (Masters et al. p. 43).

Policy Overview

ERISA establishes minimum standards with which a pension plan must comply, including (Skolnick 1974):

a. *Participation:* A full-time employee must be allowed to participate in a plan if he is at least age 25 and has worked at the firm one year.

b. *Vesting:* The employee has full legal rights over employer pension contributions after having fulfilled one of three vesting requirements (the most common being 10-year "cliff vesting"). Employee contributions are immediately vested.

c. *Information:* Employees must be provided with an annual statement on their benefit and vesting status; the Department of Labor must receive periodic reports on a plan's financial standing.

d. *Financial:* All plans promising a specified benefit to retirees (defined benefit plans) are required to accumulate funds in compliance with actuarial principles. Unfunded liabilities must be amortized over a period of 30 years in most cases. A governmental nonprofit firm, the Pension Benefit Guarantee Corporation (PBGC), insures a portion of defined benefit plans income by charging a flat per-worker premium. In case of plan illiquidity, the PBGC can claim up to 30 percent of a firm's assets to cover benefits promised.

e. *Fund management:* Pension plan sponsors are personally liable for pension investment performance if their investment advice is not in conformity with accepted money management practice (the "Prudent Man" rule). (This applies to both defined benefit and defined contribution plans, where the latter specify how much is contributed to the plan, but not payouts.)

f. *Individual plans:* Workers with no employer-sponsored plan may establish an Individual Retirement Account (IRA) or a Keogh plan (for the self-employed) into which tax-deferred contributions (up to a limit) may be deposited.

The law does not require employers to provide a pension nor

does it interfere with the determination of pension contributions or benefit levels. The purpose of the minimum standards, therefore, is to increase the chances that a worker promised a pension actually receives some form of retirement income from the employer making the promise.

Administration and enforcement of ERISA policy is allocated to several different entities: the Labor Management Services Administration of the Labor Department monitors pension plan reporting and disclosure and pension fund asset holdings. The Internal Revenue Service has responsibility for evaluating plans' compliance with participation, vesting, and funding standards established in ERISA. In addition, the PBGC oversees plans' long-term and short-term financial status. Finally, individual employees are empowered to file suit against plan administrators if benefits are illegally withheld.

Judicial decisions in the last few years have also modified the way in which employers and employees look at private pensions. In *International Brotherhood of Teamsters* v. *Daniel*,[13] the Supreme Court decided that defined benefit pensions should not be compared to savings or private securities, since investment performance was only one of several factors affecting their payout capabilities. *Nachman Corp.* v. *PBGC*[14] discussed the rights of employees to vested pension benefits in circumstances where the plan was experiencing financial difficulties. The way in which private pension benefits were integrated with workers' compensation payments was considered in *Alessi* v. *Raybestos Manhattan Inc.*[15] These cases and others currently pending highlight the continuing developments in the structure and function of employer-sponsored pensions.

The Impact of Pension Reform Regulation

One group of studies evaluating the impact of pension policy classifies pensions as deferred wages (Schiller and Weiss 1979). In this view, workers like group pensions because (1) they permit tax deferral of income, and (2) they offer a higher return on savings and lower insurance costs than individual plans could provide (Mitchell and Andrews 1981).

[13] — U.S. —, 100 LRRM 2260 (1979).
[14] 48 U.S.L.W. 4524 (1980).
[15] 49 U.S.L.W. 4503 (1981).

This approach has been criticized for not explaining why most pension plans require the employee to work for several years before vesting, why benefits are often independent of earnings, and why many pension systems are underfunded (Logue 1979). An alternative theory holds that pensions are an implicit contract between workers and employers, designed to improve worker productivity and lower turnover (Lazear 1979c). Vesting and participation requirements are understandable in this light. Pension underfunding has been interpreted along the same lines (Treynor, Regan, and Priest 1976, Feldstein and Seligman 1980, Smith 1981). The underfunded pension will pay off if the firm is in good financial health, which induces workers to internalize incentives to become more productive, exhibit lower turnover, and require less supervision. The existence of defined benefit plans which are unrelated to workers' salaries may be explained by the view that workers are risk-averse and prefer a flat dollar benefit with certainty to a benefit based on a worker's own (uncertain) income stream as he nears retirement age.

Though the different theories emphasize distinct aspects of the private pension system, no one yet knows what role pensions actually play in the labor market. For this reason there is some disagreement in the literature about the expected impact of ERISA regulations. Those who believe the labor market behaves according to neoclassical rules predict that ERISA lowers the riskiness of a pension promise, by virtue of which the pension promise becomes more expensive. In response to more costly but more secure pensions, workers' wages and/or benefit levels may fall; however, expected total compensation over individuals' lifetimes would not necessarily change (Schiller and Weiss 1980). On the other hand, the justification for ERISA might be different in a less neoclassical labor market. Research by Hamermesh (1981a), for instance, suggests that workers have very imprecise ideas about their own health and life expectancies, the implication being that they do need help in planning their retirement savings. Employees, especially at younger ages, tend to put a relatively low value on pensions (Mitchell 1980, 1981), suggesting that unions and other institutions are useful in making them more aware of the need for pensions (Gustman and Segal 1972, Lester 1967), and in redistributing income via pensions (Freeman 1978). ERISA is needed in this non-neoclassical environment because it protects workers against the possibility of not receiving a pension because of fraud. There is also some evidence that pension managers are less than perfectly "rational" in the economic sense[16] and might not reduce other elements of the compensation package in response to the greater security of pensions.

Before turning to the results of empirical studies on the effects of ERISA, several comments are in order on the severe data problems encountered by any would-be empirical researcher in this area. Perhaps the single most serious problem is that there is no way to measure the outcome variable of greatest interest to many researchers—that is, the lifetime consumption and pension benefits eventually received by today's workers, as compared to what they were promised (and, perhaps, to previous cohorts' benefits). Until today's workers retire from the labor market, it will be impossible to determine what they actually received in total compensation. An additional problem is that it has been difficult to quantify the appropriate policy variable(s) associated with ERISA. For these reasons, empirical research on ERISA is almost nonexistent. The few available studies have focused on other (nonbenefit) factors: for instance, analysts have examined pension portfolios (Cummins et al. 1980), the impact of underfunding on firms' stock prices (Feldstein and Seligman 1980, Gersovitz 1980), and the costs of administering pension plans (Mitchell and Andrews 1981, Andrews and Mitchell 1981). No one has carefully and systematically analyzed whether and how ERISA has changed wage and/or pension benefit levels and employees' rights to pensions; no one has determined whether pension plan termination patterns are attributable to the regulation or the poor financial market; and there are virtually no representative pre-ERISA data that can be used to determine scientifically whether the regulations had any effect on any outcome variable over time. Therefore we must conclude at the outset that empirical evidence on the impact of ERISA is almost nonexistent and the few available studies do not examine the effect of the regulation on compensation levels, income distribution, employment patterns, or many other dependent variables of interest.

---

[16] For instance, Bulow's paper (1979) indicates that pension funds do not invest solely in bonds, though economic theory predicts that they should.

Two descriptive and two quantitative empirical studies focus directly on the impact of ERISA reforms. Logue (1979) and Ture and Fields (1979) sketch evidence on vesting and participation rules before and after ERISA, but do not develop a systematic empirical model. Cummins et al. (1980) and Cummins, Percival, and Westerfield (1979) analyze nonlabor-market aspects of the regulatory impact; the first paper focuses on plan administrators' attitudes about extra costs attributable to the law, while the latter report attempts to determine whether ERISA had any significant impact on the portfolio composition of pension funds (Chapters 3 and 4). Both studies found little if any evidence that ERISA affected pension plan operation, though the former article suggested that costs for multiemployer plans may have been increased somewhat.

Two additional studies examine the impact of ERISA indirectly by focusing on pension underfunding patterns. Gersovitz (1980) finds that pension underfunding tends to lower a firm's stock prices, but only to the extent that underfunding is less than one-third of the firm's assets. This is significant because, under ERISA, a pension plan has claim to that proportion of the company's assets; this study thus implies that ERISA indeed influences the probability of retirees receiving promised pensions. Nonetheless, the report by Bulow (1979) shows that ERISA's regulations on pension underfunding are likely to be ineffective since actuarial assumptions are not specified in the law, and firms can alter their reported level of underfunding simply by selecting different actuarial assumptions. Finally, two studies (Mitchell and Andrews 1981, Andrews and Mitchell 1981) find that larger pension plans benefit from scale economies, and suggest that ERISA may encourage plan mergers by standardizing pension characteristics.

Effects of ERISA on Levels of Well-Being

Has the change in policy expressed in ERISA had any significant impact on society's level and distribution of well-being? As should be clear from the preceding discussion, the paucity of studies evaluating the effects of ERISA on the labor market makes it impossible to answer this equity question. Some overall descriptive material on the income distribution of retirees is available from various sources; for instance, the Presidents' Commission on

Pension Policy (1981) finds that poverty among those over 65 years of age has declined relatively and absolutely over time, in part due to increases in private pension income.[17] However, no one has attempted to evaluate how much of this change in income was due to ERISA regulation and how much to other causes. No study has determined whether groups who traditionally received little from pension plans, such as women and blacks, have indeed benefited from ERISA as a result of the less strict vesting and participation requirements. Impacts on the rest of the economy have been largely ignored this far: Cummins et al. (1980) suggest that small firms might be most seriously affected by the regulation, but careful analysis of this topic remains to be done.

Conclusions

The most surprising features of the literature on ERISA is that there is so little of it and that it is so unsystematic. In part this is explained by recognizing that pensions have become a topic of research interest only recently, and their role in the labor market and the economy as a whole is as yet not completely clear. This review of studies available to date suggests that ERISA has had no significant effects on the outcome variables examined—pension portfolios and administrative costs—but no data are yet available to address the issue of whether ERISA has affected benefit levels and/or benefit security for current or future retirees. It is hoped that researchers in the 1980s will devise better ways to fill some of the gaps identified here.

We also suggest that various reform proposals discussed in the last decade deserve serious research scrutiny. Some analysts suggest that existing regulations governing investment of fund assets are too restrictive and should be relaxed to permit a more innovative investment pattern (Rifkin and Barber 1978). Others recommend looser participation and vesting provisions, to benefit workers with short job tenure who have difficulty qualifying for benefits.[18] A few researchers have begun to investigate the pros and cons of indexing pension benefits to inflation (Feldstein 1981, Bodie 1980). Some urge the establishment of a mandatory private

[17] Most of the increase is probably attributable to real improvements in Social Security benefits.

[18] See, for instance, the hearings summarized in the President's Commission on Pension Policy (1981).

pension system covering all workers, a position particularly favored by the Presidents' Commission on Pension Policy (1981). Finally, several researchers have proposed that the PBGC be revamped in light of its low level of reserves and its lack of experience rating (Treynor, Regan, and Priest 1976). As yet, however, all of these proposed reforms remain in the planning stages.

III. Federal Minimum Wage Policy

Minimum wage legislation grew out of national concern over workers' standards of living and how to best improve them. During the 1920s and 1930s, proponents of the policy argued that employers should not be permitted to pay workers below-subsistance income. Thus a wage floor was expected to be and is still touted as an antipoverty strategy (Levitan and Belous 1979). Opponents then and now contended that a legislated wage floor would be ineffective against poverty, since low wages reflect low productivity rather than exploitative employer practices (F. Welch 1978). This portion of the paper reviews theoretical and empirical minimum wage research over the last decade.

Policy Overview

The Fair Labor Standards Act (FLSA), enacted in 1938, was to bring about a "minimum standard of living necessary for health, efficiency, and general wellbeing of workers . . . without substantially curtailing employment or earning power."[19] The bill was of necessity born of compromise; several earlier efforts to implement state-specific wage floors had failed in the courts, and Roosevelt's attempt to establish industrial wage minimums under the National Recovery Act met a similar fate in 1935. Initially the FLSA was limited to the 20 percent of the workforce engaged in interstate commerce. For employees subject to the law, the Act set a wage floor of 25 cents an hour for both men and women, or about half of the average hourly wage in manufacturing at the time.[20] The minimum has risen over time and now stands at about

[19] For a summary of historical precedents to the FLSA and the Act's major provisions, see the Report of the Minimum Wage Study Commission (1981). Here we focus only on the wage-floor provisions of the Act.

[20] Most of the minimum wage literature refers to "covered workers" though "subject workers" is the more technically correct terminology. The distinction here is that a covered worker may be exempt from the Act while a subject

half the average manufacturing wage (F. Welch 1978).[21] Coverage increased over the last 40 years from about 40 to about 80 percent of nonagricultural civilian nonsupervisory employees. Administrative and enforcement powers under the FLSA were granted to a special Wage and Hours Division of the Department of Labor. The Labor Department was given responsibility for granting exemptions to the law, and has done so for companies with annual gross sales under a third of a million dollars (as well as for some students and handicapped workers).

The Impact of Minimum Wage Policy

A simple neoclassical model of the effect of a minimum wage was first stated four decades ago (Stigler 1946). If employers and workers are competitive, a minimum wage set above the competitive level will reduce employment because firms cannot pay workers more than the value of their marginal product and thus the wage floor induces layoffs of workers that would otherwise be earning less than that floor. The extent of disemployment is a function of labor demand elasticity when coverage is universal and the wage floor uniform across workers (F. Welch 1978) and of how high the wage floor is set. Incomes fall to zero for those who lose their jobs, and the overall distribution of earnings becomes more unequal.[22]

Theoretical neoclassical research of the 1970s elaborated on this simple textbook approach in several ways. Hashimoto and Mincer (1970) recognized that some firms are exempt from FLSA provisions, implying that they may lower wages and absorb those laid off from covered-sector jobs. Wachter and Kim (1979) pointed out that some individuals may be unwilling to take uncovered-sector jobs, preferring instead to remain unemployed in the hope of finding a job at a higher covered-sector wage. Therefore, Mincer

---

worker is both covered by the Act and not exempt from its provisions. In fact, it has recently been estimated that one-quarter of the employed wage and salary workers are covered, though exempt from the minimum wage provision of the Act (S. Welch 1981).

[21] Many states also established their own legislation governing wages and hours. These state floors are typically less than or equal to the federal level, but the statutes may cover more workers.

[22] Gramlich (1976) and Ragan (1977) recognize that worker hours rather than employment might adapt, particularly if the firm bears hiring and training costs. This does not materially affect the conclusions drawn from the model with respect to total earnings and employment changes, however.

(1976) concludes that unemployment rates are not particularly good measures of the impact of wage minimums. Other authors (Hamermesh 1981b) stress that firms' responsiveness to a wage floor depends on the ease of substitution between skilled and unskilled workers. A general equilibrium long-run theoretical model of the impact of a minimum wage which takes into account both physical and human capital formation has not yet been analyzed in detail, though recent efforts by Cox and Oaxaca (1981) are promising.

Though neoclassical models of the minimum wage impact grew increasingly sophisticated over the last decade, their theoretical predictions became less and less clear cut. For example, while the theories do clearly support the conclusion that a wage floor will reduce labor demanded in firms covered by the minimum, the quantity and distribution of labor cutbacks depend on the level and coverage of the real minimum, labor and product demand elasticities, substitutability of capital and labor of various types, and labor supply. In contrast, the theories do not unambiguously predict whether *aggregate* employment or *aggregate* unemployment will rise or fall. Nor is the effect of minimum wages on the overall income distribution predictable on an a priori basis from these models. Resolution of these theoretical ambiguities clearly requires empirical analyses in the years ahead.

Theoretical neoclassical models of the minimum wage have been challenged from three directions. All three emphasize labor market inefficiencies due to *employer* behavior; in contrast to the literature on other forms of labor market regulation, virtually no attention has been devoted to *other* labor market structures that might justify government regulation.

One interesting case, mentioned by Stigler (1946) and others, arises when employers are monoposonists and control labor purchases completely. In this type of market, a wage floor set high enough forces the monopsonists to raise wages and employment without reducing efficiency.[23] The single quantitative paper on this topic (West and McKee 1980) reports that firms' output indeed tends to rise significantly after the wage minimum is raised. If this

[23] It is unlikely that a national uniform wage minimum could be "correct" for all firms, though how the correct levels might be set has not generated much debate in the literature.

finding is supported with other data, it would constitute an important argument in favor of minimum wage policy.

A second rationale for a wage floor was elaborated in the early writings of Webb (1912). He held that workers respond to higher wages by becoming more productive, so that a wage floor may improve earnings without lowering employment at all. Why employers do not pay enough to benefit from this wage-productivity interaction is as yet unclear in the literature. A third argument for a minimum wage is usually termed the "shock theory." It states that employers are slow to adopt productive new technology, but a wage floor induces them to overcome this lethargy by investing in more innovative production techniques. Whether or not innovation in this form contributes to net employment increases or not, and why employers are slow to adjust, is unclear. These two rationales for a wage minimum seem to raise more questions than they answer, and they require more theoretical and empirical attention before they can stand on their own.

The empirical literature on minimum wages is voluminous, perhaps larger than on any other single labor market regulation. Its quality is, however, uneven.[24] Most studies identify employment rates (or levels) as the dependent variable of most interest, though some concentrate on unemployment. In part, this relatively narrow empirical focus was a result of data shortcomings: aggregate figures on employment were typically easier to obtain than were other data. One disadvantage of an aggregate focus is that changes in group composition when people leave and enter the ranks of the unemployed may affect results. As individual level micro data became available, this problem of sample selection began to be addressed. Relatively few studies focus on the distribution of individual or family *income*. Fewer studies still analyze changes in income patterns over time and over peoples' lifetimes.

Data problems have also made it difficult to develop good measures of the appropriate policy variables. In any particular cross-section of firms, all covered employers must offer the same

[24] Several early efforts sponsored by the Department of Labor in the 1950s focused on low-wage sectors such as the garment and lumber industries. Although these studies usually concluded that the minimum wage had little or no deleterious effect on employment in these sectors, their empirical conclusions did not stand up to reanalysis by Peterson and Stewart (1969) and Brown, Gilroy, and Kohen (1980).

minimum.[25] This uniformity means that cross-section data do not contain a "control group" with which firms covered by the law can be compared. Some cross-section studies develop a variable which is the ratio of the federal wage minimum to some area-specific average wage, often multiplied by a variable proxying for coverage. This approach may be criticized by recognizing that regional variation in wage levels often reflects not minimum wage level differences, but other labor market features (like industrial structures) which may more readily explain regional disemployment. Other analysts use time-series data, arguing that changes in the price level and in the nominal wage floor over time should provide the empirical variation required for quantitative analysis. Time-series studies have drawbacks, too, because they pick up changes in workforce composition as females and youths enter the labor market. Finally, both cross-section and time-series studies have found it difficult to distinguish between the impact of the minimum *level* and *coverage*, since policy changes usually alter both variables at the same time.

With few exceptions, empirical studies tend to focus on teenage employment patterns because this demographic group is the most numerous, the least killed, and probably most susceptible to disemployment effects.[26] When the methodological and data differences across studies are kept in mind, the time-series evidence suggests that a 10 percent increase in the minimum wage is associated with a 0.5 to 1.5 percent decline in youth employment; cross-sectional evidence is more variable but also spans that range (Brown, Gilroy, and Kohen 1980). Some analysts claim that the wage floor has a larger disemployment effect on blacks than on whites, but this contention is as yet only weakly supported in the data.

Studies on adult employment response to the minimum wage are even more inconclusive; analysts disagree not only on the

[25] Ashenfelter and Smith (1979) argue, however, that compliance varies across firms and over time, depending on the cost and the probability of being caught and penalized. Compliance is also influenced by regional and sectoral differences in wages and prices. Recent evidence indicates that minimum wage violations are concentrated in the retail and trade sectors of the economy and disproportionately impact women and teenagers (Sellekaerts and Welch 1981).

[26] Teenagers under 18 years old are also covered by FLSA restrictions on child labor. Hence, for that subset of teenagers, the minimum wage may not be the only cause of disemployment.

magnitude but also the sign of the impact. Hamermesh (1981b) claims that adult employment is marginally enhanced by the minimum wage, while Gramlich (1976) finds no response. Mincer (1976) concludes that older males and many females lose jobs, but Parsons (1980) argues that adult females are, on net, not adversely affected. This evidence is thus contradictory and will remain so until empirical work controls for compositional changes in the groups under study and identifies substitution between different kinds of labor and capital.

While the majority of studies takes a static perspective, a few analysts examine labor market dynamics as workers and firms adjust to new wage minimums over time. Here the conclusions are also in disagreement: Zucker (1973) reports that about four-fifths of the total employment changes occurred within six months of a change in the minimum. This rapid adjustment is confirmed by Hamermesh (1981), but Moore (1971), in earlier work, found a much slower adjustment pattern. More research that employs a dynamic view of labor market adjustments is needed on this topic in future years.

Effects on Well-Being

Many have inquired about the distributional effects of the minimum wage. Welch (1978) and Parsons (1980) conclude that many minimum wage workers are from reasonably well-to-do families. Gilroy (1981) puts it differently (pp. 179–81): "As one might expect, a large proportion—43 percent—of those workers in families below the official poverty level are making the minimum wage or less. . . . What is surprising is that these workers account for only 11 percent of all minimum wage workers." In general, the policy does not appear to benefit the poor relatively more when evaluated in cross-section data or even over short periods of time. This conclusion may be altered as new data become available on the impact of the wage floor on workers' skills and lifetime income patterns: studies by Mincer and Leighton (1980) and Ehrenberg and Marcus (1980) conclude that the lifelong impact of minimum wage coverage may lower income for low-wage workers.

Conclusion

The literature on one of the oldest forms of labor market regulation, the minimum wage, contains some strengths and some weaknesses. To a great degree, applied researchers in the last decade have tested only neoclassical empirical models. The available evidence suggests that, as a result of wage floors, teenage employment is somewhat lower than it could be, though effects in the long run are as yet uncertain. A less clear picture emerges about the impact of the minimum wage on adult employment. Our understanding of how the policy affects the distribution of income is as yet rudimentary; as better micro data on firms and workers are developed, this shortcoming must be remedied.

It must also be recognized that existing empirical studies have not viewed broadly enough the context in which minimum wage policy operates. Other institutions, regulations, and social policies also affect the eventual income distribution of earnings and nonlabor income, and these should be taken into account as well. For instance, levels of benefits and eligibility rules for welfare programs vary across regions and over time, influencing the payoff to work and participation as well as unemployment. Unemployment insurance plays a major role for some workers. Income and other taxes alter the relative returns to working, as do in-kind transfers and their eligibility requirements. Nor has the role of labor unions in establishing and maintaining prevailing wages been taken into account in studies which purport to evaluate the minimum wage. The interactions of politics and institutions should be examined in order to develop a clearer understanding of the contribution of each to the distribution of income and employment. They are usually not, however.

Even this brief review of minimum wage policy would be incomplete without mentioning some of the more controversial topics surfacing in recent years.[27] The Report of the Minimum Wage Study Commission (1981) touches on several: What would result from a special subminimum for youth? On this topic, Brown (1981b), Hamermesh (1981), and Freeman, Gray, and Ichniowski

[27] Goldfarb (1974) has a well-organized review of papers appearing up to the early 1970s. The Report of the Minimum Wage Study Commission (1981) provides a bibliography and review of several works the Commission sponsored as well as independent research. The paper by Brown, Gilroy, and Kohen (1980) is perhaps the most comprehensive.

(1981) come to quite different conclusions. Should the wage floor be indexed to inflation? Does the minimum wage cause wage structure compression, or do employers maintain traditional wage differentials? Should the minimum be tailored to specific industries and regions? Evaluating these questions will, no doubt, receive a great deal of attention in the 1980s. Whether the wage minimum is the best way to alleviate poverty is an additional important concern that must also be examined in the next decade.

IV. Antidiscrimination Policy

Prior to the 1960s individual states had a variety of bills on the books protecting workers treated unequally because of race, sex, or age (Landes 1968). At the federal level, some concern over discriminatory practices was embodied in the 1938 Fair Labor Standards Act, but this law protected mainly against long hours and poor working conditions. Not until the 1960s did federal regulation directly confront the labor market problems of minorities and women. This section evaluates what we have learned in the last decade about the impact of federal antidiscrimination policy on blacks and women.[28]

Policy Overview

Government policy toward labor market discrimination in the 1960s found expression in two major pieces of legislation: the Equal Pay Act of 1963, and Title VII of the 1964 Civil Rights Act. The Equal Pay bill focuses specifically on sex discrimination by prohibiting employers from maintaining separate pay scales for males and females. The law specifies that men and women must receive the same wage when they work at the same establishment, performing work which requires the equal skill, effort, and responsibility ("equal pay for equal work"). It does permit pay differences across workers performing different jobs, or where seniority and piece-rate systems produce different earnings outcomes.

Title VII of the Civil Rights bill contrasts with the Equal Pay Act because it proscribes discrimination due to race, religion, and national origin as well as gender. Its pay provisions are broader than those in the Equal Pay Act because they are not explicitly

[28] Antidiscrimination policy also covers workers identifiable by religion, age, handicap, and veteran status. Less attention has been devoted to these areas, however.

limited to comparisons across equal jobs. Employment provisions figure prominently in this law: it prohibits unequal practices in hiring, training, promotion, or discharge. A novel feature of this bill is that it establishes an enforcement arm, the Equal Employment Opportunity Commission (EEOC), charged initially with conciliation and preparation of court briefs and later permitted to initiate court proceedings and represent employees.

A second important antidiscrimination tool wielded by the federal government is its leverage as a purchaser of goods and services. Executive Order 11246 (as amended in 1968) requires government contractors not only to abide by existing antidiscrimination law, but also to take affirmative action in hiring, training, and promoting minorities and women. If a firm is found in noncompliance, it may be penalized in several ways, including debarment in the most extreme case.

In addition to congressional acts and administrative practice, a third antidiscrimination tool became important during the 1960s and 1970s—judicial action.[29] The Supreme Court took active stances in several important cases. In *Griggs* v. *Duke Power*,[30] it prohibited pre-employment tests which selected against racial minorities more often than whites, when they did not predict successful performance on the job. The principle of retroactive back pay was examined in a case involving American Telephone and Telegraph, culminating in a $38 million negotiated settlement for women employees (Wallace 1976). More recently the Court has examined particular affirmative action plans. In the *Weber* case,[31] for instance, the Supreme Court found that a degree of reverse discrimination was permissible under Title VII.

Cases involving yet another principle have begun to emerge in the last few years. The controversy here is the principle of "equal pay for comparable worth," which holds that men's and women's pay rates should be equalized for jobs which are in some sense comparable though not identical (Livernash 1980, Lindsay 1980, Milkovich 1980). The Supreme Court's recent (1981) decision in *County of Washington* v. *Gunther*[32] was less than definitive

[29] See Smith (1980), Gold (1981), and Wallace and Driscoll (1981) for a review and discussion of legislative issues.

[30] 401 U.S. 424 (1971).

[31] 443 U.S. 193 (1979).

[32] 101 S.Ct. 2242, 25 FEP Cases 1521 (1981).

on this new principle, because of several narrow interpretations of the legislative record. It is likely that this topic will continue to find its way to court during the 1980s.

The Impact of Antidiscrimination Policy

One of the most interesting features of national antidiscrimination policy is that it regulates labor market *outcomes* rather than labor market *processes*. Thus it differs from, say, health and safety policy which establishes standards for working conditions but does not specify worker health levels. This focus on outcome has some drawbacks: if the nature of discrimination is poorly understood, required changes in labor market processes may not occur as a result of policy (Marshall 1974). On the other hand, a result of the law's focus on outcomes is that policy-makers have been forced (with some difficulty) to focus directly on workers' earnings and employment patterns.

Because the regulatory approach is so direct, it might be thought that antidiscrimination policy might be more successful than other laws in attaining its goals. Neoclassical theorists find some ground for disagreement, however. Analysts in this tradition note that federal pay provisions, in particular, can have unexpected results: raising blacks' or womens' wages may encourage employers to hire fewer of them, in favor of (now relatively cheaper) white males (Madden 1973). The simple theoretical approach suggests, then, that higher pay may be offset by employment losses for blacks and women.

Though equal pay regulations may be ineffective, employment and affirmative action provisions are more likely to reduce barriers confronting minorities and females, according to neoclassical analysts. These barriers arise from what Becker (1957) calls "tastes for discrimination" on the part of employers, fellow workers, and/or consumers. (For further discussion, see the Flanagan and Mitchell chapter in this volume.) When equal employment legislation is effectively enforced, employers will find it expensive to avoid hiring women or blacks and will increase their demand for these types of workers. If qualified females and minorities are available for hire, the policy should, on net, improve their earnings and employment both in absolute terms and in comparison with white male workers. The effectiveness of this policy is further enhanced if misinformed employers do not realize that women and minorities are as productive as white males, and the law forces them to revise their expectations (Cain 1976).

Challenges to the neoclassical view of the labor market and policy are quite numerous. Some authors emphasize that unequal outcomes occur because workers face difficulties in other markets. For instance, black workers have often paid more than whites for housing, transportation, and education (or received lower quality for the same price) as well as other services (Kain 1968, Danziger and Weinstein 1976, F. Welch 1973, Butler 1981). Women also face nonlabor market barriers of various types (Loury 1981, Frank 1978). To the extent that these nonlabor market factors determine entry to jobs and training opportunities, females and minorities find good jobs less accessible. Antidiscrimination policy was thus complemented by housing and educational subsidies of the last decade.

A second and influential group challenging the neoclassical model is the dual labor market analysts (Doeringer and Piore 1971). Writers in this group postulate that various institutional labor market features explain the lower job attainment of blacks and women, including co-workers' unwillingess to bring blacks and women into training and apprenticeship programs (Briggs and Foltman 1981), inability of employees to turn educational skills into monetary rewards (Oaxaca 1973), and difficulties of women and minorities in holding jobs once hired (Marston 1976). In this view, vigorous affirmative action was likely to be quite valuable in altering discriminatory labor market structures.

Monopoly and monopsony have been emphasized in still other studies as factors contributing to the persistence of unequal pay and employment for women and blacks. Stiglitz's (1973) analysis led him to conclude that employer monopsonies were not strong enough to explain lower earnings for females and minorities, but more recent researchers find that monopolistic firms pay black workers less (Haessel and Palmer 1978). Few alternative job opportunities for women is given as the explanation for lower wages in other studies (Frank 1978; Cardwell and Rosenzweig 1978); thus firm-side market power appears to depress the earnings of women as well as blacks. Others note that craft unions were discriminators in the past (Wallace and Driscoll 1981), barring entry to all but white males. High union wage levels might also have facilitated employer discrimination indirectly, by creating a labor pool from which employers could select only the workers whom they favored. Analysts writing in this vein tended to conclude that the equal pay and especially the affirmative action provisions of antidiscrimination policy would be especially important in helping women and blacks override monopsonistic and union barriers.

Making the transition from theoretical to empirical policy analysis proved to be difficult for many researchers, in part because of several data problems. Freeman (1973), Butler and Heckman (1977) and Brown (1981a) have written extensively on the fact that aggregate data can conceal flows of workers in and out of the labor market, so that increases in reported earnings attributed to policy initiatives must be spurious. Almost equally problematic has been the empirical difficulty of finding policy variables that adequately reflect antidiscrimination policy. Studies of compliance by federal contractors typically use companies without any federal contract as the "control group" for purposes of evaluating the impact of affirmative action policy. However, Brown (1981c) points out that federal contractors may differ systematically from noncontractors, making the comparison erroneous. Osterman's (1981) policy measure is more precise, since the term he uses is an industry-specific tally of contract reviews and compliance agreements. EEO studies have even more difficulty quantifying the policy variable of interest: Beller (1980) focuses on EEO investigations by type, but is forced by data constraints to limit her attention to state-level data rather than individual company and employee groups.

Empirical studies of antidiscrimination policy may be divided into federal contract compliance studies and research on EEO. Prominent in the first literature is a set of studies appearing in the *Industrial and Labor Relations Review* in 1976, as well as the review by Brown (1981c). Ahart (1976), for instance, provides a descriptive account of the difficulties encountered in enforcing the policy. The papers by Goldstein and Smith (1976) and Heckman and Wolpin (1976) are some of the better-known econometric evaluations of the microeconomic data. Flanagan (1976) and Brown (1981c) compile and examine the evidence from time series and other studies. Overall these studies indicate that federal contract compliance efforts were rather ineffective, at least with respect to relative employment rates of blacks and whites. Employment gains for black males are detected in a few studies (Brown (1981) concludes "no more than 10% in the long run"), but specific policy variables like contract reviews are usually not responsible. No effect is found for black females in most cross-sectional studies. Smith and Welch (1977) and Freeman (1973) examine relative earnings of blacks, and suggest that racial earnings differences between males were not strongely influenced by contract compliance policy. Only the Osterman (1981) study detects a significant policy impact, and that paper looks at turnover rates rather than earnings.

Less quantitative research analyzes the direct impact of EEO, in part because of data problems noted earlier. A cross-section study by Beller (1980) uses data on the probability of EEO apprehension and of having to pay a penalty to the EEOC or to state Fair Employment Commissions, derived from actual data on EEO investigations by state. Interestingly enough, the effectiveness of the law appears to differ across minorities and women: on net, policy variables are found to reduce black employment and have virtually no effect on black-white relative earnings; in contrast EEO policy significantly narrowed the sex difference in earnings over time by 3 to 8 percent.[33] A time-series analysis by Freeman (1973) found that cumulative EEOC expenditure had a positive and significant effect on relative black earnings. Butler and Heckman (1977) correct for the sample composition bias noted above and find virtually no effect of EEO variables. Smith and Welch (1979) also challenge Freeman's conclusion, saying that an improvement in educational quality was more likely the responsible factor in improving black relative earnings. Arriving at a firm conclusion in this area is difficult, but the available evidence indicates that women's relative earnings were marginally improved by EEO policy, while black/white employment and earnings differentials were probably not significantly affected.

Impact on Well-Being

It is difficult to evaluate the impact of antidiscrimination policy

[33] The reduction in the earnings gap was largely due to lower male wages. Wage increases for white females attributable to the antidiscrimination policy were estimated to be between 3 and 8 percent, higher in years of lower unemployment.

on the overall level and distribution of well-being. The consensus to date might be summarized as follows: overall employment probably was little affected by the policy, and relative earnings growth was largest for women. Both highly skilled females and minorities benefited more than did others (Freeman 1973). No one has yet attempted an overall assessment of the short-run costs and benefits of antidiscrimination policy, nor a complete analysis of its effect on individual and family income and expectations. Long-run impacts have generally been neglected; two exceptions are found in Lazear's (1979a, 1979b) work, which concludes that job advancement is much more likely for females as a result of the policy initiatives, but not for blacks. Much research remains to be done in this area.

Conclusion

The main contribution of antidiscrimination analysis over the last decade has been its new insights into real-world labor market institutions. Structures coming under scrutiny include the role of hiring and personnel policy, on-the-job training and apprenticeship, and the relationship between earnings, worker characteristics and firm-level variables. More analysis is needed on each of these elements in order for us to more fully understand how antidiscrimination policy works when it does, and why it failed when it did. In general, existing analysis indicates that antidiscrimination policy probably improved women's earnings and had little effect on black workers' earnings and employment.

V. Concluding Remarks

Previous sections discussed the available research on workplace health and safety, pensions, minimum wages, and discrimination in pay and employment. It is also instructive to look across the policy areas to appraise the literature as a whole.

Did the Government Policies Attain Their Goals?

Neoclassical and institutional research is uneven on the direct impact of the four regulatory policies. The evidence indicates that EEO and OSHA reforms had a positive though small effect on the outcomes they sought to alter, the minimum wage probably did not improve earnings for most low-skilled workers, and no study examined whether ERISA improved pension security. More analysis needs to be done on the direct as well as the second-round effects of these labor market regulations, including their impact on total compensation and employment, collective bargaining, organizational structure, and whether they alter employer and worker attitudes. Most studies take a fairly narrow perspective, looking only at one particular program or policy at a time. A wider net must be cast to understand how any given policy initiative interacts with other political and economic entities in the labor market.

What Were the Costs and Benefits of These Regulatory Policies and to Whom Did They Accrue?

Rational social decision-making should be based on an understanding of the level and distribution of costs and benefits associated with a given policy, yet the literature is far from helpful in this regard. No researcher has fully examined the direct costs of any of the four policies, including compliance and enforcement expenditures. In only a few instances have analysts investigated which labor market groups benefited from regulations—the minimum wage studies stand out as exceptions. There are also very few studies of the effect of these regulations on overall productivity (see Denison 1979 and Gray 1981) and virtually no analyses on how the regulations altered the distribution of power between labor and management, if at all, and between these parties and the government. Each of these questions should be addressed in the next decade.

Was the Actual Regulatory Package the Best Possible Set of Policy Instruments Available to Attain the Desired Goals?

In evaluating existing programs, it is important to ask whether more beneficial outcomes might have been achieved with a different set of policies, given the same budget allocation and the same socioeconomic circumstances. Most of the regulations impose standards on employers, but a variety of other schemes might be devised. For instance, many safety and health studies mention alternative policy tools to reduce risks; the various options should be enumerated and analyzed in other areas as well. We still have only a rudimentary understanding of regulatory agencies' behavior, goals, and constraints; this gap must be filled, too, if realistic and feasible policy alternatives are to be considered.

How Did Research During the 1970s Differ from That Which Came Before, and What Research Is Likely to Be the Most Useful in the Next Decade?

Research on labor market regulation during the 1970s distinguished itself in some very important ways from policy analysis of earlier decades. First and foremost, applied researchers have grown increasingly sensitive to statistical and measurement problems encountered in the course of examining empirical data. This is a welcome development and should continue in the future. Another contribution of recent research has come about because labor market analysts are increasingly interested in understanding the behavior and motivations of labor market actors. In so doing, they have recognized the unexpected and sometimes unwanted side-effects of well-intentioned policies, as in the case of possible wage responses to job or pension risks. Perhaps the work which most clearly enhanced our understanding of institutional behavior was in the discrimination area.

These strengths have unfortunately been viewed as weaknesses in recent years, however, by those who expect unambiguous answers from social science research as well as by those who prefer that project evaluation not be done at all. Clearly applied social science research cannot settle debates where philosophical issues rather than empirical magnitudes are at issue. On the other hand informed policy-makers cannot remain ignorant of how labor market entities respond to the regulatory and economic incentives if they are to spend resources wisely and regulate effectively.

Three directions of research are suggested as most useful in the upcoming decade. First, we need to know more about why regulatory policy comes into being—how research findings and other influences find their way into labor market regulation. Second, continuing attention must be devoted to ways in which regulation affects labor market outcomes. This decade may provide a valuable "natural experiment" in the case of the policies discussed above, since the current Administration appears to be altering substantially the direction and intensity of regulatory efforts. The third strategy very much worth pursuing would examine organizational responses to regulatory and other environmental shifts. In particular, more work needs to be done on how employers, unions, and other advocacy groups react to new regulatory policy and practice and, in turn, how legal and executive institutions adapt to changing organizational behavior.

The questions that remain to be answered are challenging. More complete and sophisticated answers are beginning to emerge. However, if this trend is to continue, more and better data are required than have been available in the past—particularly with respect to union, firm-level, and government behavior. It is hoped that recent cutbacks in federal support for data gathering and research programs will not retard this endeavor too seriously.

References

Ahart, Gregory J. "A Process Evaluation of the Contract Compliance Program in Nonconstruction Industry." *Industrial and Labor Relations Review* 29 (July 1976): pp. 565–71.

Andrews, Emily S., and Olivia S. Mitchell. "Evaluating a National Pension Plan Data Base." *Proceedings of the American Statistical Association Meetings* (Summer 1981).

Ashenfelter, Orley, and Robert S. Smith. "Compliance with the Minimum Wage Law." *Journal of Political Economy* 87 (April 1979): pp. 333–50.

Ashford, Nicholas A. *Crisis in the Workplace: Occupational Disease and Injury.* Cambridge, Mass.: MIT Press, 1976.

Bacow, Lawrence S. *Bargaining for Job Safety and Health.* Cambridge, Mass.: MIT Press, 1980.

Becker, Gary S. *The Economics of Discrimination.* Chicago: University of Chicago Press, 1957.

Beller, Andrea H. "The Effect of Economic Conditions on the Success of Equal Employment Opportunity Laws: An Application to the Sex Differential in Earnings." *Review of Economics and Statistics* 62 (August 1980): pp. 379–87.

Bodie, Zvi. "Purchasing Power Annuities: Financial Innovation for Stable Real Retirement Income in an Inflationary Environment." NBER Working Paper No. 442, February 1980.

Briggs, Vernon, and Felician F. Foltman, eds. *Apprenticeship Research.* Ithaca: New York State School of Industrial and Labor Relations, Cornell University, 1981.

Brown, Charles. "Black/White Earnings Ratios Since the Civil Rights Act of 1964: The Importance of Labor Market Dropouts." NBER Working Paper No. 617, 1981a.

———. "Estimating the Effects of a Youth Differential on Teenagers and Adults." In *Report of the Minimum Wage Study Commission,* Vol. V. Washington: U.S. Government Printing Office, 1981b.

———. "The Federal Attack on Labor Market Discrimination: The Mouse That Roared?" NBER Working Paper No. 669, May 1981c.

Brown, Charles, Curtis Gilroy, and Andrew I. Kohen. "Effects of the Minimum Wage on Youth Employment and Unemployment." Minimum Wage Study Commission Working Paper No. 1, May 1981 (revised).

Butler, Richard J. "Smaller Apples: Trends in Racial and Sexual Discrimination Among South Carolina School Teachers." Unpublished paper, New

York State School of Industrial and Labor Relations, Cornell University, July 1981.

Butler, Richard, and James J. Heckman. "The Government's Impact on the Labor Market Status of Black Americans: A Critical Review." NBER Working Paper No. 183, June 1977.

Carwell, Lucy A., and Mark R. Rosenzweig. "Economic Mobility, Monopsonistic Discrimination and Sex Differences in Wages." Yale University, March 1978.

Chown, Paul. "Workplace Health and Safety: A Guide to Collective Bargaining." Berkeley: Center for Labor Education, Institute of Industrial Relations, University of California, 1980.

Cain, Glen G. "The Challenge of Segmented Labor Market Theories to Orthodox Theory: A Survey." *Journal of Economic Literature* 14 (December 1976): pp. 1215-51.

Cooke, William N., and Frederick H. Gautschi III. "The Impact of OSHA Citations and Plan-Specific Safety Programs on Lost Days Due to Injuries." *Industrial Relations* (Fall 1981).

Cox, James, and Ronald L. Oaxaca. "Effect of Minimum Wage Policy on Inflation and Output Prices, Employment, and Real Wage Rates by Industry." In *Report of the Minimum Wage Study Commission*, Vol. VI. Washington: U.S. Government Printing Office, 1981.

Cummins, J. David, John Percival, Randolph Westerfield, and J. G. Ramage. "Effects of ERISA on the Investment Policies of Private Pension Plans: Survey Evidence." *Journal of Risk and Insurance* 46 (September 1979).

Cummins, J. David, John Percival, and Randolph Westerfield. "The Impact of ERISA on the Investment Policies of Private Pension Funds and Capital Market Efficiency." Final Report to the U.S. Department of Labor, July 1979.

Danziger, Sheldon, and Michael Weinstein. "Employment Location and Wage Rates of Poverty-Area Residents." *Journal of Urban Economics* 3 (April 1976): pp. 127–45.

Denison, Edward F. *Accounting for Slower Economic Growth: The U.S. in the 1970's.* Washington: Brookings Institution, 1979.

Doeringer, Peter, and Michael J. Piore. *Internal Labor Markets and Manpower Analysis.* Lexington, Mass.: D.C. Heath, 1971.

Ehrenberg, Ronald G., and Alan Marcus. "Minimum Wage Legislation and the Educational Outcomes of Youth." In *Research in Labor Economics*, ed. Ronald G. Ehrenberg. Greenwich, Conn.: JAI Press, 1981.

Feldstein, Martin. "Private Pensions and Inflation." *American Economic Review* 71 (May 1981): pp. 424–28.

Feldstein, Martin, and Stephanie Seligman. "Pension Funding, Share Prices and National Saving." NBER Working Paper No. 509, July 1980.

Flanagan, Robert J. "Actual Versus Potential Impact of Government Anti-Discrimination Programs." *Industrial and Labor Relations Review* 29 (July 1976): pp. 486–507.

Frank, Robert J. "Why Women Earn Less: The Theory and Estimation of Differential Overqualification." *American Economic Review* 68 (June 1978): pp. 360–73.

Freedman, Audrey. *Industry Response to Health Risk.* New York: The Conference Board, 1981.

Freeman, Richard B. "The Effects of Trade Unionism on Fringe Benefits." NBER Working Paper No. 292, October 1978.

———. "Changes in the Labor Market for Black Americans, 1948–72." *Brookings Papers on Economic Activity* 4 (1:1973).

Freeman, Richard, Wayne Gray, and Casey Ichniowski. "Low Cost Student Labor: The Use and Effects of the Subminimum Wage Provisions for Full-Time Students." NBER Working Paper No. 765, September 1981.

Gersovitz, Mark. "Economic Consequences of Unfunded Vested Pension Benefits." NBER Working Paper No. 480, May 1980.

Gilroy, Curtis. "A Demographic Profile of Minimum Wage Workers." Minimum Wage Study Commission Working Paper No. 4, September 1980 (revised).

Gold, Michael. "Some Thoughts on the Disparate Impact Definition of Employment Discrimination." Unpublished paper, New York State School of Industrial and Labor Relations, Cornell University, April 1981.

Goldfarb, Robert S. "The Policy Content of Quantitative Minimum Wage Research." *Proceedings of the 27th Annual Meeting, Industrial Relations Research Association, 1974.* Madison, Wis.: IRRA, 1975. Pp. 261–68.

Goldstein, Morris, and Robert S. Smith. "The Estimated Impact of the Anti-Discrimination Program Aimed at Federal Contractors." *Industrial and Labor Relations Review* 29 (July 1976): pp. 523–43.

Gramlich, Edward M. "Impact of Minimum Wages on Other Wages, Employment, and Family Incomes." *Brookings Papers on Economic Activity* 7 (2:1976).

Gray, Wayne. "The Impact of Government Regulation on Productivity." Unpublished paper, Harvard University, December 1981.

Greenough, William, and Francis King. *Pension Plans and Public Policy.* New York: Columbia University Press, 1976.

Gustman, Alan L., and Martin Segal. "Wages, Wage Supplements, and the Interaction of Union Bargains in the Construction Industry." *Industrial and Labor Relations Review* 25 (January 1972): pp. 179–85.

Haessel, Walter, and John Palmer. "Market Power and Employment Discrimination." *Journal of Human Resources* 13 (Fall 1978): pp. 545–60.

Hamermesh, Daniel S. "A General Empirical Model of Life-Cycle Effects in Consumption and Retirement Decisions." Unpublished paper, Michigan State University, June 1981a.

———. "Minimum Wages and the Demand for Labor." NBER Working Paper No. 656, April 1981b.

Hashimoto, Masanori, and Jacob Mincer. "Employment and Unemployment Effects of Minimum Wages." NBER Working Paper, April 1970.

Heckman, James J., and Kenneth I. Wolpin. "Does the Contract Compliance Program Work?" *Industrial and Labor Relations Review* 29 (July 1976): pp. 544–64.

Kain, John F. "Housing Segregation, Negro Employment and Metropolitan Decentralization." *Quarterly Journal of Economics* 82 (May 1968): pp. 175–97.

Kochan, Thomas A. *Collective Bargaining and Industrial Relations.* Homewood, Ill.: Richard D. Irwin, 1980.

Kochan, Thomas A., Lee Dyer, and David G. Lipsky. *The Effectiveness of Union-Management Safety and Health Committees.* Kalamazoo, Mich.: W. E. Upjohn Institute for Employment Research, September 1977.

Landes, William M. "The Economics of Fair Employment Laws." *Journal of Political Economy* 76 (July/August 1968): pp. 507–52.

Lazear, Edward. "Male/Female Wage Differentials: Has the Government Had Any Effect?" In *Women in the Labor Market,* eds. Cynthia Lloyd, Emily Andrews, and Curtis Gilroy. New York: Columbia University Press, 1979a.

———. "The Narrowing of Black/White Wage Differentials Is Illusory." *American Economy Review* 69 (September 1979b): pp. 353–64.

———. "Why Is There Mandatory Retirement?" *Journal of Political Economy* 87 (December 1979c): pp. 1261–84.

Lester, Richard. "Benefits as a Preferred Form of Compensation." *Southern Economic Journal* 33 (April 1967).

Levitan, Sar A., and Richard S. Belous. "The Minimum Wage Today: How Well Does It Work?" *Monthly Labor Review* 102 (July 1979): pp. 17–21.

Lindsay, Cotton Mather. *Equal Pay for Comparable Worth: An Economic Analysis of a New Antidiscrimination Doctrine.* An LEC Occasional Paper, Law and Economic Center, University of Miami, 1980.

Livernash, E. Robert. *Comparable Worth: Issues and Alternatives.* Washington: Equal Employment Advisory Council, 1980.

Logue, Dennis E. *Legislative Influence on Corporate Pension Plans.* Washington: American Enterprise Institute for Public Policy Research, 1979.

Loury, Glenn C. "Is Equal Opportunity Enough?" *American Economic Review* 71 (May 1981): pp. 122–26.

Lucas, Robert E. B. "Hedonic Price Functions." *Economic Inquiry* 13 (June 1975): pp. 157–78.

MacAvoy, Paul W. "The Nondecision Cotton Dust Decision." *The New York Times,* July 5, 1981.

Madden, Janice Fannery. *The Economics of Sex Discrimination.* Lexington, Mass.: D.C. Heath, 1973.

Marshall, Ray. "The Economics of Racial Discrimination: A Survey." *Journal of Economic Literature* 12 (September 1974): pp. 849–71.

Marston, Stephen T. "Employment Instability and High Unemployment Rates." *Brookings Papers on Economic Activity* 7 (1:1976).

Masters, Stanley, David Zimmerman, Karen Holden, James E. Jones, Jr., Richard Kaluzny, Susan Meives, and Craig Olson. "Potential for Planned Experimentation in the Department of Labor Regulatory Area." Institute for Research on Poverty Special Report 23. Madison: University of Wisconsin, undated.

Mendeloff, John. *Regulating Safety: An Economic and Political Analysis of Occupational Safety and Health Policy.* Cambridge, Mass.: MIT Press, 1979.

Milkovich, George T. "Pay Inequalities and Comparable Worth." *Proceedings of the 33rd Annual Meeting, Industrial Relations Research Association, 1980.* Madison, Wis.: IRRA, 1981.

Mincer, Jacob. "Unemployment Effects of Minimum Wages." *Journal of Political Economy* 84 (2:August 1976): pp. S87–104.

Mincer, Jacob, and Linda S. Leighton. "Effects of Minimum Wages in Human Capital Formation." NBER Working Paper No. 441, February 1980.

Mitchell, Olivia S. "Fringe Benefits and the Costs of Changing Jobs." Labor Economics Working Paper, Cornell University, 1980.

———. "Fringe Benefits and Labor Mobility." *Journal of Human Resources* 17 (Spring 1982): pp. 286–98.

Mitchell, Olivia S., and Emily S. Andrews. "Scale Economies in Private Multi-employer Pension Systems." *Industrial and Labor Relations Review* 34 (July 1981): pp. 522–30.

Moore, Thomas. "The Effect of Minimum Wages on Teenage Unemployment Rates." *Journal of Political Economy* 79 (July/August 1971): pp. 897–902.

Oaxaca, Ronald. "Sex Discrimination in Wages." In *Discrimination in Labor Markets,* eds. Orley Ashenfelter and Albert Rees. Princeton, N.J.: Princeton University Press, 1973.

Oi, Walter Y. "On the Economics of Industrial Safety." Working Paper No. 48, Industrial Relations Section, Princeton University, June 1974.

Osterman, Paul. "Affirmative Action and Opportunity: The Impact of the Federal Contract Compliance Program Upon the Turnover of Women Workers." Department of Economics Working Paper No. 70, Boston University, August 1981.

Parsons, Donald O. *Poverty and the Minimum Wage.* Washington: American Enterprise Institute for Public Policy Research, 1980.

Peterson, John, and Charles Stewart, Jr. *Employment Effects of Minimum Wage Rates.* Washington: American Enterprise Institute for Public Policy Research, 1969.

President's Commission on Pension Policy. *Coming of Age: Toward a National Retirement Income Policy.* Final Report. Washington: February 1981.

Ragan, James F., Jr. "Minimum Wages and the Youth Labor Market." *Review of Economics and Statistics* 59 (May 1977): pp. 129–36.

Report of the Minimum Wage Study Commission. Washington: U.S. Government Printing Office, 1981.

Rifkin, Jeremy, and Randy Barber. *The North Will Rise Again.* Boston: Beacon Press, 1978.

Rosen, Sherwin. "Hedonic Prices and Implicit Markets: Product Differentiation in Pure Competition." *Journal of Political Economy* 82 (January/February 1974): pp. 34–55.

———. "Valuing Health Risk." *American Economic Review* 71 (May 1981): pp. 241–45.

"Safety Agency to Forgo 'Cost-Benefit Analysis.'" *The New York Times,* July 13, 1981.

Savelson, Donald W., and Mark A. Wainger. "New Problems and Recent Developments in Occupational Safety and Health Law." *Proceedings of the New York University 31st Annual National Conference on Labor,* June 14–16, 1978.

Schiller, Bradley R., and Randall D. Weiss. "The Impact of Private Pensions on Firm Attachment." *Review of Economics and Statistics* 61 (August 1979): pp. 369–80.

———. "Pensions and Wages: A Test for Equalizing Differences." *Review of Economics and Statistics* 62 (November 1980): pp. 529–38.

Sellekaerts, Brigitte, and Stephen W. Welch. "Violations of the Fair Labor Standards Act: Inferences from the 1979 Noncompliance Survey." In *Report of the Minimum Wage Study Commission,* Vol. III. Washington: U.S. Government Printing Office, 1981.

Skolnik, Alfred M. "Pension Reform Legislation of 1974." *Social Security Bulletin* 37 (December 1974): pp. 35–41.

Smith, Arthur B., Jr. "The Law and Equal Employment Opportunity: What's Past Should Not Be Prologue." *Industrial and Labor Relations Review* 33 (July 1980): pp. 493–505.

Smith, James P., and Finis Welsh. "Black/White Wage Ratios: 1960–1970." *American Economic Review* 67 (June 1977): pp. 323–38.

———. "Race Differences in Earnings: Survey and New Evidence." Rand Report P5883, 1979.

Smith, Robert S. "The Feasibility of an 'Injury Tax' Approach to Occupational Safety." *Law and Contemporary Problems* 38 (Summer-Autumn 1974).

———. *The Occupational Safety and Health Act: Its Goals and Its Achievements.* Washington: American Enterprise Institute for Public Policy Research, 1976.

———. "Compensating Wage Differentials and Public Policy: A Review." *Industrial and Labor Relations Review* 32 (April 1979a): pp. 339–52.

———. "The Impact of OSHA Inspections on Manufacturing Injury Rates." *Journal of Human Resources* 14 (Spring 1979b): pp. 145–70.

———. "Pensions, Underfunding and Salaries in the Public Sector: Testing the Theory of Compensating Differentials." *Review of Economics and Statistics* 63 (August 1981): pp. 463–67.

Stigler, George J. "The Economics of Minimum Wage Legislation." *American Economic Review* 36 (June 1946): pp. 358–65.

Stiglitz, Joseph E. "Approaches to the Economics of Discrimination." *American Economic Review* 63 (May 1973): pp. 287–95.

Thaler, Richard, and Sherwin Rosen. "The Value of Saving a Life: Evidence from the Labor Market." Paper presented at the NBER Conference on Income and Wealth, Household Production and Consumption, Washington, November 1973.

Traynor, J. L., W. Priest, and P. Regan. *The Financial Reality of Pension Funding under ERISA*. Homewood, Ill.: Dow-Jones Irwin, 1976.

Ture, Norman, with Barbara A. Fields. *The Future of Private Pension Plans*. Washington: American Enterprise Institute for Public Policy Research, 1979.

Viscusi, W. Kip. "Job Hazards and Worker Quit Rates: An Analysis of Adaptive Worker Behavior." *International Economic Review* 20 (February 1979): pp. 29–58.

Wachter, Michael, and S. Kim. "Time Series Changes in Youth Joblessness." NBER Working Paper No. 384, August 1979.

Wallace, Phyllis A., ed. *Equal Employment Opportunity and the AT&T Case*. Cambridge, Mass.: MIT Press, 1976.

Wallace, Phyllis A., and James W. Driscoll. "Social Issues in Collective Bargaining 1950–80: A Critical Assessment." Sloan School of Management Working Paper 1203-81, MIT, April 1981.

Webb, Sydney. "The Economic Theory of a Legal Minimum Wage." *Journal of Political Economy* 20 (December 1912).

Welch, Finis. "Black/White Differences in Returns to Schooling." *American Economic Review* 63 (December 1973): pp. 893–907.

———. *Minimum Wages: Issues and Evidence*. Washington: American Enterprise Institute for Public Policy Research, 1978.

Welch, Stephen W. "FLSA Coverage, Exemptions and Violations: Some Institutional Considerations." In *Report of the Minimum Wage Study Commission*, Vol. III. Washington: U.S. Government Printing Office, 1981.

West, E. G., and Michael McKee. "Monopsony and 'Shock' Arguments for Minimum Wages." *Southern Economic Journal* 46 (January 1980): pp. 883–91.

Williams, Harold W. "A Job for Congress." *The New York Times*, July 16, 1981.

Wood, Michael. "An Assessment of Three Years of OSHA: Labor View." *Proceedings of the 27th Annual Meeting, Industrial Relations Research Association*, 1974. Madison, Wis.: IRRA, 1975. Pp. 43–51.

Zucker, Albert. "Minimum Wages and the Demand for Low-Wage Labor." *Quarterly Journal of Economics* 87 (May 1973): pp. 267–77.

CHAPTER 5

Personnel/Human Resource Management Research

LEE DYER
Cornell University

DONALD P. SCHWAB
University of Wisconsin-Madison

The purpose of personnel/human resource management (HRM) is to shape such significant organizational outcomes as employee performance, length of service (tenure), attendance, and satisfaction. These outcomes are influenced most directly by characteristics of individuals interacting with characteristics of jobs. Functional activities such as external staffing, internal staffing, employee development, and compensation are used to affect the characteristics of individuals and jobs and, thus, the various outcomes. Other HRM activities, such as job analysis, performance appraisal, and personnel planning serve largely to support the functional activities. Of course, HRM does not take place in a vacuum; the various components of the model as well as the interactions among them are influenced by several external factors, including laws and regulations, labor unions, and labor markets.

In reviewing a field as diverse as human resource management, choices must be made. One concerns subject matter. Here we limited ourselves to four prominent substantive themes of the 1970s. Two are fundamentally scientific and recurrent throughout the social sciences, namely, the measurement of, and relationships among, the major constructs of the field. To reflect the content of the literature, we focused on four such constructs, all outcomes as shown in Figure 1: satisfaction, which is attitudinal, and performance, turnover, and absenteeism, all behavioral.

More applied, perhaps, is the third substantive theme—the

FIGURE 1
A Model of Personnel/Human Resource Management

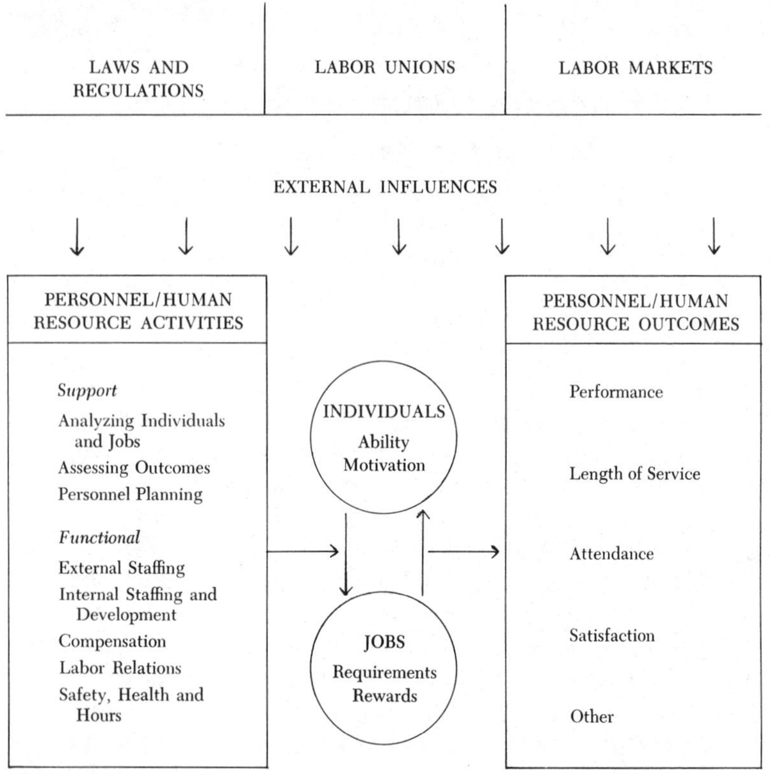

Adapted from H. G. Heneman III, D. P. Schwab, J. A. Fossum, and L. Dyer, *Personnel/Human Resource Management* (Homewood, Ill.: Richard D. Irwin, Inc., 1980).

effects of functional HRM activities on various outcomes, especially the four noted above. Several such activities received attention during the 1970s, including recruiting (for example, Reilly, Tenopyr, and Sperling 1979), selection procedures (for example, Schmidt, Hunter, McKenzie, and Muldrow 1979), employee feedback (for example, Ilgen, Fisher, and Taylor 1979), and such motivational techniques as goal-setting, job enrichment, and participative decision-making (for example, Locke, Feren, McCaleb, Shaw, and Denny 1980). Since space limitations precluded a complete review, we chose one activity, pay, for comprehensive treatment. Pay was picked because it is a pervasive and potentially powerful human resource management activity whose significance has consistently been underestimated, if not denigrated, in the social science and business literature. Moreover, there is no current review of this literature (the most recent being Heneman and Schwab 1975).

HRM decision-making about employees constitutes the fourth substantive theme. This choice was motivated by two considerations. First, the literature is voluminous. Second, while there are reviews of decision-making in specific activity areas—selection, for example (see Arvey 1979, Schmitt 1976)—no one has yet attempted to integrate the decision-making literature across the full spectrum of HRM activities.

With the subject matter in hand, a second choice involved the nature of the literature to be reviewed. Personal preference and inclination led us toward the research literature; thus, in this review reference is made to conceptual articles and books only where the contributions seemed particularly noteworthy. A third choice involved sources, and here we opted to review systematically six of the major research-oriented journals in the field: *Academy of Management Journal, Industrial Relations, Industrial and Labor Relations Review, Journal of Applied Psychology, Organizational Behavior and Human Performance,* and *Personnel Psychology.* Although this decision obviously excluded some worthy contributions, we feel that much, if not most, of the best research was covered.

Our methodology was straightforward. Independently, we scanned the six journals noted to (1) select those studies which fell within the purview of the review, and (2) determine in which of the four substantive areas each relevant article belonged.[1] Upon completion of this task for each year (1970 to 1979), we compared our selections and categorizations and resolved any differences. Generally the rate of agreement on both scores was well over 90 percent, and the disagreements were easily resolved. This

[1] The authors wish to thank Martha Garcia, Mark Rosen, and Paul Biesiadecki for their research assistance and, for their financial support, the Research Fund of the New York State School of Industrial and Labor Relations, Cornell University, and the Graduate School of the University of Wisconsin-Madison.

procedure resulted in the identification of 279 studies for inclusion. Detailed analysis of these studies was then performed, and the results formed the basis for this review.[2]

Measuring Human Resource Management Outcomes

We found 84 articles pertaining to the measurement of human resource outcomes in the journals reviewed. Performance measurement received the most attention (56 studies) with satisfaction running a distant second (24). Turnover (1) and absenteeism (3) were also-rans.

Satisfaction

The 1960s witnessed substantial interest and some progress in satisfaction measurement research. Two methodologies based on discontinuous theories of human needs were developed and widely implemented: Herzberg's (1966) story-telling method and Porter's (1961) *Need Satisfaction Questionnaire* (NSQ), which was motivated by Maslow's (1954) need hierarchy. In addition, two carefully validated measures, designed to assess the dimensionality of satisfaction, were also published: Smith, Kendall, and Hulin's (1966) *Job Descriptive Index* (JDI) and Weiss, Dawis, England, and Lofquist's (1967) *Minnesota Satisfaction Questionnaire* (MSQ). Extensive psychometric data were provided for both. Finally, Locke (1969) capped off the decade with a solid theoretical paper that raised a number of issues with direct implications for satisfaction measurement.

Given this activity level, it was perhaps necessary for the area to lie fallow for a time, which is indeed what happened during the 1970s. For the most part, efforts during this decade were characterized by mopping up issues raised in the previous 10 years.

Chief among these was research performed on the NSQ. Eight studies were found that addressed the psychometric properties of that instrument. Since NSQ research has been reviewed in depth elsewhere (Schwab 1980), only the conclusion bears repeating, ". . . the NSQ fails to measure the need hierarchy as intended . . ." (p. 29). Unfortunately, the NSQ was used in a great deal of sub-

[2] In the chapter are cited only those sources which for one reason or another we wish to highlight. A complete list of references can be obtained from either author.

stantive research before its psychometric deficiencies were revealed.

Several other residual issues attracted some attention during the early part of the seventies. Among these were three studies that investigated the value of weighting satisfaction responses by the perceived importance of the work dimensions of interest. The results supported earlier findings that such weighting does not improve the measurement of satisfaction. Herzberg's typology also stimulated an occasional measurement-oriented investigation, but by the mid-1970s his two-factor conceptualization of satisfaction had generally lost scholarly favor.

There was relatively little research on new measures of satisfaction. This quiescence can undoubtedly be traced in part to the authors of the JDI and MSQ. Both groups engaged in extensive studies of scale construction and evaluation prior to publication. By example, they no doubt discouraged one-shot, ad hoc measurement efforts.

At the same time, we were surprised to find that the JDI and MSQ themselves have not been subject to much measurement-oriented research. Only three studies were found on the JDI and none on the MSQ, per se. Two studies compared the two instruments. Interestingly, the maximum shared variance (convergence) on any of the four scales common to both instruments was only 38 percent in one study (Dunham, Smith, and Blackburn 1977), and only 49 percent in the other (Gillet and Schwab 1975). Thus, though they are obviously carefully constructed, they do not appear to measure the same things. Substantive satisfaction research including both measures could be helpful in sorting out the common, as well as the unique, variance in these instruments.

Performance

Performance measures range from purely "objective" procedures that tally, often mechanically, quantity and quality of output to more "subjective" procedures in which someone, typically a supervisor, makes judgments about employees' attributes, behaviors, or results. The latter measures, typically referred to as performance appraisal, received the research attention during the 1970s.

As researchers and practitioners know, performance appraisal is a complex and problematical process. A fundamental objective is validity; that is, appraisals that accurately reflect employees' true performance. While difficult to access directly, there is considerable evidence showing that the performance appraisal process is subject to unreliability and systematic error, both illustrative of invalid assessments.

During the 1970s investigators used two broad strategies in attempting to account for the lack of validity in performance appraisals. One approach assumed that invalid appraisal variance is largely attributable to the design of the instrument itself. This approach has a long, if not noble, history among psychometrically oriented HRM researchers. The second was broader in scope and made fewer a priori assumptions about the probable sources of appraisal error, focusing rather on a number of situational variables that transcend instrumentation alone.

Instrumentation Research. In the 1950s and 1960s instrumentation-oriented performance appraisal research frequently focused on forced-choice procedures, typically with little success. Only two such studies were found in our review, and both were published at the beginning of the decade. More recently, Blanz and Ghisselli (1972) described and recommended the mixed-standards scale (MSS) which, like forced-choice, relies on the juxtaposition of items within the instrument to alleviate common appraisal errors. The MSS failed to titillate but a handful of the psychometrically inclined, a fact that is probably less attributable to the nature of the MSS than to the allure of yet another approach to instrumentation: behaviorally anchored rating scales (BARS).

Rather than obscure item identification and meaning, as the forced-choice and MSS procedures do, the BARS procedure welcomes—and indeed requires—rater participation in the instrument development. Many psychometric virtues are hypothesized to result from this participative approach. Briefly, since development begins with a representative set of critical incidents, that are then carefully dimensionalized, BARS supposedly represents the performance domain of the job(s) involved in a valid fashion. At the same time, the developmental procedures allegedly aid in understanding and agreement on items in the final instrument, thus enabling raters to evaluate with less unreliability and systematic error and with a greater degree of validity.

Thirty-one empirical studies (more than half of all the performance-measurement studies reviewed) were published on BARS during the 1970s. In most, investigators varied developmental or appraisal procedures and compared the psychometric results (for example, leniency error) obtained with BARS against those obtained with alternative performance appraisal measure(s).

A review of this research in the mid-1970s concluded that "... there is little reason to believe that BARS are superior to alternative evaluation instruments" (Schwab, Heneman, and DeCotiis 1975, p. 557). The evidence generated since does not suggest the need to modify that conclusion. Thus, it is hoped that research in the 1980s will shift from an excessive preoccupation with instrumentation to focus on other, potentially more fruitful aspects of the appraisal process.

Other Aspects of the Appraisal Process. In comparison with instrumentation, other aspects of the performance appraisal process received limited attention during the 1970s. Two issues attracting some research were the positions occupied by raters and the amount or type of training they receive.

Three studies treated the job level of raters as an independent variable, and five more compared others' ratings against self-reports of performance. The most dramatic finding emerging from these studies was a consistently low degree of convergence between evaluations generated by raters in different positions. To cite one example, Heneman (1974) observed correlations between superior and self ratings ranging between .02 and .39. Unfortunately, results such as these provide little information concerning the reasons for the variance unique to each source. Some undoubtedly is attributable to random error which apparently is present under the best of conditions (Borman 1978). Other unique variance may be due to differences in the ability or motivation of raters to provide valid ratings.

Can training be used to increase the ability, or perhaps even the motivation, to rate accurately? We found seven studies tangentially related to this issue (some are reviewed in Spool 1978). Most attempted to use training to eliminate rating errors such as leniency and central tendency, and most of these were successful. What is not clear, however, is whether these efforts actually resulted in more valid performance appraisals.

Summary. As far as performance appraisal is concerned, we are left at the end of the 1970s with little positive to report. Research convincingly showed that instrumentation has minimal impacts on psychometric errors, but that conclusion was pretty well established before.

The truly important psychometric issue to emerge during the 1970s received little attention. Specifically, judicial decisions involving equal employment opportunity called for job-related personnel decisions. For example, in *Moody* v. *Albemarle*[3] the Supreme Court held that unless supervisory appraisals were founded in job requirements, they could not serve as a defensible criterion for such HRM decisions as promotions and layoffs.

BARS would appear to satisfy this judicial mandate since the performance dimensions are specified on a job-by-job basis. However, given the inordinate cost of developing such instruments for each job and the absence of other than legal justification for the expense, efforts to identify acceptably homogeneous jobs for purposes of performance appraisal are clearly called for. Unfortunately, only one study directed toward this purpose was uncovered in our review (Cornelius, Hakel, and Sackett 1979).

Of continuing concern is accounting for the unexplained variance in performance appraisal results. As noted, studies during the 1970s established that some of the unreliability was due to the position of the evaluator. Remaining to be explained are the reasons for these differences, and whether they can be overcome, for example, through rater training. We believe that additional research should be aimed at examining sources of invalid appraisals other than instrumentation. In this research it should be kept in mind that the ultimate objective is not to identify, and ultimately ameliorate, appraisal errors per se, but rather to identify, and ultimately bring to pass, those conditions contributing to the attainment of valid performance appraisal results.

Turnover and Absenteeism

We have combined our review of the measurement research on turnover and absenteeism, not because they lack the significance to stand alone, but because of the previously mentioned paucity of research. In one sense, both constructs are similar, and

[3] 422 U.S. 405, 10 FEP Cases 1181 (1975).

simple, since they represent dichotomies. The simplicity, however, is deceptive and measurement issues plague the operationalization of the two constructs.

A frequent difficulty in measuring turnover is to distinguish reliably between various reasons for leaving. Indeed, Price (1977) argued that making the distinction between voluntary (employee initiated) and involuntary (employer initiated) turnover is the single most difficult measurement task facing researchers in this area. One study (Hinrichs 1975) attempted to examine the reliability of the reasons for departure given by former employees as a function of measurement procedure (company exit interview, follow-up questionnaire, and exit interview by external consultant) and time (unfortunately, perfectly confounding the two). As with an earlier study (Lefkowitz and Katz 1969), this study showed low convergence across methods/time, strongly suggesting that the turnover measures conventionally employed in substantive investigations contain significant amounts of error. Until the sources of this error are identified and the causes alleviated, the findings of the substantive research must be called into question.

Evidence on absenteeism was generated which suggested that alternative methods for assessing the construct had remarkably low convergence. This is especially problematical when most substantive studies failed to report the measurement method employed (Muchinsky 1977). Also problematical were findings suggesting that various absenteeism measures are not stable over time. Employees who are absent in one time period are not the same ones who are absent in other time periods. The entire logic of individual prediction models is called into question if this measured instability reflects the true state of affairs.

Summary

In a significant sense, research on the measurement of behavioral outcomes (performance, turnover, and absenteeism) is hampered since in practice organizations frequently have existing measurement methods that researchers must adopt and adapt to their purposes. This presents obvious problems when attempting to design and execute research that is aimed at assessing and improving measurement.

The problem is exacerbated by the fact that each organization typically has its own unique measurement method(s). Standardization, as has occurred in satisfaction instrumentation, is difficult to achieve. While such standardization may not be appropriate in performance measurement (due to the uniqueness of jobs), it would clearly be advantageous in measuring absenteeism and turnover. Toward that end, the Bureau of National Affairs (BNA) has started to report organizational data on both variables (Miner 1977). Unfortunately, both measures were chosen because of the frequency of their use, and not their probable validity.

Efforts such as BNA's could be helped if researchers attuned to measurement issues devoted more energy to developing valid measures of turnover and absenteeism. Indeed, we recommend that more attention be given to the measurement of these constructs in the future, with a corresponding deemphasis on performance appraisal instrumentation research.

Relationship Among Human Resource Management Outcomes

Along with several conceptual pieces, our review uncovered 51 research articles on relationships among human resource outcomes: 25 focused on satisfaction-performance linkages, 18 on satisfaction and turnover, 11 on satisfaction and absenteeism, three on performance and turnover, two on performance and absenteeism, and six on turnover and absenteeism. (The figures add to more than 51 since some articles addressed more than one relationship.)

Satisfaction and Performance

To what extent are satisfaction and performance related? Is the relationship causal? And if so, in which direction does the causal arrow run? As Schwab and Cummings (1970) pointed out early in the decade, these questions have a long and venerable history in HRM research, a history to which the 1970s contributed much heat, but only a small amount of light.

Theoretically, the simplified notion that satisfied employees are more productive employees was laid to rest, although a number of authors took pains to point out that under certain (and quite complex) conditions it is at least reasonable to expect variations in satisfaction to cause variations in performance motivation and, subsequently, performance (Locke 1976, as an example). Gaining in popularity, however, was the notion that it is more likely to expect that performance is the cause and, again under certain (reward) conditions, satisfaction is the effect (Locke 1976, Schwab and Cummings 1970). Still another view, put forth by Mahoney (1979), incorporated both of the earlier stated positions, postulating that the causal arrow in fact runs in both directions. And, finally, there are those who argue in favor of treating satisfaction and performance as two separate outcomes, expecting correlational, let alone causal, relationships between them only under very special circumstances (Locke 1976, Schwab and Cummings 1970).

It would be pleasurable to report that this theoretical diversity generated a flood of germane, carefully conducted research designed to test the various views. Alas! Nonetheless, a few researchers did address the causality issue, while many more searched for significant moderators of the satisfaction-performance relationship.

The Causal Research. Included here are longitudinal studies using (primarily) cross-lagged correlational techniques (and hence not truly causal), as well as the true experiments. We found 10 such studies, four of which can be interpreted as supporting the satisfaction-leads-to-performance view (Greenhaus and Rodin 1974 as an example), four the performance-leads-to-satisfaction view (example—Leonard and Weitz 1971) and three neither view (example—Sheridan and Slocum 1975). This, sad to say, represents the state of the research that can arguably be described as causal.

The Correlational Research. Fifteen cross-sectional studies were found that examined the moderating effects of various variables on satisfaction-performance relationships. In general, these studies support the view that some organizational and individual factors do in fact significantly moderate the relationships between some facets of satisfaction and some measures of performance (for example, Jacobs and Soloman 1977, Inkson 1978). Correlations in the 40s and 50s, and occasionally even higher, have been reported. Unfortunately, however, little more can be said. In the 15 studies, fully 12 different moderators were examined, and in all cases the theoretical justification for the moderators chosen was unclear. Thus, it is difficult to know what the results mean.

In short, few empirical insights were added during the 1970s to the causal questions involved with performance and satisfaction. For the moment, the four different hypotheses concerning the relationship between satisfaction and performance still await adequate empirical tests.

Satisfaction and Turnover

In theory, dissatisfaction causes turnover because it is an aversive emotion (Locke 1976) that stimulates a desire to leave the offending situation. And, in fact, virtually all reviewers from Brayfield and Crockett (1955) to Locke (1976) and Mitchell (1979) have found a consistent, if modest, negative relationship between satisfaction and turnover. We did also.

That the observed relationship is modest comes as no surprise. An aversion to the job may not lead to departure because (1) it might be dealt with in other ways (for example, rationalization, psychological withdrawal, toleration), (2) there may be no reasonable employment alternatives, and (3) an employee may be pulled rather than pushed from a job (Locke 1976). All three explanations are incorporated in a comprehensive model of the turnover process put forth late in the decade by Mobley, Griffeth, Hand, and Meglino (1979).

Turnover research in the 1980s could increase understanding by systematically testing the Mobley model. In this context, Locke (1976) has recommended in-depth case studies of individual decision-making with particular emphasis on the off-quadrant cases (for example, dissatisfied employees who do not leave). Another possible approach is to use expectancy theory to construct a model incorporating both the force to stay and the force to leave (Parker and Dyer 1976).

Satisfaction and Absenteeism

In general, research into the satisfaction-absenteeism relationship has paralleled research into the satisfaction-turnover relationship in concept, methods, and assumptions. With respect to results, however, the situation is less clear. Some reviewers (Porter and Steers 1973, for example) have concluded that satisfaction predicts absenteeism and turnover about equally, while others (for example, Nicholson, Brown, and Chadwick-Jones 1976) argue that the former relationship has been found to be less consistent, weaker, and more tenuous.

Our own review supports the latter view. We uncovered six studies offering unambiguous interpretations. These studies involved 38 correlations between various measures of satisfaction and absenteeism. Of these, only 12 were negative and significant; the median correlation was .12. Further, of 240 correlations reported by Nicholson et al. (1976), only 22 were negative and significant; seven were positive and significant, and 211 were nonsignificant.

In 1978, Steers and Rhodes developed a process model of absenteeism and conducted an extensive review of the relevant research. Implicitly at least the model distinguishes between voluntary and involuntary absenteeism and suggests that attendance motivation is a function of satisfaction and pressures to attend, and that actual attendance is a function of attendance motivation and the ability to attend. Steers and Rhodes suggest that the model is consistent with the research reviewed. But, in fact, no evidence is cited to support the view that satisfaction increases attendance motivation.

In our view, the satisfaction-attendance linkage is likely to be every bit as complex as the satisfaction-performance motivation linkage mentioned earlier. For example, while Ilgen and Hollenback (1977) found that pressure to attend increased the explained variance in absenteeism over and above that explained by satisfaction alone, together the two variables accounted for only about 7 percent of the variance in total absences. It is doubtful that ability to attend alone would explain the rest. Thus, while Steers and Rhodes (1978) have begun a useful discussion of the role of satisfaction in determining absenteeism, much remains to be done. Essentially, we agree with Nicholson et al. (1976) that ". . . further advances in our understanding of absences are only likely to accrue from research that is prepared to look at the behavior in greater depth . . . , over longer periods of time . . . , in relation to a wider range of independent variables . . . , and at more than a single level of analysis" (p. 735).

Performance and Turnover

Normative statements abound suggesting that organizations should strive to assure a negative relationship between performances and both voluntary and involuntary turnover. Only a few attempts have been made, however, to ascertain empirically the extent to which various organizations manage in this way, the conditions under which low performers choose to leave, are eased out, or are summarily dismissed, and the organizational implications of various policies and programs to control performance turnover.

In a Navy setting, LaRocco, Pugh, and Gunderson (1977) found performance to be unrelated to voluntary turnover (as measured by officer reenlistment), but negatively related to involuntary turnover (as measured by the Navy's decision to separate officers or to deny them the opportunity to reenlist). Further, Farris (1971) found that different variables operate in the turnover of high and low performers. While his list of 25 discriminators lacked a theory base, making the results difficult to interpret, the idea of identifying environments in which good performers are inclined to stay and poor performers to leave (and vice versa) is intuitively appealing. More work in this direction would appear to promise high potential payoff.

Another issue worthy of consideration is the possibility that turnover is not necessarily a negative factor from the standpoint of individual (or organizational) effectiveness. Dalton and Todor (1979) discussed the conceptual issues involved here, but thus far the issue has not been considered in empirical studies.

Performance and Absenteeism

While little research was performed in the performance-absenteeism linkages, Hackman and Lawler (1971) did find generally negative relationships in a large correlational study. While this is what one might expect, in a more intensive analysis Staw and Oldham (1978) found the opposite, and suggested that absenteeism may serve a maintenance function for those who otherwise might not be able to cope with their jobs. They concluded that absenteeism may not always be negative in its consequences, and put forth the possibility that programs designed to reduce absenteeism may actually yield negative organizational results.

Turnover and Absenteeism

Virtually all of the theorizing about the turnover-absenteeism relationship deals with the voluntary components of these variables. Three views are common (Lyons 1972, Porter and Steers 1973). One postulates a continuum of withdrawal behavior progressing from absenteeism to turnover. The second views absenteeism as an alternate form of withdrawal behavior, especially when other employment is not available. And the third suggests that the two constructs are qualitatively different. Note that the first two views suggest that turnover and absenteeism are withdrawal behaviors that should be related—positively in the first instance, negatively in the second—only among employees intending or at least wishing to withdraw. The third suggests no necessary relationship between the two constructs.

The empirical evidence tends to support the continuum, rather than the substitute, hypothesis. Acceptance should be provisional, however, since many nonsignificant correlations are found, and even when significant the correlations generally are of low magnitude. In all probability, for many employees the decision to stay or leave is essentially independent of the decision to attend or not attend work on any given day. Unfortunately, researchers have yet to get close enough to turnover and absenteeism decisions to test the independence hypothesis adequately. It is possible that these low correlations reflect nothing more than the measurement problems alluded to earlier.

Discussion

By far the greatest amount of research on dependent variable relationship has been devoted to possible attitudinal-behavior linkages, and more particularly to the satisfaction-performance relationship. During the decade, however, researchers continued to find no consistent causal or correlational relationship between satisfaction and performance. Satisfaction does seem to be fairly consistently, if weakly, related to (voluntary) turnover, but not to absenteeism.

The belief that performance and turnover should be negatively related is apparently so well accepted that researchers have not troubled themselves to study it. Thus we know very little about the conditions under which good performers stay, while poor performers (voluntarily and involuntarily) leave. Perhaps worse, we know very little about the individual or organizational consequences in situations where performance and turnover are entirely unrelated.

Similarly, the widespread belief that performance and absenteeism are negatively related has apparently stifled research as well. But here Staw and Oldham (1978) have challenged conventional wisdom, and we will likely see a spate of follow-up research in the next few years.

Widespread, too, is the tendency to treat turnover and absenteeism as related forms of withdrawal or escape behavior. While it is true that turnover and absenteeism tend to be positively related, and more strongly so when the turnover decision is imminent, the extent to which this indicates withdrawal or escape behavior is less clear. Certainly some who leave are pulled rather than pushed, but many who grab an occasional day off have no intention of quitting their jobs (indeed, following Staw and Oldham's [1978] logic, they may be doing it so that they can continue to face their jobs). Clearly, more intensive studies are needed that link the decision-making processes leading to turnover and absenteeism.

Although not always explicit, virtually all of the turnover and absenteeism theory and research reviewed here deals only with the voluntary component. Some consideration of the involuntary components would appear to be warranted, given their organizational significance.

The research on which we base these conclusions ranged in quality from excellent to awful. In general, there were too many cross-sectional studies and too few longitudinal studies and laboratory and, especially, field experiments. And intensive case studies, despite their obvious applicability (Locke 1976), continued to be eschewed. Further, theory rarely drove the research, and the choice of complementary independent and moderator variables appeared to be more a matter of convenience than a calculated attempt to build a cumulative body of knowledge. Further, the measurement problems noted in the previous section persisted.

Nevertheless, the latter part of the decade produced a number of interesting theoretical and conceptual developments (compare Locke 1976, Mahoney 1979, Mobley et al. 1979, Steers and Rhodes 1978, Staw and Oldham 1978). And the quality of the research began to improve. Thus, there is reason to hope that in the next few years advances will be made in untangling the complex nature of the relationships among the major outcomes of the HRM field.

Pay and Human Resource Management Outcomes

A major issue in human resource management is the extent to which activities such as recruitment, selection, internal staffing, training, job design, performance appraisal feedback, compensation, and hours of work affect various attitudinal and behavioral outcomes (Dyer 1980). Here, for reasons previously given, we focus on just one activity, pay, to review in depth. Correlational research was generally excluded to concentrate on laboratory and field experiments (or quasi-experiments) in which one or more aspects of pay was manipulated to examine the effects on one or more of the four major outcomes: satisfaction, performance, turnover, and absenteeism. In all, we found 38 such studies, most of them focused on pay and performance.

Satisfaction with Pay

Lawler (1971) and Dyer and Theriault (1976) have both proposed models of the determinants of pay satisfaction. While neither model has been tested in its entirety, both have received partial support. For example, both hypothesize that one determinant of pay satisfaction is the perceived amount of pay received. The latter, of course, is highly correlated with the actual pay level. Several survey studies and three laboratory experiments found that pay satisfaction is moderately related to amount of pay received. The models also suggest that the pay level–pay satisfaction relationship will be moderated by perceptions of the amount of pay that should be received. This hypothesis also received support in some of the equity theory research (for example, Pritchard, Dunnette, and Jorgenson 1972).

The Dyer and Theriault model also hypothesizes that pay satisfaction will be influenced by the perceived appropriateness of pay criteria. It is further hypothesized that managerial and professional employees prefer performance criteria (see Dyer, Schwab, and Theriault 1975), and that other types of employees prefer seniority (Lawler 1971). These hypotheses received some support from Pritchard, Leonard, and Von Bergen (1976) who found that students (aspiring managers and professionals?) were more satisfied with a fixed ratio incentive schedule than an hourly pay plan and from Schwab and Wallace (1974) who found blue-collar workers to be more satisfied with an hourly than a piece-rate plan (other factors equal). The hypothesis was not supported, however, among the students studied by Baird and Hamner (1979).

In general, research on pay satisfaction was added to studies whose primary purpose was the investigation of employee performance. Although findings were often consistent with satisfaction conceptualizations, the studies themselves were not theoretically oriented. As a consequence, relatively little was learned that might reasonably constitute a basis for theory testing or even development.

Performance

During the seventies, four motivational perspectives dominated the research relating pay with performance. Most prevalent and enduring were the reinforcement theories. The others were Adams's (1965) equity theory, Deci's (1975) cognitive evaluation (intrinsic motivation) theory, and Locke's (1968) goal-setting theory.

Under the rubric of reinforcement theory we include both expectancy theory and operant conditioning. Although quite different in underlying philosophies, the two theories yield the same prescription concerning pay: namely, pay motivates to the extent its receipt is made contingent upon desired behaviors. This principle, in turn, leads to two obvious research questions. First, do pay plans in which pay is contingent upon performance result in higher levels of performance than pay plans based on other factors (for example, time worked)? And second, under what types of reinforcement schedules are the greatest performance improvements attained?

We found four field studies and eight laboratory experiments that addressed the first question, and in all cases the results were supportive of reinforcement theory. Three of the four field studies involved the introduction of individual incentive plans among rather unique groups of employees: tree planters (Yukl and Latham 1975) and beaver trappers (Latham and Dossett 1978, Latham and Pursell 1976). All resulted in superior performance over prior levels or over control groups receiving hourly pay. The fourth field study involved the discontinuation of an incentive plan among a group of welders in an industrial setting (Rothe 1970) with a resulting (but temporary) decrease in productivity. All of the laboratory experiments showed the superiority of individual incentive pay plans over hourly schemes among college students working on simulated jobs.

Many of the same studies also examined the efficacy of various reinforcement schedules. In all cases continuous reinforcement schedules (in which every desired behavior is rewarded [for example, a piece-rate plan]) were compared with variable reinforcement schedules (in which only some of the desired behaviors are rewarded and the reward pattern varies around some fixed number set). The results were mixed, showing no clear-cut superiority for either approach.

A related issue concerns the relative effectiveness of individual and group incentive plans. Reinforcement theory, and some of the earlier research (Lawler 1971, as an example) suggests that the former are superior since they make a closer link between an individual's performance and his or her pay. Only two studies were found that made direct comparisons between the two types of plans; both found individual incentive plans to be superior.

Equity theory (Adams 1965) postulates that individuals who perceive themselves as under- or overpaid may alter their performance levels as one behavioral choice to restore equity. Equity theory was the subject of considerable research in the late 1960s, and we found four laboratory studies published during the 1970s. Three provided no support for the theory, and the fourth obtained mixed results. Perhaps these findings help explain why equity theory was dropped after 1972 as a basis for pay-performance research.

Deci (1975) postulated that so-called extrinsic rewards (pay, for example) in situations where individuals already have a high degree of so-called intrinsic motivation may lead to a reduction in overall motivation and, thus, performance. Some support for the hypothesis has been obtained when measures of motivation and task perseverance were used as dependent variables (Mitchell 1979), but the few laboratory studies using performance as a dependent variable have yielded mixed results. This line of inquiry, too, seems to have been dropped.

In his early work on goal-setting, Locke (1968) postulated that incentives, including pay, have their effects on performance through their influence on individual goals. Initial research (for example, Locke, Bryan, and Kendall 1968) supported this position, but several studies conducted during the seventies refute it, as Locke (Locke, Shaw, Saari, and Latham 1981) recently acknowledged. In these studies high goals led to higher levels of performance than "do best" or no goals irrespective of the pay plan used, and incentive pay led to higher levels of performance than hourly pay whether or not goals were set. No interaction effects were found. As Tolchinsky and King (1980) pointed out, however, these studies were not without their methodological problems. And, in another context, Locke et al. (1980) showed that incentive pay plans involving explicit goal-setting (so-called task and bonus plans) have resulted in even greater overall performance improvements (median = 40 percent) than traditional incentive plans (median = 35 percent). Thus, it would seem to be an open question at this point whether the motivational effects of goal-setting and contingent pay are independent, additive, or interactive.

In sum, an important feature of the research literature on pay and performance during the seventies was its dominance by scholars who were more interested in motivation theory than pay per se. Thus, while strides were made in sifting and winnowing among motivation theories (Campbell and Pritchard 1976), many important HRM issues remained unexamined, at least empirically. For example, most jobs in our society are not amenable to the adoption of true incentive pay plans because the outputs of the work cannot be objectively measured. Thus, merit pay plans in which performance appraisals are used to determine (typically) annual increases in pay are widely employed. The effectiveness of merit pay plans, particularly in periods of high inflation, has been questioned. Yet, during the 1970s no experimental studies of its effects on performance (or motivation) were published. Do, or can, merit pay plans show the same impressive performance improvements that Locke and his colleagues (Locke et al. 1980) found for incentive pay plans?

Research is also needed on whether pay interacts with other motivational systems and various work and social conditions to produce the performance results observed. Concerning motivational systems, some evidence (reviewed earlier) is accumulating concerning goal-setting, but there is little beyond speculation regarding participative decision-making, job enrichment, and other such programs (Dyer 1975, Lawler 1981). Research on the significance of other, more administrative issues has been virtually nonexistent. Many of these are amenable to laboratory research, but eventually a concern for external validity must lead researchers to the field and to longer term studies. Pay plans are changed constantly. It is time for investigators to avail themselves of these naturally occurring "experiments."

Turnover

The role of pay in determining employee turnover (or retention) has not captured the interest of personnel scholars. As part of a larger study, Goodman and Salipante (1976) reported that, among a group of formerly hard-core unemployed, starting wages had no effect on subsequent turnover. However, number of months to the first raise, size of first raise, and pay level at the end of three months all did. But this was about it.

Useful research on pay and turnover is extremely difficult to do. Satisfactory simulations in the laboratory are virtually impossible, as are pure field experiments. Nonetheless, there are naturally occurring quai-experimental situations where pay levels and pay systems are changed (sometimes to cut down on turnover) or exist in variable forms across roughly comparable groups. In either situation, fairly rigorous comparisons of employee attitudes and leaving behavior should be possible. Such research would have the potential to make a significant contribution to both the labor market and the compensation and turnover literatures.

Absenteeism

If pay can induce people to work hard, it also ought to induce them to come to work in the first place. So goes the logic underlying a number of studies in which reinforcement principles were employed in the design of pay systems to reduce absenteeism. In one (Pedalino and Gamboa 1974), the intervention resembled a poker game. It resulted in an 18.27 percent decrease in an already modest absentee rate. In another (Stephens and Burroughs 1978), it was a cash drawing among nurses and ward clerks in two hospitals and it, too, resulted in significant declines in absenteeism. A third (Scheflen, Lawler, and Hackman 1971) employed a more traditional incentive concept, but found similar results, among janitors.

Again, then, the motivational power of money has apparently been demonstrated. But many questions remain, not the least of which has to do with the conditions when these types of reinforcement programs, especially those involving card games and lotteries, can be successfully introduced and sustained. And what, if any, are their effects on other relevant outcomes such as satisfaction, performance, or turnover (Baum and Youngblood 1975)? Another interesting issue involves the relative effectiveness of these types of programs vis-à-vis more traditional approaches to absenteeism control.

Summary

During the 1970s, pay reemerged as an interesting (researchable) personnel activity. Comprehensive models of pay satisfaction were developed and partially tested. The motivational power of pay was reinforced using as outcomes both performance and absenteeism. (In fact, Locke et al. [1980] showed the motivational power of pay to be greater than that of several other, and perhaps more fashionable, motivational techniques, including goal-setting, job enrichment, and participative management.) Expectancy and operant conditioning theories were generally supported (although the explanatory power of the former was shown to be low [Schwab, Olian, and Heneman 1979]) while equity theory and cognitive evaluation (intrinsic motivation) theories were not. The role of pay in the turnover decision was little studied, perhaps because of the practical difficulties of carrying out such research.

In general, the experimental research on pay was well formulated and designed. It was, however, conducted mostly by researchers whose primary interest was in motivation theory rather than pay per se, and thus showed a far greater concern with internal than external validity. It is hoped that in the decade ahead researchers will build on these efforts and begin to tackle the many administrative issues involved in the installation and perpetuation of various types of pay plans.

HRM Decision-Making

Human resource management activities are largely implemented through managers' decisions. Job applicants, for example, are typically made offers by managers who have made clinical interpretations of interview, biographical, and other data. Salary-increase decisions generally follow a subjective review of performance through appraisal or other less formal methods. HRM policies and procedures serve as guidelines, to be sure, but managerial judgment is a major determinant of how the organization actually affects individual employees.

During the 1970s a number of investigators began to focus on managerial decisions affecting employees. Our review uncovered 106 such studies. By far the largest group, 67, were cast in a selection context. Another 29 involved ratings of current employees. Some of the latter focused on promotion decisions, while others examined various aspects of performance appraisals. Fifteen studies addressed compensation decisions. Other decisions studied one or more times were employee discipline, grievances, and retirement. (The subtotals add to more than 106 because multiple decisions were considered in some studies.)

Selection

The emphasis on selection decision-making appears to have been stimulated by two specific events. One was Mayfield's (1964) influential review of the selection interview research in the mid-1960s. He showed that such interviews typically lacked reliability and validity and argued that improvements were likely only if investigators disaggregated the process to determine variables that influence interviewer decision-making. The second event, also occurring in 1964, was passage of Title VII of the Civil Rights Act. Its prohibition of discrimination in employment based on race, color, national origin, religion, and sex stimulated researchers to consider the possibility that those "protected" attributes of employees or prospective employees affect managerial judgments in HRM decision-making.

Interviewing Process. In the early 1970s researchers were primarily interested in understanding the interviewing process as Mayfield recommended. By way of illustration, contrast effects (that is, the extent to which an interviewer's evaluation of an interviewee depends on the qualifications of others considered at about the same time) was the subject of six studies. Five others examined the effect of the location of positive and negative information within a job applicant's resume.

These and other studies investigating the interviewing process were reviewed by Schmitt (1976). On balance, his review clearly showed that a variety of factors other than applicants' qualifications influence interviewer judgments of employability. Unfortunately, these potential sources of error generally showed no consistent pattern. Across studies, for example, contrast effects accounted for as little as 2 percent, and as much as 67 percent, of the variance in interviewer evaluations.

EEO Characteristics. Following a detailed review of the studies examining the effects of applicant sex on hiring decisions, Arvey (1979) concluded that, other things equal, resumes from females tended to receive lower evaluations than those from males. In a somewhat more inclusive review, Schwab and Olian (1981) found ten experimental investigations favoring males, nine showing no differences, and two favoring females. Both reviews noted that only a small amount of evaluation variance was typically attributable to sex even when the effect was statistically significant.

In our review, we found only five investigations of the effect of race on selection judgments. None reported evidence suggesting that minorities are evaluated less favorably than majority candidates. No published research was found investigating whether color, national origin, or religion (the other attributes covered by Title VII) influence selection judgments.

Even though the substantive emphasis of the interviewing and EEO research differed, similar methodologies were employed. Almost without exception, the studies used experimental designs. Characteristics of hypothetical applicants and/or other features of the selection context were varied, with treatment levels being randomly assigned to subjects (decision-makers). In 39 of the studies, subjects were either practitioners (for example, college recruiters enlisted to participate) or a mixture of practitioners and college students. In 28 studies they were exclusively college students.

In almost all cases, subjects were asked to provide their evaluations by making an employment-suitability rating of the stimulus candidate(s). The data, in turn, were usually provided through written resumes rather than in the form of actual job applicants. Exceptions are the more recent studies focusing on the effect of nonverbal communication where role-playing has been used (for example, Imada and Hakel 1977, Sterrett 1978).

Overwhelmingly, researchers have examined the main and interaction effects of applicant, decision-maker, and/or situation using between-group designs. Consequently, the studies have generally determined, at most, whether various characteristics influence average evaluations of decision-makers, and not how decision-makers utilize the information to make employment judgments.

A few studies, however, assessed the decision-making process using within-subject policy-capturing methodologies (see, for example, Roose and Doherty 1976). Such investigations presented subjects with a set of hypothetical job applicants varying on several attributes (personal characteristics). The subjects' task was to provide an overall suitability rating of each alternative. The subjects' judgmental policy was modeled using multiple regression or analysis of variance (ANOVA) techniques by assessing the amount of variance in the overall rating that was attributable to various applicant attributes.

While the number of policy-capturing studies is too small for confident generalizing, all provide evidence of substantial individual differences in decision-making. In particular, they suggest systematic judgmental differences in the importance of different attributes in making overall evaluations. To a lesser extent, they also suggest differences in the way evaluators combine information (for example, linearly or configurally) in making selection decisions.

Employee Evaluations

Much of the research on decisions regarding current employee behavior (performance appraisal) and predicted future behavior (promotions) during the 1970s was, once again, stimulated by Title VII of the Civil Rights Act of 1964. Most frequently studied was the effect of sex (of rater and/or ratee) on appraisal and promotion decisions. Nine such studies were found. In general, the methodologies employed, and the findings, were similar to those already noted in the context of selection decision-making.

An interest in policy-capturing also stimulated some research on appraisal and promotion decisions. Zedeck and Kafry (1977), for example, used policy-capturing to assess rating decisions and then went on to cluster raters by apparent decision model usage. Ogilvie and Schmitt (1979) explored both linear and configural model usage. At least two studies (Taylor 1975, Zedeck and Kafry 1977) found that subjects' self-reported decision models were inconsistent with models inferred from policy-capturing.

Several studies investigated promotion decisions in an assessment center context. A frequent finding was that overall promotability ratings could be "predicted" with just a few of the many measures usually used in an assessment center (Sackett and Hakel 1979, Schmitt 1977). A similar finding was also observed by Taylor and Wilsted (1976) who studied Air Force cadets. Finally, four studies (most recently, Muldrow and Bayton 1979) investigated a variety of process issues (for example, information retention) involved in making promotion decisions.

Compensation

Research on managerial compensation decisions received substantial attention during the 1970s. Seven such studies were performed in a selection context, and another two were attached to appraisal studies. In all of these cases, the pay decision was simply added to the other decisions as an additional dependent variable.

Another six studies were found that focused primarily on compensation decisions. These were about evenly divided between those studying the personal characteristics of the pay allocatee (handicapped status, equity of past rewards, and strength of demand for an increase) and allocator (sex, authoritarianism, equity of rewards, and magnitude of rewards). Generally all found support for the hypothesized effects.

Discussion

The substantial amount of research attention given to human resource management decision-making is justified in our view. Prior emphasis on HRM technologies has not only been of limited value (as is perhaps overly well illustrated by our review of the performance appraisal measurement research), but suggests an erroneously mechanized view of actual practice. Investigations of decision-making processes can potentially do much to shed light on the "real world" of HRM.

Unfortunately, the research conducted during the 1970s, although voluminous, made only limited progress. We believe future efforts might be made more productive by attending to three issues. First, HRM decision-making research needs to be more concerned with substantive theory. The relatively few studies on compensation decisions have found a large number of variance sources in allocatees, allocators, and the environment. Continuation of atheoretical searches for significant variance sources could easily go on forever. Much more valuable, however, would be conceptual efforts to specify important variance sources and the nature of their probable interrelationships before undertaking additional empirical research.

Second, in both conceptual and empirical efforts, greater emphasis should be placed on external validity. Taking interviewing research as the illustration, it is questionable whether the findings obtained to date generalize to practice. While there are reasons to assume that student subjects may serve as suitable proxies for organizational recruiters (Bernstein, Hakel, and Harlan 1975), the use of hypothetical and especially "paper" applicants (see, for example, Gorman, Clover, and Doherty 1978), and the use of suitability ratings rather than the choice/rejection of applicants as the dependent variable are both questionable in terms of external validity.

Finally, researchers interested in HRM decisions need to attend more carefully to the literature from the decision sciences (for a recent partial review, see Einhorn and Hogarth [1981]). As noted, most such researchers have focused on decision results and have simply identified the collective effects on these of various manipulated characteristics. Although of some interest, such investigations do not provide information about individual differences in decision-makers or about the way these decision-makers combine information in making judgments. As our review has shown, a few researchers have begun to adopt policy-capturing methodologies to study these issues, and we feel this pattern should continue. Further, it is time to go beyond studies of decision results to examine the decision-making process itself. Illustrative issues of interest include the ways that decision-makers search for alternatives, as well as the ways they search for and ultimately evaluate the attributes of the alternatives considered. From such studies should come the understanding needed to improve the quality of human resource management decisions that are so vital to both organizational and individual success.

Conclusions

Among the substantive issues we chose to review, it was the theoretically based, experimental research that most often moved the field along. For example, experimental studies of motivation theories clearly established the positive power of contingently based pay programs on employee performance and absenteeism. While one can properly note that this represents no more than substantiation of a hypothesis formulated at least eight decades ago, the research was sufficiently well designed to facilitate sorting among competing motivational theories, while lending confidence to the substantive results. Further, some of the BARS and managerial decision-making research was methodologically sound, although the absence of conceptual grounding meant that the results tended to be noncumulative and often difficult to decipher.

Interestingly, even in the studies researching pay, the major contributions were made by scholars more interested in intervening variables—in this case motivation—than in either pay or HRM outcomes. This, in turn, greatly influenced their choice of research questions and designs. We would like to have found a better balance in terms of both content and method. One major challenge, it would seem, is for HRM scholars to reassert the preeminence of HRM activities and outcomes as topics of research, calling on appropriate theories from the social sciences and elsewhere as they are useful in framing hypotheses and interpreting results. Another is to elevate a concern for external validity to the stature accorded the concern for internal validity during the 1970s. This means that laboratory experiments must be designed to more closely resemble the "real world," and that the number of field experiments and quasi-experiments conducted must be greatly increased.

We would also suggest a shift in emphasis with respect to HRM outcomes. During the 1970s (and before as well) performance and satisfaction were dominant, both from a measurement and substantive perspective. Without denying the importance of these outcomes to organizations and society at large, we believe that employee turnover and absenteeism deserve more attention. Some conceptual developments were made on behalf of these variables during the decade just past. We hope that empirical efforts, especially regarding measurement, will flourish in the decade ahead.

Finally, in terms of new emphasis, researchers would do well to recall that HRM policies and practices are neither initiated nor administered in a vacuum. Rather, they and their efforts are constantly affected by public policy and economic constraints. The 1970s were characterized by dramatic changes in both, including emerging enforcement mechanisms for the social policies formulated during the 1960s, rapid inflation, and increasingly effective international competition. But, during the decade these environmental factors were essentially ignored by HRM researchers. As we enter the 1980s the environment is no less tumultuous, and it should no longer be ignored.

Writing for the IRRA a decade ago, Strauss (1970) foresaw the demise of human resource management as an academic discipline and, indeed, predicted that at the end of the 1970s there would be no such review. Having thus been made fully cognizant of the perils of prognostication, we nevertheless offer our own prediction for the years ahead. Despite our frequent criticism, we are mildly optimistic. As investigators build on the best research of the recent past, we feel that in the next few years they will make noticeable strides toward a better understanding of the ways in which organizational policies and practices influence the major HRM outcomes, and the ways in which important HRM decisions are made. With a little luck, these developments may even result in some improvements in practice as well.

References

Adams, J. S. "Inequality in Social Exchange." In *Advances in Experimental Social Psychology,* ed. L. Berkowitz. New York: Academic Press, 1965. Pp. 276–99.

Arvey, R. D. *Fairness in Selecting Employees.* Reading, Mass.: Addison-Wesley, 1979.

Baird, L., and W. C. Hamner. "Individual vs. System Rewards: Who's Dissatisfied, Why, and What Is Their Likely Response?" *Academy of Management Journal* 22 (1979): pp. 783–92.

Baum, J. F., and S. A. Youngblood. "Impact of an Organizational Control Policy on Absenteeism, Performance, and Satisfaction." *Journal of Applied Psychology* 60 (1975): pp. 688–94.

Bernstein, V., M. D. Hakel, and A. Harlan. "The College Student as Interviewer: A Threat to Generalizability?" *Journal of Applied Psychology* 60 (1975): pp. 266–68.

Blanz, F., and E. E. Ghiselli. "The Mixed Standard Scale: A New Rating System." *Personnel Psychology* 25 (1972): pp. 185–200.

Borman, W. C. "Exploring Upper Limits of Reliability and Validity in Job Performance Ratings." *Journal of Applied Psychology* 63 (1978): pp. 135–44.

Brayfield, A. H., and W. H. Crockett. "Employee Attitudes and Employee Performance." *Psychological Bulletin* 52 (1955): pp. 396–424.

Campbell, J. P., and R. D. Pritchard. "Motivation Theory in Industrial and Organizational Psychology." In *Handbook of Industrial and Organizational Psychology,* ed. M. D. Dunnette. Chicago: Rand McNally, 1976. Pp. 63–130.

Cornelius, E. T. III, M. D. Hakel, and P. Sackett. "A Methodological Approach to Job Classification for Performance Appraisal Purposes." *Personnel Psychology* 32 (1979): pp. 283–98.

Dalton, D. R., and W. D. Todor. "Turnover Turned Over: An Expanded and Positive Perspective." *Academy of Management Review* 4 (1979): pp. 225–35.

Deci, E. L. *Intrinsic Motivation: Theory and Research.* New York: Plenum, 1975.

Dunham, R. B., F. J. Smith, and R. S. Blackburn. "Validation of the Index of Organizational Reactions with the JDI, the MSQ, and Faces Scales." *Academy of Management Journal* 20 (1970): pp. 420–32.

Dyer, L. "Implications of New Theories of Work for the Design of Compensation Systems." *Proceedings of the Annual Meeting of the Industrial Relations Research Association,* 1975. Pp. 160–67.

———. "Personnel Policy Theory and Research: The Need and the Reality." Paper delivered at the annual meeting of the Academy of Management, Detroit, Mich., August 1980.

Dyer, L., and R. D. Theriault. "The Determinants of Pay Satisfaction." *Journal of Applied Psychology* 61 (1976): pp. 596–604.

Dyer, L., D. P. Schwab, and R. D. Theriault. "Managerial Perceptions Regarding Salary Increase Criteria." *Personnel Psychology* 29 (1976): pp. 233–42.

Einhorn, H. J., and R. M. Hogarth. "Behavioral Decision Theory: Process of Judgment and Choice." *Annual Review of Psychology* 32 (1981): pp. 53–88.

Farris, G. F. "A Predictive Study of Turnover." *Personnel Psychology* 24 (1971): pp. 311–28.

Gillet, B., and D. P. Schwab. "Convergent and Discriminant Validities of Corresponding Job Descriptive Index and Minnesota Satisfaction Questionnaire Scales." *Journal of Applied Psychology* 60 (1975): pp. 313–17.

Goodman, Paul, and Paul Salipante, Jr. "Organizational Rewards and Retention of the Hard-Core Unemployed." *Journal of Applied Psychology* 61 (1976): pp. 12–21.

Gorman, C. D., W. H. Clover, and M. E. Doherty. "Can We Learn Anything About Interviewing Real People from 'Interviews' of Paper People? Two Studies of the External Validity of Paradigm." *Organizational Behavior and Human Performance* 22 (1978): pp. 165–92.

Greenhaus, J. H., and I. F. Badin. "Self Esteem, Performance and Satisfaction: Some Tests of a Theory." *Journal of Applied Psychology* 59 (1974): pp. 722–26.

Hackman, J. R., and E. E. Lawler III. "Employee Reactions to Job Characteristics." *Journal of Applied Psychology* 55 (1971): pp. 259–86.

Hammer, T. H., and J. Landau. "Methodological Issues in the Use of Absence Data." *Journal of Applied Psychology* 66 (1981): pp. 574–81.

Heneman, H. G. III. "Comparisons of Self- and Superior Ratings of Managerial Performance." *Journal of Applied Psychology* 59 (1974): pp. 638–42.

Heneman, H. G. III, and D. P. Schwab. "Work and Rewards Theory." In *Motivation and Commitment,* eds. D. Yoder and H. G. Heneman, Jr. Washington: Bureau of National Affairs, 1975. Pp. 1–22.

Heneman, H. G. III, D. P. Schwab, J. A. Fossum, and L. Dyer. *Personnel/Human Resource Management.* Homewood, Ill.: Richard D. Irwin, 1980.

Herzberg, F. *Work and the Nature of Man.* Cleveland: World, 1966.

Hinrichs, J. P. "Measurement of Reasons for Resignation of Professionals: Questionnaires vs. Company and Consultant Exit Interviews." *Journal of Applied Psychology* 60 (1975): pp. 530–32.

Ilgen, D. R., and J. H. Hollenback. "The Role of Job Satisfaction in Absence Behavior." *Organizational Behavior and Human Performance* 19 (1977): p. 148–61.

Ilgen, D. R., C. D. Fisher, and M. S. Taylor. "Consequences of Individual Feedback on Behavior in Organizations." *Journal of Applied Psychology* 64 (1979): pp. 349–71.

Imada, A. S., and M. D. Hakel. "Influence of Nonverbal Communication and Rater Proximity on Impressions and Decisions in Simulated Employment Interviews." *Journal of Applied Psychology* 62 (1977): pp. 275–300.

Inkson, J. H. "Self Esteem as a Moderator of the Relationship Between Job Performance and Job Satisfaction." *Journal of Applied Psychology* 63 (1978): pp. 243–47.

Jacobs, L., and T. Soloman. "Strategies for Enhancing the Prediction of Job Performance from Job Satisfaction." *Journal of Applied Psychology* 62 (1977): pp. 417–21.

LaRocco, J. M., W. M. Pugh, and E. K. Gunderson. "Identifying Determinants of Retention Decisions." *Personnel Psychology* 30 (1977): pp. 199–215.

Latham, G. F., and D. L. Dossett. "Designing Incentive Plans for Unionized Employees: A Comparison of Continuous and Variable Ratio Reinforcement Schedules." *Personnel Psychology* 31 (1978): pp. 47–61.

Lawler, E. E. III. *Pay and Organization Development.* Reading, Mass.: Addison-Wesley, 1981.

———. *Pay and Organizational Effectiveness: A Psychological View.* New York: McGraw-Hill, 1971.

Lefkowitz, J., and M. L. Katz. "Validity of Exit Interviews." *Personnel Psychology* 22 (1969): pp. 445–56.

Leonard, S. and J. Weitz. "Task Enjoyment and Task Perseverance in Relation to Task Success and Self Esteem." *Journal of Applied Psychology* 55 (1971): Pp. 414–21.

Locke, E. A. "The Nature and Causes of Job Satisfaction." In *Handbook of Industrial and Organizational Psychology,* ed. M. D. Dunnette. Chicago: Rand McNally, 1976. Pp. 1237–350.

———. "Toward a Theory of Task Motivation and Incentives." *Organizational Behavior and Human Performance* 3 (1968): pp. 157–89.

———. "What is Job Satisfaction?" *Organizational Behavior and Human Performance* 4 (1969): pp. 309–36.

Locke, E. A., J. F. Bryan, and L. M. Kendall. "Goals and Intentions as Mediators of the Effects of Monetary Incentives on Behavior." *Journal of Applied Psychology* 52 (1968): pp. 104–21.

Locke, E. A., D. B. Feren, V. M. McCaleb, K. N. Shaw, and A. T. Denny. "The Relative Effectiveness of Four Methods of Motivating Employee

Performance." In *Changes in Work Life*, eds. K. D. Duncan, M. M. Gruneberg, and D. Wallis. New York: Wiley, 1980. Pp. 363–88.

Locke, E. A., K. N. Shaw, L. M. Saari, and G. P. Latham. "Goal Setting and Task Performance: 1969–1980." *Psychological Bulletin* 90 (1981): pp. 125–52.

Lyons, T. F. "Turnover and Absenteeism: A Review of Relationships and Shared Correlates." *Personnel Psychology* 25 (1972): pp. 271–81.

Mahoney, T. A. *Compensation and Reward Perspectives*. Homewood, Ill.: Richard D. Irwin, 1979.

Maslow, G. H. *Motivation and Personality*. New York: Harper & Row, 1954.

Mayfield, E. C. "The Selection Interview: A Re-evaluation of Published Research." *Personnel Psychology* 17 (1964): pp. 239–60.

Miner, M. G. "Job Absence and Turnover: A New Source of Data." *Monthly Labor Review* 100 (October 1977): pp. 24–31.

Mitchell, T. R. "Organizational Behavior." In *Annual Review of Psychology*, eds. M. R. Rosenzweig and L. W. Porter. Palo Alto, Calif.: Annual Reviews Inc., 1979. Pp. 243–81.

Mobley, W. H., R. W. Griffeth, H. H. Hand, and B. M. Meglino. "Review and Conceptual Analysis of the Employee Turnover Process." *Psychological Bulletin* 86 (1979): pp. 492–522.

Muchinsky, P. M. "Employee Absenteeism: A Review of the Literature." *Journal of Vocational Behavior* 10 (1977): pp. 316–40.

Muldrow, T. W., and J. A. Baynton. "Men and Women Executives and Process Related to Decision Accuracy." *Journal of Applied Psychology* 64 (1979): pp. 99–106.

Nicholson, N., C. A. Brown, and J. H. Chadwick-Jones. "Absence from Work and Job Satisfaction." *Journal of Applied Psychology* 61 (1976): pp. 728–37.

Ogilvie, J. R., and N. Schmitt. "Situational Influences on Linear and Nonlinear Use of Information." *Organizational Behavior and Human Performance* 23 (1979): pp. 292–306.

Parker, D. F., and L. Dyer. "Expectancy Theory as a Within-Person Behavioral Choice Model: An Empirical Test of Some Conceptual and Methodological Refinements." *Organizational Behavior and Human Performance* 17 (1976): pp. 97–117.

Pedalino, E., and V. U. Gamboa. "Behavior Modification and Absenteeism: Interventions in One Industrial Setting." *Journal of Applied Psychology* 59 (1974): pp. 694–98.

Porter, L. W. "A Study of Perceived Need Satisfaction in Bottom and Middle Management Jobs." *Journal of Applied Psychology* 45 (1961): pp. 1–10.

Porter, L. W., and R. M. Steers. "Organizational, Work, and Personal Factors in Employee Turnover and Absenteeism." *Psychological Bulletin* 80 (1973): Pp. 151–76.

Price, J. L. *The Study of Turnover*. Ames: Iowa State University Press, 1977.

Pritchard, R. D., M. D. Dunnette, and D. O. Jorgenson. "Effects of Perceptions of Equity and Inequity on Worker Performance and Satisfaction." *Journal of Applied Psychology* 56 (1972): pp. 75–94.

Pritchard, R. D., D. W. Leonard, C. W. VonBergen, Jr., and R. Kirk. "The Effects of Varying Schedules of Reinforcement on Human Task Performance." *Organizational Behavior and Human Performance* 16 (1976): pp. 205–30.

Reilly, R. R., M. L. Tenopyr, and S. M. Sperling. "Efforts of Job Previews on Job Acceptance and Survival of Telephone Operator Candidates." *Journal of Applied Psychology* 64 (1979): pp. 218–20.

Roose, J. E., and M. E. Doherty. "Judgment Theory Applied to the Selection of Life Insurance Salesmen." *Organizational Behavior and Human Performance* 16 (1976): pp. 231–49.

Rothe, H. F. "Output Rates Among Welders: Productivity and Consistency Following Removal of a Financial Incentive System." *Journal of Applied Psychology* 54 (1970): pp. 549–51.

Sackett, P. R., and M. D. Hakel. "Temporal Stability and Individual Differences in Using Assessment Information to Form Overall Ratings." *Organizational Behavior and Human Performance* 23 (1979): pp. 120–37.

Scheflen, K. C., E. E. Lawler III, and J. R. Hackman. "Long-Term Impact of Employee Participation in the Development of Pay Incentive Plans: A Field Experiment Revisited." *Journal of Applied Psychology* 55 (1971): pp. 182–86.

Schmidt, F. L., J. E. Hunter, R. C. McKenzie, and T. W. Muldrow. "Impact of Valid Selection Procedures on Work-Force Productivity." *Journal of Applied Psychology* 64 (1979): pp. 609–26.

Schmitt, N. "Interrater Agreement in Dimensionality and Combination of Assessment Center Judgments." *Journal of Applied Psychology* 62 (1977): pp. 171–76.

———. "Social and Situational Determinants of Interview Decisions: Implications for Employment Interview." *Personnel Psychology* 29 (1976): pp. 79–101.

Schwab, D. P. "Construct Validity in Organizational Behavior." In *Research in Organizational Behavior,* Vol. 2, eds. B. M. Staw and L. L. Cummings. Greenwich, Conn.: JAI Press, 1980. Pp. 3–43.

Schwab, D. P., and L. L. Cummings. "Theories of Performance and Satisfaction: A Review." *Industrial Relations* 9 (1970): pp. 408–30.

Schwab, D. P., and J. D. Olian. "From Applicant to Employee: Gatekeeping in Organizations." Mimeo, 1981.

Schwab, D. P., and M. J. Wallace, Jr. "Correlates of Employee Satisfaction with Pay." *Industrial Relations* 13 (1974): pp. 78–89.

Schwab, D. P., H. G. Heneman III, and T. A. DeCotiis. "Behaviorally Anchored Rating Scales: A Review of the Literature." *Personnel Psychology* 28 (1975): pp. 549–62.

Schwab, D. P., J. D. Olian, and H. G. Heneman III. "Between Subject Expectancy Theory Research: A Statistical Review of Studies Predicting Effort and Performance." *Psychological Bulletin* 86 (1979): pp. 139–47.

Sheridan, John E., and John W. Slocum, Jr. "The Direction of the Causal Relationship Between Job Satisfaction and Work Performance." *Organizational Behavior and Human Performance* 14 (1975), pp. 159–72.

Smith, P. C., L. M. Kendall, and C. L. Hulin. *The Measurement of Satisfaction in Work and Retirement.* Chicago: Rand McNally, 1969.

Spool, M. D. "Training Programs for Observers of Behavior: A Review." *Personnel Psychology* 31 (1978): pp. 853–88.

Staw, B. M., and G. R. Oldham. "Reconsidering our Dependent Variables: A Critique and Empirical Study." *Academy of Management Journal* 21 (1978): pp. 539–59.

Steers, R. M., and S. R. Rhodes. "Major Influences on Employee Attendance: A Process Model." *Journal of Applied Psychology* 63 (1978): pp. 391–407.

Stephens, T. A., and W. A. Burroughs. "An Application of Operant Conditioning to Absenteeism in a Hospital Setting." *Journal of Applied Psychology* 63 (1978): pp. 518–21.

Sterrett, J. H. "The Job Interview: Body Language and Perceptions of Potential Effectiveness." *Journal of Applied Psychology* 63 (1978): pp. 388–90.

Strauss, G. "Organizational Behavior and Personnel Issues." In *A Review of Industrial Relations Research,* Vol. I, eds. W. L. Ginsburg, E. R. Livernash, H. S. Parnes, and G. Strauss. Madison, Wis.: Industrial Relations Research Association, 1970. Pp. 145–206.

Taylor, R. N. "Preferences of Industrial Managers for Information Sources in Making Promotion Decisions." *Journal of Applied Psychology* 60 (1975): pp. 269–72.

Taylor, R. L., and W. D. Wilsted. "Capturing Judgment Policies in Performance Rating." *Industrial Relations* 15 (1976): pp. 216–24.

Tolchinsky, P. D., and D. C. King. "Do Goals Mediate the Effects of Incentives on Performance?" *Academy of Management Review* 5 (1980): pp. 455–68.

Weiss, D. J., R. V. Dawis, G. W. England, and L. H. Lofquist. *Manual for the Minnesota Satisfaction Questionnaire.* Minnesota Studies in Vocational Rehabilitation, Vol. 22. Minneapolis: University of Minnesota, 1967.

Yukl, G. A., and G. P. Latham. "Consequences of Reinforcement Schedules and Incentive Magnitudes for Employee Performance: Problems Encountered in an Industrial Setting." *Journal of Applied Psychology* 60 (1975): pp. 294–98.

Yukl, G. A., G. P. Latham, and E. D. Pursell. "The Effectiveness of Performance Incentives Under Continuous and Variable Ratio Schedules of Reinforcement." *Personnel Psychology* 29 (1976): pp. 221–31.

Zedeck, S., and D. Kafry. "Capturing Rater Policies for Processing Evaluation Data." *Organizational Behavior and Human Performance* 18 (1977): pp. 269–94.

CHAPTER 6

Organizational Behavior and Industrial Relations

JEANNE M. BRETT
Northwestern University

TOVE HELLAND HAMMER
Cornell University

This chapter presents an in-depth review of the behavioral theory and empirical research relevant to three topics of interest to scholars and practitioners in the fields of organizational behavior and industrial relations. The three are participative decision-making, the decision to vote for or against union representation, and bargaining. We chose these topics because sufficient theoretical and empirical work has been done on them to highlight the contributions of organizational behavior theory.

The grounding of industrial relations research in behavioral theory is by no means solely a phenomenon of the 1970s; recall that much of the interdisciplinary industrial relations research in the 1950s was so grounded. However, the flavor of the behavioral research in the 1970s is distinctly *organizational* and decidedly different from that of the earlier period. The dearth of industrial relations research based on behavioral theory during the 1960s and early 1970s coincided with the growth of the field of organizational behavior, as scholars in the latter field were adapting, mixing, merging, and anthropomorphizing theory from psychology and sociology to explain causal events in organizational contexts. Industrial relations research began to feel the impact of the organizational behavior area of study as scholars trained in organizational behavior theory and research methods occasionally tried to understand causal events in interorganizational contexts.

There are numerous areas other than participative decision-making, the decision to vote for or against union representation, and bargaining where organizational theory is having an impact on industrial relations research. We hope, however, that the three we have chosen for self-contained reviews illustrate well the application of organizational behavior theory to research in union-management contexts.

Participative Decision-Making

The forms, processes, and outcomes of joint decision-making between workers and management are described in this section. In traditional capitalist economies, decision-making power over the uses of capital, labor, and profits belongs to the owners of capital or their management representatives. In programs of joint decision-making, some of these rights of ownership are transferred to nonowning workers either by law or by grants from the employer.

Worker participation in management has been a topic of heated and value-laden debate since the early demonstration experiments of the Human Relations School (Coch and French 1948; French, Israel, and Aas 1960; Morse and Reimer 1956). At the time, the arguments for worker participation were a mixture of the pragmatic and economic, the moral and ideological. Both the employer and the employees, it was argued, would benefit if workers were allowed to grow and develop psychologically through increased involvement in organizational decision-making, which would channel workers' creative energies toward the fulfillment of organization goals (Argyris 1964, Likert 1961, Trist and Bamforth 1951).

In the 1970s participation came to be seen as a mechanism for the redistribution of power within the enterprise and, ultimately, within the broader society (Dahl 1970, Emery and Thorsrud 1976, Pateman 1970, Vanek 1975). At that time several European countries enacted legislation dictating minimum requirements for formal participation in the running of organizations by nonmanagerial workers (IDE International Research Group 1981a). In the United States, concern over declining productivity and quality in the face of foreign competition and American workers' unwillingness to accept physically and psychologically debilitating work (U.S. Department of HEW 1973) stimulated a pragmatic interest in worker participation. The U.S. government funded the American Center for Quality of Working Life which, in turn, funded a series of demonstration projects.

A result has been enormous interest in the forms and processes of participation in the last decade. The literature available on participation has expanded exponentially and is at the moment galloping out of control. The bulk of it is oriented toward generating change in organizations through the implementation of the new organizational democracy laws or the new programs of worker autonomy designed to improve the quality of working life, not toward evaluation (see Elden [1978] for a discussion of the tradeoffs between action and evaluation, and Taylor [1977a, 1977b] for a critique of the evaluation research). Nevertheless, there have been some serious efforts to examine the effects of different forms of worker participation (for example, Bolweg 1976, Engelstad and Qvale 1977, Goodman 1979, IDE International Research Group 1981b). This review uses these studies to describe the conceptual foundations upon which the participation models rest and then to assess the effect of various forms of participation on three factors: workplace democracy, organizational effectiveness, and the role of the local union.

The Participation Model

Participation means the involvement of workers or their representatives in the decision-making processes of the firm. Participation models differ considerably in the scope of decisions they include, the number of workers involved in decision-making, and the amount of power workers can exercise vis-à-vis management. Participation can be direct or indirect, formal or informal, prescribed by law (for example, the 1976 German Codetermination Act), through contracts (collective bargaining, for example), or by individual management grants (autonomous work groups, quality circles as examples).

It is convenient to place the different forms of participation in two categories, based on their origins—legal statutes and employer grants—because research on the effects of the two forms differs in focus. Legally based, or prescribed, structures such as worker representation on boards of directors, workers' councils, or collective bargaining are formal systems of participation with written rules and regulations for involving workers in decision-making. These systems usually provide uniform guidelines for participation in all organizations that come under the jurisdiction of the law or contract. Employer-granted participation usually does not specify an individual's or a group's legal rights to be involved in decision-making. To the extent that formal written agreements exist in granted models, they are specific to a given organization. Examples of granted participation systems are quality of working life (QWL) programs, sociotechnical designs, labor-management committees, and quality control (QC) circles.[1]

With both legally based and granted participation there can be gaps between the formal blueprints for participation and actual involvement of workers in the decision-making process. Therefore we distinguish between *de jure* participation, which is the formal written prescription for worker involvement, and *de facto* participation, which is the actually experienced involvement in decision-making (IDE International Research Group 1981b).

While de facto or experienced participation is not the central purpose of most granted participation models (QWL and sociotechnical design programs are instituted to improve directly such outcomes as organizational effectiveness and worker satisfaction), the theoretical foundation of these programs contains assumptions about worker autonomy as well as responsibility and readiness for involvement in organizational governance (Herzberg 1966, Trist 1979). In practice, many of these programs include de facto participation, often through autonomous workgroups on the shop floor and joint labor-management decision-making bodies.

The major research question then is whether de jure participation leads to de facto participation and eventually to outcomes beneficial to workers, employers, and society at large, such as positive worker attitudes and behaviors, better mental and physical health, organizational productivity, organizational growth, and national labor stability and industrial peace. We now turn to an examination of different types of legally based and granted forms

---

[1] Granted participation is not totally devoid of legislative roots, in the sense that it sometimes grows up around the implementation of legislation. The Occupational Safety and Health Act (1973) has instigated labor-management committees and QWL programs (Goodman 1979). The distinction to be made here is that legislation is not the immediate antecedant of granted participation.

of participation to see if our current research answers this question.

First we will examine the effects of different models of de jure participation where the central dependent variable is industrial democracy: legal models, experiments to further industrial democracy, worker representation on company boards of directors, and employee ownership. Next we discuss the different forms of granted participation—sociotechnical systems, quality of working life experiments, quality control circles—where the central dependent variable is organizational effectiveness. Finally we address the different roles that local unions have chosen to take with respect to worker participation.

Legally Based Participation: Toward Industrial Democracy

There is considerable debate over the conceptual definition of industrial democracy (see Bernstein 1976, Blumberg 1968, Gustavsen 1973, and Vanek 1975 for differing points of view). To cover the spectrum of studies with industrial democracy as a dependent variable, the definition used here is the extent to which workers and their representatives influence the outcome of organizational decisions. The core of this construct is the degree of power-sharing between labor and management, and the research tests the hypothesis that participation leads to industrial democracy.[2]

The extent of democratization is defined along two dimensions: scope of decisions—the subject matter open to worker involvement and influence—and the level or degree of influence over the decisions made. Scope ranges from issues of immediate concern to workers, such as wages and benefits, working conditions, standards, and job design, to the organization-level concerns of employment policies, hiring of executives, choices of markets and products, investments, and the distribution of earnings. Level of influence ranges from workers simply being informed by management about decisions to be made, through consultation, joint decision-making, to full worker control or self-management (Bernstein 1976, IDE International Research Group 1981b).

Research with workplace democracy as a dependent variable is predominantly European and centers on legally based participa-

[2] Participation and industrial democracy are distinguished by the involvement of workers or their representatives in the decision-making process versus the influence they exert over decisions.

tive structures where participation is usually indirect—that is, where workers' interests are represented by a small number of delegates.

Legal Models. The Industrial Democracy in Europe research group, in the most comprehensive evaluation of participative structures to date, examines the effects of de jure participation on worker influence and involvement in 12 countries (IDE International Research Group 1981a, 1981b). The research covers 134 firms in the service (banking and insurance) and manufacturing (metal industries) sectors, stratified by organization size and worker skill-level.

The study attempts to answer several questions. The central hypothesis is that de jure participation influences the intraorganizational distribution of de facto participation. Also examined are the differences in de jure and de facto participation between hierarchical levels in organizations, the extent of involvement and influence in decision-making by representative bodies internal and external to the firm, and the differential effectiveness of de jure participative structures as determinants of actual participation. Levels of participation are examined for seven groups: nonsupervisory employees, first-line supervisors, middle management, top management, bodies above the firm level (supervisory boards, boards of directors, conglomerate management, shareholders and owners), representative bodies at the firm level (workers' councils, local unions), and institutions outside the firm/company (national unions, banks, community councils, etc.).

The amount of prescribed (de jure) participation by each of these groups over 16 decisions covering short-term (working hours, task assignments), medium-term (hiring decisions, reorganizations of the work process), and long-term (investments, new products) issues is assessed through structured interviews with key management and union representatives at the firm level. Degrees of worker involvement in decision-making (de facto participation) is measured through representative samples from the various hierarchical organizational levels.

The findings point to a high degree of formalized (de jure) participation in most countries for both worker and management representatives. (An exception is Britain which has few written prescriptions for involvement by any level in the organizational hierarchy.) Nevertheless, a surprising amount of legal and contractual (de jure) power over all kinds of decisions, including day-to-day operations, is concentrated in the hands of top management and supervisory bodies. It appears that the European industrial democracy legislation has formalized worker rights to participation without limiting managerial prerogatives.

The effect of hierarchy is even stronger in the de facto participation data. Across organizations and countries, workers have the least and top management the most influence in all areas of decision-making. The more strategic the decision (of a long- versus a short-term nature), the larger is the influence gap between hierarchical levels. Workers participate in the execution rather than in the formulation of organizational goals and policies. Similar conclusions about workers' role in the decision-making process are reached by the Decisions in Organizations (DIO) research group from a smaller cross-cultural study of participation (Heller et al. 1970).

De jure participation has a significant effect on the distribution of de facto influence between hierarchical levels: the more extensive the formal regulations prescribing worker participation, the smaller the difference between labor and management's influence over decisions. Furthermore, the correlation between de jure and de facto participation is greater for more strategic, long-term decisions, and greater with respect to representative bodies and workers than to top management. About 40 to 60 percent of the variance in workers' influence over medium- and long-term decisions is explained by written prescription, but their de facto influence over short-term decisions is poorly explained.

The IDE research comparisons of the effectiveness of laws, contracts, and formal written management policies as instigators of de facto participation show that collective bargaining contracts are the most important in both promoting worker and representative-body influence in decision-making and guaranteeing the implementation of de jure participation. European unions have played an active role in the passage of industrial democracy legislation through their close relationships with dominant political parties (IDE International Research Group 1981a), but more important, they have been able to ensure adherence to regulations through collectively bargained contracts and in-plant contract management.

Norwegian Industrial Democracy Experiments. Experimentation with direct participation to further industrial democracy took place in Europe well before the codetermination legislation of the 1970s. The Norwegian Industrial Democracy project experimented with the use of autonomous workgroups as a vehicle for worker control in organizations. In several field experiments, sponsored jointly by the Federation of Trade Unions and the Employers' Confederation, workgroup members were given control over technical decisions (planning and choice of work methods, work scheduling and task allocations, materials ordering, quality control, machine set-up and maintenance) and personnel (social) decisions (hiring of new workers, discipline, distribution of leadership functions, work hours, shift composition). Cross-training of tasks created a broader set of job skills and allowed rotation through different job classifications. The immediate purpose of the job-redesign experiments was better utilization of labor and more satisfactory work environments, but the ultimate goal was the democratization of the entire organization through shop-level democracy. Job redesign was just the first step in a continuous process of organizational and social change.

The original evaluation study was a concurrent research design, with standard research instruments used to assess differences between experimental and control plants on autonomy, productivity, job satisfaction, and worker control over decision-making (Bolweg 1976). This was replaced by an action research design where the evaluation emphasis is on the processes of change and the active involvement of the research subjects in continuous assessment of the experiment and in the change of experimental conditions *during* the experiment (Herbst 1974). This departure from the classical evaluation research paradigm tends to produce in-depth case studies with data in the form of interviews, observations, and archival records.

Very limited support was found for the hypothesis that direct participation through shop-floor autonomy leads to increased worker involvement in organizations. Worker influence was not diffused upwards and, in fact, did not even spread to other workgroups on the same hierarchical level. More recent experiments with the introduction of autonomous workgroups on board ships in the merchant marine further illustrate that while sociotechnical designs are somewhat successful in changing work process technology and low level organizational control systems, they have to be supplemented with representative participation to give workers influence over the full scope of organizational decisions (Johansen 1977, Roggema and Hammarstrom 1975).

Representation on Boards of Directors. Worker representation on company boards of directors is the law in Austria, Denmark, Germany, Norway, and Sweden.[3] Empirical evaluation research is limited and tends to focus on institutional constraints which keep board representation from furthering industrial democracy.

Case studies of worker directors on the supervisory boards of the British Steel Corporation show that they have a minimal effect on board procedures and decision outcomes (Bank and Jones 1977, Brannen, Batstone, Fatchett, and White 1976). Their influence is limited to personnel and job-security issues, which shows an adherence to, if not an outright acceptance of, the narrow "shop-floor specialist" role defined for them by the regular board members.

An extensive cross-sectional study, covering 130 firms, examined the effects of the 1973 Norwegian Codetermination Act (which prescribes one-third representation on company boards by nonsupervisory employees) on workplace democracy (Engelstad and Qvale 1977). The researchers found a strong moderator effect of organization size; two years after the law went into effect labor representatives in small organizations (with small boards) had attained measurable influence over decisions on a wide variety of issues. In large organizations their influence was minimal. Size also moderated the effects of worker representation on board procedures and processes. In large firms the board tended to absorb or swallow up the worker-directors, corroborating findings from the British research (Brannen et al. 1976). In smaller firms the workers' presence had a "shock effect" on the boards, leading them to adhere more strictly to the regulations of board procedures and

[3] Worker representation on supervisory boards has an extreme form in the Yugoslav workers' councils. Because Yugoslav organizations are social property, however, Yugoslavia is an off-quadrant case and will not be considered here.

forcing the directors to be better prepared for meetings and more involved in their prescribed supervisory activities.

However, Engelstad and Qvale (1977) conclude that despite increased influence by labor on company supervisory boards, this form of codetermination is not likely to lead to democratization of the enterprise.[4] There is no trickle-down effect of participation. A study evaluating Sweden's 1972 Codetermination Act closely replicates these findings and shows that the worker constituency does not view board representation as an effective form of power-sharing (Statens Industriverk 1975). Brannen et al. (1976), from a survey of 2400 steelworkers, draw the same conclusion.

Employee Ownership. It has been argued that an effective sharing of power is impossible as long as ownership of the means of production eludes labor (Vanek 1975). While control is not always contingent on ownership or managerial status, it is generally the case that ownership means governance. In the U.S., employee-owned companies in the form of producers' cooperatives, in which workers commonly own and manage the business, have existed since the 1790s (Jones 1977, Shirom 1972). In today's cooperatives, such as the West Coast plywood factories (Berman 1967) and the San Francisco scavenger firms (Perry 1978), ownership shares are equally distributed, giving each member one vote in the decision-making process. The more common form of company ownership, shareholding, has been extended to workers through Employee Stock Ownership Plans (ESOPs) (Kelso 1958) and through employee purchases of plants scheduled for closure (Stern and Hammer 1978).

ESOPs, which are deferred compensation programs whereby workers accumulate company stock held in trust for them, is a potential source of worker power if the stock is voting stock and workers control the trust. It is not the purpose of the ESOP to increase worker control, however, and studies show that the contingency of workplace democracy arising from stock-bonus plans is exceedingly remote (Stern and Comstock 1978).

Where employee ownership is the result of corporate divesti-

[4] The term codetermination, from the German *Mitbestimmung*, means worker participation at several levels of the organizational hierarchy, from supervisory boards at the level of the enterprise down to works councils on the shop floor. In the German industrial relations system, this is not limited to company board representation.

tures, workers without previous ownership rights hold substantial amounts of stock (Gurdon 1978, Hammer and Stern 1980, Long 1980). However, Hammer and Stern show that worker-owners do not show a strong preference for exercising their full legal rights to the management of the organization.[5] The workers see themselves as traditional financial investors, and the more stock they own, the stronger is their preference for a traditional decision-making structure, favoring the expertise of management. Furthermore, worker-owners want any joint decision-making to go through their union representatives, using the collective bargaining process, which suggests that employee stock ownership by itself does not create a common class of capital owners out of labor and management.

The worker-ownership research demonstrates clearly that financial ownership is not sufficient to make either workers or managers break down well-established hierarchical delineations of power and make changes in internal decision-making processes. For worker-ownership to be translated into worker control, both formal structures for participation in decision-making on all levels of the organization and an active interest in worker participation must exist within labor and management.

Conclusion. Bernstein (1976) offers a list of six necessary conditions for a democratic workplace. These include the formal structures of participation and a participatory/democratic consciousness among labor and management, an economic return to the workers on the surplus they produce, ready access to management-level information, guaranteed individual rights, and an appeals procedure to protect workers from possible management reprisals when they criticize existing procedures or oppose proposed policy changes. These requirements go well beyond what is currently available to labor through either legal statutes or employer grants. The results of the evaluation research, which show a rather limited effect of participation programs on organizational democracy, are understandable in light of the modest changes that

[5] This does not mean that worker-owners have no interest in power-sharing. In particular, local union leaders in employee-owned firms have taken an active role in ensuring some form of worker participation. However, rank-and-file workers prefer consultation to active direct involvement in the decision-making process.

actually take place in the decision-making strategies in organizations under the label of "industrial democracy."

Granted Participation: Strategies in Search of Organizational Effectiveness

The goal of managers in implementing voluntary or "granted" worker participation programs is improved organizational effectiveness. Old, established programs, such as the labor-management productivity committees of the 1920s and the Scanlon Plan (Lesieur 1968), have improved productivity as a publicly stated goal. Newer programs, such as QWL, quality control circles, and sociotechnical system designs, avoid a public emphasis on productivity. Instead, their stated goals are an improved quality of working life, worker involvement in the labor process, commitment to the organization, reduction of hierarchies, quality of performance, and flexibility in staffing. Eventually, organizations expect such first-level goals to pay off in bottom-line figures of increased productivity and decreased labor costs, absenteeism, and turnover.

The theoretical model which links participation to organizational effectiveness is built on an assumption that employees have untapped reserves of both energy and talent that will be released when workers are granted the opportunity to participate.[6] To facilitate the release and diffusion of this knowledge and energy, some participation programs (in particular, sociotechnical designs) require a change in the organizational structure, toward a reduction in hierarchical levels and the formation of autonomous work-groups with overlapping members. Workers are cross-trained to different jobs surrounding their own specialty area, which increases their span of competence and makes staffing more flexible as workers can be assigned to a variety of jobs across classifications. It is hypothesized that productivity will increase due to the positive effects of participation on intrinsic work motivation and worker commitment and involvement and because the expanded

[6] There are few explicit and detailed theoretical statements in the literature that explain the participation-organizational effectiveness relationship. Hypotheses and underlying assumptions are implicit and incomplete. The assumption that participation can release untapped knowledge and energy appears repeatedly in the case study literature on participation through QWL, QC circles, and sociotechnical design programs. However, it is not always clear when the case study writers are presenting public relations motivated arguments for worker participation and when they are stating serious hypotheses.

skills and untapped knowledge which can accompany participation will be directed to the solution of work-related problems (see, for example, Goodman 1979, Trist 1981).

Programs of direct participation vary considerably in the scope of active worker involvement and in the quality of their evaluations. To illustrate these differences, we will describe two organizational interventions currently in vogue among American employers—the quality control (QC) circle and the QWL program.

QC circles originated in Japan in the early 1960s as part of a large-scale effort to improve the quality of manufactured products. A QC circle consists of a small group of workers (from 3 to 20 people) from the same work area who meet on a regular basis to identify and solve workshop problems. The workers receive training in simple statistical methods of data analysis and the process of selecting and solving real production problems. Participation is voluntary. Ideally, a circle operates as an autonomous workgroup, with the right to call in technical experts in the organization to assist in data-gathering, problem solution, and implementation. The intended purpose of this form of worker participation is to improve product quality, and, to pay off, it requires an organizational infrastructure of support in the form of trainers, facilitators, and steering committees, and a long-term commitment from both workers and management. The success of the QC circle approach depends heavily on a managerial philosophy of open communications, trust, and broad worker participation.

QC circles are proliferating in the U.S. They were initiated at Lockheed in 1974 (and dropped in 1978 when their founders left to start their own consulting firms). Experts estimate that there will be more than 6000 circles operating in U.S. companies by the end of 1981 (Cole 1980). Part of this spread is due to a promise of quick payoffs and high returns on investment in a program which requires only modest structural changes in an organization (Metz 1981). The promise of fast dollar gains for the price of a steering committee and a few training sessions is an illusion, however. Circles will not succeed as either worker participation programs or quality improvement ventures unless they are implemented with a full managerial commitment to participation (Cole 1980, Yager 1981).

Despite a clear-cut operational definition of the independent variable and highly specific criteria for assessing the effectiveness of QC circles, there is no published research that evaluates either the process of participation or the outcomes of circle activities. The only form of "evaluation" available is accounts of the savings which companies experience in the weeks and months after the circles are installed and enthusiastic journalistic case studies provided by consultants (Hutchins 1980 and Irwin 1978, for example).[7]

In contrast to the relatively narrow QC circle programs discussed above, QWL and sociotechnical designs result in a number of changes in organizational structures and systems beyond worker participation. These include redesign of job tasks, formation of autonomous workgroups, labor-management committees, abolition of first-line supervisors, multiskilling, and a reward system of equal wages within workgroups and group bonuses as opposed to individual pay based on job classifications (Trist 1981). With such system-wide changes it is impossible to isolate the effects of participative decision-making on organizational effectiveness. However, in sociotechnical design and QWL programs, the individual changes made in the organization are not separate independent variables. They constitute an integrative whole which is more than the sum of its parts. In an evaluation of these programs, the entire intervention must be seen as one independent variable.[8]

The dominant form of empirical evaluation of QWL and sociotechnical programs is the case study. Cases of interventions are available in company technical reports, business and management journals, volumes of readings, and review articles. Examples of the most famous cases are General Foods' Topeka plant, Volvo's Kalmar plant, Donnelly Mirror, and Philips of Holland (Davis and Cherns 1975, Glaser 1976, Taylor 1977a and 1977b, Wild 1975).

A review of this literature shows that positive changes in or-

[7] The literature on other modest participation programs, such as labor-management committees and Scanlon Plans, shows that there are no comparative longitudinal or cross-sectional studies of the former, even in the very recent research in this area (Meek 1981), and very inadequate research on the Scanlon Plan (see Bullock and Lawler 1980). An exception is a very recent study (Schuster 1982) which employs a longitudinal design and shows significant productivity gains in several Scanlon Plans and related gain-sharing programs.

[8] In reviewing this literature, interventions which only redesign the labor process (the job itself) are not included. Job redesign exemplified by the Hackman and Oldham (1980) research does not automatically lead to increased worker participation.

ganizational effectiveness are reported in a large number of cases. There are percentage changes in production output, labor costs, rejects, absenteeism, and turnover after the implementation of worker participation and organizational restructuring. It is not possible to tell if these changes are significant, however, or caused by other factors in the organizational environment because statistical tests are not reported and experimental controls for contaminants, such as improvement in technology, are not used. There is also considerable divergence between cases in the choice of operational definitions of effectiveness. Taylor (1979) describes the results reported as "serendipitous," in the sense that they seem unplanned and unexpected. When evaluations are not planned with intended outcomes specified in advance in accordance with the theoretical model underlying the organizational change, it is not surprising that the case studies are idiosyncratic. They clearly cannot be viewed as evidence supporting the hypothesis that these programs increase organizational effectiveness.

The research on the effects of participation on intangible, or "soft," outcomes such as job satisfaction, worker commitment, involvement, and psychological health, is more respectable. While a part of the literature comes in anecdotal form (for example, Gyllenhammar 1977, Norstedt and Aguren 1973), more methodologically rigorous presentations are available (Wall and Lischeron 1977, for example). The research on employee attitudes will not be examined in detail. Suffice it to say that both case studies and cross-sectional research show that direct participation, properly implemented, with adjustments made for individual differences in values and expectations, appears to contribute positively to job satisfaction, involvement, and commitment. Indirect participation through representation, on the other hand, does not seem to affect attitudes toward work and organizations (IDE International Research Group 1981b, Emery and Thorsrud 1976, Nightingale 1979, Tannenbaum et al. 1974).

Programs of worker participation are organizational interventions. An evaluation of their effectiveness therefore requires a before-and-after experimental design with control groups. The complexity of the theoretical model with its network of interactions between organizational characteristics, employee cognitions, attitudes and behavior, and an experimental design requirement of random assignment of subjects to treatments, makes it very difficult to carry out field tests of the entire model.

The most comprehensive evaluation of a sociotechnical design and QWL project is Goodman's (1979) study of the Rushton Mining Company. The Rushton experiment was one of a series of labor-management demonstration projects in unionized firms initiated by the American Center for Quality of Working Life. The study had a textbook evaluation research design built into the intervention before it started, a set of hypotheses and statistical prediction models specified in advance, and carefully developed conceptual and empirical definitions of the dependent variables.

The intervention involved restructuring of several facets of the organization: the coal mining task, the pay system, the communication system, and the organizational hierarchy. The focus of the intervention was three mining crews which were transformed into autonomous workgroups. A labor-management committee was established to diagnose problems arising from the new program and to introduce changes in the experiment if necessary. The program was introduced in one of the mine's three sections, with other sections serving as control groups. The experiment lasted one year, after which it was terminated by a close worker vote.

The specific purpose of the evaluation was to assess the effects of the entire QWL program on worker attitudes, productivity, safety, and job skills, to establish the time that changes in attitudes and behaviors were most pronounced, and to test the persistence of change over time. Data on all subjects were collected at four time periods—one before, one during, and two after the experiment. Comparison of time periods and of the experimental and control subjects form the statistical basis of evaluation. In addition to quantitative data on attitudes, coal production, safety infractions, accidents, absenteeism, and grievances, qualitative information from interviews and on-site observations was collected.

The data on workers' job satisfaction, commitment, and motivation support previous research: QWL interventions have positive effects. The increases in work motivation did not translate into productivity, however. It had been hypothesized that coal production would increase because the miners would be working "smarter," with better coordination across teams, more productivity-related suggestions in the autonomous workgroups, and less absenteeism. Job-switching, which increased flexibility of staffing and intershift coordination, took place, but there were no significant increases or decreases in the amount of coal produced.[9] However, more effort was put into safe labor practices in the experimental crews, and safety was better there than among the control crews. Neither absenteeism nor the number of grievances decreased significantly.

While the tangible economic data did not show the expected effects of change, the qualitative information on intangible dimensions of organizational effectiveness did. Workers and managers reported improvement in skills, increased and more positive interaction between labor and management, and better communication throughout the experimental section of the mine. It is worth noting that most other evaluations of QWL and sociotechnical interventions rely heavily on such anecdotal evidence. The findings from the Goodman study suggest that the qualitative data do not cross-validate in rigorous quantitative analyses and should be interpreted with great caution.

Organizational attachment, operationalized as absenteeism or turnover, is a frequently noted criterion in the QWL case study literature. Absenteeism has also been used to assess the effectiveness of more limited participation programs (Bragg and Andrews 1973, Lawler and Hackman 1969, Scheflen, Lawler, and Hackman 1971). The common finding is a reduction in absence rates, which is interpreted to mean that the intervention has made employees more motivated to come to work. Recent research suggests that the relationship between worker participation and absenteeism is not uniformly linear, however. Hammer, Landau, and Stern (1981) examined absenteeism patterns of workers who had become financial participants in their firm in efforts to avoid a plant shutdown and loss of their jobs. Worker ownership meant both financial and psychological commitment to the organization and the motivation to be present at work to ensure its economic survival and success. Their study showed an expected negative relationship between

[9] The interpretation of the Rushton productivity data has caused some controversy. There was a slight positive effect on production as weekly tonnage in the experimental section was greater than in comparison group sections, but the positive differences are not statistically significant. When N is small, which is the case in a number of demonstration experiments, experimental differences may have to be unrealistically large to satisfy statistical test criteria.

worker commitment and voluntary (or illegitimate) absenteeism, as well as a significant decrease in such absences after the workers had come to ownership. However, this beneficial effect of ownership was cancelled out by a significant increase in involuntary absenteeism. The researchers conclude that the need to withdraw from work on occasion does not necessarily disappear with an organizational change that ties the worker closer to the organization. People with high commitment and involvement, and coworkers who depend on their carrying a fair share of the workload—which is the case in autonomous workgroups, for example—will still take time off. But with organizational change to worker ownership, or to self-governed workgroups, or to membership in labor-management committees comes personal visibility and the need to legitimize one's behavior. Officially acceptable explanations for the behavior take the place of no explanation and result in a significant change in the absence *records,* but not in overall absenteeism.

The Hammer et al. (1981) study supports Goodman's (1979) finding of no decrease in overall absence rates after the QWL intervention. In neither study is the finding of "no significant differences" a result of methodological shortcomings or carelessness in measurement. Their conclusions, which go counter to the case study research, are derived from extensive data gathering, the use of conceptually and empirically sound definitions, and correct statistical models. It is bothersome, however, that the very few careful studies done should contradict the many positive case reports on the effectiveness of worker participation programs.

Taylor (1979) and Hopwood (1979) argue that the lack of serious attention to evaluation comes from several sources. There is a general reluctance to use economic and behavioral measures because the process of evaluation and its outcomes are threatening to the organization, to the employees, and to the change agents. Assessment is not neutral. It involves a value judgment about the relative importance of organizational outcomes. An evaluation of QWL programs stressing cost-benefit analysis and workgroup productivity will signal to workers and unions that worker participation means working harder, not necessarily smarter, which reinforces already strong suspicions. Furthermore, the instigators of programs that are implemented with the political power maneuvers necessary to mount and manage organizational change have much to lose if the programs are seen as purely resource-consuming rather than resource-generating activities. Therefore, many times concerns with the economic consequences of different programs reflect more a desire to legitimize than to assess and learn. The "reporting bias" described by Cummings and Salipante (1976) of making public information on only those experiments which are successful is the result of the high personal and political costs of failure for both the change agents and the organizations serving as demonstration cases.

In summary, it is far from clear whether granted forms of worker participation—programs like Scanlon Plans, QC circles, sociotechnical system designs, and QWL—have the hypothesized positive effects on worker performance, attachment to work, and better utilization of human resources. The findings related to social outcomes—such as job satisfaction, worker commitment, involvement, and motivation—are more encouraging. What is lacking in the research are systematic tests of the hypothesized linkages between worker reactions to granted participation and organizational restructuring and behavioral outcomes. To test either all or parts of the effectiveness model will require an acknowledgement from the researchers acting as change agents that evaluations must be designed into the interventions before they begin, and not added on as an afterthought.

The Role of the Union

Worker participation in management outside collective bargaining has not been enthusiastically received by American union leaders. Participation through QWL projects, sociotechnical design programs, labor-management committees, and employee ownership has been perceived as a means to divide the loyalty of the rank and file, which weakens the union, and to coopt the workers into management, which neutralizes labor as a special interest group. In the U.S., management has shown a preference for cooperation with employee groups outside the collective bargaining process (Davis and Cherns 1975, Katzell, Yankelovich, and Associates 1975), and so have union leaders (Kochan, Lipsky, and Dyer 1975). Despite the unions' stated preference for limited direct involvement by workers in management, survey data show that labor-management committees in areas of safety and health, productivity, and QWL have grown in number and importance in the private and public sectors in the 1970s. The entry of labor into cooperative programs has often come as a reaction to local economic crises, with threats of plant-closures, layoffs, and unemployment (for example, Batt and Weinberg 1978, Martin 1976).

In contrast, European unions have taken a proactive stance toward an expanded mandate for worker involvement. While there are exceptions (French and Italian unions, in particular, view participation outside collective bargaining as a capitalistic means of eroding working class consciousness), national unions have played an active role in the design and passage of legislation furthering worker control. Local unions have pushed for and organized union-controlled selection of representatives to councils, boards, and committees and have established elaborate educational programs for those selected to serve (IDE International Research Group 1981a).

The research on the effect on the union of worker participation is mostly anecdotal information, hypotheses, and advice on how to overcome the obstacles to joint decision-making set up by both union and management (for example, Edelstein 1979, Lawler and Ozley 1979, Schlesinger and Walton 1977). However, the few systematic studies suggest that the effect of worker participation on the union depends on whether the union takes a proactive or reactive stance.

Stern and O'Brien (1980) argue that employee ownership and the ensuing participation in decision-making should strengthen the local union because the union's representation function will be crucial where workers are minority stockholders, know little about the rights of stock ownership, and have expectations of sharing decision-making responsibilities. Support for this hypothesis comes from Hammer and Stern (1980), who found that among blue-collar workers the local union continues to be seen as the sole representative of workers in joint decision-making and as the protector of worker ownership rights vis-à-vis management. However, the researchers found some erosion of the union's representative role among white-collar unionized employees who consider direct worker participation outside collective bargaining as a likely development in addition to union representation.

The board of director studies (Brannen et al. 1976, Engelstad and Qvale 1977) show that the union strengthens its position vis-à-vis management where it takes control over the representative function. Where the union elects, trains, and monitors the labor representatives to supervisory boards and manages the communication flow between representatives and the rank and file, worker representatives have a better chance of being effective worker advocates on the board because they are perceived by management as being interest group representatives with union power. Where the union plays a minor role in the management of the worker participation and limits itself to collective bargaining and contract management, the chances of worker cooptation by management, exactly what the union fears, are much higher.

The research to date on the union role in worker participation programs is limited and thus we cannot draw firm conclusions about increases or decreases in union strength. However, the research suggests that the union can strengthen its function as interest group representative when it takes a proactive instead of a reactive stance toward participation, power-sharing, or joint ownership. Data from both the U.S. and Europe show that labor-management cooperation in an area of common interest, such as the firm's economic survival, does not forge one common interest group from the two parties. If anything, the cooperation tends to define more sharply areas where interests diverge, such as the distribution of earnings (Brannen et al. 1976, Engelstad and Qvale 1976), which reinforces the need for union representation to protect worker interests. To strengthen its position in both ownership and participation programs, the union may have to retain its role as the workers' voice but change its role vis-à-vis management from pure adversarial to more of a managing partner.

Conclusion

The flourishing interest in worker participation which began in the early 1970s has left us in the usual state of the applied social sciences: our knowledge about the processes and outcomes of joint labor-management decision-making is more extensive now, but we have more questions seeking answers.

It is clear that the legislative and organizational enthusiasm which has enveloped participative decision-making has not resulted in widespread workplace democratization. The potential for worker influence in the running of the enterprises which is offered by legally based participation programs has not been realized. Workers participate in the execution but not in the setting of organization policies. We do not know what factors individually, or in combination, hinder or facilitate democracy in the workplace, and research which goes beyond the documentation of the IDE study is needed on the participation model. We also cannot specify with any certainty whether worker participation leads to more effective organizations in the long run.

Further, the findings to date do not show how extensive the involvement of workers is even in the execution of company policies. Where participation is by representation, the vast majority of the workforce remains outside the decision-making process. Where participation is direct, it appears that most workers are still only marginally involved. As a rule, the case studies describe small groups of workers who over time become isolated in the organization. When participative structures are diffused throughout organizations, some workers are more active than others. The evaluation research has been silent on the questions of the extent and depth of participation. It has assumed that a participation program "takes" once it is implemented, as suggested by positive changes in job satisfaction, worker involvement, and motivation.

There is a need for research that examines the participation process itself and addresses the relatively simple questions of who participates, how participation occurs, and what program and organizational characteristics facilitate or hinder their participation. Such questions are being raised by organizational behavior researchers in current work on union participation (Gordon et al. 1980), and they should be raised with respect to organizational participation as well.

When answering these questions, reliance on the one presently dominant method of participation research—the qualitative case study—should be avoided. We have learned far more about the effects of legal and granted participation from the few carefully designed studies than from the numerous case reports available. It is high time for participation researchers to move beyond evaluation by story-telling.

The Decision to Vote For or Against Union Representation

Empirical research and theorizing about the decision to vote for or against union representation are reviewed in this section.[10] The 1970s produced a substantial amount of empirical research and some theorizing about factors leading to union organization. As is typical in the organizational behavior literature, the theoretical articles are propositional and the empirical research is distinctly atheoretical. Factors assumed to influence employee decisions about union organizing are measured and the decisions modeled use correlational (not causal or confirmatory) techniques. As a result, it is relatively easy to identify the major factors that appear to influence attitudes toward unions (or are at least correlated with votes), attitudes about working conditions, attitudes about influence, and possibly the perceived company and union campaigns.[11] In this section we take on the formidable task of proposing a structural model which indicates the causal order and causal direction among these variables and a theory of decision-making which explains the causal relationships. First, the literature is reviewed to identify potential causal connections. Then a model is proposed, along with a theoretical rationale which justifies the proposed causal connections.

The Decision to Vote For or Against Union Representation

Union Attitudes. A significant correlation between some measures of attitudes toward unions and vote has been found in every study reviewed which measured these two constructs (see Table 1). Measures include attitudes toward unions in general, or what Kochan (1979) calls "Big Labor Image," attitudes or beliefs about union instrumentality, and attitudes about the suitability of collective bargaining. The employees who vote for union representation are those who are favorable toward unions in general and/or who believe a union can be instrumental in improving their con-

[10] There is little behavioral research on decertification (see Anderson et al. 1980, Chafetz and Fraser 1979); the theories and models that explain individual decisions to vote for union representation seem appropriate for explaining similar individual decisions to vote to decertify union representation.

[11] We have not included intent because it is most likely a pure mediating variable between these factors and vote (e.g., these variables have no direct effect on vote other than the effect which is mediated by intent). See Cook and Campbell (1979) and James et al. (1982) for an explanation of mediating variables.

ditions of employment and/or who believe collective bargaining is appropriate for employees like themselves. This relationship is powerful and it holds in both blue- and white-collar samples. Attitudes toward unions predict vote (Getman et al. 1976), are associated with union membership (Flango 1975, Martin 1978, Walker and Lawler 1979), and are associated with vote intent (Kochan 1979).

While the research does not identify the unique causes of pro-union attitudes, there appear to be general trends. Kochan (1979), whose random sample survey data provide a good basis for drawing inferences about trends, concludes that there is a tremendous organizing opportunity for the labor movement among unorganized minority employees and white-collar women because of their prounion attitudes, but that no other group characterized by age, education, or industry is likely to show a strong preference for union representation in the abstract. It is true that in certain elections members of one or more demographic or job groups tend to have similar attitudes toward unions and to vote in a similar manner. This appears to be due to characteristics of their shared experiences and is only predictable based on knowledge of those experiences. For example, Getman et al. (1976) report that in several elections in which the union was successfully characterized as discriminatory against blacks, black employees voted overwhelmingly against union representation. Farber and Saks (1980) show that employees who were relatively well paid compared to others in their unit were antiunion. The several studies of university faculty representation show that similar groups—for example, untenured faculty—have different attitudes toward collective bargaining depending on their peculiar circumstance (Feuille and Blandin 1974, Flango 1975, Muczyk et al. 1975, Seidman et al. 1974, Walker and Lawler 1979).

There appears to be a significant but moderate correlation between attitudes toward unions and attitudes toward working conditions. In general, employees who are dissatisfied with their working conditions are more positive toward unions both in the abstract (Kochan 1979) and in the midst of a union representation election (Getman et al. 1976). Attitudes toward working conditions may be a causal factor influencing attitudes toward unions—that is, as an employee becomes more dissatisfied (satisfied) with the job, he/she becomes more positive (negative) toward unions, but there is no research that either confirms or refutes this causal direction.

Union Campaign and Union Attitudes. Only Getman et al. (1976) have data which show that the union's campaign may contribute to prounion attitudes. While employees who were initially prounion apparently attended more closely to the union campaign than did other employees, a change in union attitudes and a switch from a procompany vote to a prounion vote *was* associated with familiarity with the union campaign and attending union campaign meetings.[12]

Attitudes Toward Working Conditions. Table 1 also shows studies which have found an association between attitudes toward working conditions and union activity, union membership, and vote or vote intent. There is a bit more variability in the power and significance of the relationships between various measures of satisfaction with working conditions and the dependent variables than was the case with the relationships between measures of attitudes towards unions and the dependent variable. There are some general trends, however. Dissatisfaction with wages and other extrinsic working conditions, such as security and promotion, are frequently associated with vote, union membership, and vote intent in white- and blue-collar settings (Kochan 1979; see also Hammer and Berman 1981, Le Louarn 1980). Getman et al. (1976), with their largely blue-collar sample, found satisfaction with work itself to be the least highly correlated with vote of any of the working conditions measured. Several studies find treatment by supervisors to be an important variable, and Hamner and Smith (1978) find that morale (a group's average satisfaction with supervision) predicts the future degree of union activity in that group.

Many of the studies in white-collar units find dissatisfaction with, or desire for, some form of employee influence to be a significant factor. Unfortunately, desire for influence was not always measured in the blue-collar samples. Kochan's (1979) data pro-

[12] The correlation which supports this statement and the conclusions in Getman et al. (1976, p. 145) are not reported. The correlation between familiarity with the union campaign and independent change in attitudes toward unions $r = .10$; $p \leq .01$. While we are hesitant to draw causal inferences from results that are not based on a full confirmatory analysis, the analytic procedures on which the Getman et al. attitude change data were based (Tucker et al. 1966) meet many of the conditions necessary for causal inference.

TABLE 1

Studies Showing Relationships Between Union Attitudes and Union Membership, Vote and Vote Intent

Study	Type of Attitude	Dependent Variable	Causes of Union Attitude	Type of Unit	Company Attitude
Alutto & Belasco 1974	Collective bargaining	Collective bargaining	Demographics, Job characteristics	White-collar	
Belasco & Alutto 1969	Collective bargaining	Collective bargaining	Demographics, Job characteristics	White-collar	Influence
Bigoness 1978	Collective bargaining	Collective bargaining	Wages	White-collar	
Brett 1980a,[a] Brett 1980b,[a]	Instrumentality	Vote		Same as Getman et al.	Promotion, Job security
Farber & Saks 1980					
Feuille & Blandin 1974	Collective bargaining	Collective bargaining	Demographics, Job characteristics	White-collar	$, Fringes, Influence
Flango 1975[b]	Collective bargaining	Preelection union membership		White-collar	$
Getman et al. 1976	Labor image, Instrumentality	Vote	Demographics, Job characteristics, Union campaign	Primarily blue-collar	$, Fringes, Promotion, Job security, Treatment by supervisors
Hammer & Berman 1981		Vote (post hoc)		White-collar	Trust, Job content, Security, $

TABLE 1 (*Continued*)

Study	Type of Attitude	Dependent Variable	Causes of Union Attitude	Type of Unit	Company Attitude
Hamner & Smith 1978		Degree of union activity		White- and blue-collar	Supervision
Hellriegel et al. 1970	Collective bargaining	Collective bargaining	Job characteristics	White-collar	
Herman 1973[a]					
Kochan 1979	Labor image, Instrumentality	Intent	Demographics, Job characteristics	White- and blue-collar	$, Fringes, Job content, Influence
Le Louarn 1980	Instrumentality	Vote (post hoc)		White-collar (nurses)	Stress, Role conflict, Role ambiguity, Supervision, $, Influence
Martin 1978	Collective bargaining	Union membership		White-collar (clerical)	$, Coworkers, Supervision
Muczyk et al. 1975	Collective bargaining	Vote (post hoc)		White-collar (professors)	$
Schriesheim 1978	Labor image, Instrumentality	Vote (post hoc)		Blue-collar	$, Security, Working conditions, Independence
Seidman et al. 1974		Intent	Demographics, Job characteristics	White-collar	$, Promotion, Organizational commitment
Walker & Lawler 1979	Collective bargaining	Union membership		White-collar	

[a] See Getman et al. 1976.

[b] Lack of statistical analysis makes this study difficult to present.

vide aid in drawing conclusions here. He reports that the desirability of participation is more highly correlated with vote intent than perceived difficulty in exerting influence for white-collar workers, but both variables contribute significantly for both groups.

The research on union organizing does not identify the unique conditions that cause dissatisfaction with working conditions. Organizational behavior researchers typically assume that experiences in the work environment, either real or perceived, stimulate the formation of attitudes and attitudes cause behaviors, such as absenteeism (Steers and Rhodes 1978) or turnover (Porter and Steers 1973).[13]

While there is some evidence that objective differences in wages within a firm are related to differences in voting behavior, presumably through the mediating variable of attitudes (Farber and Saks 1980), objective differences between firms do not necessarily correspond to differences in vote outcome. The best evidence for this conclusion is in Susan Catler's unpublished bachelor's thesis (1978). With data from 10 years of files of the AFL-CIO's Organizing Department, she was able to evaluate the relationships among a number of economic, legal, and organizational variables and vote outcome in over 1200 campaigns. While her sample is probably not representative of the National Labor Relations Board (NLRB) elections which were held during this period, it is large, and there is substantial variance on both the independent and dependent variables. She found no significant correlations between the election outcome and the local unemployment rate, change in the unemployment rate, inflation, degree of unionization in the local area, whether or not the election occurred in a right-to-work state, geographical region, industry, firm size, or average wage compared to the industry wage. Getman et al.'s (1976) data on 30 elections support Catler's findings; they find no significant correlations between the election outcome and the local unemployment rate, cost of living, degree of unionization in the local area, type of industry, or firm size.

It seems likely that objective differences between firms are not always mirrored by substantive differences in attitudes and be-

[13] This theory—that attitudes cause behavior rather than vice versa—is a long-standing argument in the organizational behavior literature (Lawler and Porter 1967, Weick 1969 and 1979).

liefs. Getman et al.'s data clearly indicate that it is the subjective factors which carry the relationship to vote.

There are simply no data indicating that prounion attitudes are causes as opposed to mere correlates of dissatisfaction with working conditions and the desire for influence. To the extent that employees bring their pro- or antiunion attitudes with them when they accept employment in a firm, these attitudes are likely to act as a filter that affects the development of the employees' attitudes toward working conditions. Yet, attitudes toward unions may be strongly influenced by the union attitudes of coworkers and supervisors. Hence, it is extremely difficult to propose that union attitudes are either direct or reciprocal causes of attitudes toward working conditions and desire for participation, or whether they are merely correlates, both caused by other factors.

Attitudes Toward Working Conditions and the Campaign. There are also no data to indicate that either the company or union campaign causes changes in attitudes toward working conditions *which are not predictable from employees' initial attitudes.* Getman et al. (1976) is the only study with data relevant to this issue. They measured the actual campaign—that is, the issue content of letters, speeches, and meetings; they had an independent determination made of the legality of the campaign; and they measured employees' perceptions of the campaign. There are significant correlations between switch and change in attitudes toward working conditions (Getman et al. 1976, Table 3-10), but no significant correlations between change in attitudes toward working conditions and company campaign familiarity, perception of the unlawful campaign, or actual occurrence of unlawful campaigning.[14] They suggest that the correlation between attitude change and switch might be due to cognitive dissonance (McGuire 1960) or what Weick (1979) today calls retrospective sense-making —that is, I voted against union representation, so I think conditions are pretty good around here. There is no evidence in the Getman et al. study to support cognitive information processing theory that information from the company campaign caused attitude change and vote switch, in that order.

[14] The data supporting these statements do not appear in Getman et al. (1976). The correlations are with company campaign familiarity $r = .00$, NS; perceptions of unlawful campaigning: reprisal $r = -.07$, NS; benefit $r = -.07$, NS; total $r = -.05$, NS; occurrence of unlawful campaigning $r = -.06$, NS.

Union Campaign. Given Getman et al.'s (1976) results, it seems reasonable to propose that the union campaign has a direct, independent effect on vote. Figure 1 shows an incomplete structural model of the cognitive decision process leading to a decision to vote for or against union representation.[15] It is also a somewhat atypical cognitive model in that attitudes, not perceptions, are represented as the primary causal factors. This is because employees have attitudes about unions in general, the instrumentality of unions, the appropriateness of collective bargaining for employees like themselves, their working conditions, and their influence when there is no imminent union representation election (Kochan 1979). The figure shows the relationship between union attitudes and the perceived union campaign as reciprocal, because Getman et al. find that employees who are prounion are more likely to attend to the union campaign and employees who attended union meetings became more prounion. The relationship between company attitudes, including attitudes toward working conditions and influence and perceptions of the union campaign, is also reciprocal because Getman et al. find that employees who are satisfied with working conditions are less likely to attend to the union campaign, but that exposure to the union campaign in the form of attendance at union meetings is related to change in attitudes toward the company.

Company Campaign. Figure 1 shows direct causal relationships between union and company attitudes and the perceived company campaign. These two causal propositions do not rule out the possibility that company and union attitudes and the company's response to the union organizing drive (for example, the company campaign) are affected by the company's general orientation toward unions (a factor which is exogenous and not represented in Figure 1). Some companies are actively and overtly antiunion, and this climate may affect employee attitudes prior to the particular organizing drive under investigation. The company's response to a particular union organizing attempt is not represented as having a reciprocal effect on attitudes or a direct effect on vote. This is because Getman et al. (1976) find no significant

[15] This figure is incomplete because it does not show all the exogenous causes of attitudes and perceptions; hence it is not a self-contained system.

FIGURE 1

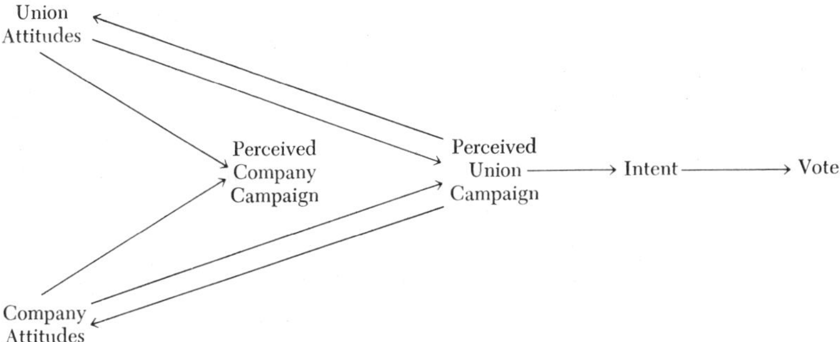

relationships between the company campaign and vote or switch and attitude change.[16]

Brett (1980) suggests that two aspects of the company campaign might have an indirect effect on vote by impacting on attitudes about the instrumentality of unions. If the company campaigns hard, some union supporters may interpret such campaigning as evidence that the employer has "seen the light" and will improve working conditions without the union. Alternatively, a strong antiunion campaign may convince some union supporters that their employer is so antiunion that a union is not going to be able to improve working conditions.

The Decision-Making Theory. Figure 1 models a social influence theory of decision-making. Currently four theories dominate the organizational behavior literature on decision-making (Pfeffer 1981, Allison 1971): rational theory, bounded rational theory, social influence theory, and garbage can, which is not technically an individual process (though see Martin 1981). Rational theories assume the decision-maker approaches a choice by searching the environment for information about outcomes, their contingent links to alternative choices, and their personal value, and then selects the choice that maximizes the probability of favorable outcomes. Bounded rational theory (Simon 1957) emphasizes the decision-maker's cognitive limits, positing that the decision-maker will search only when motivated or stimulated by some dissatis-

[16] Note that while a significant correlation does not imply causality, a nonsignificant correlation between constructs that are reliably measured on a sufficiently large and representative sample implies lack of causality.

faction with current outcomes, then search, probably sequentially, until a satisfactory alternative is identified.

Despite the fact that the decision to vote for or against union representation is limited by two alternatives (in most units more than 88 percent of the eligible voters vote [NLRB 1980, p. 31]), there is no evidence of rational decision-making. Employees do not approach the decision in a state of uncertainty, gathering and weighing the contingencies and valences of outcomes associated with choices. The bounded rational model might be applied to this decision process—for example, as soon as the choice opportunity becomes known, the employee considers the alternatives and makes a quick decision which persists despite numerous influence attempts. Social influence theory is the most parsimonious theoretical explanation of the causal relations among the events in Figure 1 because of the importance placed on the effect of prior preferences on choice and information processing. This theory, unlike the rational or bounded rational theories, does not assume that the decision-maker searches for information. Indeed, just the opposite: the decision-maker may intentionally avoid exposure to information that is likely to conflict with preferences and, if exposed to such information, may distort it during cognitive processing, such that upon retrieval the information appears to support rather than conflict with the original preference.

The garbage can may model the ideas of some employees whose votes cannot be modeled by social influence theory. While this theory has been most widely applied at the organizational level to describe decision-making in organized anarchies or loosely coupled systems, its metaphors, if not its constructs, can be easily translated to the individual decisions. According to Cohen, March, and Olson (1972), decisions are opportunities into which problems and solutions are dumped. The decision-maker moves through the environment (the can) in a more or less random fashion, bumping into information and social influence attempts (the garbage) which either glance off or influence him, possibly in obvious, but more likely in subtle and initially imperceptible ways. The decision-maker is assumed not to have predefined known preferences. Indeed, March (1978) and Weick (1979) argue that choice may cause preferences rather than vice versa. The decision-maker also does not search extensively to identify alternatives and evaluate them, since such search is assumed to be costly, but decides based on information that happens to be available at the time the decision must be made.

Conclusion

Figure 1 is an inductive model derived from a large number of separate empirical investigations of attitudes and vote and one empirical study of attitudes, the campaign, and vote. The attitude-vote studies fit neatly with the social influence theory of decision-making. Even without the attitude, campaign, and vote study, one could predict simply from social influence theory that the campaign would have little independent impact on vote. The Getman et al. (1976) results confirm this proposition in a post hoc sort of way. Further research on the decision to vote for or against union representation needs to pose a priori theoretical decision models and test their fit to data using sophisticated confirmatory procedures. It may be that one or more of the causal parameters in Figure 1 is wrong or even that social influence theory is not the optimal model of this individual decision process, but it is only by posing theoretical models and testing them for confirmation/refutation that we shall advance our understanding of causal relationships.[17]

Bargaining

Organizational behavior theory and empirical research on labor-management conflict and bargaining are reviewed in this section. In order to set the stage for this review, it is essential that the reader be aware of the profound change in the theoretical conceptualization of conflict that has occurred in the organizational behavior literature in the 1970s. Organizational theory and industrial psychology have long been dominated by a norm of rationality and a management perspective. For example, the strategic contingencies theories of organizational design, which argue that some optimal organizational design exists, given the organization's

[17] What Hammer calls the "turbulence" associated with the Getman et al. findings is not discussed here. The authors have responded to their critics elsewhere (Goldberg et al. 1981). However, it is interesting to consider that social influence theory would predict the turbulence that occurred. Parties with a stake in putting on union or antiunion campaigns would be expected to reject as invalid evidence suggesting the campaign has little impact on vote independent of employees' prior attitudes.

technology, size, or environmental uncertainty (Lawrence and Lorsch 1967, Galbraith 1973, Woodward 1965, Pennings 1975), assume that if such contingencies could be uncovered, the implementation of rational structures would be straightforward (Pfeffer 1981, p. 14). Likewise, expectancy theories of motivation, choice, and attitude formation, which argue that behavior is a function of subjective utilities (Vroom 1964, Lawler 1973, Fishbein and Ajzen 1975), assume that if alternatives and outcomes could be specified, behavior would be predictable. Intraorganizational conflict, much less collective bargaining with a union, has no legitimate role in organizations which are rationally structured and rationally managed. Indeed, because this view assumes that conflict adversely affects individual efficiency and organizational performance (Pfeffer 1981), much of organizational development has been geared toward the elimination of conflict through techniques such as interpersonal peace-making (Walton 1969) and process consultation (Schein 1969).

Models that view organizations as political systems in which workgroups, interest groups, and coalitions vie for power are receiving increased attention in the organizational behavior literature (Bacharach and Lawler 1980, Pfeffer 1978 and 1981, Weick 1969 and 1979). While a unionized organization is an anathema to the functional-rational view of organizations, from the political perspective the union is just another interest group participating in the power struggle. Not only does conflict have a legitimate role in the political models of organizations, but conflict and bargaining are considered to be basic aspects of organizational decision-making. The presence of conflict does not mean the organization is in the process of destroying itself, but only that there is a heterogeneity of preferences and values within the organization.[18] Theorists, Weick (1979), for example, who take an evolutionary perspective, argue further that such heterogeneity is necessary for an organization to adapt effectively to a complex and changing environment. From this perspective, conflict must be managed,

[18] To be sure, classical bargaining theorists typically assume that bargainers act rationally, comparing costs and benefits of no agreement to costs and benefits of particular settlements (Bacharach and Lawler 1981, p. 4). Modern theorists such as Bacharach and Lawler (1980, 1981) point out that bargaining is so fraught with uncertainty and ambiguity that purely rational bargaining behavior is not possible. Furthermore, even if rational bargaining were possible, it would not eliminate conflict.

not eliminated—and managed in such a way as to preserve the internal heterogeneity of preferences and values. Organizational development, far from trying to eradicate conflict, should be geared toward the preservation of heterogeneity by designing structures and processes within which effective bargaining and problem-solving can occur (Brett et al. 1980).[19]

In this respect the theory and practice of industrial relations in the U.S. is far ahead of the theory and practice of organizational behavior. The system of laws that governs industrial relations in both the public and private sectors legitimizes the conflict between union and management and provides a normative structure—bargaining—within which conflict can be at least partially contained and the heterogeneity of values preserved. An effective union-management relationship is one in which the conflict can be controlled through bargaining, perhaps with the aid of a third party such as a mediator or arbitrator, but without the intervention of the legal system within which the industrial relations system is embedded (Brett 1980).

Failure of the industrial relations system to contain such conflict suggests the need for structural changes and experimentation with new forms of conflict management. Much of the behaviorally oriented research on bargaining in the 1970s can be viewed in just this way—attempts to evaluate how various structures and strategies impact on the effectiveness of bargaining. The research has been done in both laboratory and field settings and occurs in the context of both contract and grievance negotiations.

Bargaining occurs between parties linked in power-dependency relationships with each other and with their respective constituencies, within the limits of formal and normative structures, under conditions of incomplete information, and sometimes with the assistance of a third party. This section reviews the literature, both theoretical and empirical, that discusses the impact of these conditions on the effectiveness of bargaining. It ends with a review of the literature on bargaining processes, with a focus on bargaining strategies, tactics, and outcomes.

---

[19] A review of the organizational development literature is beyond the scope of this paper, but see, for example, Szilagyi and Wallace's (1980, Ch. 7) discussion of the use of lateral systems, liaisons, integrating departments, task forces, teams, and matrix structures to preserve heterogeneity or preferences and manage intergroup conflict.

Power-Dependency Relationships

Pfeffer (1981) points out that power is tricky to define but easy to recognize: a powerful party is one which is able to get outcomes it desires. Bacharach and Lawler review the theoretical literature on power in two very important books (1980 and 1981), and in their most recent book they conclude that power is a primitive term and refuse to define it. Their very thorough theoretical discussion, however, lays the groundwork for defining power as the subjective appraisal of the dependence of parties linked in a social exchange relationship *and* of the likelihood that that dependence will be exploited. Party A's power is partly a function of Party B's dependence on A. Party B's dependence on A is a function of the availability to B of alternative sources of outcomes which can be obtained from the relationship with A and the value to B of those outcomes[20] (see also Emerson 1962 and 1972). Bacharach and Lawler (1981) argue further that the punitive capability aspect of power be distinguished from the dependence aspect. Punitive capability, following Tedeschi, is the magnitude of B's valued outcomes that A has the ability to remove times the credibility of A's removing them (Bacharach and Lawler 1981, p. 116).

This view of power is particularly useful when studying union-management relationships because it distinguishes between the stake parties have in the relationship (dependence) and their ability to control each other's outcomes (punitive capability), the latter characteristic being useless if the parties need not interact. Moreover, this definition of power is useful in considering both inter- and intraorganizational bargaining in the union-management context, since not only are union and management dependent on each other for outcomes, but chief negotiators and bargaining teams on both union and management sides have power-dependency exchange relationships with their respective constituencies.

Constituencies

The literature on the effect of constituencies illustrates a power-dependency exchange relationship in action. Real, imagined, or anticipated pressure from a constituency changes a negotiator's

[20] Bacharach and Lawler (1981) use the term commitment instead of value.

behavior in the direction that the bargainer thinks will be positively evaluated by the constituency (Rubin and Brown 1975). At least in the laboratory, this means the bargainer's behavior becomes more aggressive. Peterson and Tracy (1976), in a field study, show that anticipated constituency approval, measured prior to bargaining, correlates with bargainers' perceived success in problem-solving, measured after negotiations. Constituencies that are anticipated to support the bargainer apparently free him/her for problem-solving. Bargainers that do not anticipate constituency approval are not successful in problem-solving, by their own evaluation. Deutsch's (1973) research suggests why: Bargainers under constituency pressure reduce their problem-solving behaviors. Their search for alternative ways to resolve issues becomes limited, as does their ability to take each other's roles and see the situation from the opponent's point of view (see also Klimoski 1972, Klimoski and Ash 1974).

Formal and Normative Bargaining Structures

Formal and normative bargaining structures are the rules under which bargaining occurs. Formal structures are statutory in the case of contract negotiation (that is, a state law requiring arbitration of public-sector impasses) and contractual in the case of grievance negotiation (that is, the grievance procedure). Normative structures are general expectations about patterns of interaction that develop over time—that is, a bargaining norm or equality or equity. These structures are intended to impact on bargaining through their effect on the parties' power, particularly the likelihood that parties will use their punitive capability.

The 1970s produced substantial research on structures relevant to contract negotiation and some research and theorizing about structures that affect grievance negotiation. This section reviews that research.

Contract Negotiation. The proliferation of state labor laws and the variety of Canadian provincial labor laws provide rich research material for studying the impact of various statutory provisions for resolving impasses. Alternatives include mediation, fact-finding (where the third party issues written recommendations for settlement of the dispute), conventional arbitration, and final-offer arbitration (where a third party chooses the final offer of one party or the other). From a theoretical perspective, each technique can be viewed as a structure which, because it reduces the parties' control over bargaining outcomes, should stimulate them to avoid this loss of control and to bargain effectively to a settlement. If they do reach an impasse, each loses some control as a third party intervenes in a more or less controlling manner, depending upon statutory provisions.

There are numerous issues in evaluating the effectiveness of these techniques: Are these statutory provisions for impasse resolution better than no statutory provisions at all? If so, which provision or set of provisions is most effective and under what conditions? Are contracts resulting from one or another of the procedures more or less acceptable to the parties?

While the effectiveness of these impasse resolution procedures has been thoroughly researched in the 1970s (see Anderson [1981] for a review), the results are equivocal. Kochan (1980b) concludes that any impasse resolution procedure is better than no provision in terms of avoiding impasses and strikes. The literature, however, is replete with references to the procedures' "side effects" (Feuille 1975, Anderson and Kochan 1977, Kochan et al. 1979). In particular, it is presumed that they "chill" bargaining and become "addictive." Chilling implies that parties bargaining under an impasse resolution statute defer making concessions until the third party becomes involved, and chilled bargaining is believed to be addictive or to have a narcotic effect in that once parties have made use of the impasse procedure, they are likely to do so in future negotiations. While Anderson (1981) maintains that the evidence is ambiguous as to whether or not chilling and addiction occur, Kolb (1981a) argues that these structures can be and are being used strategically (that is, to exert control over valued outcomes) to set patterns, to help chief negotiators bargain intraorganizationally, to justify politically risky arguments, and to manage professional negotiators' images. Her argument suggests that while these structures do impact on the parties power, the impact is not always equal. One party may actually perceive greater control once the third party becomes involved—that is, it may be easier to convince the arbitrator than the opponent of the merits of one's position.

No research compares all four impasse resolution procedures

directly. There appear to be higher settlement rates under statutes providing for final-offer as opposed to conventional arbitration (Feuille 1975, Notz and Starke 1978, Kochan et al. 1979).

The research on mediation shows that it is more effective under certain conditions (Kochan 1980). Specifically, the more intense the impasse, especially when the issue turns on the employer's ability to pay, the less effective is mediation. Mediation is more effective when the parties perceive the mediator to be experienced, able, and aggressive than when they do not, and when the parties are strongly motivated to settle than when they are not. With respect to issues, mediation appears to be more effective when negotiations break down because one party or the other has become overcommitted to a position than when they break down over an economic issue, such as ability to pay, or there is an intra-organizational dispute.

There are numerous descriptions of the mediation process (Kressel 1972, Kochan 1980a) and of mediator tactics (Fisher and Ury 1978, Kolb 1981b), but little research on the relationships between a mediator's tactics and outcomes. Kolb (1981b) concludes that factors beyond the mediator's control, not mediator tactics, are most important in determining bargaining outcomes. Kochan's (1980b) intermediate criteria—number of issues resolved and the parties' movement on issues—might be more useful for evaluating the effectiveness of mediator tactics. For example, Rubin and Brown (1975), after reviewing the sparse literature on third parties, concludes that mediators may be successful in breaking an impasse and getting the parties to begin to make concessions because mediator-initiated concessions allow the parties to avoid giving an impression of weakness.

Future research on mediation ought to be informed by Kolb's (1981b) recent field study. Contrary to previous literature which suggests that mediators approach an impasse with a bag full of tactics from which they select an initial strategy based on the characteristics of the situation and choose among the strategies as the mediation phase of bargaining develops, Kolb finds that there are brands of mediation. She observed nine state mediators' and six FMCS mediators' work on 16 cases and found that, throughout their cases and regardless of whether the case was in the public or private sector, state mediators played a deal-maker role and the federal mediators played the role of orchestrator. These differences in role orientation accounted for how they structured their strategy throughout the case as well as their perception of the parties. She attributes these differences in behavior to the way federal mediators are socialized and the state mediators' lack of socialization.

So while mediation may be an art whose effectiveness is difficult to gauge, mediators do get settlements using techniques that can be learned either through reinforcement by outcomes (the state mediators in Kolb's study) or by training and reinforcement through socialization (the federal mediators in Kolb's study).

Grievance Negotiation. There is little variation in the structure of grievance procedures in the U.S., but a great deal of variation in rates of grievance filing, settlements prior to arbitration, and resort to wildcat strikes (Goldberg and Brett 1982). Research has identified the parties' attitudes toward each other (Brett and Goldberg 1979, Thomson and Murray 1976, Turner and Robinson 1972) as well as technological change, technologies requiring high levels of worker responsibility, and centralization and formalization of management decision-making as correlates of high grievance rates (Thomson and Murray 1976, Peach and Livernash 1974). While this research does not establish causal order or rule out the possibility that the correlations are spurious (due to another factor, for example), there have been several attempts to use organizational development techniques to change factors that are assumed to cause distressed grievance procedures—procedures that become overloaded because of the parties' inability to resolve grievances at lower levels of the system.

The Federal Mediation and Conciliation Service has been using a program designed around behavioral science principles of attitudinal and perceptual restructuring and superordinate goal-setting (see Blake et al. 1954). The program is usually initiated in particularly troubled labor-management situations after a contract has been successfully mediated. There are numerous descriptions of the relations-by-objectives program in the literature (Brett et al. 1980, Kochan 1980a, Popular 1976, Hoyer 1979), but no evaluation studies have been published.

To deal with distressed grievance procedures, Brett and Goldberg (1979) propose a variety of organizational development techniques that focus on changing behavior, not by changing attitudes, but by changing the structure or process by which grievances are handled and, hence, by changing the power relationships. Their suggestions include establishing limits within which first-level supervisors can resolve grievances, making the grievance or strike rate a dimension of managers' performance evaluations and rewarding managers with low rates (see Lawler and Rhode [1976] for a discussion of the potential dysfunctional effects of the latter procedure), and moving grievance authority from operations to staff personnel. On the union side, they suggest having a group decide whether or not to take a grievance to arbitration (group decision-making diffuses responsibility and tends to be riskier than individual decision-making; see Wallach, Kogan, and Bem 1962).[21] To deal with wildcat strikes in the coal industry, they even suggested negotiating a local agreement giving the union the right to strike after a majority vote. Brett, Goldberg, and Ury (1980) describe a case (27 wildcat strikes in 23 months) in which three of these techniques were tried—adding a labor relations expert whose role was to absorb some, but not all, of the labor relations responsibilities at the mine; establishing limits within which foremen could settle grievances and providing incentives for them to do so; and designing and implementing a normative system, consisting of a pattern of behaviors for each party if a strike threatened. Supplementing the latter was two months of process consultation during which the third party acted more like an organizational-development consultant than a mediator in that he did not try to mediate particular issues, but suggested ways to improve the parties' negotiating behaviors when difficult issues arose. While it is impossible to determine which, if any, of the techniques were successful in reducing the number of wildcat strikes at this mine (which remained strike free for nine months from the onset of the intervention to the expiration of the wage agreement), the case illustrates intervention techniques that recognize conflict as legitimate, but try to control it with formal and normative structures.

There was some experimentation in the 1970s with expedited

---

[21] In the coal industry, about which Brett and Goldberg were writing, the decision to take a grievance to arbitration is made by an elected district representative. There are political pressures on this individual to take grievances to arbitration.

arbitration as a system intended to reduce costs and the delays associated with a heavy volume of arbitration. Pioneered in the steel industry (Fischer 1972), an expedited arbitration structure usually requires that the hearing will be informal, that the rules of evidence shall not apply, that there will be no transcript or posthearing briefs, and that the arbitrator will give his/her decision either immediately or within a few days. Most expedited arbitration decisions are not precedential. Because of this latter limitation and the parties' desire for rapid decisions that are final and binding, access to expedited arbitration is normally limited to grievances involving minor discipline (Sandver, Blaine, and Woyar 1981).

Expedited arbitration is an example of a structural change that probably will not solve the problem of an overloaded arbitration system because it does not address the underlying reasons why the system became overloaded in the first place, since it does not effect a change in the parties' power. It simply speeds up the process and makes the parties' access to a third party less costly, and it possibly could have a negative effect on the settlement rate prior to arbitration if, as suggested previously, a party perceives that it will have more influence over the outcome if a third party makes the decision than if a negotiated solution is reached. One laboratory study suggests that this may be particularly so in grievance negotiation. LaTour et al. (1976) asked bargainers participating in a simulation for their preferences for three types of bargaining—bargaining with no third party intervention, bargaining with mediation, and bargaining with binding arbitration. The subjects preferred arbitration over mediation and no third party when a standard was available.

Goldberg (1982) describes a procedure for mediating grievances which inserts a structural change—a voluntary mediation step—in the grievance procedure prior to arbitration. With this procedure, grievances should be resolved as quickly, as cheaply, and with higher acceptability than with expedited arbitration. It plays on the parties' power not by changing their control over outcomes, but by changing their value for outcomes. Additionally, it has the potential for reducing the overall load on both the mediation and arbitration steps of the grievance procedure since the mediator is serving largely as a process consultant, and over time and with reinforcement, the parties' negotiating skills should improve.

Goldberg and Brett (1982) report that in a six-month experiment with grievance mediation, the mediators were able to settle 86 percent of the grievances heard at one-quarter of the cost and in one-quarter of the time that would have been required to arbitrate these grievances. Furthermore, there was no change in the step-3 settlement rate from the period prior to the experiment to the experimental period, suggesting that mediation has no adverse effect on lower level settlements. It is too soon to tell if mediation is having the predicted impact on the abilities of the parties to negotiate successfully without third-party help, but the experiments are continuing.

Bargaining Process and Outcome

Bargaining in the labor-management context is inherently distributive (Walton and McKersie 1965). During the negotiations process, the parties make tactical choices and exchange individual concessions; the end product is a collective act—the agreement. These individual choices about concessions and tactics are assumed to be rational—that is, directed toward the goal of maximizing a party's own outcomes—within the very real limits of a bargaining situation where information is limited and ambiguous. Laboratory research indicates that choices associated with concessions and tactics are associated with a party's subjective assessment of own or opponent's power (Bacharach and Lawler 1981, Hamner 1980, Magenau and Pruitt 1979, Rubin and Brown 1975). This section discusses the theoretical relationships between power, concessions, tactics, and outcomes and associated empirical evidence, most of which is based on laboratory research.

Concessions. Concessions are behaviors that reduce the difference between parties on an issue and are attempts to influence the concession behavior or perceptions of the opponent. For example, party A's round-1 concession provides party B with some behavior from which to draw inferences about A's aspirations and intentions and on which to base a decision about party B's response. A pattern of concessions is called a bargaining strategy.

Five different models of concession behavior are identified in the theoretical literature: Schelling's (1960) fair strategy; Osgood's

(1962) strategy of reciprocity, sometimes called the soft strategy; Siegel and Fouraker's (1960) strategy of no reciprocation, usually called the tough strategy; Komorita and Brenner's (1968) moderately tough strategy of only enough reciprocation to avoid impasse; and Wall's (1977a, 1977b, 1981) strategy of reinforcement.[22]

Schelling's (1960) fair strategy is governed by an a priori norm of equity. The parties are assumed to approach bargaining from the normative perspective that there must be a fair solution to the conflict. Bargaining is dominated by open information exchange as the parties search for the fair solution. This is an ideal bargaining process for integrative issues and is theoretically viable for distributive issues. Fair, in the distributive situation, could be interpreted as equitable given the distribution of power between the parties. The model assumes that the parties can agree on what is fair in their situation and will use coercive power only to keep the other party from straying from the fair solution.

Osgood's (1962) strategy of graduated reciprocation is governed by an a priori norm of reciprocity, or tit for tat. A reciprocates B's concessions and expects his own concessions to be reciprocated. The model assumes that both parties must make concessions in order for impasses to be avoided, but that concession-making is inhibited by lack of trust. An opening unilateral concession is supposed to be followed by subsequent unilateral concessions until the opponent gains trust in the negotiator and initiates a reciprocal exchange in which A's small concessions are reciprocated by small concessions by B and A's large concessions are reciprocated by large concessions by B. Osgood suggests that this bargaining norm is valid in situations where two parties have equal power, an impasse has been reached, or the parties are being mutually pressured to reach agreement.

Siegel and Fouraker's (1960) model is a process strategy which unfolds in the course of negotiations. Bargainers are assumed to open the negotiations at their highest points of aspiration. Opponent's concessions are assumed to modify bargainer's aspiration levels according to the following model: B's concessions, large or small, are assumed to increase A's aspirations, hence inhibiting A

[22] Concession strategies that are shared by the parties and that remain in force throughout the negotiating period become normative structures which, while they reduce uncertainty in the system about bargaining norms, may or may not reduce the likelihood of impasse.

from making concessions at all. This model leads quickly to impasse unless B is willing to continue to make concessions in response to A's recalcitrance or A is willing to break the impasse by making small concessions until B begins to participate again or A's minimum aspiration level has been reached.

Komorita and Brenner's (1968) model is a variant of Siegel and Fouraker's model. They suggest a tough but reasonable strategy to avoid an impasse. B's concessions, large or small, are assumed to increase A's aspiration, but rational A ignores his greedy instinct not to concede at all and makes small concessions to avoid impasse and to keep B making concessions.

Wall's (1977a, 1977b, 1981) reinforcement model is also a process strategy which unfolds in the course of negotiations. Bargainers are assumed to value concessions because of the need to avoid impasse, but their concession-making behavior is governed by rules of reinforcement, not norms of reciprocity. When B responds to A's concession with a large concession, A will repeat his previous concession which will be smaller than B's concession. When B does not respond with a large concession, A's subsequent concession will be significantly different from his previous concession and from B's concession.

There has been a substantial amount of empirical research on these models, but unfortunately it does not provide a very strong basis for drawing conclusions and prescriptions. Much of the laboratory research on bargaining uses prisoner's dilemma games or trucking games (where parties have to negotiate over sharing a one-lane road or taking separate but longer routes) and does not simulate the type of bargaining that goes on between union and management. Much of the research that does use bilateral monopoly settings, where the parties are linked in a dependency-exchange relationship, fails to have the subject negotiators bargaining under the surveillance of a constituency. Finally, few studies build in mutual pressure to reach agreement which, according to Komorita and Barnes (1969) results in larger average concessions, more rapid agreement, and reciprocity.[23]

Strict adherence to these three boundary conditions rules out so much of the research that almost nothing could be said about

[23] Many studies have a zero payoff for both parties if no agreement is reached, but this is hardly the same as the negative outcomes that accrue to collective bargaining negotiations when a strike occurs.

the effects of different strategies on bargaining outcomes. By loosening the constituency and mutual pressure condition, conclusions can be drawn about two important research questions: Do uninstructed bargainers actually use these strategies? Which strategy is superior with respect to avoiding impasse and to the parties' satisfaction with the outcome?

Harnett and Cummings (1980) find that most bargainers' behavior can be classified into theoretical categories.[24] Table 2 presents the operational distinctions used for classification. Harnett and Cummings report that the intermediate strategy was the most frequently used, followed by the tough, soft, and fair strategies. There was no evidence of bargainers following a reciprocating

TABLE 2

Bargaining Strategy and Outcomes from Harnett and Cummings 1980

Strategy	Definition	Percent Using Strategy[a]	Time to Reach Decision	Average Payoff
Tough (Siegel & Fouraker)	Start high, concede infrequently in moderate or small amounts	23%	71 min.	$8.35
Intermediate (Komorita & Brenner)	Start intermediate concede in moderate amounts	29%	57 min.	$7.94
Soft (Osgood)	Start high, concede frequently in small amounts	18%	72 min.	$7.90
Fair (Schelling)	Start at fair position or move rapidly to it, concede little or nothing after fair position reached	15%	60 min.	$7.17

[a] Fifteen percent of the subjects could not be classified.

[24] This study makes an important contribution to understanding bargaining behavior because of its design. Subjects, an international sample of managers, played against each other in a bilateral monopoly game. Subjects had information about their own payoff matrices, but not about their opponent's, and the payoff matrices were asymmetric—both realistic conditions. Subjects were allowed to keep their profits (less than $10 on the average). Subjects had plenty of time, 90 minutes, to strike a bargain and to exhibit bargaining strategies for the experiments to model. The only important bargaining conditions that were not present in this study were constituencies and pressure to reach agreement, though all but four groups did reach agreement.

strategy.[25] Wall (1981) corroborates this finding and shows further that although subjects expected reciprocity on the first round, when they did not get a reciprocal concession (from a subject opponent) they quickly ceased expecting reciprocity and shortly became quite accurate in predicting their opponent's concessions.

The low correlations between bargainers' concession patterns in these two studies does not necessarily mean that a bargainer's concession behavior has no impact on his opponent's concession behavior. Wall (1977a, 1977b, 1981) has shown, in a series of laboratory experiments, that bargainers' behavior can be altered both by opponent concession behavior (reinforcement) and constituency reinforcement. In the study which crosses opponent and constituency reinforcement (all bargainers had constituencies; some constituencies gave no feedback), accountability to a constituency appeared to wipe out the main effect of opponent reinforcement. This study provides further evidence of the impact of a constituency on a bargainer's behavior.

Several reviews (Rubin and Brown 1975, Ch. 9; Bacharach and Lawler 1980, p. 125; Magenau and Pruitt 1979) conclude that an overall tough strategy with a high opening offer and only enough concessions to avoid impasse yields the highest bargaining payoff. Table 2 show that in the Harnett and Cummings (1980) study, differences in time to reach agreement between strategies were not large, though they report much more variability in time in the fair group than in the others. Average payoffs differed significantly only between the fair groups and the others. When they broke strategy down into initial offer, size of concession, and frequency of concession, size of initial offer and average size of concession were negatively correlated and related to payoff. Bargainers who started high and made smaller concessions had larger profits than bargainers who started at a more intermediate level and who also tended to make larger concessions. The frequency of bargainers' concessions was not related to payoffs in the univariate analysis, but added a significant increment to the multiple correlation after size of concession.

Hamner (1974) simulated a stalemate and then had subjects bargain against an experimenter who was programmed to follow a tough strategy, an intermediate strategy, a soft strategy (tit for

[25] Note the soft strategy was not defined as reciprocating.

tat), and a fair strategy—a single concession to the middle of the bargaining range and no concessions thereafter. The soft strategy resulted in significantly higher payoffs for the experimenter than any other strategy. It also resulted in more agreements in a shorter period of time than did any tougher strategies.

These studies suggest that the fair strategy is probably not as effective as the others. The soft strategy may be best following an impasse. The tough strategy may be a marginally better initial strategy. While these studies have made significant contributions to our understanding of bargaining behavior, there is substantial room for more research. One major unanswered question is which strategy is superior when played against which other strategy. For example, the tough strategy may be superior when played against a soft or fair strategy, but not when played against a tough or intermediate strategy. Another question is how a negotiator can get his/her opponent to change strategies. Wall (1981) suggests a reinforcement strategy as a possible answer, but not when under the watchful eye of a constituency. Yet another question is, how do bargaining strategies and bargaining tactics interact?

Tactics. Tactics are attempts to influence the opponent's perceptions via argumentation. There are basically two types of tactics: those that attempt to change the opponent's perceptions of his/her own power, and those that attempt to change the opponent's perceptions of the party's power. Sanctions are a special case of the latter type. For example, party A could attempt to increase the opponent's (party B's) perception of party A's power by threatening to withhold from B outcomes that B values and depends upon A to provide. Alternatively, A may try to convince B that an outcome B provides to A is available to A elsewhere or is not highly valued by A.

Bacharach and Lawler (1980) point out two important cautions regarding the use of tactics. First, tactics can be countered by blocking or matching. In example 1 above, B could block A by protecting B's relationship with its alternatives. In example 2, B could block A from acquiring alternatives. Alternatively, B could counter A's tactics by matching A's behavior. In example 1, B could act to increase A's dependency on B by reciprocally reducing A's alternative sources of outcomes. Or in example 2, B could act to decrease dependency on A by increasing its own sources of outcomes. Second, the actual use of coercive tactics, as opposed to the threat, results in a decrease in the power of the party that used the tactic. For example, if B is dependent on A because A pays high wages, and A threatens and then reduces B's wages, A becomes less powerful because A no longer provides the outcome B values—high wages. Hence, while threats are potentially powerful tactics, they are effective only if the threatened party believes the threatener will act, and the threatener does not want to act because the act of coercion will reduce his power.

Other problems with tactical action are whether or not B perceives what A intends to convey by a tactical argument and whether or not B believes A. Perceptual accuracy in bargaining is apparently no different from perceptual accuracy in any other organizational setting—it is poor. Balke et al. (1973) applied the paradigm used in human judgment studies to an enacted contract negotiation and found that even after the negotiation was over and the final outcome was known to all parties, in reenacting different stages of face-to-face bargaining, negotiators were inaccurate not only about their opponents' judgments, but also about their own. Further research shows that negotiators do not always believe accurately perceived communications. For example, threats that are not backed by power, low cost to the threatening party, high status, and the party's reputation for carrying out threats are unlikely to be believed (Tedeschi et al. 1973).

There is almost no empirical research on the use of noncoercive tactics (Magenau and Pruitt 1979, Bacharach and Lawler 1980). Relevant research issues include identifying determinants of a bargainer's choice of tactics and assessing the effectiveness of various tactics or combinations of tactics in changing bargaining strategies and breaking impasses. Bacharach and Lawler (1980) provide a number of testable hypotheses about tactical choice.

The research on sanctions is greatly enriched by a study reported in Bacharach and Lawler's 1981 book.[26] They report finding a pattern of tactical reciprocity that is particularly strong when the factors are sanctions. This pattern is not related to the party's punitive capacity, nor is it related to concession behavior. Apparently once one party begins threatening, the other, regardless of his/her punitive capability, reciprocates the threats. As bar-

[26] Unfortunately this study's methods are only briefly described.

gaining continues, the threats turn into sanctioning acts and concession behavior actually decreases. Bacharach and Lawler's findings are consistent with conclusions about the relationship between sanctioning tactics and bargaining outcome drawn from the literature by Magenau and Pruitt (1979) and Rubin and Brown (1975).

Conclusion

In the preceding discussion of behavioral theory and research relevant to conflict and bargaining, we made a number of points —among them that models which view organizations as political systems in which workgroups, interest groups, and coalitions vie for power are receiving increasing attention in organizational behavior. This perspective is particularly useful in looking at union-management relations because it means that the union is just another interest group vying for power, conflict is legitimate, and conflict does not mean the organization is in the process of destroying itself. Indeed, just the opposite. Conflict that can be managed in such a way as to resolve issues without destroying the heterogeneity of parties' views may be the key to effective organizational adaptation and survival. The behavioral research on bargaining in the 1970s can be viewed as an attempt to evaluate how various bargaining structures and processes impact on the effectiveness of bargaining.

The dependency definition of power was developed to provide a basis for understanding the relationship between bargaining power and bargaining outcome. We also reviewed the effects of various bargaining structures, strategies, and tactics on bargaining outcomes.

Conclusion

It was our intention in this chapter to illustrate the application of organizational behavior theory to research in union-management contexts by reviewing the theory and empirical research on participative decision-making, the decision to vote for or against union representation, and bargaining. The reviews show, first, that there has been a substantial amount of empirical research on these topics in the past ten years, including several landmark studies. Second, they show that while there is much well-developed theory available in the literature, few of the empirical studies test theory explicitly and many are not even theory driven. Third, the empirical research often has substantial methodological limitations. For example, there is an overabundance of case studies in the participation research area and an overreliance on cross-sectional data for drawing causal inferences in the voting studies. While the conflict and bargaining literatures are balanced between field studies and laboratory experiments, few of the laboratory experiments adhere strictly to the boundary conditions of collective bargaining. As a result of the theoretical and methodological limitations of this earlier research, there are substantial research gaps to be filled during the next decade.

We suspect that had we cast our topic net broadly and presented only the merest highlights of our reviews of the theoretical and empirical literature, our conclusion would have been the same: Due to theoretical and methodological limitations of past research, there is much more research to be done. This general, two-pronged criticism is as solid when applied to traditional organizational behavior topics, such as leadership and organizational design, as it is to these industrial relations topics. Much of the problem can be attributed to the training and proclivities of the scholars.

Theory in organizational behavior tends to be borrowed from the disciplines of psychology and sociology. In psychology, theoretical development has been closely tied to programs of experimental research. Nonexperimental researchers in psychology have long been trained to avoid drawing causal inferences from correlational data. Hence, their studies, while testing hypotheses about relationships, do not test hypotheses about causal relationships. Sociologists and economists have been using path analysis and structural equation techniques for some time to test hypotheses about causal relationships. After a flurry of such studies in the organizational behavior literature in the mid-1970s, the techniques seem to be little used now. There are several reasons. First, path analysis and structural equation techniques have only recently been introduced into the psychology and organizational behavior curriculums; thus, the use of these techniques was not widely understood in the mid-1970s. Second, the analytic technology vastly outstripped the researchers' theoretical technology; that is, until recently the theoretical requirements for using these techniques were not widely known. Third, psychologists and psychology-trained organizational behavior researchers are always worried about measurement error. Manifest variable models, such as path analysis, assume perfectly reliable data. Computer programs for structural equation modeling with latent variables have become widely available recently, and these latent variable models, assuming their assumptions are met, avoid reliability problems. Thus, this diffusion of knowledge of structural equation techniques should increase the degree of theory-testing in nonexperimental research in both organizational behavior and industrial relations in the coming years.

We do not foresee a similar breakthrough in research methodology which will solve the problem of nonreliance on a particular method. Ethnomethodology is currently "hot" in organizational behavior (see Van Maanen, Dabbs, and Faulkner 1981). But the problem is not so much one of increasing the number of research methodologies available (see Campbell and Stanley 1963, Cook and Campbell 1979, James, Mulaik, and Brett 1982, as well as Van Maanen et al.) as of generating research on a particular topic that utilizes more than one method. Two factors cut against progress along these lines. First, while most Ph.D. students are trained in multiple methods, they become experts, through experience, in only one or two, and as scholars, they tend to stick with the methods of their expertise. We accept this practice as almost inevitable. Second, research funding is so sparse, and promises to continue to be, that it seems unlikely that there will be resources to utilize broadly different methodologies within the same study.

Despite our pessimism about methodology and funding, we think that the trend of research on topics that interface between organizational behavior and industrial relations will continue in the 1980s. There is a small but growing group of scholars who have already staked out this interface for research. Even though a dwindling percentage of the U.S. labor force is unionized, the issues at this interface are important because they have implications for both union and nonunion labor.

References

Adams, J. S. "Inequity in Social Exchange." In *Advances in Experimental Psychology*, ed. L. Berkowitz. New York: Academic Press, 1965.

Allison, G. T. *Essence of Decision*. Boston: Little, Brown, 1971.

Alutto, J., and J. A. Belasco. "Determinants of Attitudinal Militancy Among Nurses and Teachers." *Industrial and Labor Relations Review* 27 (January 1974): pp. 216–27.

Anderson, J. C., C. A. O'Reilly III, and G. Busman. "Union Decertification in the U.S.: 1947–1977." *Industrial Relations* 19 (Winter 1980): pp. 100–107.

Anderson, J. C. "Evaluating the Impact of Compulsory Arbitration: A Methodological Assessment." *Industrial Relations* 20 (Spring 1981): pp. 128–48.

Anderson, J. C., and T. A. Kochan. "Impasse Procedures in the Canadian Federal Service: Effects on the Bargaining Process." *Industrial and Labor Relations Review* 30 (April 1977): pp. 283–301.

Argyris, C. *Integrating the Individual and the Organization*. New York: Wiley, 1964.

Bacharach, S. B., and E. J. Lawler. *Bargaining, Power, Tactics, and Outcomes*. San Francisco: Jossey-Bass, 1981.

———. *Power and Politics in Organizations*. San Francisco: Jossey-Bass, 1980.

Balke, W. M., K. R. Hammond, and G. D. Meyer. "An Alternate Approach to Labor-Management Relations." *Administrative Science Quarterly* 18 (September 1973): pp. 311–27.

Bank, J., and K. Jones. *Worker Directors Speak*. Westmead, England: Gower Press, 1977.

Batt, W., and E. Weinberg. "Labor-Management Cooperation Today." *Harvard Business Review* (January 1978).

Belasco, J. A. and J. A. Alutto. "Organizational Impact of Teacher Negotiations." *Industrial Relations* 9 (October 1969): pp. 67–79.

Benton, A. A. "Accountability and Negotiations Between Group Representatives." *Proceedings*, 80th Annual Convention, American Psychological Associations, 1972. Pp. 227–28.

Berman, K. V. *Worker-Owned Plywood Companies: An Economic Analysis*. Pullman: Washington State University Press, 1967.

Bernstein, P. *Workplace Democratization: Its Internal Dynamics*. Kent, Ohio: Kent State University Press, 1976.

Bigoness, W. "Correlates of Faculty Attitudes Toward Collective Bargaining." *Journal of Applied Psychology* 63 (April 1978): pp. 228–33.

Blake, R., H. Shepard, and J. S. Mouton. *Managing Intergroup Conflict in Industry*. Houston: Gulf Publishing, 1954.

Blumberg, P. *Industrial Democracy: The Sociology of Participation*. London: Constable, 1968.

Bolweg, J. F. *Job Design and Industrial Democracy: The Case of Norway*. Leiden, The Netherlands: Martinus Nijhoff, 1976.

Bragg, J. E., and I. R. Andrews. "Participative Decision-Making: An Experimental Study in a Hospital." *Journal of Applied Behavioral Science* 9 (1973): pp. 727–36.

Brannen, P., E. Batstone, D. Fatchett, and P. White. *The Worker Directors: A Sociology of Participation*. London: Hutchinson, 1976.

Brett, J. M. "Behavioral Research on Unions and Union-Management Systems." In *Research in Organizational Behavior*, Vol. 2, eds. B. M. Staw and L. L. Cummings. Greenwich, Conn.: JAI Press, 1980a.

———. "Why Employees Want Unions." *Organizational Dynamics* (Spring 1980b): pp. 47–59.

Brett, J. M., and S. B. Goldberg. "Wildcat Strikes in Bituminous Coal Mining." *Industrial and Labor Relations Review* 32 (July 1979): pp. 465–83.

Brett, J. M., S. B. Goldberg, and W. Ury. "Mediation and Organizational Development: Models for Conflict Management." *Proceedings of the 33rd Annual Meeting, Industrial Relations Research Association,* 1980. Madison, Wis.: IRRA, 1981. Pp. 195–202.

Brickman, P. "Role Structures and Conflict Relationships." In *Social Conflict,* ed. P. Brickman. Lexington, Mass.: D. C. Heath, 1974.

Brief, A., and D. E. Rude. "Voting in Union Certification Elections: A Conceptual Analysis." *Academy of Management Review* 6 (1981): pp. 261–67.

Brown, B. R. "The Effects of Need to Maintain Face on Interpersonal Bargaining." *Journal of Experimental Social Psychology* 4 (1968): pp. 107–22.

Bullock, R. J., and E. E. Lawler III. "Incentives and Gainsharing-Stimuli for Productivity." Paper presented at American Productivity Center, Productivity Research Conference, Houston, April 1980.

Campbell, D. T. "Ethnocentric and Other Altruistic Motives." In *Nebraska Symposium on Motivation,* ed. D. Levine. Lincoln: University of Nebraska Press, 1965.

Campbell, D. T., and J. C. Stanley. "Experimental and Quasi-Experimental Designs for Research." In *Handbook of Research on Teaching.* Chicago: Rand McNally, 1963.

Cartwright, D. "Influence, Leadership, Control." In *Handbook of Organizations,* ed. J. March. Chicago: Rand McNally, 1965.

Catler, Susan. "Labor Union Representation Elections: What Determines Who Wins." B. A. thesis, Department of Economics, Harvard College, 1978.

Chafetz, I., and C. R. P. Fraser. "Union Decertification: An Exploratory Analysis." *Industrial Relations* 18 (Winter 1979): pp. 59–69.

Clegg, H. *A New Approach in Industrial Democracy.* London: Blackwell, 1960.

Coch, L., and J. R. P. French. "Overcoming Resistance to Change." *Human Relations* 1 (1948): pp. 512–33.

Cohen, M. D., J. G. March, and J. P. Olsen. "A Garbage Can Model of Organizational Choice." *Administrative Science Quarterly* 17 (March 1972): pp. 1–25.

Cole, R. E. "Will QC Circles Work in the U.S.?" *Quality Progress* (July 1980): pp. 30–33.

Cook, T., and D. T. Campbell. *Quasi-Experimentation: Design and Analysis Issues for Field Settings.* Chicago: Rand McNally, 1979. Ch. 1.

Cronbach, L. J., and L. Furby. "How Should We Measure Change—Or Should We?" *Psychological Bulletin* 74 (July 1970): pp. 68–80.

Cummings, G. T., and P. F. Salipante. "Research-Based Strategies for Improving Work Life." In *Personal Goals and Work Design,* ed. P. Warr. New York: Wiley, 1976.

Dachler, H. P., and B. Wilpert. "Conceptual Dimensions and Boundaries of Participation in Organizations." *Administrative Science Quarterly* 23 (March 1978): pp. 1–39.

Dahl, R. A. *After the Revolution.* New Haven, Conn.: Yale University Press, 1970.

Davey, H. W. "Arbitration as a Substitute for Other Legal Remedies." *Proceedings,* 25th Annual New York University Conference on Labor, 1973.

Davis, L. E., and A. B. Cherns. *The Quality of Work Life: Vols. I and II.* New York: Free Press, 1975.

Derber, M. "Collective Bargaining: The American Approach to Industrial Democracy." *Annals of the American Academy of Political and Social Science* 431 (May 1977): pp. 83–94.

Deutsch, M. *The Resolution of Conflict.* New Haven, Conn.: Yale University Press, 1973.

Driscoll, J. W. "Working Creatively with a Union: Lessons from the Scanlon Plan." *Organizational Dynamics* (Summer 1979): pp. 61–80.

Edelstein, J. D. "Trade Unions in British Producers' Cooperatives." *Industrial Relations* 18 (Fall 1979): pp. 358–63.

Elden, M. *Three Generations of Work Democracy Experiments in Norway: Beyond Classical Sociotechnical Analysis.* Trondheim, Norway: IFIM Rapport, June 1978.

Emerson, R. M. "Exchange Theory, Part I: A Psychological Basis for Social Exchange." In *Sociological Theories in Progress,* Vol. 2, eds. J. Berger, M. Zelditch, and B. Anderson. Boston: Houghton Mifflin, 1972.

———. "Exchange Theory, Part II: Exchange Relations, Exchange Networks, and Groups as Exchange Systems." In *Sociological Theories in Progress,* Vol. 2, eds. J. Berger, M. Zelditch, and B. Anderson. Boston: Houghton Mifflin, 1972.

———. "Power Dependence Relations." *American Sociological Review* 27 (February 1962): pp. 31–41.

Emery, F. E., and E. Thorsrud. *Democracy at Work.* Leiden: The Netherlands: Martinus Nijhoff, 1976.

Engelstad, P. H., and T. U. Qvale. *Innsyn og Innflytelse i Styre og Bedriftsforsamling.* Olso: Tiden Norsle Forlag, 1977.

Farber, H. S., and D. H. Saks. "Why Workers Want Unions: The Role of Relative Wages and Job Characteristics." *Journal of Political Economy* 88 (April 1980): pp. 349–69.

Feuille, P. "Final Offer Arbitration and the Chilling Effect." *Industrial Relations* 14 (October 1975): pp. 302–10.

Feuille, P., and J. Blandin. "Faculty Job Satisfaction and Bargaining Sentiments: A Case Study." *Academy of Management Journal* 17 (1974): pp. 678–92.

Fischer, B. "Arbitration: The Steel Industry Experiment." *Monthly Labor Review* 95 (November 1972): pp. 7–10.

Fishbein, M., and I. Ajzen. *Belief, Attitude, Intention and Behavior.* Reading, Mass.: Addison-Wesley, 1975.

Fisher, R., and W. Ury. *International Mediation: A Working Guide.* New York: International Peace Academy, April 1978.

Flango, V. E. "Faculty Attitudes and the Election of a Bargaining Agent in the Pennsylvania State College System—1." *Journal of Collective Negotiations in the Public Sector* 4:2 (1975): pp. 157–74.

Freeman, R. B., and J. L. Medoff. "The Two Faces of Unionism." *The Public Interest* 57 (Fall 1979): 69–93.

French, J. R. P., J. Israel, and D. Aas. "An Experiment on Participation in a Norwegian Factory." *Human Relations* 13 (February 1960): pp. 3–19.

Galbraith, Jay R. *Designing Complex Organizations.* Reading, Mass.: Addison-Wesley, 1973.

Getman, J. G., S. B. Goldberg, and J. B. Herman. *Union Representation Elections: Law and Reality.* New York: Basic Books, 1976.

Glaser, E. M. *Productivity Gains Through Worklife Improvements.* New York: Harcourt Brace Jovanovich, 1976.

Goldberg, S. B. "The Mediation of Grievances Under a Collective Bargaining Contract: An Alternative to Arbitration." Chicago: Northwestern Law School, 1982.

Goldberg, S. B., and J. M. Brett. "Mediation of Grievances." Technical Report submitted to the U.S. Department of Labor under Contract J-9-P-1-0034, 1982.

Goldberg, S. B., J. C. Getman, and J. M. Brett. "Union Representation Elections: Law and Reality: The Authors Respond to the Critics." *Michigan Law Review* 79 (1981): pp. 564–93.

Gordon, M. E., J. W. Philpot, R. E. Burt, C. A. Thompson, and W. E. Spiller. "Commitment to the Union: Development of a Measure and an Examination of Its Correlates," Monograph. *Journal of Applied Psychology* 65 (August 1980): pp. 479–99.

Gurdon, M. A. "The Structure of Ownership: Implications for Employee Influence and Organizational Design." Doctoral dissertation, New York State School of Industrial and Labor Relations, Cornell University, 1978.

Gustavsen, B. "Environmental Requirements and the Democratization of Industrial Organizations." *Proceedings,* International Sociological Conference on Participation and Self-Management, 4 (1973): pp. 5–22.

Gyllenhammar, P. *People at Work.* London: Addison-Wesley, 1977.

Hackman, J. R., and G. R. Oldham. *Work Redesign.* Reading, Mass.: Addison-Wesley, 1980.

Hammer, T. H., and M. Berman. "The Role of Noneconomic Factors in Faculty Union Voting." *Journal of Applied Psychology* 66 (August 1981): pp. 415–21.

Hammer, T. H., J. C. Landau, and R. N. Stern. "Absenteesim When Workers Have a Voice: The Case of Employee Ownership." *Journal of Applied Psychology* 66 (October 1981): pp. 561–73.

Hammer, T. H., and R. N. Stern. "Employee Ownership: Implications for the Organizational Distribution of Power." *Academy of Management Journal* 23 (1980): pp. 78–100.

Hamner, W. C. "Effects of Bargaining Strategy and Pressure to Reach Agreement in a Stalemated Negotiation." *Journal of Personality and Social Psychology* 30 (1974): pp. 458–67.

———. "The Influence of Structural, Individual and Strategic Difference." In *Bargaining Behavior: An International Study,* eds. D. L. Harnett and L. L. Cummings. Houston: Dame Publications, 1980.

Hamner, W. C., and F. J. Smith. "Work Attitudes as Predictors of Unionization Activity." *Journal of Applied Psychology* 63 (August 1978): pp. 415–21.

Harnett, D. L., and L. L. Cummings. *Bargaining Behavior: An International Study.* Houston: Dame Publications, 1980.

Heller, F., P. J. D. Drenth, P. L. Koopman, and V. Rus. "A Longitudinal Study in Participative Decision Making." *Human Relations* 30 (1977): pp. 567–87.

Hellriegel, D., W. French, and R. B. Peterson. "Collective Negotiations and Teachers: A Behavioral Analysis." *Industrial and Labor Relations Review* 23 (April 1970): pp. 380–96.

Herbst, P. G. *Socio-technical Design: Strategies in Multidisciplinary Research.* London: Tavistock, 1974.

Herman, J. B. "Are Situational Contingencies Limiting Job Attitude–Job Performance Relationships?" *Organizational Behavior and Human Performance* 10 (1973): pp. 208–24.

Herzberg, F. *Work and the Nature of Man.* New York: World, 1966.

Hirschman, A. O. *Exit, Voice and Loyalty.* Cambridge, Mass.: Harvard University Press, 1970.

Homans, G. C. *Social Behavior: Its Elementary Forms.* New York: Harcourt Brace, 1961.

Hopwood, A. G. "Towards the Economic Assessment of New Forms of Work Organizations." In *The Quality of Working Life in Western and Eastern Europe,* eds. C. L. Cooper and E. Mumford. London: Associated Business Press, 1979.

Hoyer, D. T. "A Program of Conflict Management: An Exploratory Study." *Proceedings of the 32nd Annual Meeting, Industrial Relations Research Association,* 1979. Madison, Wis.: IRRA, 1980. Pp. 334–35.

Hutchins, D. "How Quality Goes Round in Circles." *Management Review* (1980): pp. 27–32.

IDE, Industrial Democracy in Europe International Research Group. *European Industrial Relations.* Oxford: Clarendon Press, 1981a.

———. *Industrial Democracy in Europe.* Oxford: Clarendon Press, 1981b.

Irwin, R. R. "QC Circles Spur Productivity, Improve Product Quality." *Iron Age* (June 1978): pp. 61–62.

James, L. R., S. Mulaik, and J. Brett. *Confirmatory Analysis.* Innovations in Research Methodology Conference, Center for Creative Leadership, Greenboro, N.C., 1982.

Janus, I. L. *Victims of Groupthink.* Boston: Houghton Mifflin, 1972.

Janus, I. L., and L. Mann. *Decision Making.* New York: Free Press, 1977.

Johansen, R. "Changes in Work Planning Increase Shipboard Democracy." *National Labour Institute Bulletin* 3 (1977): pp. 9–18.

Jones, D. "The Economic and Industrial Relations of Producers' Cooperatives in the United States, 1791–1929." *Economic Analysis and Worker Management* 3-4 (1977): 295–317.

Katzell, R., D. Yankelovich, and Associates. *Work, Productivity, and Job Satisfaction.* New York: Psychological Corp., 1975.

Kelso, L. O. *The Capitalist Manifesto.* New York: Random House, 1958.

Kilman, R. H., and K. W. Thomas. "Four Perspectives on Conflict Management: An Attributional Framework for Organizing Descriptive and Normative Theory." *Academy of Management Review* 3 (1978): pp. 59–68.

Klimoski, R. J. "The Effects of Intragroup Forces on Intergroup Conflict Resolution." *Organizational Behavior and Human Performance* 8 (1972): pp. 363–83.

Klimoski, R. J., and R. A. Ash. "Accountability and Negotiator Behavior." *Organizational Behavior and Human Performance* 11 (1974): pp. 409–25.

Kochan, T. A. *Contemporary Views of American Workers Toward Trade Unions.* Report to the Office of Assistant Secretary for Policy, Evaluation, and Research, U.S. Department of Labor, Contract B-9-E-8-2899. See also "How American Workers View Labor Unions." *Monthly Labor Review* 102 (April 1979): pp. 23–31.

———. "Collective Bargaining and Organizational Behavior Research." In *Research in Organizational Behavior,* Vol. 2, eds. B. M. Staw and L. L. Cummings. Greenwich, Conn.: JAI Press, 1980a. Pp. 129–76.

———. *Collective Bargaining and Industrial Relations.* Homewood, Ill.: Richard D. Irwin, 1980b.

Kochan, T. A., D. Lipsky, and L. Dyer. "Collective Bargaining and the Quality of Work: Reflections of Union Activists." *Proceedings of the 27th Annual Meeting, Industrial Relations Research Association,* 1974. Madison, Wis.: IRRA, 1975. Pp. 150–62.

Kochan, T. A., M. Mironi, R. G. Ehrenberg, J. Baderschneider, and T. Jick. *Dispute Resolution Under Factfinding and Arbitration: An Empirical Analysis.* New York: American Arbitration Association, 1979.

Kolb, D. "Good Reasons for Chilled Bargaining and Procedural Addiction: Some Observations on Strategic Decision Making Under Impasse." Unpublished manuscript, Simmons College, 1981a.

———. "Roles Mediators Play: State and Federal Practice." *Industrial Relations* 20 (Winter 1981b): pp. 1–17.

Komorita, S. S. "Tacit Communication and Cooperation in a Two-Person Game." In *Proceedings, Vol. III,* Workshop on Experimental Economics, Frankfurt, Germany, 1972.

Komorita, S. S., and M. Barnes. "Effects of Pressures to Reach Agreement in Bargaining." *Journal of Personal and Social Psychology* 13 (1969): pp. 245–52.

Komorita, S. S., and A. R. Brenner. "Bargaining and Concession Making Under Bilateral Monopoly." *Journal of Personal and Social Psychology* 9 (1968): pp. 15–20.

Kressel, K. *Labor Mediation: An Exploratory Survey.* Albany, N.Y.: Asssociation of Labor Mediation Agencies, 1972.

LaTour, S., P. Houlden, L. Walker, and J. Thilbaut. "Some Determinants of Preference for Modes of Conflict Resolution." *Journal of Conflict Resolution* 20 (June 1976): pp. 319–56.

Lawler, E. E. III. *Motivation in Work Organizations.* Monterey, Calif.: Brooks-Cole, 1973.

Lawler, E. E. III, and J. R. Hackman. "Impact of Employee Participation in the Development of Pay Incentive Plans: A Field Experiment." *Journal of Applied Psychology* 53 (December 1969): pp. 467–71.

Lawler, E. E. III, and L. Ozley. "Winning Union-Management Cooperation on Quality of Worklife Projects." *Management Review* (March 1979): pp. 19–24.

Lawler, E. E. III, and L. W. Porter. "The Effect of Performance on Job Satisfaction." *Industrial Relations* 7 (October 1967): pp. 20–28.

Lawler, E. E. III, and J. G. Rhode. *Information and Control in Organizations.* Santa Monica, Calif.: Goodyear Publishing, 1976.

Lawrence, P. R., and J. W. Lorsch. *Organization and Environment.* Boston: Graduate School of Business Administration, Harvard University, 1967.

Le Louarn, J. Y. "Predicting Union Vote from Worker Attitudes and Perceptions." *Proceedings of the 32nd Annual Meeting, Industrial Relations Research Association,* 1979. Madison, Wis.: IRRA, 1980. Pp. 72–82.

Lesieur, F., ed. *The Scanlon Plan—A Froniter in Labor-Management Cooperation.* Cambridge, Mass.: MIT Press, 1968.

Likert, R. *New Patterns of Management.* New York: McGraw-Hill, 1961.

Long, R. J. "Job Attitudes and Organizational Performance Under Employee Ownership." *Academy of Management Journal* 23 (1980): pp. 726–37.

Magenau, G. M., and D. G. Pruitt. "The Social Psychology of Bargaining: A Theoretical Analysis." In *Industrial Relations: A Social Psychological Approach,* eds. G. M. Stephenson and J. Brotherton. Chichester, England: Wiley, 1979.

March, J. G. "Bounded Rationality, Ambiguity and the Engineering of Choice." *Bell Journal of Economics* 9 (Autumn 1978): pp. 587–608.

March, J. G., and H. A. Simon. *Organizations.* New York: Wiley, 1958.

Martin, J. E. "Union-Management Committees in the Federal Sector." *Monthly Labor Review* 99 (October 1976): pp. 30–31.

———. "State Employee Affiliation and Attitude Differences." *Journal of Applied Psychology* 63 (October 1978): pp. 654–57.

———. *A Garbage Can Model of the Research Process.* Innovations in Research Methodology Conference, Center for Creative Leadership, Greensboro, N.C., 1981.

Matsui, T., M. Kagawa, J. Nagamatsu, and Y. Ohtsuka. "Validity of Expectancy Theory as a Within-Person Behavioral Choice Model for Sales Activity." *Journal of Applied Psychology* 62 (December 1977): pp. 764–67.

McGuire, W. "A Syllogistic Analysis of Cognitive Relationships." In *Attitude, Organization and Change,* eds. M. J. Rosenberg, C. I. Hoveland, W. J. McGuire, R. P. Abelson, and J. W. Brehm. Chicago: Rand McNally, 1960.

Meek, Chris. "An Evaluation of the Jamestown Labor-Management Committees." Doctoral dissertation, New York State School of Industrial and Labor Relations, Cornell University, 1981.

Metz, E. J. "Caution: Quality Control Circles Ahead." *Training and Development Journal* (August 1981): pp. 71–76.

Mitchell, T. R. "Expectancy Models of Job Satisfaction, Occupational Preference and Efforts: A Theoretical, Methodological and Empirical Appraisal." *Psychological Bulletin* 81 (December 1979): pp. 1053–77.

Morse, N. C., and E. Reimer. "The Experimental Change of a Major Organizational Variable." *Journal of Abnormal Social Psychology* 52 (1956): pp. 120–29.

Muczyk, J. P., R. T. Hise, and M. J. Gannon. "Faculty Attitudes and the Election of a Bargaining Agent in the Pennsylvania State College System,

II." *Journal of Collective Negotiations in the Public Sector* 4:2 (1975): pp. 175–89.

National Labor Relations Board (NLRB). *45th Annual Report.* Washington: U.S. Government Printing Office, 1980.

Nightingale, D. V. "The Formally Participative Organization." *Industrial Relations* 18 (Fall 1979): pp. 310–21.

Norstedt, J. P., and S. Aguren. *The Saab-Scania Report.* Stockholm: Swedish Employers' Confederation, 1973.

Notz, W. W., and F. A. Starke. "Final Offer Versus Conventional Arbitration as a Means of Conflict Management." *Administrative Science Quarterly* 23 (June 1978): pp. 189–203.

Osgood, C. E. *An Alternative to War and Surrender.* Urbana: University of Illinois Press, 1962.

Pateman, C. *Participation and Democratic Theory.* London: Cambridge University Press, 1970.

Peach, D. A., and E. R. Livernash. *Grievance Initiation and Resolution: A Study in Basic Steel.* Boston: Graduate School of Business Administration, Harvard University, 1974.

Pennings, J. M. "The Relevance of the Structural-Contingency Model for Organizational Effectiveness." *Administrative Science Quarterly* 20 (September 1975): pp. 393–410.

Perry, S. *San Francisco Scavengers: Dirty Work and the Pride of Ownership.* Berkeley: University of California Press, 1978.

Peterson, R. B., and L. N. Tracy. "A Behavioural Model of Problem-Solving in Labour Negotiations." *British Journal of Industrial Relations* 14 (July 1976): pp. 159–73.

Pfeffer, J. *Organizational Design.* Arlington Heights, Ill.: AHM Publishing, 1978.

———. *Power in Organizations.* Marshfield, Mass.: Pitman Publishing, 1981.

Popular, J. J. "Labor-Management Relations: U.S. Mediators Try to Build Common Objectives." *World of Work Report* 1 (September 1976): pp. 1–3.

Porter, L. W., and R. M. Steers. "Organizational, Work and Personal Factors in Employee Turnover and Absenteeism." *Psychological Bulletin* 80 (1973): pp. 151–76.

Roggema, J., and N. K. Hammarstrom. *Nye Organisasjonsformer Til Sjos.* Oslo: Tanum-Norli, 1975.

Ross, A. M. "Distressed Grievance Procedures and Their Rehabilitation." In *Labor Arbitration and Industrial Change,* Proceedings of the 16th Annual Meeting, National Academy of Arbitrators. Washington: Bureau of National Affairs, 1963.

Rubin, J. Z., and B. R. Brown. *The Social Psychology of Bargaining and Negotiation.* New York: Academic Press, 1975.

Sandver, M., H. Blaine, and M. Woyar. "Time and Cost Savings Through Expedited Arbitration Procedures: Evidence from Five Industrial Settings." *Arbitration Journal* 36 (December 1981): pp. 11–21.

Scheflen, K. C., E. E. Lawler III, and J. R. Hackman. "Long-Term Impact of Employee Participation in the Development of Pay Incentive Plans: A Field Experiment Revisited." *Journal of Applied Psychology* 55 (June 1971): pp. 182–86.

Schein, E. H. *Process Consultation: Its Role in Organization Development.* Reading, Mass.: Addison-Wesley, 1969.

Schelling, T. C. *The Strategy of Conflict.* New York: Oxford University Press, 1960.

Schlesinger, L. A., and R. E. Walton. "The Process of Work Restructuring and Its Impact on Collective Bargaining." *Monthly Labor Review* 100 (April 1977): pp. 52–54.

Schriesheim, C. A. "Job Satisfaction, Attitudes Toward Unions and Voting in a Union Representation Election." *Journal of Applied Psychology* 63 (October 1978): pp. 548–52.

Schuster, M. "The Impact of Union Management Cooperation on Productivity and Employment." Paper presented at the Arden House Conference, Columbia University, New York, January 1982.

Seidman, J., L. Kelley, and A. Edge. "Faculty Bargaining Comes to Hawaii." *Industrial Relations* 13 (February 1974): pp. 5–22.

Shirom, A. "The Industrial Relations Systems of Industrial Cooperatives in the United States, 1880–1935." *Labor History* 13 (Fall 1972): pp. 533–51.

Siegel, S., and L. E. Fouraker. *Bargaining and Group Decision-Making.* New York:McGraw-Hill, 1960.

Simon, H. *Models of Man.* New York: Wiley, 1957.

Slichter, S., J. Healy, and E. R. Livernash. *The Impact of Collective Bargaining on Management.* Washington: Brookings Institution, 1960.

Statens Industriverk. *Styrelse Representation for Anstallda.* Stockholm: Liber Forlag, 1975.

Staw, B., L. Sandelands, and J. Dutton. "Threat Rigidity Effects in Organizational Behavior: A Multilevel Analysis." *Administrative Science Quarterly* (forthcoming).

Steers, R. M., and S. R. Rhodes. "Major Influences on Employee Attendance: A Process Model." *Journal of Applied Psychology* 63 (August 1978): pp. 391–407.

Stern, R. N., and P. Comstock. *Employee Stock Ownership Plans (ESOPs): Benefits for Whom?* (Key Issue No. 23) Ithaca: New York State School of Industrial and Labor Relations, Cornell University, 1978.

Stern, R. N., and T. H. Hammer. "Buying Your Job: Factors Affecting the Success or Failure of Employee Acquisition Attempts." *Human Relations* 31 (December 1978): pp. 1101–17.

Stern, R. N., and P. R. O'Brien. Unpublished manuscript, New York State School of Industrial and Labor Relations, Cornell University, 1980.

Stevens, C. M. *Strategy and Collective Bargaining Negotiations.* New York: McGraw-Hill, 1963.

Szilagyi, A. D., Jr., and M. J. Wallace, Jr. *Organizational Behavior and Performance.* Santa Monica, Calif.: Goodyear, 1980.

Tannenbaum, A. S., B. Kavcic, N. Rosner, M. Vianello, and G. Wiesner. *Hierarchy in Organizations: An International Comparison.* San Francisco: Jossy-Bass, 1974.

Taylor, J. C. "Experiments in Work System Design: Economic and Human Results, Part I." *Personnel Review* 6 (Summer 1977a).

———. "Experiments in Work System Design: Economic and Human Results, Part II." *Personnel Review* 6 (Autumn 1977b).

———. "The Measurement Dilemma and Some Thoughts for Its Solution." In *The Quality of Working Life in Western and Eastern Europe,* eds. C. L. Cooper and E. Mumford. London: Associated Business Press, 1979.

Tedeschi, J. T., B. R. Schlenker, and T. V. Bonoma. *Conflict, Power and Games.* Chicago: Aldine-Atherton, 1973.

Thomson, J. D., and V. V. Murray. *Grievance Procedures.* Lexington, Mass.: D. C. Heath, 1976.

Trist, E. "Adapting to a Changing World." In *Industrial Democracy Today,* ed. G. Sanderson. New York: McGraw-Hill-Ryerson, 1979.

———. "The Evolution of Socio-technical Systems. A Conceptual Framework and an Action Research Program." In *Perspectives on Organizational Design and Behavior,* eds. A. Van de Ven and W. Joyce. New York: Wiley, 1981.

Trist, E. L., and K. W. Bamforth. "Some Social and Psychological Consequences of the Longwall Method of Coal-Getting." *Human Relations* 4 (1951): pp. 3–38.

Tucker, L., R. Damarin, and S. Messick. "A Base-Free Measure of Change." *Psychometrika* 31 (1966): pp. 457–73.

Turner, J. T., and J. W. Robinson. "A Pilot Study of the Validity of Grievance Settlement Rates as a Predictor of Union Management Relationships." *Journal of Industrial Relations* 14 (1972): pp. 314–22.

U.S. Department of Health, Education, and Welfare (USHEW). Task Force Report on *Work in America.* Cambridge, Mass.: MIT Press, 1973.

Vanek, J. *Self-Management.* Baltimore: Penguin, 1975.

Van Maanen, J., J. Dabbs, and R. Faulkner. "Innovative Ways of Allocating and Analyzing Qualitative Data." APA Innovations in Methodology Conference, 1981.

Vroom, V. *Work and Motivation.* New York: Wiley, 1964.

Walker, J. M., and J. J. Lawler. "Dual Unions and Political Processes in Organizations." *Industrial Relations* 18 (Winter 1979): pp. 32–43.

Wall, J. A., Jr. "Effects of Opposing Constituent Stances, Opposing Representative's Bargaining, and Representative's Locus of Control." *Journal of Conflict Resolution* 21 (September 1977a): pp. 459–74.

———. "Operantly Conditioning a Negotiator's Concession Making." *Journal of Experimental Social Psychology* 13 (1977b): pp. 431–40.

———. "An Investigation of Reciprocity and Reinforcement Theories of Bargaining Behavior." *Organizational Behavior and Human Performance* 27 (1981): pp. 367–85.

Wall, T., and J. Lischeron. *Worker Participation: A Critique of the Literature and Some Fresh Evidence.* Maidenhead, Berkshire, England: McGraw-Hill, 1977.

Wallach, M. A., N. Kogan, and D. J. Bem. "Group Influence on Individual Risk Taking." *Journal of Abnormal and Social Psychology* 65 (1962): pp: 75–86.

Walton, R. *Interpersonal Peacemaking: Confrontations and Third-Party Consultation.* Reading, Mass.: Addison-Wesley, 1969.

Walton, R., and R. McKersie. *A Behavioral Theory of Labor Negotiations.* New York: McGraw-Hill, 1965.

Webb, J. "Behavioral Studies of Third Party Intervention." In *Social Psychological Approach,* eds. G. M. Stephenson and C. J. Brotherton. Chichester, England: Wiley, 1979.

Weick, K. *The Social Psychology of Organizing.* Reading, Mass.: Addison-Wesley, 1969.

———. *The Social Psychology of Organizing,* 2nd ed. Reading, Mass.: Addison-Wesley, 1979.

Wild, R. *Work Organization.* New York: Wiley, 1975.

Woodward, J. *Industrial Organization: Theory and Practice.* London: Oxford University Press, 1965.

Yager, E. G. "The Quality Control Circle Explosion." *Training and Development Journal* (April 1981): pp. 98–105.

Zack, A. M. "Suggested New Approaches to Grievance Arbitration." In *Arbitration—1977,* Proceedings of the 30th Annual Meeting, National Academy of Arbitrators. Washington: Bureau of National Affairs, 1978.

Zajonc, R. B. "Feeling and Thinking: Preferences Need No Inferences." *American Psychologist* 35 (1980): pp. 151–75.

CHAPTER 7

Labor History in the 1970s: A Question of Identity

JONATHAN GROSSMAN
U.S. Department of Labor

WILLIAM T. MOYE
U.S. Bureau of Labor Statistics

If disciplines or subdisciplines mirror the surrounding culture, labor history during the 1970s certainly reflected the vitality and pluralism, if not anarchy, so characteristic of U.S. society in the decade. In a generational passage, younger historians challenged the old standards of the Wisconsin School. No new consensus emerged, although three works published at the end of the decade may represent the initial presentations of a new synthesis.

In the major development of the period, some labor historians, moved by ideological as well as methodological concerns, rebelled against the prevailing influence of institutional economics in a lively effort to highlight alternative interpretations and to shift the focus of research. Ironically, the very charm of the new literature created problems for the discipline, blurring its distinctiveness by introducing interdisciplinary approaches. Moreover, it has not captured the interest of the worker and has provided little assistance to policy-makers, remaining too much an academic exercise.

New Approaches

Although the academic flowering has its roots into the 1950s, when resurgent scholars launched activities that, for example, led to the founding of *Labor History*,[1] the so-called "new labor history" of the 1970s truly springs from the soil of the 1960s. The English-

[1] Robert H. Zieger, "Workers and Scholars: Recent Trends in American Labor Historiography," *Labor History* (Spring 1972), pp. 247–28.

man E. P. Thompson published his monumental *The Making of the English Working Class* in 1963. The continuing civil rights campaigns and the growing antiwar movement on college campuses from 1968 on fed a spirit of rebellion. Moreover, many American labor historians were infected by events in Europe, David Montgomery specifically pointing to "France's May Events of 1968, the Prague Spring, Italy's 'Hot Autumn' of 1969."[2] Thus aroused, they confronted many of the conclusions reached by their predecessors and, more significantly, attacked those who had largely prevailed in the field for some 50 years, namely, John R. Commons, Selig Perlman, and Philip Taft of the Wisconsin School. Following Thompson, they concentrated on cultural factors in an attempt to write "history from the bottom up."

At the beginning of the decade, publication of three books signalled, to many critics, the coming of age of labor history as the equal of the other subdisciplines: Melvyn Dubofsky, *We Shall Be All: A History of the IWW* (1969); Sidney Fine, *Sit-Down: The General Motors Strike of 1935–36* (1969); and Irving Bernstein, *The Turbulent Years: A History of the American Worker, 1933–41* (1970). For instance, Bernstein's volumes [*The Lean Years* appeared in 1960] present perhaps the most comprehensive treatments since the Commons and others, *History of Labour in the United States*. Alice and Staughton Lynd's *Rank and File* (1973), though a flimsy book, marked a new, more radical approach, probably spurred by the example of the French student-worker revolt of 1968.[3] Herbert Gutman, however, exerted a crucial influence through his collected essays, *Work, Culture and Society in Industrializing America*, published in 1976.

According to David Brody, a friend of the movement, Gutman expressed the "hallmark of labor history in the 1970s: namely, a persistent effort to capture the total historical experience of American working people rather than only that part expressed through

[2] David Montgomery, *Workers' Control in America: Studies in the History of Work, Technology, and Labor Struggles* (Cambridge: Cambridge University Press, 1979), p. 6. It might be noted that Thompson is a leader of the British Committee for Nuclear Disarmament.

[3] David Brody, "Labor and the Great Depression: The Interpretive Prospects," *Labor History* (Spring 1972), p. 231; "Labor History in the 1970s: Toward a History of the American Worker," originally delivered at Organization of American Historians (1978), printed in *Labor History* (Winter 1979), p. 1; "Radical Labor History and Rank-and-File Militancy," *Labor History* (Winter 1975), pp. 119–20.

the labor movement." Another friend, David Montgomery, writes of the two basic themes of Gutman's essays, the "vitality and distinctiveness" of working-class subculture and its "ubiquitous impact" on the daily activities of nineteenth-century Americans. A disciple, Alan Dawley, emphasizes another basic characteristic: Gutman's focus on human activity rather than deterministic economic laws or abstract social structures.[4]

In his "Introduction," Gutman complained that "altogether too little attention has been given to the ways in which the behavior of working people affected the development of the larger culture and society." That is, Commons, Perlman, and the institutional economists, in their concentration on those workers belonging to unions, neglected most workers and their culture. And, Gutman continued, this culture, even in times of great stress, exhibited strong conservative aspects as family, class, and ethnic ties persisted. Montgomery, having viewed Gutman's scheme of the working-class culture these themes pervaded, points to a major difference with the Commons approach—whereas Commons analyzed the worker as economic man, Gutman showed that working-class culture rejected strict economic rationality.[5]

Maurine W. Greenwald speaks of the shift in social history in recent years from emphasis on institutions and individual leaders to the "collective experience and structure of peoples daily work and home life." Carl N. Degler says of his own experience in labor history, "When we talked about labor in the late 1940s, we meant organized labor. Today, scholars in the field have relatively little interest in the institutional side of labor history, but they do have a great deal of interest in the working class, its family life, its community existence, and its degree of class consciousness."[6]

---

[4] Brody, "Labor History in the 1970s," p. 1; Montgomery, "Gutman's Nineteenth Century America," *Labor History* (Summer 1978), p. 417; Alan Dawley, "E. P. Thompson and the Peculiarities of the Americans," *Radical History Review* (Winter 1978–1979), p. 34.

[5] Herbert G. Gutman, *Work, Culture and Society in Industrializing America* (New York: Vintage Books, 1977), pp. xii, 10, 17–18, 41; Montgomery, "Gutman's Nineteenth Century America," p. 419. Despite his influence, Gutman has not fulfilled the promise shown in these essays. One might have expected a comprehensive treatment of the American working class by now.

[6] Maurine Weiner Greenwald, "Historians and the Working-Class Woman in America," *International Labor and Working Class History* (Spring 1979), p. 23; Carl N. Degler, "Remaking American History," *Journal of American History* (June 1980), p. 10.

Many of these "new" labor historians were stimulated by the upsurge of rebellious activities in the late 1960s. Montgomery mentions a wave of strikes, including the historically important walkouts at General Electric and the U.S. postal system—coming on top of the civil rights campaigns and antiwar crusades and the European experiences. Dawley summarizes the feeling of many in writing of "the hopes of a generation of radical scholars that common people could make their own history, and that sympathetic historians could write it using such imaginative tools as reading upper class sources 'upside down,' pursuing oral history of the living, and 'decoding' the behavior of the dead." David Brody concludes, "The New Left enthusiasm for participatory democracy translated among historians into rallying cries for 'history from the bottom up' and for a 'history of the inarticulate.'"[7]

Growing out of the "New Left" causes and focusing on the worker and his culture rather than the organized labor institutions, much of the "new labor history" not only challenges the traditional framework of the discipline, but attacks the unions themselves as conservative, stagnant, and corrupt. Robert H. Zieger observes that Samuel Gompers, who once towered over American labor historiography, is now the object of assault. Zieger continues, "Much of this revisionism has carried with it ideological implications. The critique of the Gompers-AFL tradition parallels the New Left political view that American society is corrupt and devious in all of its manifestations and that no institutions are more worthy of contempt than those, such as the labor movement and the universities, which seek reform within the corrupt context of the larger society."[8]

The other, and primarily academic, stimulus to the "new labor history" came predominantly from E. P. Thompson. Indeed, Brody declares that, except for Frederick Jackson Turner's frontier thesis, probably no other historical interpretation has spurred such schol-

---

[7] Montgomery, *Workers' Control,* p. 6; Dawley, "E. P. Thompson," p. 39; Brody, "Labor History in the 1970s," p. 6. The whole profession was affected by the events, and many in other fields joined the rebellion. However, thousands dropped their membership in the American Historical Association, the largest professional organization, because they felt that the radical scholars sacrificed objectivity for social militancy. The second largest, the Organization of American Historians, in the late 1970s, elected as their president Eugene D. Genovese, a Marxist who had welcomed the Vietcong victory in Vietnam.

[8] Zieger, "Workers and Scholars," pp. 250, 257.

arly activities among American craftsmen as Thompson's *The Making of the English Working Class.* Emulating Thompson, many Americans have undertaken local studies, focusing on the detailed and specific.[9]

Eric J. Hobsbawm, another Englishman and major influence, commented that a great deal of traditional labor history treated workers from above and provided only an occasional glimpse of what the militant rank-and-file thought of the labor movement. Newer, historians, Hobsbawm noted, dealt with the followers as as well as the leaders, the unorganized as well as the organized, the more staid and conservative workers as well as the radicals and revolutionaries. "In short," he summed up, "with the class rather than the movement or party." Norman Baker writes that both Thompson and Hobsbawm are seeking to rescue certain social groups from obscurity.[10]

The same is true of Gutman, Brody, Dubofsky, Montgomery, and other American writers of the new movement who have, as Michael Kammen notes, "rediscovered history 'from the bottom up.'" Kammen explains that "rediscovered" is a significant word, because some historians of the 1930s and 1940s, particularly those dealing with immigration and ethnic groups, had already engaged in what was termed "grass-roots history."[11]

Leon Stein and Philip Taft make interesting comments to this point in their introduction to the Arno Press/New York Times reprint of *Workers Speak, Self Portraits* (1971), a collection of cameos of working-class lives first published at the start of the twentieth century. These autobiographies, remarkable for their intimacy and insights, foreshadowed the current vogue for oral history, describing not the exploits of the rich and famous, but of "undistinguished Americans whom journalism and history tend to ignore."[12]

---

[9] Brody, "Labor History in the 1970s," pp. 6–7.

[10] Eric J. Hobsbawm, "Labor History and Ideology," *Journal of Social History* (Summer 1974), pp. 374–75; Norman Baker, contribution in George G. Iggers, *New Directions in European Historiography* (Middletown, Conn.: Wesleyan University Press, 1975), p. 170.

[11] Michael Kammen, "Introduction," in Kammen, ed., *The Past Before Us: Contemporary Historical Writing in the United States* (Ithaca, N.Y.: Cornell University Press, 1980), p. 24.

[12] Leon Stein and Philip Taft, "Introduction," in *Workers Speak, Self-Portraits,* American Labor from Conspiracy to Collective Bargaining Series (New York: Arno Press and The New York Times, 1971), pp. vii-viii.

These comments also emphasize the considerable cross-fertilization and boundary-jumping taking place in the general field of social history and the subdiscipline of labor history. Kammen believes that American historical research has become more cosmopolitan and pluralistic due to heavy borrowing from other social sciences. Brody highlights the erosion of compartmentalization with the increasing cross-stimulation among ethnic history, community studies, and researchers of political behavior, the city, social mobility, and blacks.[13]

In their intensity and comprehensiveness, some of the new studies reflect the influence of the French *Annales* school with its microscopic investigation of many aspects of community life. But the French influence is, quite logically, more apparent among American students of French labor—such as Joan W. Scott, *The Glassworkers of Carmaux* (1974)—than in American labor historiography.

The broad scope of interests and the push for alternative approaches and interpretations have benefited from methodological developments. Hobsbawm himself commented, "Much of labor history—especially the social history of the working class—must use new methods and techniques."[14] Thus, many recent works, especially in community and workforce studies, reflect the popularity of quantitative methods, while many authors have also relied extensively on oral history techniques.

Alan Dawley's *Class and Community: The Industrial Revolution in Lynn* (1976) certainly stands as one of the more provocative of the new histories. Relying heavily on census manuscripts, city directories, and union membership lists, Dawley developed the character of the Knights of St. Crispin as representing a cross section of the labor force, thus challenging the traditional view of the Crispins and their response to technological change in the shoe industry. John R. Commons and Don D. Lescohier had based their institutional interpretation on the nature of the union's organization; its proceedings, constitution, and oaths; the strikes fought; and the economic competition faced by the manufacturer.

---

[13] Kammen, "Introduction," p. 26; Brody, "Labor History in the 1970s," pp. 7–8.

[14] Hobsbawm, "Labor History," p. 378.

Whereas Commons and Lescohier emphasized Crispin concern for "green hands," Dawley claimed a wider consciousness.[15]

Alexander Saxton's *The Indispensable Enemy: Labor and the Anti-Chinese Movement in California* (1971) is one of the important ethnic studies, showing the influence exerted by negative identification. Other significant ethnic studies include Virginia Yans-McLaughlin, *Family and Community: Italian Immigrants in Buffalo, 1880–1930* (1977); John Bodnar, *Immigration and Industrialization: Ethnicity in an American Mill Town* (1977); and Michael Feldberg, *The Philadelphia Riots of 1844: A Study of Ethnic Conflict* (1975).

Barbara W. Wertheimer presents an extensive account of women in the labor movement before World War I in *We Were There* (1977). Thomas Dublin's *Women at Work* (1979) provides important insights into women's response to and experience with industrialization. In a short, derivative article, "Working Women and the 'Women's Question,'" Dublin argues, "Working women also came to challenge the dominant ideology of the Cult of True Womanhood and the view of female gender that it promoted."[16]

Anthropologist Anthony F. C. Wallace contributes an important intensive cultural study and cross-disciplinary approach in *Rockdale: The Growth of an American Village in the Early Industrial Revolution* (1978)—winner of a 1979 Bancroft Prize as a book "of exceptional merit and distinction" in American history. Bruce Laurie's *Working People of Philadelphia, 1800–1850* (1980) is a valuable addition to that literature. In his review, Walter Licht highlights Laurie's discussion of the formal and informal activities of Traditionalist communities, including "gangs, saloon life, and volunteer fire companies."[17]

In *Worker City, Company Town: Iron and Cotton-Worker Protest in Troy and Cohoes, New York, 1955–84* (1978), Daniel J.

[15] Brody, "Labor History in the 1970s," p. 11; John R. Commons, "American Shoemakers, 1648–1895," in *Labor and Administration* (New York: Macmillan Co., 1913), pp. 255–58; Don D. Lescohier, *The Knights of St. Crispin, 1867–1874*, American Labor from Conspiracy to Collective Bargaining Series (New York: Arno Press and The New York Times, 1969).

[16] Tom Dublin, "Working Women and the 'Women's Question,'" *Radical History Review* (Winter 1979–1980), p. 94. See also Leslie W. Tentler, *Wage-Earning Women: Industrial Work and Family Life in the United States, 1900–1930* (New York: Oxford University Press, 1979).

[17] Walter Licht, "Labor and Capital and the American Community," *Journal of Urban History* (February 1981), p. 224.

Walkowitz chronicles worker responses to industrialization in two very different environments. John Cumbler, in *Working-Class Community in Industrial America: Work, Leisure, and Struggle in Two Industrial Cities, 1800–1930* (1979), likewise attempts a comparative study of two communities, Lynn and Fall River, Massachusetts.

Susan E. Hirsch, in *Roots of the American Working Class: The Industrialization of Crafts in Newark, 1800–1860* (1978), provides another of the intensive community studies. But her presentation is of somewhat different texture, as it is heavily quantitative and structurally oriented.[18]

A special edition of *Radical History Review* (Spring 1978) presents a collection of articles under the overall title "Labor and Community Militance in Rhode Island." Written by members of the Providence Editorial Collective of the Middle Atlantic Radical History Organization, the articles concentrate on twentieth-century experience, although there are two nineteenth-century studies. Interspersed with the articles are two lively oral histories.[19]

The development of the "new labor history" and its emphasis on working-class culture has prompted the establishment of new journals, some of which lead precarious lives. *International Labor and Working Class History* is published by the Study Group of that name and edited by David Montgomery.

Southern Exposure, a regional interdisciplinary journal growing out of the civil rights movement, published considerable material on labor-related topics. For example, "No More Moanin': Voices of Southern Struggle" (Winter 1974) includes extensive material on the Southern Tenant Farmers' Union and the 1929 Gastonia textile strike. "Here Come a Wind: Labor on the Move" (Winter 1977) covers the campaign at J. P. Stevens and presents an in-depth report on Harlan County, Kentucky.

Of somewhat different genre but definitely kin are the popular —and highly valuable—works by Studs Terkel: *Hard Times: An Oral History of the Great Depression in America* (1970) and *Working: People Talk About What They Do All Day and How They Feel About What They Do* (1974). Terkel's *American*

[18] See also Tamara K. Hareven and Randolph Langenbach, *Amoskeag: Life and Work in an American Factory-City* (New York: Pantheon, 1978).

[19] The articles are by Gary Kulik, Paul Buhle, Scott Molloy, Judith Smith, Gary Gerstle, Kate Dunnigan, and Richard Quinney.

Dreams: Lost and Found appeared in 1980. H. L. Mitchell's reminiscences, *Mean Things Happening in this Land* (1979) retain a sense of outrage—and meanness.

Division and Dispute

Practitioners of the "new labor history" broke valuable ground and established benchmarks, but failed to sweep the field. For one thing, proponents have not agreed on a common approach beyond fairly general statements. A critic, James O. Morris, puts his view rather sternly, declaring, "I must confess, in all candor, that I do not see the outlines of a new synthesis in anything so broad, so diverse, and so vague as work undefined and unqualified."[20] But sympathizers have aired their differences, too.

Hobsbawm himself warned, "If we do not formulate questions first and look for the material in the light of these questions, we risk producing merely a leftwing version of antiquarianism, work which is the equivalent of that of amateur folklore collectors." In his review of the Lynds' *Rank and File: Personal Histories of Working-Class Organizers*, Brody echoes a similar complaint, that rank-and-file oral historians too frequently merely record what the informants volunteer. The Lynds, Brody argues, had not done their homework and did not ask probing questions—in contrast to those scholars building the Columbia University Oral History Project.[21]

Brody also criticizes Gutman, charging that Gutman's "Work, Culture and Society in Industrializing America" [the essay] is a "strategic retreat from Thompson's basic formulation. Class is, in fact, wholly jettisoned from Gutman's analysis." Gutman's anthropological distinction between culture and society, Brody continues, limits his discussion to a narrow band of working-class experience —the moment when generation after generation of newcomers, steeped in pre-industrial culture, comes in contact with industrial society.[22]

Montgomery also emphasizes Gutman's focus on the moment of contact, pointing out the existence of "two distinct, but not mutually exclusive groups. One was made up of recent migrants

[20] James O. Morris, "Communications: To the Editor," *Labor History* (Fall, 1979), p. 629.

[21] Hobsbawm, "Labor History," p. 375; Brody, "Radical Labor History," p. 120.

[22] Brody, "Labor History in the 1970s," pp. 17–18.

to the industrial areas from the American countryside or from Europe and Asia. The other consisted of those who had been born and raised in the industrial world, the veteran working class, if you will." Montgomery complains that Gutman's fixation on the recent migrant and the moment of contact ignores the veteran element which "produced most of the labor organizations of the age."[23]

Montgomery alleges another Gutman shortcoming, characterizing Gutman's observations on working-class political power as "more tantalizing than satisfying." He writes that Gutman contributed some valuable insights, but comments that Gutman's examples of the power of workers in operation were generally negative. Furthermore, he notes that Alexander Saxton and Alan Dawley have written superior studies which show that flashes of worker anger quickly burned out and that their fleeting rebellions had little long-range effect.[24]

Gutman is also challenged by Marxists. Mary Nolan writes that Gutman focuses "on culture and the family at the expense of larger economic and political issues." She, however, argues that the historian must do more than reconstruct the past from one group's view, but should make comparisons, explain events and ideas, and evaluate the long-range importance of various forms of culture, consciousness and political behavior.[25]

James Weinstein, in joining the criticism of the Lynds' oral history approach, establishes a major theme of early revolutionary critique of the "new labor history." Writing of Staughton Lynd, Weinstein explains that Lynd failed to analyze the nature of trade unions. According to Weinstein, Lynd never acknowledged that, by concentrating on union recognition and collective bargaining, militant workers may have been diverted from working-class goals and tied closer to the corporate system.[26]

Weinstein continues the criticism in his review of James Matles and James Higgins's *Them and Us: Struggles of a Rank and File Union* (1974). Under the title "The Grand Illusion," Weinstein

[23] Montgomery, "Gutman's Nineteenth Century America," pp. 420–21.

[24] Montgomery, "Gutman's Nineteenth Century America," pp. 426–27.

[25] Mary Nolan, "New Perspectives on Social History," *Socialist Review* (May-June 1978), pp. 125–26, 134n.

[26] James Weinstein, "Can a Historian Be a Socialist Revolutionary?" *Socialist Revolution* (May-June 1970), pp. 103, 105.

posits the shortcomings of even such a militant union as the United Electrical, Radio, and Machine Workers of America. That militancy which Matles and Higgins chronicle is considered tactical maneuvering by Weinstein: "This means that militancy is not a principle in itself, but is subordinate to the union's goal of achieving the best possible settlement within a given set of circumstances."[27]

The "old" left has continued to produce. Philip S. Foner published *Organized Labor and the Black Worker, 1619–1973* (1974), *Labor and the American Revolution* (1976), and *Women and the American Labor Movement: From Colonial Times to the Eve of World War I* (1979). Foner has also continued his valuable series, *History of the Labor Movement in the United States*—which Zieger labels "perhaps the most impressive product of radical labor historiography in recent years"—with the fifth volume, *The AFL in the Progressive Era, 1910–1915* (1980) and the same predetermined interpretation.[28]

Martin Glaberman, in *Wartime Strikes, The Struggle Against the No Strike Pledge in the UAW During World War II* (1980), provides a leftwing analysis by a participant. For example, he writes that the social unionism practiced by such leaders as Walter P. Reuther represented a tendency toward incorporation of the labor movement into the "welfare state." He continues, "Social unionism represented the demand of the state for the social control of the workers at least as much as it represented the generalized interests of the membership of the unions."[29]

Other labor historians, neither leftist not radically chic, question the basis for much of the "new" literature. Robert H. Zieger, himself the author of the excellent *Madison's Battery Workers, 1934–1952* (1977), writes, "The term 'New Left' is vague and undescriptive, carrying with it specific criticisms of existing society but no clear and positive social perspective." More pointedly, he declares, "By holding high the banner of the masses and by rejecting so

[27] Weinstein, "The Grand Illusion: A Review of 'Them and Us,'" *Socialist Revolution* (June 1975), p. 90.

[28] Zieger, "Workers and Scholars," p. 259; Henry P. Gyzda, "Labor History in Black and White," *Monthly Labor Review* (March 1981), pp. 77–78.

[29] Martin Glaberman, *Wartime Strikes: The Struggle Against the No-Strike Pledge in the UAW During World War II* (Detroit: Bewick Editions, 1980), p. 8.

completely American trade unionism, recent scholars may in fact be pursuing a will-of-the-wisp and turning their backs upon a valid, if ambiguous, American tradition."[30]

Such scholars as Dubofsky, Montgomery, and Gutman, Zieger warns, must be careful not to romanticize workers and their culture. In fact, Zieger even turns Montgomery's own criticism back upon him, pointing out that most of the popular resistance movements failed. Besides, many workers rejected militance and radicalism and accepted consumerism and "job-conscious" unionism. Yet, Zieger concludes, mass organization in the 1930s owed more to those AFL unions which supported industrial organization than to the idealistic traditions of the Knights of Labor and the Industrial Workers of the World.[31]

An observation by John Saville on British labor historians seems pertinent, reflecting the same concern for the tendency to romanticize working-class culture that "encourages both a whiggish understanding of the labour movement's general evolution and, at times, a somewhat antiquarian approach to the subject."[32]

Robert Ozanne, author of *A Century of Labor-Management Relations at McCormick and International Harvester* (1967), offers more trenchant charges, alleging that "new" historians intentionally distort the findings of the Wisconsin School, and Commons specifically, in an effort to make their own ideological statements. On Dawley's *Class and Community,* Ozanne states, "It appears to me that Dawley has pretty much made up a straw man by misrepresenting Commons' view." According to Ozanne, Dawley's main criticism of Commons is ideological: Commons's analyses deny Marxist theories.[33]

Ozanne then turns to Montgomery and his "Workers' Control of Machine Production in the Nineteenth Century" (1976). Of Montgomery's comment that Commons supported Frederick W. Taylor's antiunion views, Ozanne writes that the interpretation is "totally erroneous." In fact, Ozanne continues, the quotation from

[30] Zieger, "Workers and Scholars," pp. 258, 264.

[31] Zieger, "Workers and Scholars," p. 263.

[32] John Saville, "The Radical Left Expects the Past to Do Its Duty," *Labor History* (Spring 1977), p. 272.

[33] Robert Ozanne, "Trends in Labor History," originally read at Industrial Relations Research Association (1979), printed in *Labor History* (Fall 1980), pp. 4–6.

Commons cited by Montgomery had nothing to do with Taylor or scientific management—Commons does not even mention Taylor or his ideas in the entire chapter from which Montgomery takes the quote. Ozanne also challenges Montgomery's conclusions in *Workers' Control in America, Studies in the History of Work, Technology, and Labor Struggles* (1979), especially what he considers Montgomery's nostalgic picture of late nineteenth-century labor politics. He notes that the Knights of Labor could scarcely count five supporters in the House of Representatives.[34]

Ozanne writes that "Gutman laces his writing with deprecating generalizations about 'traditional labor historians'." He then counters, declaring that the concerns of Commons and Perlman "are still relevant to labor historians." Commons's extension of markets theory, says Ozanne, exerts as much impact on labor-management relations today, in a world of wider and wider markets, as on the Philadelphia shoemakers of 1805—witness management and labor in the auto and steel industries joining to seek government loan guarantees and import restrictions.[35]

Rather than denigrating others or pronouncing strictures, Ozanne advocates variety. He welcomes the diversity of focus, methods, sources, and framework of recent works as a sign of strength and calls on sociologists, political scientists, labor economists, practitioners of industrial relations, and lawyers to join in writing labor history.[36]

Some have been studying the institutional responses to the civil rights movement, the shift toward the service industry, the growth of government, and leadership crises with more traditional tools. For example, August Meier and Elliott Rudwick, who distinguished themselves in the field of black history, have written *Black Detroit and the Rise of the UAW* (1979), a dramatic account of the growth of black influence in Detroit in general and in organized labor in particular.

Richard B. Morris edited *The American Worker* (1976–1977), a Bicentennial history project of the U.S. Department of Labor, which presents articles by a diverse group of authors: Edward Pessen, David Montgomery, Philip Taft, Irving Bernstein, Jack

---

[34] Ozanne, pp. 6–7, 10.

[35] Ozanne, pp. 8–9.

[36] Ozanne, p. 11.

Barbash, and Morris himself. The text, richly supplemented by pictures and illustrations, provides a rare, general treatment.[37]

Several fine biographies have appeared, for example, Melvyn Dubofsky and Warren Van Tine's excellent *John L. Lewis* (1977). In addition, participants, journalists, and others not necessarily trained as historians have produced such interesting studies as Frank Cormier and William J. Eaton's *Reuther* (1970) and George W. Martin's *Madam Secretary, Frances Perkins* (1976). Joseph C. Goulden's *Meany* (1972) is especially valuable because of his access to rarely opened records of the AFL-CIO executive council. David Dubinsky combined with A. H. Raskin to write his memoirs, *David Dubinsky, a Life with Labor* (1977).

Two of the better products of investigative reporting were John Herling's *Right to Challenge: People and Power in the Steelworkers Union* (1972)—a dramatic account of democracy in action—and Dan T. Moldea's *The Hoffa Wars: Teamsters, Rebels, Politicians, and the Mob* (1978).

On a slightly different point, both the newer and the more traditional literature have benefited from the development of new resources. The Archives of Labor and Urban Affairs at Wayne State University in Detroit, under the leadership of Philip P. Mason, has become a major research and resource center. Founded in 1958, it houses the historical records of seven major international unions, among them the UAW. It has also developed a large collection of personal papers, as well as files of several dissident groups. The Archives are housed in the Walter P. Reuther Library, a gift to the University from the UAW.[38]

In 1970, the Southern Labor Archives was established at Georgia State University in Atlanta, with a focus on the Southeast. Other regional archives have been located at the University of Texas at Arlington (1967) and Pennsylvania State University (1967). In 1977, the Tamiment Labor Library at New York University expanded with the addition of the Robert F. Wagner Archives.

A number of international unions have started official archives,

[37] Morris's own *Government and Labor in Early America* (1946) stands as a monumental work in its own right. The last general text was Joseph G. Rayback, *A History of American Labor* (1966).

[38] Philip P. Mason, "Labor Archives in the United States," *Archivum* (Paris) 27 (1980).

and the American Federation of Labor–Congress of Industrial Organizations (AFL-CIO) has announced plans for an archives at the George Meany Educational Center at Silver Spring, Maryland.

The State Historical Society of Wisconsin, with an old and distinguished labor collection, has joined with the University of Maryland and Pace University in a joint project to microfilm and index the Samuel Gompers Papers—the first installment of which is now available. Director of the project is Stuart B. Kaufman, whose *Samuel Gompers and the Origins of the American Federation of Labor, 1848–1896* appeared in 1973.

The Arno Press/New York Times reprint series, "American Labor: From Conspiracy to Collective Bargaining," provides yet another helpful type of resource with 105 titles in two series.

Transition Time

Labor history, then, as an academic entity, stands at a very important transition point. Having challenged the *ancien regime*, the "new" labor historians have not erected a coherent substitute. Tony Judt's comment on similar developments in European labor historiography seems especially pertinent: "The upshot of all this has been to explode labor history as such and produce a marked tendency to re-integrate it into a new and wider stream, that of modern social history."[39]

Indeed, a version of Commons's extension-of-markets theory seems at work. As practitioners seek to expand the subject area, introduce new approaches, and emphasize different aspects, they seem to lose for labor history, as a specific subdiscipline, some of its identity and distinctiveness. Thus, subjects once considered elements of labor history now stand on their own, and workers from other disciplines invade the field.

For partisans of labor history, Michael Kammen's observation sounds a warning: a steadily expanding social history threatens to encircle its sibling disciplines. As confirmation of the vulnerability, for example, Lawrence Stone, in his list of six major historical fields "still in their heroic phase of primary exploration and rapid development," counts history of mass culture, or *mentalités*—

[39] Tony Judt, "Minerva's Owl and Other Birds of Prey: Reflections on the Condition of Labor History in Europe," *International Labor and Working Class History* (Fall 1979), p. 32.

citing E. P. Thompson as a leading figure, but never mentioning labor history.[40]

Zieger points to a danger in this diffusion: labor history could become a "peripheral" concern. In the great era of industrialization, the plight of the worker seemed crucial. His strikes and internal controversies, his militancy or lack thereof, all concerned the nation. However, technological advances render the manual labor force less vital to the postindustrial age, and other issues hold the public attention. In that situation, Zieger says, "The embattled worker *and his chroniclers* [emphasis added] may seem anachronistic and isolated from overriding social concerns."[41]

Carl Degler speaks of this problem in the broad context of general American history: "We were clearly right to have shaken off the old WASP-imposed and WASP-centered unity of American history, but we have not yet created a new, equally holistic conception of American history to replace it." Samuel P. Hays writes of his disappointment with social history, where, in his view, the "proliferation of subject matter" has retarded the development of a conceptual framework. Brody's conclusions about the lack of structure or framework in the "new labor history" parallel Hays: the thrust of the movement militates against a cohesive reconstruction.[42]

The subdiscipline of labor history is experiencing a sort of mid-life crisis. The old order has been challenged and, to some extent, surpassed, while new research and new approaches continue to percolate, but no new standards have won general acceptance. So no new identity has emerged, and some are calling for the erection of a new, comprehensive, interpretive analysis. Yet no new consensus is imminent.

Steps Toward a New Focus

Even so, a number of students are focusing on the workplace

---

[40] Kammen, "Introduction," p. 34; Lawrence Stone, "History and the Social Sciences in the Twentieth Century," in *The Future of History, Essays in the Vanderbilt University Centennial Symposium*, ed. Charles F. Delzell (Nashville, Tenn.: Vanderbilt University Press, 1977), pp. 22–23.

[41] Zieger, "Workers and Scholars," p. 263.

[42] Degler, "Remaking American History," p. 17; Samuel P. Hayes, "A Systematic Social History," in *American History: Retrospect and Prospect*, eds. George A. Billias and Gerald B. Grob (New York: Free Press, 1971), pp. 316–17; Brody, "Labor History in the 1970s," p. 16.

as the starting point for understanding the workers' experience. Brody himself has suggested as a rallying point an economic approach beginning, not with culture but with work and the job, and expanding from there—that is, shop-floor history. Montgomery tries to explain the attraction and the significance: "On the job, workers must define their own world for themselves. . . . The working class has always formulated alternatives to bourgeois society in this country, particularly on the job."[43]

One approach in studying the workplace focuses on the actions of management, the general thesis being that the owners and their representatives, especially since the turn of the century, have used various tactics of scientific management, technological innovation, corporate welfare schemes, and political manipulation to mold the workplace and the workers' consciousness to their benefit. Harry Braverman presents this argument in his stimulating Marxist interpretation, *Labor and Monopoly Capital* (1974).

A similar analysis is found in Richard Edwards's *Contested Terrains: The Transformation of the Workplace in the 20th Century* (1979). A radical labor economist, Edwards compares the methods used by major corporations, including American Telephone and Telegraph, Ford, and United States Steel, in a basically institutional approach which argues that management was motivated primarily by profits. Daniel Nelson, in *Managers and Workers: Origins of the New Factory System in the United States, 1880–1920* (1975), presents a more positive emphasis to the managerial revolution by concentrating on the improvements in factory conditions and the substitution of hierarchical management for the arbitrary powers of the foreman. Other useful discussions, some of which deal only in part with industrial relations, are Stuart Brandes, *American Welfare Capitalism* (1976); Alfred D. Chandler, *The Visible Hand: The Managerial Revolution in Business* (1977); and David F. Noble, *America by Design: Science, Technology, and the Rise of Corporate Capitalism* (1977).[44]

---

[43] Brody, "Labor History in the 1970s," p. 19; "Once Upon a Shop Floor: An Interview with David Montgomery," *Radical History Review* (Spring 1980), pp. 48, 52.

[44] Montgomery and Brody discuss the different views. See Montgomery, "To Study the People: The American Working Class," *Labor History* (Fall 1980), pp. 491–92, and Brody "Labor History in the 1970s," pp. 13–14.

Another approach in studying the workplace focuses on the actions of the workers, their responses, and their social organizations. This view highlights worker militancy and labor's often violent rejection of management initiatives. Walter Licht, for one, sees the beginning of a new synthesis in this focusing on class conflict and shop-floor militancy.[45]

David Montgomery, in "The 'New Unionism' and the Transformation of Workers' Consciousness in America, 1909–22" (1974), writes that "mass involvement, direct challenge to managerial authority, and contempt for accepted AFL practice" characterized labor struggles from 1909 into the early 1920s. He especially emphasizes the role of the skilled workers, who "took advantage of every period of low unemployment to attack certain elements of the new managerial methods directly."[46]

James R. Green, in commenting on Montgomery's paper, suggests that the so-called "new unionism" may really have sprung from an "older form of job-conscious unionism which could generate militant resistance to changes in production methods, but which could also produce racist and elitist forms of labor organization." Green obviously sympathizes with the revolutionary Industrial Workers of the World which led so many of the mass strikes of the period, but which the operators destroyed with their superior strength and political influence.[47]

Peter N. Stearns also writes of labor struggles and culture clashes at the turn of the century, albeit the European experience. In *Lives of Labor: Work in a Maturing Industrial Society* (1975), he emphasizes the dramatic confrontation between workers, whose values are those of the past, and the new wave of technological change. Rather more poignantly than Montgomery or Green, Stearns explains the consequences: "A culture that had been painfully established or re-established after the first shock of indus-

---

[45] Licht, "Labor and Capital," p. 237.

[46] Montgomery, "The 'New Unionism' and the Transformation of Workers' Consciousness in America, 1909–22," *Journal of Social History* (Summer 1974), pp. 511, 519. See also Bruno Ramirez, *When Workers Fight: The Politics of Industrial Relations in the Progressive Era, 1898–1916* (Westport, Conn.: Greenwood Press, 1978), and Irwin Yellowitz, *Industrialization and the American Labor Movement, 1850–1900* (Port Washington, N.Y.: Kennikat Press, 1971).

[47] James R. Green, "Comments on the Montgomery Paper," *Journal of Social History* (Summer 1974), pp. 532, 534.

trialization was now challenged. What work was, what wives were for, what children were for all had to be rethought."[48]

Writing of the English experience, David Brody also shows how shop-floor differences highlight comparative development. Brody focuses on the English shop stewards' movement during World War I and the mass organization drives of the New Deal, arguing that the English workers exerted greater control over production, that the movement enjoyed strong ideological support, and that it operated in a framework of secure trade-unionism. The American mass production workers, he says, lacked control of the processes and faced virulent employer resentment.[49]

Nelson Lichtenstein shifts the focus to the World War II period in "Auto Worker Militancy and the Structure of Factory Life, 1937–1955" (1980). He writes, in disappointment, that the wartime struggles seemed to lay the basis for a postwar industrial relations system combining shop-floor bargaining over work rules and production standards with company-wide bargaining over pay, pensions, and other benefits. However, he laments, "The raw power exercised by rank and file workers under favorable wartime conditions left little institutional legacy, and worker control of production standards never became a permanent part of the postwar collective bargaining agenda."[50]

Three Books, a Potential Synthesis

Three books published at the end of the period make strides toward a new synthesis, although considerable progress is still to be made. David Brody, in *Workers in Industrial America, Essays on the Twentieth Century Struggle* (1980); David Montgomery, in *Workers' Control in America, Studies in the History of Work, Technology, and Labor Struggles* (1979); and James R. Green, in *The World of the Worker* (1980), posit as their framework a continuing conflict throughout this century over control of the means and processes of production. Each more or less begins with the workplace and moves into the broader sweeps of indus-

---

[48] Peter N. Stearns, *Lives of Labor: Work in a Maturing Industrial Society* (New York: Holmes and Meier Publishers, 1975), p. 13.

[49] Brody, "Radical Labor History," pp. 122–24.

[50] Nelson Lichtenstein, "Auto Worker Militancy and the Structure of Factory Life, 1937–1955," *Journal of American History* (September 1980), pp. 348–49.

trial relations, dealing primarily with the issue of control and the social and political ramifications of the struggle. All three definitely carry leftist implications, agreeing that capitalists have co-opted organized labor into the "liberal corporate state." On this theme they vary, with Brody's the more balanced and moderate, Montgomery more aggressive, and Green the most radical.

Brody, Montgomery, and Green basically argue that management won control over the workplace through various campaigns of scientific management and personnel administration—with the assistance of the government—culminating in the "American Plan" of the 1920s which pretty well collapsed the House of Labor built by Samuel Gompers. During the New Deal, organized labor regrouped, with militants pushing New Deal programs further to the left and unions benefiting from protective legislation—which solidified a coalition of labor with the Democratic Party. Despite the promise inherent in the wartime struggles, the three agree, post-World War II labor relations became rather circumscribed negotiations between powerful, established bureaucracies. Leadership of organized labor, they say, turned increasingly conservative and exclusionary and is now retreating before a resurgent anti-union sentiment.

All three are stronger on the years before World War II, and each treats the last 30 years rather superficially. Their comments on this period, while frequently perceptive, are often generalizations or ideological statements lacking specific detail based on original research. Nor do they give much coverage to the civil rights campaigns, the power of multinational corporations, the emergence of public employee unions, or the extension of government social and economic programs. They rather leap from the Korean War to Vietnam to the "new conservatism."

Brody, in *Workers in Industrial America*, produces a series of essays in which he covers some technological changes, managerial initiatives, union activities, and collective bargaining developments and some of their social, political, and governmental ramifications. His is certainly the most balanced—by variety of coverage and by attention to the more recent period. Some of his most pertinent comments are found in the two essays dealing with the years since World War II, but 35 such eventful years are too many to cover in two extended essays.

Significantly, reluctantly, and rather unhappily, Brody almost seems to confirm the traditional Commons-Perlman view. Indeed, in one of the essays he writes of "a rather sobering thought: that maybe Samuel Gompers was right after all and that pure-and-simple unionism was the proper match for the American working class." In another place he notes that, for most workers, money became the paramount consideration in the collective bargaining agreement and concludes that Sumner Slichter correctly described the American labor movement as fundamentally conservative.[51]

David Montgomery concentrates much more on the actual workplace in his collection of essays, *Workers' Control in America.* Five of his seven essays describe the confrontation between worker and manager in the years 1900 to 1920, Montgomery arguing that operators intentionally set out to destroy organized labor by crushing unions and eliminating the work procedures through which they exerted power.

Although Montgomery covers fewer of the social and political aspects and his treatment of the years after 1920 is impressionistic at best, he makes some important, if controversial, statements about the political sphere. According to Montgomery, the federal government, after the Democratic victories of 1910 and 1912, began to exert its power in labor questions. Whereas the National Civic Federation had proven largely ineffective on crucial issues, governmental power bolstered by political influence proved an irresistible promise for many labor leaders.[52]

Thus, Montgomery continues, "corporate liberalism" wooed the labor movement by manipulating the country's political system during the World War I era as well as in the 1930s. In writing of the later period, he points out the danger: "This government activity was simultaneously liberating and co-optive for the workers." Whereas government intervention benefited workers by protecting the right to organize and bargain, it also tied the unions to the political system—and mostly to the Democratic Party.[53]

James R. Green, an editor of *Radical America* since 1972, has also written *Grass-Roots Socialism: Radical Movements in the Southwest, 1895–1943* (1978) in which he highlights the Socialist

[51] Brody, *Workers in Industrial America: Essays on the Twentieth Century Struggle* (New York: Oxford University Press, 1980), pp. 166, 190.

[52] Montgomery, *Workers' Control,* p. 83.

[53] Montgomery, *Workers' Control,* pp. 83, 165.

Party of Oklahoma. In *The World of the Worker*, Green acknowledges the influence of Gutman, Foner, and Montgomery and declares, "By taking a rank-and-file approach, I hope to emphasize the creativity and tenacity of ordinary workers acting together with leaders of their own choosing."[54] The result is probably the most provocative of the three. It is definitely the most militant, and it is also the most episodic and impressionistic.

In one of his more pertinent points, Green writes of the antagonism between workers and the so-called "Progressives." At the city level, he argues, reformers, intent on throwing out the machine bosses, proposed remedies which increased the power of businessmen and professionals at the expense of the workers. At the federal level, business interests and bureaucrats joined to promote uniform regulations of wages, hours, safety rules, and compensation—which organized labor generally viewed with healthy skepticism as designed to enlist the state's aid in the managerial and technological revolution.[55]

With a sense of *ennui*, Green writes of the present situation: "In 1980, workers still lived and worked in a world that had been shaped during the 1940s: they were still struggling against the same corporations, now more powerful than ever. . . . [T]hey still had to contend with unions over issues of autonomy, democracy, and authority; and they still lacked a sense of control in their work."[56]

There seem to be two major gaps in the shop-floor histories as represented by Brody, Montgomery, and Green. For one thing, the whole field of collective bargaining over the last 30 years requires much more scrutiny. For the other, the range of governmental activities—which affect each worker almost every day in some way—must be studied with more care.

To the first point, Lichtenstein writes that historians have mostly left the story of shop-floor relations after 1940 to labor economists and industrial sociologists whose research is often ahistorical and management-oriented.[57] Indeed, one example of the better type is the 1980 Industrial Relations Research Association

[54] Green, *The World of the Worker* (New York: Hill and Wang, 1980), p. xi.

[55] Green, pp. 80, 82.

[56] Green, p. 211.

[57] Lichtenstein, "Auto Worker Militancy," p. 336n.

volume, *Collective Bargaining: Contemporary American Experience,* edited by Gerald G. Somers. Experts present some history and analysis of trends and practices in ten major industries, and Jack Barbash provides an excellent commentary.[58]

As to government-labor relations, a start has been made, especially on partisan activities, but recent labor historians have generally dealt with the subject only tangentially. Even Dawley complains that few American labor historians have addressed the role of the state as directly as Thompson did in *The Making of the English Working Class.*[59]

Leaving aside the ideological implications of Dawley's comments, it is true that few works contain detailed studies of government activities—other than to posit its "oppressive" or "co-optive" nature. Brody, Montgomery, and Green do provide some valuable insights, but few on programmatic content or effect. Robert H. Zieger's *Republicans and Labor, 1919–1929* (1969) is one of the better examples of the type of work needed.

There are several aspects which deserve attention, and not just the federal government's role during major strikes or the congressional convolutions in passing legislation. A multitude of governmental programs affect all classes of labor. The Fair Labor Standards Act with the minimum wage, the Davis-Bacon Act requiring payment of the "prevailing wage" on government construction, the Employee Retirement Income Security Act which protects private pensions, and the Occupational Safety and Health Act providing workplace standards have changed many of the priorities of collective bargaining, as have affirmative action and environmental protection programs. Public works, job training, welfare, social security, and unemployment insurance affect the individual's attitude toward work. Major unions and industries have joined together to seek federal assistance in times of financial crisis. In addition, the public sector comprised one of the fastest growing fields for unionization until very recent years.

The Cost of Living Adjustment, which Brody barely mentioned in connection with the 1948 United Automobile Workers–General

[58] See also Joseph P. Goldberg, Eileen Ahern, William Haber, and Rudolph A. Oswald, eds., *Federal Policies and Worker Status Since the Thirties* (Madison, Wis.: Industrial Relations Research Association, 1976).

[59] Dawley, "E. P. Thompson," p. 52.

Motors negotiations,[60] may now affect more American workers—and Americans generally—than any of the other programs or actions to which he gives much more coverage. Recent developments—specifically, announcement of a "social contract" between organized labor and the Carter Administration and election of Douglas Fraser to the Chrysler board—highlight the need for further study of the whole subject of "codetermination."[61] The lack of such concerns means that labor historians exert little influence on policy and policy-makers. That role goes to the practitioners and the actors.

Indeed, too much of the "new labor history" is an interesting intellectual exercise aimed at an academic audience. The limits of appeal are indicated to some extent by the circulation figures for *Labor History*, the principal journal in the field—less than 2000. Carl Degler, speaking of the broad field of American history, refers to "the growing gulf between professional historians and the public, including in the latter the students in the high schools and colleges where most of us teach." Ronald Filippelli also warns of the "elite nature of historical scholarship and the history profession," but he sees "new methodologies and new subject interests" and urges labor educators to "take a lead in changing the mandarin attitude" by utilizing the new social history—and especially oral history.[62]

Indeed, Americans are deeply interested in their past. And the popularity of such movies as *Norma Rae* and such television docu-dramas as *The Triangle Fire* shows the wide appeal of labor-related productions. Sylvester Stallone produces *F.I.S.T.*, and *Harlan County, U.S.A.* is featured at the New York Film Festival. The 1979 special double issue of *Film Library Quarterly* lists some 250 titles and 70 distributors of films on American working-class history, and Robert B. Toplin provides a splendid bibliography in "American History through the Media."[63]

In addition, District 1199, National Union of Hospital and

[60] Brody, *Workers in Industrial America*, p. 184.

[61] See William T. Moye's "Presidential Labor-Management Committees: Productive Failures," *Industrial and Labor Relations Review* (October 1980).

[62] Degler, "Remaking American History," p. 21; Ronald L. Filippelli, "The Uses of History in the Education of Workers," *Labor Studies Journal* (Spring 1980), pp. 3–12.

[63] Robert B. Toplin, "American History through the Media," *Organization of American Historians Newsletter* (July 1981), pp. 19–23.

Health Care Employees (New York), through its Bread and Roses Cultural Program, has developed a multifaceted project—part of which is reproduced in *Images of Labor* (1981). And the AFL-CIO, in an effort to counteract damaging media portrayals of organized labor, has recently published a brief magazine for popular distribution— *A Short History of American Labor.*

Closing Thoughts

From its beginning with George McNeill and Richard T. Ely, labor history has been written by crusaders for social justice, and the field continues to attract radicals and reformers. Spurred by the civil rights crusade and the antiwar movement, the "new" historians are following E. P. Thompson in exploring important aspects of working-class life not generally covered by the traditional institutional historians, and they are adding a refreshing spirit and vision to the field by challenging long-standing interpretations.

New authors publish, and new journals appear, even while workers in the more conventional modes also produce new contributions. And the identity of the subdiscipline is blurred by the very broadening of horizons and infusion of interdisciplinary techniques.

There is no need for rigid conformity. Indeed, one would second Ozanne's call for variety of subject and method and diversity of authorship. Even so, with their recent books, Brody, Montgomery, and Green do provide valuable possibilities for a new synthesis more closely related to the workplace experience than to institutional necessities.

What seems required is more concern for labor-government relations and more perspective on collective-bargaining developments. This means more attention to the institutions, and particularly labor organizations. Louis F. Post, distinguished "Progressive" editor, single taxer, and the first Assistant Secretary of the Department of Labor, wrote in the first Annual Report of the Department: "It is only through organization that the many in any class or of any interest become articulate with reference to their common needs and aspirations."[64]

---

[64] U.S. Department of Labor, *Report of the Secretary,* 1913, p. 8.

References

Baker, Norman. Contribution in *New Directions in European Historiography*, ed. George G. Iggers. Middletown, Conn.: Wesleyan University Press, 1975.

Brody, David. "Labor and the Great Depression: The Interpretive Prospects." *Labor History* 13 (Spring 1972).

———. "Labor History in the 1970s: Toward a History of the American Worker." *Labor History* 20 (Winter 1979).

———. "Radical Labor History and Rank-and-File Militancy." *Labor History* 16 (Winter 1975).

———. *Workers in Industrial America: Essays on the Twentieth Century Struggle.* New York: Oxford University Press, 1980.

Commons, John R. *Labor and Administration.* New York: Macmillan Co., 1913.

Dawley, Alan. "E. P. Thompson and the Peculiarities of the Americans." *Radical History Review* 19 (Winter 1978–1979).

Degler, Carl N. "Remaking American History." *Journal of American History* 67 (June 1980).

Dublin, Tom. "Working Women and the 'Women's Question.'" *Radical History Review* 22 (Winter 1979–1980).

Fahey, David M. "From Labor History to Working Class History." *Journal of Urban History* 6 (November 1979).

Filippelli, Ronald L. "The Uses of History in the Education of Workers." *Labor Studies Journal* 5 (Spring 1980).

Glaberman, Martin. *Wartime Strikes, The Struggle Against the No-Strike Pledge in the UAW During World War II.* Detroit: Bewick Editions, 1980.

Green, James R. "Comments on the Montgomery Paper." *Journal of Social History* 7 (Summer 1974).

———. *The World of the Worker.* New York: Hill and Wang, 1980.

Greenwald, Maurine W. "Historians and the Working-Class Women in America." *International Labor and Working Class History* 14/15 (Spring 1979).

Gutman, Herbert. *Work, Culture and Society in Industrializing America.* New York: Vintage Books, 1977.

Guzda, Henry P. "Labor History in Black and White." *Monthly Labor Review* 104 (March 1981).

Hays, Samuel P. "A Systematic Social History." In *American History: Retrospect and Prospect,* eds. George A. Billias and Gerald N. Grob. New York: Free Press, 1971.

Hobsbawm, E. J. "Labor History and Ideology." *Journal of Social History* 7 (Summer 1974).

Judt, Tony. "Minerva's Owl and Other Birds of Prey: Reflections on the Condition of Labor History in Europe." *International Labor and Working Class History* 16 (Fall 1979).

Kammen, Michael, ed. *The Past Before Us: Comtemporary Historical Writing in the United States.* Ithaca, N.Y.: Cornell University Press, 1980.

Labor and Community Militance in Rhode Island. Special issue, *Radical History Review* 17 (Spring 1978).

Lescohier, Don D. *The Knights of St. Crispin, 1867–1874.* American Labor from Conspiracy to Collective Bargaining Series. New York: Arno Press and The New York Times, 1969.

Licht, Walter. "Labor and Capital and the American Community." *Journal of Urban History* 7 (February 1981).

Lichtenstein, Nelson. "Auto Worker Militancy and the Structure of Factory Life, 1937–1955." *Journal of American History* 67 (September 1980).

Mason, Philip P. "Labor Archives in the United States." *Archivum* (Paris) 27 (1980).
Montgomery, David. "Gutman's Nineteenth-Century America." *Labor History* 19 (Summer 1978).
———. "To Study the People: The American Working Class." *Labor History* 21 (Fall 1980).
———. "The 'New Unionism' and the Transformation of Workers' Consciousness in America, 1909-22." *Journal of Social History* 7 (Summer 1974).
———. *Workers' Control in America, Studies in the History of Work, Technology, and Labor Struggles.* Cambridge: Cambridge University Press, 1979.
Morris, James O. "Communications: To the Editor." *Labor History* 20 (Fall 1979).
Moye, William T. "Presidential Labor-Management Committees: Productive Failures." *Industrial and Labor Relations Review* 34 (October 1980).
Nolan, Mary. "New Perspectives on Social History." *Socialist Review* 8 (May-June 1978).
"Once Upon a Shop Floor: An Interview with David Montgomery." *Radical History Review* 23 (Spring 1980).
Ozanne, Robert. "Trends in Labor History." *Labor History* 21 (Fall 1980).
Saville, John. "The Radical Left Expects the Past to Do Its Duty." *Labor History* 18 (Spring 1977).
Stearns, Peter N. *Lives of Labor, Work in a Maturing Industrial Society.* New York: Holmes and Meier Publishers, 1975.
———. "Toward a Wider Vision: Trends in Social History." In *Past Before Us: Contemporary Historical Writing in the United States,* ed. Michael Kammen. Ithaca, N.Y.: Cornell University Press, 1980.
Stearns, Peter N., and Daniel J. Walkowitz, eds. *Workers in the Industrial Revolution: Recent Studies of Labor in the United States and Europe.* New Brunswick, N.J.: Transaction Press, 1974.
Stein, Leon, and Philip Taft, eds. "Introduction." In *Workers Speak, Self-Portraits.* American Labor from Conspiracy to Collective Bargaining Series. New York: Arno Press and The New York Times, 1971.
Stone, Lawrence. "History and the Social Sciences in the Twentieth Century." In *The Future of History, Essays in the Vanderbilt University Centennial Symposium,* ed. Charles F. Delzell. Nashville, Tenn.: Vanderbilt University Press, 1977.
Toplin, Robert B. "American History through the Media." *Organization of American Historians Newsletter* 9 (July 1981).
U.S. Department of Labor. *Report of the Secretary, 1913.*
Weinstein, James. "Can a Historian Be a Socialist Revolutionary?" *Socialist Revolutionary* 1 (May-June 1970).
———. "The Grand Illusion: A Review of 'Them and Us.'" *Socialist Revolutionary* 5 (June 1975).
Young, James D. "The Problems and Progress of the Social History of the British Working Classes, 1880–1914." *Labor History* 18 (Spring 1977).
Zieger, Robert H. "Workers and Scholars: Recent Trends in American Labor Historiography." *Labor History* 13 (Spring 1972).

CHAPTER 8

A Critical Appraisal of Research on Unions and Collective Bargaining

MYRON J. ROOMKIN

HERVEY A. JURIS
Northwestern University

The 1970s were significant for the study of unions and collective bargaining. Union membership as a percentage of all employment declined and employer resistance to unions showed signs of increasing. But at the same time unions achieved considerable growth in the public sector while establishing themselves in such other industries as health care, professional sports, and private colleges.

It was also a decade in which the method of inquiry in the study of unions and collective bargaining underwent profound change. During the 1970s analytical research firmly established itself in this field. The earlier work of the institutionalists, seen as being inadequately rigorous, was supplanted in large part by model-building and testing which were judged the preferred way to advance knowledge. Measurement and quantification were pursued as ways to give clarity to vague concepts. As Derber has noted (1967), labor scholars have always been interested in the development of science. This most recent emphasis on scientism was helped along by the cadre of researchers trained in industrial relations in the late 1960s and by the economists, sociologists, and psychologists who evidenced an increased interest in industrial relations during the decade. We are to review that body of literature.

By their nature, literature reviews are selective and this review is no exception. We have concentrated on what was scholastically unique about the decade and emphasized analytical research at the expense of the large body of work that described, evaluated, or critiqued industrial relations policies and practices. "Recent Publications" listings in the *Industrial and Labor Relations Review* during the decade were our principal source of relevant published materials. Because a decade is a rather arbitrary delineation of time, we have included significant items of the late 1960s or items that appeared as unpublished working papers at the end of the 1970s.

The reviewed material is organized into the following sections: (1) the union as an institution, (2) collective negotiations and labor disputes, (3) dispute resolution, and (4) the outcomes of bargaining.

Unions as Institutions

Trade unionism since the time of the Webbs has been defined as a defensive association of workers tied together by workplace interests and a collective contract of employment. Trade unionism as an institution, however, faced several challenges during the 1970s, including a growth in employer attacks on unions, a decline in union penetration in manufacturing and construction, and an increase in the number of persons in the labor force said to be not in the need of trade union services.

These challenges led people to think about the current and future visibility of trade unionism as an institution. Did trade unionism still meet the needs of postindustrial society? Would unions need to change their traditional reliance on market power and rely instead on increased political action as a means of influence? Several thoughtful reviews appeared during the decade offering reassessment on issues such as these.

The consensus of these authors was that the classical paradigm survived yet another decade—that is, trade unionism was still a workplace institution, a union was still a defensive association of workers, and a collective agreement was still the goal (see Galenson and Smith 1978, Schmidman 1979, Juris and Roomkin 1980, Lodge and Henderson 1979). There was, however, considerable disagreement among these authors as to the future of U.S. labor-management relations. Lodge and Henderson see us on the verge of an era of cooperation. Barbash (1980) observed that unions and collective bargaining had become "civilized" and predicted that there would be very little change. Piore (1980), forecasting the prospect of greater changes, envisions a need for unions finally to shed their conservative capitalist baggage and to undertake more radical political actions. Gary Fink's (1973) evidence, revealing that state and local unions during the 1930s were more interested in government intervention into the economy than was the AFL, provides some historical support for Piore's forecast even in the face of the classical paradigm.

The above-mentioned studies notwithstanding, however, the empirical revolution had a significant impact on the study of unions as institutions. These contributions tended to concentrate on the issues of union growth and union administration.

Union Growth

Research in the 1970s brought a new dimension to the longstanding debate over the causes of unionism and the determinants of trade union growth. For years those who saw union membership linked to the cyclical behavior of the economy argued with those who believed that institutional and historical developments were the major determinants of union growth. Scholars in the 1970s attempted to settle the controversy through empirical research using three different dependent variables. Macro studies of growth and decline generally sought to explain variations in union membership or changes in membership. Another set of studies looked at union victories and losses in representation elections as measures of workers' interest in unions. Finally, some advances were made in the study of the characteristics and attitudes of individual workers toward unions.

Of the membership studies, one of the most comprehensive was Bain and Elsheikh's (1976) study of union growth in several nations. Building on the earlier econometric work of Ashenfelter and Pencavel (1969), Bain and Elsheikh regressed the rate of change in the membership of American unions for the period 1897 to 1970 on the change in wage rates, the change in prices, two measures of the unemployment rate, and the lagged value of the union's potential for growth (defined as the inverse of the portion of the workforce organized). To account for the role of government in union formation, the authors included a dummy variable representing the passage of the Wagner Act. They found that changes in membership were influenced by all of these cyclical economic variables as well as the role of government, and that their equation is superior on statistical criteria to others in the literature (especially that of Ashenfelter and Pencavel).

Not all public policy significantly affected the size of the labor movement. Contrary to public opinion, the impact of state right-to-work laws authorized by the Taft-Hartley Act has been found to be insignificant. Lumsden and Peterson (1975) regressed union membership in each state on whether or not the state possessed a right-to-work law along with other determinants of membership. They concluded that the differences captured by the coefficient estimated for the right-to-work variable actually represented interstate differences in people's attitudes toward unionism. To control for the fact that these attitudes influence both the passage of such laws and the willingness of people to join unions, Moore and Newman (1975) specified separate equations for membership and the presence of a law. Once the joint effects were removed, no separate impact of right-to-work laws on union membership could be found. Statistical research seems to support the view that right-to-work laws are symbolic and not substantive.

Research on union membership should benefit greatly in the future from advances in the measurement of this variable. In the private sector, Freeman and Medoff (1979a) supplied us with more accurate and current measures of union membership by industry. Information on public-sector membership also became more plentiful during the decade (see Burton [1979]).

The union representation election, although only one of several ways that unions can acquire members, also represented an important focus of research. This focus permitted researchers to examine the descriptive qualities of the workplace (for example, Adams and Krislov 1974, Sandver 1980), characteristics of the unions themselves (Walker and Lawler 1979), and the efficiency with which an agency conducted the election (Roomkin and Juris 1979).

While these studies added a needed dimension to the research, they were limited by the availability of published data from public agencies and by these agencies' decisions on which data to record. A more desirable approach would be the collection of data by the researcher at the time of the election so that there could be more control over variables studied and a greater chance to test a priori theoretical models of the direction of causality.

The study of management campaigns by Getman, Goldberg, and Herman (1976) in 31 single-union election cases (selected because they had a better than average chance of producing a hotly contested election) was a highly significant step in that direction. The authors interviewed employees before the election about their attitudes toward working conditions and unions, and their voting preferences. Immediately afterwards they reinterviewed employees to determine changes in those attitudes. Using tabular and correlational analysis, they found, among other things, that "employees have strong and stable predispositions to vote for or against union representation" (p. 72).

Because the authors also concluded that the election campaign (and, by extension, the public policy that regulates it) did not alter how employees voted, the Getman-Goldberg-Herman study caused considerable controversy and became the object of meticulous scrutiny. Methodological critics of the work were concerned that the elections studied were too few in number or in very small firms (Eames 1976), that the impact of the campaigns should have been isolated from other relevant variables using regression analysis (Flanagan 1976), and that the sample selection criteria may have led to sample bias (Roomkin 1977). These criticisms notwithstanding, modest support for their position came from a laboratory experiment conducted by Pichler and Fitch (1975), in which the views of undergraduate business school students about unions were not seriously altered after viewing a film the labor board had judged to be so coercive that it exceeded permissible limits of employer free speech. Irrespective of this controversy, the Getman-Goldberg-Herman study must stand as a landmark in industrial relations research because of its achievement in the collection and analysis of micro data on a labor policy issue of great significance.

Our knowledge of worker interest in unionism was advanced by those who studied the characteristics and attitudes of individuals toward unions. Looking at the correlates of membership, holding constant industry and regional factors, Scoville (1971) estimated that older, nonwhite males were most likely to be union members, but that men and women had the same propensity to join a union once differences in labor force attachment were adjusted. From studies such as the one conducted by Gerhart and Maxey (1978), it appears that workers still see unionism as a means of checking employer discretion at the workplace and as a way of improving the terms and conditions of employment. According to Kochan's study (1979b) of responses to the 1977 Quality of Employment Survey, the propensity to join a union requires, first, a perceived dissatisfaction with working conditions, and, second, a perceived desire for participation at the workplace as well as a perceived lack of effective alternatives for influencing working conditions.

Another stream of research just developing at the end of the decade was the study of decertification elections which some persons felt were becoming more significant in labor-management relations (see, for example, Dworkin and Extejt [1979, 1980] and Anderson et al. [1980]).

Even though we have achieved a fair understanding of the factors that motivate workers to join unions, there is still room for inquiry continuing to incorporate the advances discussed above and a need for dealing with the problem of exogenous shocks such as depression, war, or periods of hyperinflation. As Bain and Elsheikh (1976) have noted, the quantitative study of union growth must by its nature omit "those variables with a sporadic and unsystematic influence upon union growth" (p. 116). Yet, as Derber (1980) reminds us, union growth historically occurs in sharp spurts, usually in response to "some exceptional and often unexpected combination of factors" (p. 55) of the kind excluded from quantitative analysis. In addition, while we have a good deal of casual evidence that employers have become more sophisticated, aggressive, and successful in forestalling unionization attempts and winning union elections, and perhaps even in avoiding the signing of first contracts where unions have won, we have not yet seen studies that effectively capture this range of management influences on union growth or membership. While we recognize the difficulty of doing this type of research, it seems to represent a formidable challenge for researchers in the years ahead.

Union Administration

In reaction to the heavy emphasis during the 1960s on the issue of union democracy, John T. Dunlop (1970) proposed that we look at trade unions as if they were not-for-profit organizations. The theory of such organizations could then be applied to issues like the structure of unionism, the rationality of trade union administrative decisions or goal-setting, and the characteristics of union personnel practices. During the 1970s, research on unions as organizations did indeed adopt this perspective. The reader interested in the application of organizational behavior theories to union structure, internal processes, and performance may wish to note especially Warner's contributions to the theory of the union as an organization (1975 and 1972a) as well as Warner (1972b) and Nash (1974).

Dunlop notwithstanding, interest in the question of union democracy was maintained, only this time the interest was prompted by the desire to retest the conventional wisdom in the field using more rigorous techniques of data collection and analysis.

The field's rich tradition of case studies of unions was also continued during the decade. See, for example, Brill's (1978) study of the Teamsters; Brooks's (1977) history of the Communications Workers of America; the American Federation of Teachers, described in Braun's 1972 volume; the Airline Pilots described in Hopkins's volume (1971); and Stieber's (1973) encyclopedic treatment of public-sector unionism.

Union Administrative Practices. Students of union administration traditionally looked at governance and leadership. In the 1970s students of union administration also looked at the question of resource allocation within the union and perceptions of the rank and file as to the efficacy of the services they received.

Richard Block's 1980 study is the first in what we hope will be a series on the internal allocation of resources by unions. Block dichotomizes the union's resources into those spent on organizing the unorganized and those spent for representational services as the union organizes larger shares of its jurisdiction. To determine the conditions under which dollars are spent on organizing, he examines the factors associated with the number of union representation elections achieved per 1000 union members as a function of the union's penetration rate in the industry and several characteristics of the structure of union governance. From this he concludes that "unions that have success in organizing their primary jurisdiction organize less relative to the total availability of their resources than unions that have been less successful in organizing" (p. 112).

Although his results are statistically significant, he acknowledges that "the dependent variable used was not a direct measure of the extent to which unions allocate their resources between organizing and representation services" (p. 112). We are hopeful that others pursuing this line of research will be able to develop more direct measures. A second way of approaching the same question would be to capture the perceptions of members (and nonmembers) as to how they value the array of services potentially offered by the union. Efforts to measure rank-and-file satisfaction with union services were under way by the end of the decade. One of the more promising projects is the study of administration of large local unions being conducted by a group at Temple University.

While the personnel practices of unions have never really captured the imagination of scholars in our field, and little work has been done on the subject, an exception is the investigation to identify the determinants of the compensation policies of union officers. From a look across such studies done in this decade (for example, Ehrenberg and Goldberg 1977, Sandver and Heneman 1980, and Bressler 1971), it appears that the pay of union leaders at different levels of responsibility is influenced by the standard determinants of compensation, but that these same factors explain less variance in the pay of union leaders than they do for manager's compensation. This is not particularly unexpected since the union remains a political organization and the compensation of leaders is influenced by noneconomic as well as economic variables.[1]

On the subject of union leadership, no new ground appears to have been broken. It is hard to understand why this subject has received so little attention, in the light of numerous challenges faced by union leaders during the decade.

Academic interest in union governance and democracy slackened during the first part of the decade, but then rebounded strongly. For an excellent review of this literature, see Strauss (1977). Two approaches were evident. One school focused on

---

[1] Another subject, the unionization of union staff, has been treated as sort of a novelty by writers. See Treckel's discussion (1971).

the empirical relationship between the formal structures and processes of the union and democracy. These studies, such as Edelstein and Ruppel's (1970) examination of union conventions and oligarchic control, tend to involve comparisons across a sample of local or national unions, inferring the characteristics of union democracy from the organizational characteristics of the union and its constitution. The work by Snowbarger and Pintz (1970) and Koziara (1972) on the impact of the Landrum-Griffin Act on the tenure of national union leaders is in the same conceptual vein.

A second approach appears in the work of Anderson (1979c) who sought to develop attitudinal and behavioral measures of union democracy. Potentially, with further refinements in measurement, the behavioral approach could incorporate the insights of the structuralists by identifying the structural conditions more or less conducive to the attitudinal and behavioral measures of democracy.

Finally, the study of unionism has always benefited from those willing to develop data on the administration of unions. This tradition was carried on during the decade in several studies of union finances (Appelbaum 1971, Troy 1975, Allison 1975) and other articles appearing in a 1975 symposium on union financial data in *Industrial Relations*, and Graham and Donoian's (1974) study of union-administered pension funds.

Union Mergers. Union mergers also received attention during the decade. The 1960s had closed with a spurt of merger activity (Dewey 1971), and there was some question whether the activity would continue. Graham (1970) felt that internal and interunion political considerations might slow the rate of merger activity. On the other hand, received theory holds that the American labor movement has always adapted to its environment by undergoing structural changes. This long-held belief was reaffirmed by Freeman and Brittain (1977) who concluded, on the basis of an evaluation of time-series data on concluded mergers, that union willingness to surrender autonomy is a function of a hostile economic environment. Moreover, research by Chitayat (1979) found that in selected case studies, the type of altered economic conditions facing unions and the respective sizes of the unions involved influence the form of the combination achieved. By the end of the decade, Chaison (1980) and Janus (1978) found that the number of combinations had in fact increased in response to external change.

This research will probably continue in the 1980s. However, as Kochan (1980, p. 162) has observed, the following issues will also need to be addressed: "(1) [D]o they (combinations) produce the improved administrative and bargaining services they promise, (2) do they facilitate adaptations to technological change, and (3) do these benefits accrue without producing offsetting reductions in union membership control and internal union democracy?"

Collective Negotiations and Labor Disputes

The processes of collective bargaining continued to be a major topic for research in the 1970s. Advances were made both theoretically and empirically in two areas of concern: the causes and correlates of strikes and the question of collective bargaining as a bilateral or multilateral process. In addition, some work was done on contract rejection and some, but not enough, on contract administration.

Strike Research

Strike research, entering the 1970s, was ripe for significant advances. Interest in the subject was high among both practitioners and scholars, and an ample body of accurate data on work stoppages was available.[2] Two forms of strike research were common during the decade: work which related strike activity to worker wage and price expectations based on prior levels of economic performance, and research which looked more at the demographic or contextual characteristics of strikes. Both forms used econometric techniques to test hypotheses and untangle complex sets of relationships.

The expression of strikes as a consequence of actor expectations had its genesis in the work of Ashenfelter and Johnson, which appeared in 1969. In the tradition of the institutional literature,

[2] Important advances in the measurement of strike activity came during this decade. David Britt and Omer R. Galle (1972) gave the initial impetus to this work by conceptualizing the volume of industrial conflict as an aggregation of the proneness to, extensity of, and intensity of strikes. Further refinements came in recognizing that measures of strike activity require controls for the opportunity to strike or the frequency of negotiations (Shalev 1980, Roomkin 1976).

they argued that union leaders and rank-and-file members have different interests in collective bargaining. Workers are interested in economic gains; leaders must be concerned about the union's survival. However, because they are also elected officials, union leaders must worry about the relationship between the settlement and worker expectations. In this model the strike is the instrument by which worker expectations are modified.

To test this theory, Ashenfelter and Johnson specified the incidence of strikes as a function of, among other things, prior price and wage changes, expressed as distributive lags, and the unemployment rate. They found that strikes increased when there were increases in the rate of price changes and decreased with reductions in real wage changes and unemployment.

Several authors showed that the expectational model as captured in lagged variables explained a large amount of the variance in strike activity in several periods and several countries (Pencavel 1970, Snyder 1975 and 1977, Roomkin undated, Kaufman 1978). Douglas A. Hibbs, Jr. (1976), in perhaps one of the most important of such studies, analyzed the volume of strikes in ten advanced industrial societies from 1950 to 1968. His results show that strike data fit the expectations model and that workers in industrialized countries tend to have long memories.

While the volume of strike activity is correlated with the duration of strikes, Britt and Galle (1974) found that the two indicators have different sets of determinants. This was confirmed by Swint and Nelson (1978), who substituted strike duration for incidence as the dependent variable in an equation based upon the Ashenfelter and Johnson model and found that the model explained noticeably less variance in strike duration than in strike activity.

Where the expectational approach sought to establish relationships between strike activity and aspects of the economic environment, a second group of studies looked at the characteristics of the actors and the process as determinants of strike behavior. Whereas those working with the expectations model relied upon aggregate data and longitudinal designs, the second group used relatively disaggregated data and cross-sectional designs. In these studies measures of strike activity have been correlated, with varying degrees of success, with plant size (Eisele 1970, Shorey 1975), the characteristics of technology (Eisele 1974), community structure (Lincoln 1978, R. Stern 1976), the structure of bargaining (McLean 1977), and the internal structure of unions (Roomkin 1976).

Quantitative research on strikes must find some way of blending the two types of work done in the past decade. Information about the environment—how it contributes to or moderates expectations—should be integrated with variables that capture workplace conditions and other likely causes of militancy and conflict. For example, Robert Dubin (1973) has hypothesized that workers are more militant, the less attached they are to their jobs. Thus job attachment may play a role in forming expectations at differential rates. By necessity, research such as this will have to look at small units of analysis if synthesis is to be achieved. Interindustry strike studies (McLean 1979, for example) and interregional strike studies conducted during the decade were a step in the right direction, but were not sufficiently disaggregated to finely measure the contextual variables. In addition, scholars may wish to follow Roomkin's lead (1976) by using the bargaining unit as the level of analysis. In the long run, some way of pooling time-series and cross-sectional analyses also seems prudent since collective bargaining is not an episodic phenomenon, but an evolving relationship.

Researchers are also likely to devote attention to refining the aggregate expectations models. As they do so, some way must be found to incorporate into the model the costs of the strike to employers as well as to the workers. The few attempts to measure employer concession behavior (Farber 1978 and Comay et al. 1974) have only touched the surface of this issue. The task will be to construct a model that takes into account the inherent bilateralism of the negotiations process.

It is also important to improve our understanding of work stoppages in particular industries. In mining, for example, where the truly interesting aspects of work stoppages pertain to the causes and consequences of wildcat strikes, Brett and Goldberg's (1979) work has shown us the importance of supervisory practices in determining the incidence of wildcats. An interesting test of this finding would be to see if wildcats are caused by the same factors in industries with a nonaberrant environment—that is, one with a better developed system of grievance administration or better programs of supervisory training.

In construction, there is evidence that work stoppages are used for purposes of organizing or asserting jurisdictional claims (Lipsky and Farber 1976). This suggests that the strike is more than an adjunct of the wage-determining process. Models failing to take this into account may omit important determinants of strike activity. This message is particularly clearly stated in R. Stern (1978).

The explanation of public-sector work stoppages has also proved to be elusive. Burton and Krider's (1975) early and relatively unsatisfying effort to explain intercity variations in public-sector strikes in the period seem to be telling us that the models of private-sector stoppages assume a degree of institutional development not yet found in the public sector. Yet James L. Perry and Leslie J. Berkes (1977) and Perry (1977) were able to identify some factors that consistently explained strike behavior in municipal negotiations. An issue for the 1980s will be to see if either set of results can be replicated with more experience and more data.

Finally, while research on strikes is important, the strike is only one indicator of the larger issue of industrial conflict (Feuille and Wheeler 1981). To the extent that general theories of industrial conflict are tested on measures of strikes, we may only be seeing part of the picture. Thus the relationship of strikes to other manifestations of conflict between and among individuals and organizations should be clarified during the next decade.

Collective Bargaining as a Multilateral Process

An important process issue discussed during the decade was the concept of multilateral (more than two-party) bargaining in the public sector. As originally raised by McLennan and Moskow (1969), the idea centered around the ability of interest groups to influence public-sector collective bargaining by imposing "a cost [economic, political, or otherwise] on the parties to the agreement" (p. 31). Juris and Feuille (1973) extended the definition to include union attempts to bring additional pressure on local management through the courts, the legislature, or referendums.

Relying upon a theory of intraorganization conflict (Schmidt and Kochan 1972), Kochan (1974, 1975) looked at the conditions under which multilateral bargaining might arise. Theoretically and empirically, he showed how the characteristics of city government (most notably the diversity of goals and interests among city officials, and the dispersion of power) lead to conflict among managers and ultimately to multilateral bargaining.

Based on these findings, Juris and Maxey (1981) expected to find multilateral bargaining in collective bargaining involving public hospitals in six cities. Instead they found the presence of multilateral bargaining only in New York City—in negotiations involving both the public and private hospitals. This led them to suspect that multilateralism was related to the politicization of the environment in which bargaining took place. Anderson's (1979a) finding that internal conflict and a multilateral bargaining index did not show the same relationship with outputs in Canadian municipal bargaining as they had in the U.S. led him to suggest that maturity of the public-sector relationship may also be an important factor in evaluating the utility of this construct.[3]

Contract Rejections

Rank-and-file rejections of contract settlements were a popular subject for research in the late 1960s, but seem to have vanished from the literature in the 1970s even though the relative incidence of rejected tentative settlements remained roughly at pre-1970 levels (Federal Mediation and Conciliation Service 1981). Possibly, this is one subject the field believes it adequately understands, at least for the time being.

Odewahn and Krislov (1973), who studied 31 contracts rejected during the period from July 1966 to November 1969, give us a useful summary of our knowledge about contract rejections. On the basis of interviews with unions, managements, and neutrals, the authors conclude that economic factors and worker expectations were more important in explaining these rejections than were such alternative explanations as a rising level of social unrest among workers, the separation of a union's authority to negotiate from its authority to ratify a contract, or the provisions of the

[3] The process of bargaining in the public sector was very widely researched during the decade. However, this literature was carefully reviewed in the 1979 IRRA volume (Aaron et al. 1979), particularly Chapter 3, and thus is not mentioned here.

Landrum-Griffin Act. It would appear, therefore, that a rejected contract, like a strike, is an extension of the expectations process.

Contract Administration

In one of the rare empirical studies of shop-floor conflict, Peach and Livernash (1974) examined grievance rates in five companies in the basic steel industry and distinguished patterns of high and low rates of grievance generation based on the characteristics of the workplace and managerial styles used. However, underemphasized in this framework are the variables representing the individual—his or her wants, attitudes, and frustrations. These should be examined, because the grievance process is one of the major outlets for individuals to channel conflicts with the employer or the union.

Similarly, there is little if any empirical evidence on how grievance-arbitration procedures actually operate. Among the questions begging for analysis are: (1) How effective are grievance-arbitration procedures in reducing the number and severity of labor-management disputes during the term of the contract? (2) Are some types of grievance-arbitration procedures more effective than others in achieving voluntary settlement of disputes? (3) What impact does the grievance-arbitration process have upon the operation of the union as an organization? It also seems important to evaluate the heralded experiments with expedited arbitration which were supposed to reduce the number of cases brought to arbitration, as well as the formalism and costs of the process.

Some empirical work was conducted on grievance arbitrators as decision-makers (see Bankston, 1977, Peterson 1970, and Briggs and Anderson 1980). But we have not gone very far beyond the initial work in 1965 by R. W. Fleming on the predictability of arbitration awards (pp. 78–106).

Dispute Resolution

The resolution of interest disputes without strikes was the "hottest" topic in labor research during the 1970s because of the growth in the use of such techniques in the public sector. Academic and nonacademic investigators compiled a vast amount of evaluative information on many variables of procedures for settling bargaining impasses, drawing on the experiences in several states and cities and for different occupational groups. An excellent appraisal of the extensive literature on dispute resolution in the public sector appears in Thomas Kochan (1979a). Considerably less is known about the private sector and voluntary applications of such techniques. The sections below look at the most studied of the alternatives to the strike: mediation, fact-finding, and arbitration.

Mediation

If science progresses from description to inference and hypothesis-testing, then we are truly with a limited basis for scientific research in the area of mediation. The absence of good description prior to the 1970s may help explain why, judging from bibliographic citations (Levin and DeSantis 1978), mediation continues to be one of the most discussed but least researched areas of collective bargaining. The omission is a serious one in light of the public sector's growing use of mediation in solving disputes and a developing use of mediators to prevent disputes.[4]

Some progress was made during the decade, however. Maggiolo (1971) and Simkin (1971), each relying on their own extensive experience, developed treatises on mediation techniques which remain the best general description of what mediators do. Kressel (1972) used interview responses of mediators to identify three forms of mediation intervention—reflexive, nondirective, and directive. More recently, some initial work (Gerhart and Drotning 1981) has been done to measure how intensively these activities are pursued. Finally, Kolb (1981) provides a rich base for future analysis of the mediation process. Her 16-case participant-observer study of federal and state mediators represents the most significant study of mediation using this methodology since the publication of Ann Douglas's (1962) work. In addition to providing a rich description of what mediators do, her analysis of the contrasting styles of federal and state mediators pose a number of hypotheses that warrant further testing. All of these efforts could help bring more rigor to the study of mediation practice and the training

[4] The Federal Mediation and Conciliation Service undertook several controversial experiments in which mediators initiated and serviced labor-management committees. See Popular (1976) and Usery (1973).

of mediators and, as a consequence, help to settle the age-old debate whether mediation is an art or a science.[5]

An important unpublished project by the American Arbitration Association (1978) also contributed to research in this area by seeking to determine how various theories of dispute resolution might contribute to effectiveness in mediation. Game theorists, mediators, and advocates reviewed the mediation practices in the 1976 strike of District 1199 against the League of Voluntary Hospitals in New York City. By identifying some of the communications barriers between theoreticians and practitioners, the project laid the foundation for more fruitful interactions between these two groups.

A second research stream which can proceed parallel with research on process is research on the effectiveness of mediation—that is, whether or not third-party intervenors are effective in bringing about settlements through mediation. Kochan and Jick (1978), in the first systematic study of this question, examined 67 cases of mediation involving negotiations between police and firefighters and municipal governments in New York State. By defining mediation effectiveness behaviorally in terms of mediation's contribution to settlements, Kochan-Jick found that the intensity of the dispute, the aggressiveness of the mediator, and the ability of the employer to pay exerted a strong effect on the probability of reaching a settlement in mediation.

As an initial empirical inquiry into mediation effectiveness, Kochan-Jick is an important contribution. Before their results are generalized, however, it would be useful to replicate the study in several settings to take into account potential differences among states, occupations, and sectors. For example, some observers believe that mediation in the public sector is qualitatively different from mediation in the private sector because the issues are more complex, the parties less willing to compromise, and the processes more politicized in the public sector (Odewahn 1972, Robins 1972, Ross 1976).

Attention should also be given to distinguishing between the effectiveness of mediation and the parties' satisfaction with the process. Kochan and Jick found that the effectiveness of mediation

[5] Perhaps the best literary treatment of mediation as an art appeared in Fred C. Shapiro's (1970) *Profile of Theodore Kheel.*

declines in disputes involving more experienced negotiators. Yet in the private sector Krislov and Mead (1972) found higher levels of satisfaction with mediation among larger and presumably more sophisticated private-sector firms. Researchers might look at whether the difference can be attributed to differences in the constructs or differences in sector.

If there is to be important research on mediation in the 1980s, researchers will have to focus on a scientific agenda. This will not be easy. As Kochan and Jick observed, confidentiality of the mediation process will make it difficult to acquire primary data.

Fact-Finding

Fact-finding, or mediation with recommendations (sometimes called advisory arbitration), is used in dispute resolution in the health care, airline, and railway industries and in the public sector. The theory of fact-finding holds that the prospect of settlement may be enhanced by clarifying positions through the issuance of recommendations. These recommendations would presumably reveal the most logical settlement position and—if the fact-finder's report were made public—public pressure would encourage the disputants to settle. Additionally, where fact-finding was legally mandated, the parties would have added opportunity to reflect on possible settlement positions while hearings were being scheduled and conducted.

This theoretical rationale for fact-finding as a dispute-resolution procedure notwithstanding, Jean McKelvey (1969) expressed a fear that fact-finding would become less effective as the parties became accustomed to bargaining under the procedures. Support for her prediction has come from several sources. Gatewood (1974) found, for example, that the parties to teacher negotiations in Wisconsin showed an increasing tendency over time to reject fact-finders' reports. Another empirical finding contrary to theory came from Cimini's (1970) study of airline industry emergency boards appointed between 1936 and 1969. He concluded that "the pressure of public opinion was not adequate to force the parties to accept a board's recommendation, nor was voluntary compliance common" (p. 63). Finally, it is not testimony to the success of fact-finding that several states (for example, Pennsylvania, Michigan, and Wisconsin) felt compelled to substitute compulsory arbitration for fact-finding as the terminal step in mandatory dispute-resolution procedures in the public sector.

An important test of fact-finding's effectiveness will come in the health care industry. According to a study conducted by the Federal Mediation and Conciliation Service (1979), two years after the Taft-Hartley amendments, strikes occurred in 13 percent of the 120 situations in which Boards of Inquiry were appointed, but in only 4.6 percent of the situations in which boards were not appointed. In the absence of a controlled study, this might lead one to believe that BOIs were counterproductive. We do not know. We do know, however, that at the same time the actors—the parties and neutrals—believed fact-finding had advanced the goals of collective bargaining, while acknowledging that certain procedural changes were desirable. It remains to be seen if, as McKelvey predicted, fact-finding's effectiveness diminishes as the parties gain more experience in negotiations.

Compulsory Interest Arbitration

The large number of studies of compulsory arbitration undertaken during the decade have created a body of conflicting findings.[6] To some extent these disparate results come from important differences in the dispute procedures studied and the underlying political and economic contexts of the jurisdictions. We will deal with these concerns shortly. First, however, there are several methodological problems which also have affected the accuracy of this work which must be discussed.

Methodological Concerns. Our first concern is that many of the studies from which inferences on the utility and effect of compulsory arbitration are drawn were conducted within one or two years of the initiation of the process. Examples include Long and Feuille (1974) on Eugene, Oregon; Gilroy and Lipovac (1977) on Iowa; Holden (1976) on Massachusetts; Loewenberg (1970) on Pennsylvania; Wheeler (1977) on South Dakota; and Grodin (1974) on Nevada. Experience in other areas of industrial relations research suggest that distributed lag models, age, and maturity effects are important considerations in explaining variance in the

[6] For a thoughtful review of the varieties of interest arbitration to be found in collective bargaining, but one which deemphasizes the empirical literature, see Charles Morris (1976).

dependent variable. The same may be true here as well. One or two years' observation is not sufficient to generate definitive findings.

Second, the use of interrupted time-series or before-and-after research designs that characterize these studies does not allow for consideration of the fact that the introduction of compulsory procedures is often correlated with other significant events such as the growth in the number of negotiations or increases in the general level of wages.

Third, as Anderson (1981) points out, studies of compulsory arbitration have frequently neglected to control for other factors also operating on the parties' willingness to use these procedures. His work, which identifies criteria for evaluating studies of interest arbitration, should be useful to researchers in the 1980s.

Two studies that appear to us to deal with the three objections raised above were the one by J. Stern et al. (1975), which compares the outcomes of final-offer arbitration procedures for police and firefighters in Michigan and Wisconsin with the impact of conventional arbitration in Pennsylvania, and the one by a group at Cornell University (Kochan et al. 1979), which studies interest arbitration for police and firefighters under the Taylor Law of New York State. Both of these inquiries sought to establish appropriate base-line measures against which bargaining under arbitration could be evaluated, and both attempted to use rigorous statistical procedures to hold constant confounding influences.

These two studies represent competing designs for future work. One emphasizes comparisons across jurisdictions, the other intensive analyses within a jurisdiction. The latter design offers the advantage of allowing us to understand the complex political variables that seem to be present in public-sector bargaining. Intensive focus on a single jurisdiction may in theory also make the research more useful to policy-makers. Interjurisdictional comparisons, on the other hand, by introducing variability in the provisions of the law, offer a greater hope for isolating the net effects of compulsory arbitration on the process and outcomes of collective bargaining.

Process Effects. Received theory tells us that the availability of compulsory arbitration in the event of an impasse could remove the parties' incentive to negotiate, resulting in an unwillingness to reach agreement without third-party adjudication. It is also believed that this chilling effect (of arbitration on negotiations) would be reduced if the system mandated were final-offer rather than conventional arbitration because, by limiting arbitral discretion, such a system would increase the parties' costs of disagreement resulting from their failure to reach a final settlement. Empirically, these process effects for both conventional and final-offer arbitration have been difficult to pin down.

Lipsky and Barocci (1978), Drotning and Lipsky (1977), and Loewenberg (1970), among others, find support for the chilling effect. Each reports a *manifold* increase in impasses after the introduction of compulsory arbitration statutes. In Massachusetts, for example, the increase was more than 200 percent. However, Kochan et al. (1979) found that after other factors were controlled, the increased likelihood that negotiations would go to impasse was only 16 percent. Further studies should resolve these differences.

The proposition that final-offer has had less of a chilling effect than conventional arbitration seems, for the moment, to be empirically verified. Feuille's (1975b) secondary analysis of the data in published accounts of the incidence of arbitrated settlements in a variety of U.S. and Canadian jurisdictions leads him to conclude that "final-offer arbitration procedures appear to have less of a chilling effect on bargaining than do conventional arbitration procedures" (p. 309). His finding gains support from experience in the baseball industry where Chelius and Dworkin (1980) found that final-offer arbitration does not apparently destroy the incentive to settle.

However, while many are not convinced that the risks associated with final-offer arbitration do encourage negotiations to a greater extent than conventional arbitration, Farber (1980), in a theoretical analysis, suggests that even under final-offer rules, there are ways the parties can manipulate the process to minimize the risks of adverse settlements (such as manipulating their final offers).

If Farber is correct, then an interesting question is whether the mechanisms for controlling risks are related to the amount of experience one has with the process. For instance, the parties might become better at anticipating arbitral judgments as arbitrators reveal their preference through awards and opinions. Or the parties could become more aware of the effect of settlements achieved or arbitrated in adjacent jurisdictions. If these conditions hold, then final-offer arbitration, like fact-finding, could show declining effectiveness over time and an incidence of arbitrated settlements closer to that produced by conventional procedures. Alternatively, it could be argued that the improvements in the ability to make predictions, in fact, enhances the chances for settlement. Thus the controversy concerning the chilling effects of final-offer should carry on to the next decade.[7]

A controversy has also developed over whether compulsory arbitration creates a dependency—a so-called narcotic (or addictive) effect. Kochan and Baderschneider (1978) found a "high and constantly increasing rate of dependency on third-parties" had taken place in New York State police and firefighter negotiations under both fact-finding and arbitration procedures. That is, prior use of impasse procedures was positively related to current use. But upon reexamination of the same data, Butler and Ehrenberg (1981) uncovered a negative narcotic effect—that current use is a disincentive to subsequent use. The difference, in part, stems from the way in which the researchers specified their regression models to conform with theory.[8] However, until scholars reach agreement on a theory of bargaining processes, it may be difficult to judge which discovered impacts of arbitration or other impasse procedures on bargaining processes are accurate. And there will still remain the problem of determining just how big a narcotic effect has to be before it is considered big, given the positive aspects of strike avoidance. See Thompson and Cairnie (1973 and 1975) and Feuille (1975a) on this issue.

In this vein, there are those who feel that union leadership may view compulsory arbitration as a factor to be used in intraorganizational bargaining and attitudinal structuring. McCormick's (1977) description of interest arbitration in New York City between 1968 and 1975 showed how the unions and the city used arbitration to manage intraorganizational relationships with their constituencies. Similarly, Barnum (1977) showed how actors in the

[7] We are grateful to Thomas Kochan for bringing this point to our attention.

[8] For a discussion of the effect of methodology on results, see Freeman and Medoff (1981).

mass transit industry found it beneficial to use the arbitrator as a "lightning rod," thus reducing the criticism of leadership.

Outcome Effects. Arbitration, whether conventional or final-offer, in the view of most observers is a mechanism that diminishes the economic and political strength of the stronger party and brings the parties to the negotiations process as relative equals (J. Stern et al. 1975, p. 144). This implies that the wage rates in arbitrated and nonarbitrated settlements would tend to be equal. Support for this hypothesis can be found in Chelius and Dworkin's (1980) finding that the range of baseball player salaries declined after the introduction of final-offer arbitration in that industry and Lipsky and Barocci's (1978) conclusion that in Massachusetts police and firefighter salaries resulting from arbitrated settlements were not significantly different from salary changes that would have been achieved in the absence of arbitration.

To isolate the effect of final-offer arbitration on wages, J. Stern et al. compared the settlements achieved through final-offer procedures in one jurisdiction with the settlements achieved in a jurisdiction requiring conventional arbitration. Relying on what they call the "preponderance of the evidence," they conclude "that the institution of final-offer arbitration tended to raise the salaries of the police and firefighters in Michigan and Wisconsin by more than 1 but less than 5 percent and that the positive effect was much smaller, if it was present at all, in the subsequent year" (p. 169).

The above studies test only for the effect of the *use* of arbitration (that is, comparing arbitrated and negotiated settlements). A complete test of the effects of arbitration (or any other impasse procedure) needs also to test for the effects of the *availability* of the procedure since the existence of a procedure may change the behavior of the negotiators. Further discussion of this point is found in Kochan et al. (1979) and Farber and Katz (1979).

Voluntary Interest Arbitration

Fascination with voluntary interest arbitration has always tended to be greater than the number of negotiations concluded in this manner. Although a great deal has been written about instances of voluntary arbitration authorized by prenegotiating agreements (such as those found in the steel, mass transit, utilities, and the airlines), there have been no rigorous empirical evaluations of these innovations. Nor have there been any efforts exhaustively to identify instances of ad hoc arbitration so that they might be studied for patterns and similarities. An excellent nonquantitative treatment of voluntary interest arbitration, however, is contained in Charles Morris (1976).

It may be that voluntary arbitration does not occur more often in the private sector because this procedure seems to make the most sense in those rare instances where there is an inequality of bargaining power and where the economic and political costs of a strike are perceived to be greater than those associated with using arbitration. While these conditions may have had limited applicability in the past, the deteriorating environment for bargaining in several major unionized industries could make voluntary arbitration much more appealing in the 1980s. It behooves us, therefore, to identify and evaluate the limited experiences of the 1970s.

The Effect of Time

The published work on third-party procedures for settling labor disputes seems to indicate that experience with a procedure bears a relationship to the effectiveness of the procedure. Drotning and Lipsky's (1977) evaluation of fact-finding in teacher negotiations in New York State, Kochan and Jick's (1978) observations on mediation, and McKelvey's early observations about fact-finding strongly imply that the parties learn to manipulate the process. Similarly, Anderson and Kochan (1977), without specifying the exact causes, documented a "half-life" to the effectiveness of procedures, and J. Stern et al. (1975) found that wage effects between final-offer and conventional arbitration narrowed with time. Clearly, the effect is worth studying to learn what it is about the age of the procedure, the maturity of the parties, or the number of iterations that tends to yield these consequences.

Perhaps those best equipped to lead the investigation of this phenomenon are the game theoreticians (see Crawford [1979] and Farber and Katz [1979]) who already have contributed to our understanding of the incentives to settlement found in both conventional and final-offer arbitration procedures. They looked at such factors as the predictability of third-party decisions, the presence of bilateral or asymmetric information, and the parties' risk aversion and preferences.[9] It strikes us intuitively that although the mathematics of this modification might be complicated, this approach could incorporate learning by making assumptions about the actors' becoming more adept at predicting outcomes, evaluating information, and identifying risks. A learning model would help establish theoretical linkages between outcomes from prior negotiations and the parties' current desire to use the procedures.

The Outcomes of Collective Bargaining

"Outcomes" is a term which encompasses both the web of rules that emerges from bargaining (sometimes called bargaining outputs) and the impact of those rules on institutions and individuals. The heritage of this research is in an encyclopedic literature of case studies aimed at assessing the impact of unions on employers. Perhaps the most famous of these studies is Slichter, Healy, and Livernash's *The Impact of Collective Bargaining on Management* (1960), a report on manufacturing unionism in the 1950s. In the 1970s, a similar set of heuristic case studies was undertaken focusing on collective bargaining in education, local goverment, law enforcement, and health care—the so-called emerging sectors of collective bargaining. The decade also saw the development of a considerably different approach to the study of bargaining outcomes—one that sought to quantify the nonwage impacts much more precisely than before.

Because union impact on wages is reviewed elsewhere in this volume, in last year's volume (Freeman and Medoff 1981), and by Mitchell (1979), what follows deals with the impact of unions and collective bargaining on other conditions of employment, most notably the ability of management to allocate human and capital resources and the ability of management to make policy.

The Heuristic Case Studies

The studies of unions in emerging sectors all used techniques similar to those developed by Slichter et al. (1960). In each of

---

[9] Using this approach, one could analyze the several proposals for improving upon dispute procedures, among them Donn's (1977) suggestion to permit each party to submit multiple final offers, and Wheeler's (1977) proposal for "closed-offer arbitration"—a variant on conventional arbitration. There is also Foegen's (1974) plan to use public referendums in lieu of arbitration.

these studies samples were acknowledged as not scientifically drawn or statistically adequate, but rather as being drawn to seek variability on such dimensions thought important as geography, size of unit, relevant public policy, the unions or organizations associated with the industry, and duration of relationship. Each study examined the unions or associations involved, the legal environment, and the impact of unions on wages, hours, and conditions of work as well as management's ability to manage and the policy processes affecting the operation of the unit. The methodology typically involved interviews with the parties and a review of written documents and local press coverage of events in the industry studied. These data were aggregated and disaggregated, and passed through each researcher's "black box"; the results were presented in narrative form. Ultimately, however, each author compared the practice and impact of bargaining in the studied jurisdiction to the findings of Slichter et al. Rarely were differences found.

This characterization is not meant to denigrate these studies. Rather, it is meant to describe a style of research that added to knowledge and generated many of the hypotheses tested more rigorously and comprehensively by others. For this reason, the contents of these studies by sector are reviewed below.

Education. While there were many assessments of collective bargaining in public education, the work of Perry and Wildman (1970) is probably the best published to date. Studying two dozen school districts over the period 1964–1969, they found that unions had made strong inroads in management's ability to allocate resources and to make policy, but that, on balance, control remained with the school boards. Among the issues no longer the sole province of management were curriculum and textbook selection, promotion policies for teachers (to administration) and pupils (from grade to grade), pupil discipline, use of substitutes, grading policy, teacher transfer rights, and membership on sundry board committees. In the area of working conditions, the authors found an emphasis on due process, increased free time, increased cost for after-hours extracurricular work, some effort to control class size, and the implementation of grievance procedures.

Perry (1979) went back to nine of these districts in 1977. He found that the subjects covered formally and informally had expanded greatly since 1969. Contact hours were reduced and extra compensation for extracurricular responsibilities had been instituted. Management rights and control over policy formulation were also modified. For example, rules on promotion were extended, policy grievances allowed, and maintenance-of-standards clauses deleted. On balance, Perry concludes (as Perry and Wildman had in the earlier study) that "collective bargaining in public education is not radically different in process and results from collective bargaining in the private sector" (p. 16).

Outcomes in higher education also received a great deal of attention during the decade. Among those who studied this issue were Garbarino and Aussieker (1975), Kemerer and Baldridge (1975), and Begin (1974). On balance, these studies find that unions tend to concentrate on the traditional issues of wages, hours, and conditions of work. Impact on promotion and governance tended to be more procedural than substantive. These findings are consistent with Bognanno et al. (1978) whose content analysis of 59 of the 61 organized four-year college or university first contracts negotiated between 1967 and 1975 showed that content is independent of "union" (AAUP, NEA, AFT) or sector (public or private). Survey research at the University of British Columbia in 1977 (Ponak and Thompson 1979) found that most faculty were more strongly in favor of bargaining over issues normal to collective bargaining and that faculty would be cautious about using collective bargaining to effect fundamental change in university procedures. The Kemerer and Baldridge and Garbarino and Aussieker studies suggest that where a strong university senate participates in governance, the two systems have existed side-by-side. They questioned if this would continue. Given the economic and demographic pressures under which colleges and universities will operate in the 1980s, and in light of the Supreme Court's removal of National Labor Relations Board jurisdiction, it will be interesting to see what the future holds for faculty unionism.

Local Government. Stanley, with the assistance of Cooper (1972), studied union impacts in 19 local units of government in 1968 and 1969. His conclusions were similar to those of Perry and Wildman. In response to the question of union impacts on government's ability to translate the will of the people into effective action, Stanley answers "not much" (p. 139). Unions, he found, may impair governmental efficiency by raising costs, but they may also improve it by demanding adequate staffing and by providing what we have come to call the "voice" characteristics of a union contract—for example, grievance procedures, seniority, etc. Management's ability to designate programs was not impaired, albeit the level of program effort might be affected by the cost of a union contract. Stanley concluded that union gains in local government had not been excessive. Union efforts to get more in the future might burden the political and procedural restraints, according to Stanley, but the outcomes were not likely to be disastrous for city managers.

Law Enforcement. Using the same case study approach, Juris and Feuille (1973) studied 22 unionized police departments in 1971. In these cities, law enforcement unions were seen to have narrowed management discretion, fostered the development of management by policy, and protected employees against arbitrary or inconsistent treatment. Police unions, like the unions encountered by Perry and Wildman, Stanley, and Slichter et al. were found to be essentially reactionary and conservative.

Slightly less sanguine conclusions are reached by Margaret Levi (1977) who infers from case studies in Atlanta, New York, and Detroit that police unionism and collective bargaining were means of undermining bureaucratic processes and the authority of the state. Her viewpoint (that of a political scientist who is willing to consider both neoclassical economic and Marxist interpretations of the role of the state) is well taken. However, the three case studies may be somewhat atypical given the high degree of politicization in New York City and the complicating role of race relations in Atlanta and Detroit.

Hospitals. The 1974 amendments to the National Labor Relations Act extended the protection of the act to unionism in hospitals and thus provided another arena in which to investigate the impact of unions on management. Unlike the previous efforts, studies of hospital unionism were characterized by more systematic methods of data collections and a clearer set of a priori hypotheses.

Studies of hospital collective bargaining were pursued primarily by Miller and his colleagues at the University of Wisconsin-Madison and Juris and his colleagues at Northwestern University. A study by the Federal Mediation and Conciliation Service (1979) looked at the industry and the actors, but its focus was primarily on the impact of the amendments on bargaining processes rather than the impact of unions on management.

Miller's group was involved in two distinct but related efforts. The first (Miller et al. 1979) was a study of hospitals in Minnesota, Wisconsin, and Illinois. Primary data on costs and turnover were collected by questionnaire from 563 unionized and nonunionized respondents, with follow-up interviews in an unspecified number of hospitals to capture a "feel" for the institutional realities. A corollary analysis of 126 hospital bargaining agreements was also undertaken. Regression analysis was used to assess the impacts on wages, fringe benefits, and hospital costs. In determining the impact on costs, an effort was made to estimate the net effect of wage increases adjusted for changes in worker quality and the effect of reduced turnover. On balance, they concluded that the net effect on hospital costs in these states in 1975 was of the magnitude of 2–4 percent. Their survey of labor contracts indicated that hospital unions were placing very little restriction on the management of hospital manpower and were acquiring only a limited voice in management decisions either procedurally or substantively. By studying unionized and nonunionized hospitals (an element none of the other studies had attempted), the authors were able to conclude, "it is ironic that the impact of collective bargaining, at least in the short run, may have been greatest in nonunion hospitals" through a combination of threat and spillover effects (p. 148).

In 1981 the authors expanded the scope of their inquiry to encompass a national sample of hospitals (Becker et al. 1981). Although the main intention was to estimate the impact of unions on wage rates and hospital costs, the authors also report that some administrators admitted that union pressure had forced them to economize and improve management practices in the areas of scheduling, discipline, and supervision (p. 13).

Juris and his colleagues pursued the impact question from two perspectives. In one approach they analyzed contract clauses in 813 hospital labor agreements negotiated in 1974–1979 (Juris 1977, Juris and Bentivegna 1981, Juris and Maxey 1981). Contrary to conventional wisdom in the hospital industry (hospitals were different and hospital collective bargaining would be different), they found that contracts in hospitals were quite similar to those in all other industries and that the degree of similarity increased between 1976 and 1979.

Juris and Maxey (1981) also looked at policy formulation and resource allocation in hospitals. Along with field interviews, they administered an attitudinal survey to managers in 36 hospitals with established relationships in 1976–1977. Among their findings, Juris and Maxey report that managers perceived unionism as fostering greater formalization and consistency in personnel policies. In addition, no significant changes were reported in the role played by hospital boards or physicians, while the impact of the union on the quality of patient care was seen as negligible. At the same time, hospital administrators believed the union enhanced the effectiveness with which labor was recruited and utilized.

The Quantitative Studies

Empiricists followed two paths in the study of bargaining outcomes. Gerhart (1976) and Kochan and Wheeler (1975) led the way in bringing greater precision to the measurement of the web of rules. Freeman (1976) and Freeman and Medoff (1979b) pioneered in studies that sought to examine the behavioral consequences of the rules for the actors. In the future, the two paths may merge, but as of the early 1980s they remain parallel routes.

The Gerhart/Kochan-Wheeler Influence. Anxious to test the relationship between bargaining power and bargaining outputs, Kochan and Wheeler (1975) and Gerhart (1976) independently developed measures of nonwage bargaining outputs. Prior to this work, quantitative studies of outputs were done only by economists who studied such easily measured dimensions as wages and fringe benefits. As Kochan and Wheeler and Gerhart correctly pointed out, this limitation ignored much of the output of the bargaining relationship and overlooked the fact that tradeoffs often exist between the wage and nonwage provisions of an agreement.

Both of these researchers devised coding schemes that recorded the existence or absence of contract provisions as well as the relative favorableness of a particular provision to the union. Each also wrestled with the technical problem of what weights to give each item. Kochan and Wheeler, using an elaborate two-stage weighting and validation scheme, found that it produced no better measures than the unweighted scale. Gerhart relied on Wilkes Law which states that as the number of items becomes larger, the weights become unimportant. To hedge his bet, Gerhart also empirically verified his use of unitary weights.

Gerhart looked at 262 municipal labor agreements in effect in 1967–1968, covering many different occupations. Kochan and Wheeler looked at 121 firefighter agreements in effect in 1972. Each used different but broadly similar models: Power was seen as emanating from the environment and operating on outcomes both directly and indirectly through the parties. Both projects were able to explain about half of the observed variance in their respective contract indices. Gerhart suggested that future research would profit from looking at transient political considerations; Kochan-Wheeler advised us to disaggregate the components of the index. Both studies recommended the need for longitudinal rather than cross-sectional investigations.

Kochan and Block (1977) moved research in this area forward by adding wages and fringes to the outcome measures studied, by disaggregating the outcomes into five subindices (working conditions, job security, equity, pay supplements, and fringe benefits), and by looking at output indices across two-digit industries. Again, the model was essentially the same. The most important finding was that variance in wages and benefits was more likely to be explained by economic variables, but that the variance in the other indices was more likely to be explained by institutional variables.

Further advances were made by John Anderson. In a study of four rounds of bargaining in the Canadian federal sector (1979b), Anderson used the basic model (including political variables to account for bargaining in the public sector) to explain variance in the level of and changes in wages and the outputs index. He found that the same environmental factors were not significantly related to variance across rounds, suggesting that the parties may respond to different elements of their environment over time. Also, he speculated that some tradeoffs among wages and other outcomes may have taken place, but because of limited data, the tradeoff issue would have to await further study. In this regard it is probably unfortunate that Anderson did not employ the contract subindices developed earlier by Kochan and Block. This might have permitted a direct test of the tradeoff hypothesis.

Anderson's second study (1979a) looked at a nonrandom sample of contracts covering Canadian municipal employees in several occupations. The same underlying model was tested using wages and the outputs index as dependent variables, although the independent variables were not directly comparable to those in earlier studies. However, as in other studies, wages and the output indices were affected by different independent variables. Again, one would have wished that Anderson had used subindices to look at the relationship between selected outputs and different environmental factors.

One contribution of Anderson's work is the opportunity it presents to compare outputs at markedly different periods in the development of public-sector bargaining. The studies of emerging American public-sector bargaining showed that such sources of union power as the comprehensiveness of the enabling legislation could be significantly associated with the magnitude of the index, but that age of the relationship was not. Interestingly, Anderson's data on the more mature Canadian experience revealed just the opposite; age was statistically significant, but comprehensiveness was not. These results, combined with his finding that measures of multilateral bargaining were not statistically significant in the Canadian study, lead him to suggest that "[a]n emphasis on the difference between public and private sector labor relations may be misguided if we are only experiencing a reflection of the maturity of the system and the relationship between the parties within the system" (1979a, p. 143).

The Freeman-Medoff Influence. While some sought to measure the formalized "web of rules" as the outputs of the collective bargaining process, a second group of scholars was looking at the effect of these outputs on the behavior of workers and the firm.

"Two Faces of Unionism" by Freeman and Medoff (1979b) is a complete statement of the approach, although the idea was probably first stated in Freeman (1976). The main thesis is that, while economists generally focus on the monopoly wage aspects of trade unions (the monopoly "face" of trade unionism), they have not looked at the economic effect of these rules on employee and employer behavior (the collective voice/institutional response "face"). The inspiration here was Hirschman, whose *Exit, Voice and Loyalty* (1970) discussed the role of participation in organizational decision-making ("voice") as an alternative to leaving the organization—that is, quitting ("exit"). Freeman and Medoff argue that to the extent the rules negotiated by unions moderate those things that employees dislike about the employment relationship, quits should decline and job tenure increase. If this occurred, the employer's costs should decrease, especially those costs associated with the accumulation of human capital through on-the-job training, and constitute a positive bargaining outcome.

Empirical support for the impact of voice on exit is found in Freeman (1980) in which actual quits or separations were explained by, among other variables, union/nonunion status of the individual and characteristics of grievance procedures in the industry of the worker's employment. Wages and other measures of pecuniary rewards were held constant. Freeman's conclusions are that trade unionism is associated with significant, large reductions in exit behavior and that the difference, within specified limits, can be attributed to voice considerations.

Three other studies looked at the impact of collective bargaining on exit. Duane Leigh (1979) found that the greater wage effect of unions for blacks relative to whites is not counteracted by racial differences in the nonwage aspects of the contract. Using a cohort of young and middle-aged blacks and whites, drawn from the National Longitudinal Survey, Leigh finds no increasing propensity for blacks to exit or any systematic racial difference in the opportunities for occupational advancement for unionized blacks relative to unionized whites. He does warn us that this finding must be interpreted cautiously, given the number of court cases blacks have brought over the issue.[10]

Block (1978), using the contract-scaling techniques discussed above, looked at the relationship between seniority clauses in contracts and mean quit rates in two-digit industries from 1961 to 1972. Controlling for appropriate other variables, he found that promotion-transfer seniority (as opposed to layoff-recall seniority) was negatively related to quit rates—a finding consistent with the collective voice/institutional response hypothesis.

[10] One clue to the underlying process which may explain how both events might coexist is found in Cassell et al. (1975) which looked at the effect of entry level on internal labor market discrimination. They found that discrimination was more likely to occur through entering at a lower level than it was through the operation of rules once an individual was already in the organization.

Becker (1978), looking at the impact of unions on turnover in 144 midwestern hospitals, found that "unionized service occupations, on the average, experienced a turnover rate more than 12 percentage points lower than nonunion service occupations" (p. 99). Since the average annual turnover rate for the sample was 0.24, "this estimate suggests that unionization can reduce turnover by up to 50 percent" (p. 100).

Brown and Medoff (1978) extended the boundaries of work in this area by looking at the impact of unions on productivity. While ideally they would have liked to have measured elements of the "voice" construct directly (better management, morale, motivation, communication), instead they used value added in manufacturing as recorded across states in two-digit industries. Using a Cobb-Douglas production function with controls for quality of labor, they found a positive union-productivity effect which they said is not the result of the unionized industries being more productive for other reasons, or different capital/labor utilization rates in union and nonunion firms, or uncaptured quality differences in workers across industries.[11] They use this finding to suggest that while union workers may be more expensive, this cost may be partially offset by higher productivity.

Whither Outcomes Research

The prospect of a synthesis involving the quantification of the contract's terms and the behavioral or economic consequences of the agreement is quite exciting. The authors of the output studies were correct in first trying to measure contract clauses with adequate precision and then trying to explain outputs in terms of exogenous factors. However, as useful as that work has been, we must now recognize that the motivations of the actors to accept new contract provisions, or alter existing provisions, are also influenced by the impact of current clauses on the actors as well as the perceived impact of the proposed change. With further advances in measurement and statistics, we can foresee longitudinal studies that dynamically link changes in the outputs of bargaining

---

[11] J. Paul Leigh (1981) suggests a productivity-limiting outcome from a "voice" variable: if unions reduce the cost of being absent for the worker (that is, sick pay), then absenteeism is likely to increase. Higher absenteeism probably works to reduce the productivity gains of collective bargaining.

to both the determinants of bargaining power and the economic and behavioral consequences of past agreements.

Conclusion

In this review we have defined the research of the 1970s primarily in terms of the contributions of the empiricists. We justified this decision on the basis of what was new in the decade was the use of methodological techniques that had gained acceptance in economics, sociology, and psychology to study traditional industrial relations problems. What we learned is that empiricism in this field cannot stand alone. From time to time throughout these pages we have made suggestions for further research. More often than not the suggestions called for integrating microlevel variables identified by the institutionalists into the aggregate models specified by the empiricists.

These suggestions create a special burden for both groups—the identification of relevant variables and the creation of appropriate measures. We should get away from the use of aggregate data for testing models of individual decision-making just because published aggregate data are readily available.

If there is an overall theme that emerges from this research, it is that we must better understand the role of time, age, and maturity in industrial relations. It is apparently difficult to explain behavioral characteristics of unions and negotiations when the units of observation vary greatly on an unmeasured qualitative dimension. Sometimes we call this dimension maturity, but have no better operational measure than chronological age. Sometimes we don't deal with it at all, but draw inferences about it to explain our results. Institutionalists and empiricists could work together to disentangle these three variables and develop measures of the resulting constructs.

References

Aaron, Benjamin, Joseph R. Grodin, and James L. Stern, eds. *Public-Sector Bargaining.* IRRA Series. Washington: Bureau of National Affairs, 1979.

Adams, Arvil V., and Joseph Krislov. "New Union Organizing: A Test of the Ashenfelter-Pencavel Model of Trade Union Growth." *Quarterly Journal of Economics* 88 (May 1974): pp. 304–11.

Allison, Elisabeth K. "Financial Analysis of the Local Union." *Industrial Relations* 14 (May 1975): pp. 145–55.

American Arbitration Association, Research Institute. "Report on the Transfer Project in Collective Bargaining." Unpublished mimeo. 1978.

Anderson, John C. "Bargaining Outcomes: An IR Systems Approach." *Industrial Relations* 18 (Spring 1979a): pp. 127–43.

———. "Determinants of Bargaining Outcomes in the Federal Government of Canada." *Industrial and Labor Relations Review* 32 (January 1979b): pp. 224–41.

———. "Local Union Participation: A Re-examination." *Industrial Relations* 18 (Winter 1979c): pp. 18–31.

———. "The Impact of Arbitration: A Methodological Assessment." *Industrial Relations* 20 (Spring 1981): pp. 129–48.

Anderson, John C., and Thomas A. Kochan. "Impasse Procedures in the Canadian Federal Service: Effects on the Bargaining Process." *Industrial and Labor Relations Review* 30 (April 1977): pp. 283–301.

Anderson, John C., Charles O'Reilly III, and Gloria Busman. "Union Decertification in the U.S.: 1974-1977." *Industrial Relations* 19 (Winter 1980): pp. 100–107.

Applebaum, Leon. "Local Union Financial Structure: 1962–1966." *Labor Law Journal* 22 (November 1971): pp. 713–24.

Ashenfelter, Orley, and George Johnson. "Bargaining Theory, Trade Unions, and Industrial Strike Activity." *American Economic Review* 59 (March 1969): pp. 35–47.

Ashenfelter, Orley, and John Pencavel. "American Trade Union Growth: 1900–1960." *Quarterly Journal of Economics* 83 (August 1969): pp. 434–48.

Bain, George S., and Farouk Elsheikh. *Union Growth and the Business Cycle.* Oxford: Blackwell, 1976.

Bankston, Eddie W. "Value Differences Between Attorney and Economist Labor Arbitrators." *Proceedings of the 29th Annual Winter Meeting, Industrial Relations Research Assocation,* 1976. Madison, Wis.: IRRA, 1977. Pp. 151–60.

Barbash, Jack. "The Union as an Evolving Organization." In *The Shrinking Perimeter,* eds. Hervey A. Juris and Myron Roomkin. Lexington, Mass.: D. C. Heath, 1980. Pp. 63–80.

Barnum, Darold T. *From Private to Public: Labor Relations in Mass Transit.* Lubbock, Tex.: Texas Tech University, 1977.

Becker, Brian. "Hospital Unionism and Employment Stability." *Industrial Relations* 17 (February 1978): pp. 96–101.

Becker, Brian E., Glen C. Cain, Catherine G. McLaughlin, Richard U. Miller, and Albert E. Schwenk. "The Union Impact on Hospitals—A National Study." Prepared for the National Center for Health Services Research, U.S. Department of Health and Human Services. Unpublished. 1981.

Begin, James P. "Faculty Governance and Collective Bargaining: An Early Appraisal." *Journal of Higher Education* 45 (1974): pp. 582–93.

Block, Richard N. "The Impact of Seniority Provisions on the Manufacturing Quit Rate." *Industrial and Labor Relations Review* 31 (July 1978): pp. 474–88.

———. "Union Organizing and the Allocation of Union Resources." *Industrial and Labor Relations Review* 34 (October 1980): pp. 101–13.

Bognanno, Mario F., David L. Estenson, and Edward L. Suntrup. "Union-Management Contracts in Higher Education." *Industrial Relations* 17 (May 1978): pp. 189–203.

Braun, Robert J. *Teachers and Power: The Story of the American Federation of Teachers.* New York: Simon and Schuster, 1972.

Bressler, Barry. "The Salaries of Union Officials." Paper presented to the American Association for the Advancement of Science. Unpublished mimeo. 1971.

Brett, Jeanne M., and Stephen B. Goldberg. "Wildcat Strikes in Bituminous Coal Mining." *Industrial and Labor Relations Review* 32 (July 1979): pp. 465–83.

Briggs, Steven S., and John C. Anderson. "An Empirical Investigation of Arbitrator Acceptability." *Industrial Relations* 19 (Spring 1980): pp. 163–74.

Brill, Steven. *The Teamsters.* New York: Simon and Schuster, 1978.

Britt, David W., and Omer R. Galle. "Industrial Conflict and Unionization." *American Sociological Review* 37 (February 1972): pp. 46–57.

———. "Structural Antecedents of the Shape of Strikes: A Comparative Analysis." *American Sociological Review* 39 (October 1974): pp. 642–51.

Brooks, Thomas R. *Communications Workers of America: The Story of a Union.* New York: Mason Charter, 1977.

Brown, Charles, and James L. Medoff. "Trade Unions in the Production Process." *Journal of Political Economy* 86 (June 1978): pp. 355–78.

Burton, John F., Jr. "The Extent of Collective Bargaining in the Public Sector." In *Public-Sector Bargaining, eds.* Benjamin Aaron, Joseph R. Grodin, and James L. Stern. IRRA Series. Washington: Bureau of National Affairs, 1979. Pp. 1–43.

Burton, John F., and Charles Krider. "The Incidence of Strikes in Public Employment." In *Labor in the Public and Nonprofit Sectors,* ed. Daniel S. Hamermesh. Princeton, N.J.: Princeton University Press, 1975. Pp. 135–77.

Butler, Richard J., and Ronald G. Ehrenberg. "Estimating the Narcotic Effect of Public Sector Impasse Procedures." *Industrial and Labor Relations Review* 35 (October 1981): pp. 3–20.

Cassell, Frank H., Steven M. Director, and Samuel I. Doctors. "Discrimination Within Internal Labor Markets." *Industrial Relations* 14 (October 1975): pp. 337–44.

Chaison, Gary N. "A Note on Union Merger Trends, 1900–1978." *Industrial and Labor Relations Review* 34 (October 1980): pp. 114–20.

Chelius, James, and James B. Dworkin. "An Economic Analysis of Final-Offer Arbitration as a Conflict Resolution Device." *Journal of Conflict Resolution* 24 (June 1980): pp. 293–310.

Chitayat, Gideon. *Trade Union Mergers and Labor Conglomerates.* New York: Praeger, 1979.

Cimini, Michael H. "Emergency Boards in the Airline Industry: 1936–69." *Monthly Labor Review* 93 (July 1970): pp. 57–65.

Clarke, R. Oliver. "Labour-Management Disputes: A Perspective." *British Journal of Industrial Relations* 18 (March 1980): pp. 14–25.

Comay, Yochanan, Arie Melnik, and Abraham Subotnik. "Bargaining Yield Curves and Wages Settlements: An Empirical Analysis." *Journal of Political Economy* 82 (March 1974): pp. 303–13.

Crawford, Vincent P. "On Compulsory-Arbitration Schemes." *Journal of Political Economy* 87 (February 1979): pp. 131–59.

Derber, Milton. *Research in Labor Problems in the U.S.* New York: Random House, 1967.

———. "Comment." In *The Shrinking Perimeter,* eds. Hervey A. Juris and Myron Roomkin. Lexington, Mass.: D. C. Heath, 1980. Pp. 55–58.

Dewey, Lucretia M. "Union Merger Pace Quickens." *Monthly Labor Review* 94 (June 1971): pp. 63–70.

Donn, Clifford B. "Games Final-Offer Arbitrators Might Play." *Industrial Relations* 16 (October 1977): pp. 306–14.

Douglas, Ann. *Industrial Peacemaking.* New York: Columbia University Press, 1962.

Drotning, John E., and David B. Lipsky. "The Relations Between Teacher Salaries and the Use of Impasse Procedures Under New York's Taylor Law: 1968–1972." *Journal of Collective Negotiations in the Public Sector* 3 (1977): pp. 229–44.

Dubin, Robert. "Attachment to Work and Union Militancy." *Industrial Relations* 12 (February 1973): pp. 51–64.

Dunlop, John T. "What's Ahead in Union Government." In *Trade Union Government and Collective Bargaining: Some Critical Issues,* ed. Joel Seidman. New York: Praeger, 1970. Pp. 198–206.

Dworkin, James B., and Marian M. Extejt. "Why Workers Decertify Their Unions: A Preliminary Investigation." *Proceedings of the Academy of Management,* 1979. Pp. 241–46.

———. "Recent Trends in Union Decertification/Deauthorization Elections." *Proceedings of the 32nd Annual Meeting, Industrial Relations Research Association,* 1979. Madison: Wis.: IRRA, 1980.

Eames, Patricia. "An Analysis of the Voting Study of a Trade-Unionist's Point of View." *Stanford Law Review* 28 (July 1976): pp. 1181–93.

Edelstein, J. David, and Howard J. Ruppel, Jr. "Convention Frequency and Oligarchic Degeneration in British and American Unions." *Administrative Science Quarterly* 15 (March 1970): pp. 47–56.

Ehrenberg, Ronald, and Steven Goldberg. "Officer Performance and Compensation in Local Building Trades Unions." *Industrial and Labor Relations Review* 30 (January 1977): pp. 188–96.

Eisele, C. Frederick. "Organization Size, Technology, and Frequency of Strikes." *Industrial and Labor Relations Review* 27 (July 1974): pp. 560–71.

———. "Plant Size and Frequency of Strikes." *Labor Law Journal* 21 (December 1970): pp. 779–86.

Farber, Henry S. "Bargaining Theory, Wage Outcomes, and the Occurrence of Strikes: An Econometric Analysis." *American Economic Review* 68 (June 1978): pp. 262–71.

———. "Does Final-Offer Arbitration Encourage Bargaining?" Paper presented at Allied Social Sciences Associations Meeting. Unpublished, September 1980.

Farber, Henry S., and Harry C. Katz. "Interest Arbitration, Outcomes, and the Incentive to Bargain." *Industrial and Labor Relations Review* 33 (October 1979): pp. 55–63.

Federal Mediation and Conciliation Service. *Impact of the 1974 Health Care Amendments to the NLRA on Collective Bargaining in the Health Care Industry.* Washington: U.S. Government Printing Office, 1979.

———. *Annual Report, Fiscal Year 1979.* Washington: U.S. Government Printing Office, 1981.

Feuille, Peter. "Analyzing Compulsory Arbitration Experiences: The Role of Personal Preferences—Comment." *Industrial and Labor Relations Review* 28 (April 1975a): pp. 432–38.

———. "Final-Offer Arbitration and the Chilling Effect." *Industrial Relations* 14 (October 1975b): pp. 302–10.

Feuille, Peter, Wallace E. Hendricks, and Lawrence M. Kahn. "Wage and Nonwage Outcomes in Collective Bargaining: Determinants and Tradeoffs." *Journal of Labor Research* 2 (Spring 1981): pp. 39–53.

Feuille, Peter, and Hoyt N. Wheeler. "Will the Real Industrial Conflict Please Stand Up?" In *U.S. Industrial Relations 1950–1980: A Critical Assessment,* eds. Jack Stieber, Robert B. McKersie, and D. Quinn Mills. Madison, Wis.: Industrial Relations Research Association, 1981. Pp. 255–97.

Fink, Gary M. "The Rejection of Voluntarism." *Industrial and Labor Relations Review* 26 (January 1973): pp. 805–19.

Flanagan, Robert J. "The Behavioral Foundations of Union Election Regulation." *Stanford Law Review* 28 (July 1976): pp. 1195–1205.

Fleming, Robben W. *The Labor Arbitration Process.* Urbana: University of Illinois Press, 1965.

Foegen, John H. "Public Sector Strike-Prevention: Let the Taxpayer Decide." *Journal of Collective Negotiations* 3 (Summer 1974): pp. 221–25.

Freeman, John, and Jack Brittain. "Union Merger Process and Industrial Environment." *Industrial Relations* 16 (May 1977): pp. 173–85.

Freeman, Richard B. "Individual Mobility and Union Voice in the Labor Market." *American Economic Review* 66 (May 1976): pp. 361–68.

———. "The Exit-Voice Tradeoff in the Labor Market: Unionism, Job Tenure, Quits, and Separations." *Quarterly Journal of Economics* 94 (June 1980): pp. 643–73.

Freeman, Richard B., and James L. Medoff. "New Estimates of the Distribution of Private Sector Unionism in the U.S." *Industrial and Labor Relations Review* 32 (January 1979a): pp. 143–74.

———. "The Two Faces of Unionism." *The Public Interest* 57 (Fall 1979b): pp. 69–93.

———. "The Impact of Collective Bargaining: Illusion or Reality?" In *U.S. Industrial Relations 1950–1980: A Critical Assessment,* eds. Jack Stieber, Robert B. McKersie, and D. Quinn Mills. Madison, Wis.: Industrial Relations Research Association, 1981. Pp. 47–97.

Galenson, Walter, and Robert S. Smith. "The United States." In *Labor in the Twentieth Century,* eds. John T. Dunlop and Walter Galenson. New York: Academic Press, 1978. Pp. 11–84.

Garbarino, Joseph and Bill Aussieker. *Faculty Bargaining: Change and Conflict.* Report for the Carnegie Commission on Higher Education and the Ford Foundation. New York: McGraw-Hill, 1975.

Gatewood, Lucian. "Fact-Finding in Teacher Disputes: The Wisconsin Experience." *Monthly Labor Review* 97 (October 1974): pp. 47–51.

Gerhart, Paul F. "Determinants of Bargaining Outcomes in Local Government Labor Negotiations." *Industrial and Labor Relations Review* 29 (April 1976): pp. 331–51.

Gerhart, Paul F., and John E. Drotning. "Six State Study of Impasse Procedures in the Public Sector." Public Employment Relations Services Association of Labor Relations Agencies. *Information Bulletin* 4 (March-April 1981): pp. 3–5.

Gerhart, Paul F., and Charles Maxey. "College Administrators and Collective Bargaining." *Industrial Relations* 17 (February 1978): pp. 43–52.

Getman, Julius G., Stephen B. Goldberg, and Jeanne B. Herman. *Union Representation Elections: Law and Reality.* New York: Russell Sage Foundation, 1976.

Gilroy, Thomas P., and Jack A. Lipovac. "Impasse Procedure Utilization: Year One Under the Iowa Statute." *Journal of Collective Bargaining in the Public Sector* 3 (1977): pp. 181–91.

Graham, Harry. "Union Mergers." *Relations Industrielles/Industrial Relations* 25 (August 1970): pp. 552–66.

Graham, Harry, and Harry Donoian. "Union Role in Administering Collective Bargained Pension Plans." *Industrial Gerontology* (Spring 1974).

Grodin, Joseph R. "Arbitration of Public Sector Labor Disputes: The Nevada Experiment." *Industrial and Labor Relations Review* 28 (October 1974): pp. 89–102.

Hibbs, D. A., Jr. "Industrial Conflict in Advanced Industrial Societies." *American Political Science Review* 70 (December 1976): pp. 1033–58.

Hirschman, Albert O. *Exit, Voice and Loyalty.* Cambridge, Mass.: Harvard University Press, 1970.

Holden, Lawrence T., Jr. "Final-Offer Arbitration in Massachusetts: One Year Later." *Arbitration Journal* 31 (March 1976): pp. 26–35.

Hopkins, George E. *The Airline Pilots: A Study in Elite Unionization.* Cambridge, Mass.: Harvard University Press, 1971.

Janus, Charles J. "Union Mergers in the 1970's: A Look at the Reasons and Results." *Monthly Labor Review* 101 (October 1978): pp. 13–23.

Juris, Hervey A. "Labor Agreements in the Hospital Industry: A Study of Collective Bargaining Outputs." *Labor Law Journal* 28 (August 1977): pp. 504–11.

Juris, Hervey A., and Gail Bentivegna. "Labor Agreements in the Hospital Industry: A Study in Trends in Collective Bargaining Output, 1974–1981." In *Handbook of Health Care Personnel Management,* ed. Norman Metzger. Rockville, Md.: Aspen Systems Corp., 1981. Pp. 529–36.

Juris, Hervey A., and Peter Feuille. *Police Unionism.* Lexington, Mass.: D. C. Heath, 1973.

Juris, Hervey A., and Charles Maxey. "The Impact of Hospital Unionism." Prepared for National Center for Health Services Research, U.S. Department of Health and Human Services. Unpublished. 1981.

Juris, Hervey A., and Myron Roomkin. "The Shrinking Perimeter: Unions and Collective Bargaining in Manufacturing." In *The Shrinking Perimeter,* eds. Hervey Juris and Myron Roomkin. Lexington, Mass.: D. C. Heath, 1980. Pp. 197–211.

Kaufman, Bruce E. "The Propensity to Strike in American Manufacturing." *Proceedings of the 31st Annual Meeting, Industrial Relations Research Association,* 1978. Madison, Wis.: IRRA, 1979. Pp. 419–26.

Kemerer, Frank R., and J. Victor Baldridge. *Unions on Campus.* San Francisco: Jossey-Bass, 1975.

Klauser, Jack E. "Public Sector Impasse Resolution in Hawaii." *Industrial Relations* 16 (October 1977): pp. 283–89.

Kochan, Thomas A. "A Theory of Multilateral Collective Bargaining in City Governments." *Industrial and Labor Relations Review* 27 (July 1974): pp. 525–42.

———. "City Government Bargaining: A Path Analysis." *Industrial Relations* 14 (February 1975): pp. 90–101.

———. "Dynamics of Dispute Resolution in the Public Sector." In *Public-Sector Bargaining,* eds. Benjamin Aaron, Joseph R. Grodin, and James L. Stern. IRRA Series. Washington: Bureau of National Affairs, 1979a. Pp. 150–90.

———. "How American Workers View Labor Unions." *Monthly Labor Review* 102 (April 1979b): pp. 15–22.

———. *Collective Bargaining and Industrial Relations.* Homewood, Ill.: Richard D. Irwin, 1980.

Kochan, Thomas A., and Jean Baderschneider. "Dependence on Impasse Procedures: Police and Firefighters in New York State." *Industrial and Labor Relations Review* 31 (July 1978): pp. 431–49.

Kochan, Thomas A., Mordehai Mironi, Ronald G. Ehrenberg, Jean Baderschneider, and Todd Jick. *Dispute Resolution Under Fact-Finding and Arbitration: An Empirical Evaluation.* New York: American Arbitration Association, 1979.

Kochan, Thomas A., and Richard N. Block. "An Inter-industry Analysis of Bargaining Outcomes: Preliminary Evidence from Two-Digit Industries." *Quarterly Journal of Economics* 41 (August 1977): pp. 431–52.

Kochan, Thomas A., and Todd Jick. "The Public Sector Mediation Process. A Theory and Empirical Examination." *Journal of Conflict Resolution* 22 (June 1978): pp. 209–35.

Kochan, Thomas A., and Hoyt N. Wheeler. "Municipal Collective Bargaining: A Model and Analysis of Bargaining Outcomes." *Industrial and Labor Relations Review* 29 (October 1975): pp. 46–66.

Kolb, Deborah M. "Roles Mediators Play: State and Federal Practice." *Industrial Relations* 20 (Winter 1981): pp. 1–17.

Koziara, Karen S. "Landrum-Griffin and Union President Turnover: Criticism and Comment." *Industrial Relations* 11 (February 1972): pp. 118–19.

Kressel, Kenneth. *Labor Mediation: An Exploratory Survey.* Albany, N.Y.: Association of Labor Relations Agencies. Unpublished mimeo. 1972.

Krislov, Joseph, and John F. Mead. "Labor-Management Attitudes Toward Mediation." *Personnel Journal* 51 (February 1972): pp. 86–94.

Leigh, Duane. "Unions and Nonwage Racial Discrimination." *Industrial and Labor Relations Review* 32 (July 1979): pp. 439–50.

Leigh, J. Paul. "The Effects of Union Membership on Absence from Work Due to Illness." *Journal of Labor Research* 2 (Fall 1981): pp. 329–36.

Levi, Margaret. *Bureaucratic Insurgency: The Case of Police Unions.* Lexington, Mass.: D. C. Heath, 1977.

Levin, Edward, and Daniel V. DeSantis. *Mediation, An Annotated Bibliography.* Ithaca: New York State School of Industrial and Labor Relations, Cornell University, 1978.

Lincoln, James R. "Community Structure and Industrial Conflict: An Analysis of Strike Activity in SMSAs." *American Sociological Review* 43 (April 1978): pp. 199–220.

Lipsky, David B., and Thomas A. Barocci. "Final-Offer Arbitration and Public-Safety Employees: The Massachusetts Experience." *Proceedings of the 30th Annual Winter Meeting, Industrial Relations Research Association,* 1977. Madison, Wis.: IRRA, 1978. Pp. 65–80.

Lipsky, David B., and Henry S. Farber. "The Composition of Strike Activity in the Construction Industry." *Industrial and Labor Relations Review* 29 (April 1976): pp. 388–404.

Lodge, George, and Karen Henderson. "United States of America." In *Towards Industrial Democracy: Europe, Japan and the United States,* ed. Benjamin C. Roberts. Montclair, N.J.: Allanheld, Osmun, 1979. Pp. 240–82.

Loewenberg, J. Joseph. "Compulsory Arbitration for Police and Fire Fighters in Pennsylvania in 1968." *Industrial and Labor Relations Review* 23 (April 1970): pp. 367–79.

Long, Gary, and Peter Feuille. "Final-Offer Arbitration: 'Sudden Death' in Eugene." *Industrial and Labor Relations Review* 27 (January 1974): pp. 186–203.

Lumsden, Keith, and Graig Peterson. "The Effect of Right-to-Work Laws on Unionization in the U.S." *Journal of Political Economy* 83 (December 1975): pp. 1237–48.

Maggiolo, Walter A. *Techniques of Mediation in Labor Disputes.* Dobbs Ferry, N.Y.: Oceana Publications, 1971.

McCormick, Mary. "A Functional Analysis of Interest Arbitration in New York City Muncipal Government, 1968–1975." *Proceedings of the 29th Annual Winter Meeting, Industrial Relations Research Association,* 1976. Madison, Wis.: IRRA, 1977. Pp. 249–57.

McKelvey, Jean T. "Fact Finding in Public Employment Disputes: Promise or Illusion." *Industrial and Labor Relations Review* 22 (July 1969): pp. 528–43.

McLean, Robert A. "Coalition Bargaining and Strike Activity in the Electrical Equipment Industry, 1950–1974." *Industrial and Labor Relations Review* 30 (April 1977): pp. 356–63.

———. "Interindustry Differences in Strike Activity." *Industrial Relations* 18 (Winter 1979): pp. 103–109.

McLennan, Kenneth, and Michael H. Moskow. "Multilateral Bargaining in the Public Sector." *Proceedings of the 21st Annual Winter Meeting, Industrial Relations Research Association,* 1968. Madison, Wis.: IRRA, 1969. Pp. 31–40.

Miller, Richard U., Brian E. Becker, and Edward B. Krinsky. *The Impact of Collective Bargaining on Hospitals.* New York: Praeger, 1979.

Mitchell, Daniel J. B. "The Impact of Collective Bargaining on Compensation in the Public Sector." In *Public-Sector Bargaining,* eds. Benjamin Aaron, Joseph R. Grodin, and James L. Stern. IRRA Series. Washington: Bureau of National Affairs, 1979. Pp. 118–49.

Moore, William, and Robert Newman. "On the Prospects for American Trade Union Growth: A Cross-Section Analysis." *Review of Economics and Statistics* 57 (November 1975): pp. 435–45.

Morris, Charles J. "The Role of Interest Arbitration in a Collective Bargaining System." *Industrial Relations Law Journal* 1 (Fall 1976): pp. 427–531.

Nash, Al. "Local 1199, Drug and Hospital Union: An Analysis of the Normative and Institutional Orders of a Complex Organization." *Human Relations* 27 (June 1974): pp. 547–66.

Odewahn, Charles A. "Mediator in the Public Sector—A New Breed?" *Labor Law Journal* 23 (October 1972): pp. 643–48.

Odewahn, Charles A., and Joseph Krislov. "Contract Rejections: Testing the Explanatory Hypotheses." *Industrial Relations* 12 (October 1973): pp. 289–96.

Peach, David A., and E. Robert Livernash. *Grievance Initiation and Resolution.* Boston: Harvard University, 1974.

Pencavel, John H. "An Investigation into Industrial Strike Activity in Britain." *Economica* 35 (August 1970): pp. 239–56.

Perry, Charles R. "Teacher Bargaining: The Experience in Nine Systems." *Industrial and Labor Relations Review* 33 (October 1979): pp. 3–17.

Perry, Charles R., and Wesley A. Wildman. *The Impact of Negotiations in Public Education.* Worthington, Ohio: Charles A. Jones Publishing Co., 1970.

Perry, James L. "Public Policy and Public Employee Strikes." *Industrial Relations* 16 (October 1977): pp. 273–82.

Perry, James L., and Leslie J. Berkes. "Predicting Local Government Strike Activity: An Exploratory Analysis." *Western Political Quarterly* 30 (December 1977): pp. 513–27.

Peterson, Donald J. "Union Prediction in Arbitration." *Labor Law Journal* 21 (December 1970): pp. 787–93.

Pichler, Joseph A., and H. Gordon Fitch. "And Women Must Weep: The NLRB as Film Critic." *Industrial and Labor Relations Review* 28 (April 1975): pp. 395–410.

Piore, Michael J. "Unions and Politics." In *The Shrinking Perimeter*, eds. Hervey Juris and Myron Roomkin. Lexington, Mass.: D. C. Heath, 1980. Pp. 173–94.

Ponak, Allen M., and Mark Thompson. "Faculty Attitudes and the Scope of Bargaining." *Industrial Relations* 18 (Winter 1979): pp. 97–102.

Popular, John J. "Labor-Management Relations: U.S. Mediators Try to Build Common Objectives." *World of Work Report* 1 (September 1976): pp. 1–3.

Robins, Eva. "Some Comparisons of Mediation in the Public and Private Sector." In *Collective Bargaining in Government: Readings and Cases*, eds. J. Joseph Loewenberg and Michael H. Moskow. Englewood Cliffs, N.J.: Prentice-Hall, 1972. Pp. 323–29.

Roomkin, Myron. "Union Structure, Internal Control, and Strike Activity." *Industrial and Labor Relations Review* 29 (January 1976): pp. 198–217.

———. "Book Review—Union Representation Elections: Law and Reality." *Case Western Reserve Law Review* 27 (Summer 1977): pp. 1056–61.

———. "The Performance of the Ashenfelter and Johnson Strike Model." Unpublished mimeo. Undated.

Roomkin, Myron, and Hervey A. Juris. "Unions in the Traditional Sectors: The Midlife Passage of the Labor Movement." *Proceedings of the 31st Annual Meeting, Industrial Relations Research Association*, 1978. Madison, Wis.: IRRA, 1979. Pp. 212–22.

Ross, Jerome H. "Federal Mediation in the Public Sector." *Monthly Labor Review* 99 (February 1976): pp. 414–45.

Sandver, Marcus H. "Predictors of Outcomes in NLRB Certification Elections." Paper presented at the Midwest Meetings. The Academy of Management, 1980.

Sandver, Marcus Hart, and Herbert G. Heneman III. "Analysis and Prediction of Top National Union Officers' Total Compensation." *Academy of Management Journal* 23 (September 1980): pp. 534–43.

Scearce, James F., and Lucretia Dewey Tanner. "Health Care Bargaining: The FMCS Experience." *Labor Law Journal* 27 (July 1976): pp. 387–98.

Schmidman, John. *Unions in Postindustrial Society.* University Park: Pennsylvania State University, 1979.

Schmidt, Stuart M., and Thomas A. Kochan. "Conflict: Toward Conceptual Clarity." *Administrative Science Quarterly* 17 (September 1972): pp. 368–70.

Scoville, James G. "Influences on Unionization in the U.S. in 1966." *Industrial Relations* 10 (October 1971): pp. 354–61.

Shalev, Michael. "Trade Unionism and Economic Analysis—The Case of Industrial Conflict." *Journal of Labor Research* 1 (Spring 1980): pp. 133–73.

Shapiro, Fred C. "Profiles: Mediator, Theodore Kheel." *The New Yorker* 46 (August 1, 1970): pp. 36–44+.

Shorey, John. "The Size of the Work Unit and Strike Incidence." *Journal of Industrial Economics* 23 (March 1975): pp. 175–88.

Simkin, William E. *Mediation and the Dynamics of Collective Bargaining.* Washington: Bureau of National Affairs, 1971.

Slichter, Sumner H., James J. Healy, and E. Robert Livernash. *The Impact of Collective Bargaining on Management.* Washington: Brookings Institution, 1960.

Snowbarger, Marvin, and Sam Pintz. "Landrum-Griffin and Union President Turnover." *Industrial Relations* 9 (October 1970): pp. 475–76.

Snyder, David. "Industrial Setting and Industrial Conflict: Comparative Analyses of France, Italy and the United States." *American Sociological Review* 40 (June 1975): pp. 259–78.

———. "Early North American Strikes: A Reinterpretation." *Industrial and Labor Relations Review* 30 (April 1977): pp. 325–41.

Stanley, David T. *Managing Local Government Under Union Pressure.* Washington: Brookings Institution, 1972.

Stern, James L., Charles M. Rehmus, J. Joseph Loewenberg, Hirschel Kasper, and Barbara D. Dennis. *Final-Offer Arbitration.* Lexington: Mass.: D. C. Heath, 1975.

Stern, Robert N. "Intermetropolitan Patterns of Strike Frequency." *Industrial and Labor Relations Review* 29 (January 1976): pp. 218–35.

———. "Methodological Issues in Quantitative Strike Analysis." *Industrial Relations* 17 (February 1978): pp. 32–42.

Stieber, Jack. *Public Employee Unionism.* Washington: Brookings Institution, 1973.

Strauss, George. "Union Government in the U.S.: Research Past and Future." *Industrial Relations* 16 (May 1977): pp. 215–42.

Swint, Michael J., and William B. Nelson. "The Influence of Negotiators' Self-Interest on the Duration of Strikes." *Industrial and Labor Relations Review* 32 (October 1978): pp. 56–66.

Thompson, Mark, and James Cairnie. "Compulsory Arbitration: The Case of British Columbia Teachers." *Industrial and Labor Relations Review* 27 (October 1973): pp. 3–17.

———. "Analyzing Compulsory Arbitration Experiences: The Role of Personal Preference—Reply." *Industrial and Labor Relations Review* 28 (April 1975): pp. 432–38.

Treckel, Karl F. "The Unionization of Union Organizers and International Representatives." *Labor Law Journal* 22 (May 1971): pp. 266–77.

Troy, Leo. "American Unions and Their Wealth." *Industrial Relations* 14 (May 1975): pp. 134–44.

Usery, William J. "A More Activist Approach by Mediators." *Monthly Labor Review* 96 (September 1973): p. 59.

Walker, J. Malcolm, and John J. Lawler. "Dual Unions and Political Processes in Organizations." *Industrial Relations* 18 (Winter 1979); pp. 32–43.

Warner, Malcolm. "An Organizational Profile of the Small Trade Union: A Composite Case Study." *Industrial Relations Journal* 3 (Winter 1972a): pp. 51–64.

———. "Trade Unions and Organizational Theory: A Preliminary Analysis of Union Environment, Structure and Performance." *Journal of Industrial Relations* 14 (March 1972b): pp. 47–62.

———. "Unions as Complex Organizations: Strategy, Structure and the Need for Administrative Innovation." *Relations Industrielles/Industrial Relations* 30 (April 1975): pp. 43–59.

Wheeler, Hoyt N. "Closed-Offer: Alternative to Final-Offer Selection." *Industrial Relations* 16 (October 1977): pp. 298–305.

CHAPTER 9

Appraising a Decade's Research: An Overview

THOMAS A. KOCHAN
Massachusetts Institute of Technology

DANIEL J. B. MITCHELL
University of California, Los Angeles

LEE DYER
Cornell University

If it is impossible to review a decade's research in a single volume, then it is clearly also impossible to summarize all of the key developments in a single chapter. Therefore, in this final chapter we will highlight a number of the key points raised by the authors in the previous chapters, compare the record established in the 1970s with the images we have of research from earlier time periods, and pose a set of challenges for industrial relations researchers to consider as they shape their research agendas in the decade ahead.

International and Comparative Industrial Relations

It is perhaps fitting that we start the volume with a chapter on international and comparative industrial relations research since this topic is potentially the broadest in scope of any of the subjects covered. It is also fitting since the cycle of activity and research output in this area appears to reflect what at least some observers (Strauss and Feuille 1978) saw as representative of industrial relations research in general. That is, following the high level of activity described by Scoville in the early 1960s, the volume and visibility of international and comparative research declined through the mid- to late-1970s. In recent years there appears to be a budding revival at work. The relative importance of topic areas in the international field also changed and mirrors a message driven home in other chapters of this book. Broad issues concerning the theory of the labor movement and industrial conflict were surpassed in importance by issues involving economic development and trade policies, workers' participation in managerial decision-making, and the behavior and effects of multinational organizations.

Still another area in comparative research that has been growing in recent years has been comparative wage determination. Econometric studies have compared international differences in the sensitivity of wage inflation to various explanatory factors. Institutional differences between the U.S.—with its widespread use of multiyear union contracts—and other countries (where multiyear contracts are rare) have received increased attention from labor economists.

It is likely that the current awareness of the effects of worldwide competition, the interdependence of national economies, and the popularized comparisons of differences in national systems of industrial relations and management processes will further spur interest in comparative and international industrial relations research. Indeed, the recent flurry of popular books on Japan will likely give rise to additional and perhaps more detailed analysis of the diversity of industrial relations systems that exist around the world. The debate over whether industrial relations practices can be exported is clearly alive and well in the popular press. It may well reemerge in the 1980s as an important topic of analytical research.

Wage Determination and Public Policy

Flanagan and Mitchell point out that the decade of the 1970s saw strong theoretical advances in neoclassical human capital theory and its application to various aspects of wage behavior through the use of larger and better data sets. While the evidence accumulated through this work allows the authors to reach a number of substantive conclusions regarding various "stylized facts" about wage differentials, some things, such as the stability of wages over recent business cycles, remain to be explained. Presumably, as the authors suggest, this might be done through a better integration of neoclassical and institutional or segmented labor market theory. Flanagan and Mitchell, like many others, see implicit contracts theory as a promising avenue of research for explaining some of these stylized facts and integrating neoclassical and institutional theories. One question that must be asked is whether implicit contracts theory is really a new idea or simply a new term for describing ever-evolving employer personnel policies and collective bargaining practices. That is, employers and employees continuously or periodically adjust the mix of compensation and working conditions to meet their particular needs and maintain their employment relationship over time. Just as practices adjust with a lag to changing external pressures, managerial fads, and employee aspirations, the characteristics of the efficient but implicit contract that economists seek to model will also change over time. Economists will then be forced to live with the same amount of change as do other social scientists who study compensation practices.

As Flanagan and Mitchell note, wage determination researchers, like those in other areas, will respond to shifting public policy interests and major economic events. Thus, we might expect to see research on public-sector wage determination make a comeback in the mid-1980s as observers attempt to sort out the effects of the cutbacks in local and state government revenue on wages, employment, and the quality and quantity of public services. New estimates of the elasticity of public-sector labor demand will be needed to replace the estimates obtained during the period of relative stability and moderate employment growth of the late 1960s. In this area, as in private-sector wage research, we are likely to see a new stream of studies that debate whether or not the recession and other economic and political events of the early 1980s produced a discontinuity in wage-setting practices and outcomes in union and nonunion sectors. Here the analytic techniques Flanagan and Mitchell discussed as appropriate for estimating the effects of incomes policies on the wage structure and on wage changes will undoubtedly prove helpful.

Perhaps no area is more ripe for a new theoretical leap forward (or, to put it another way, there is little perceptible net return to another study using the conventional methods and models of the 1970s) than the effects of unions on wages. The exhaustive reviews and critiques of this research published in recent years all show the need for a paradigm shift that is more firmly grounded in the dynamic adjustments unions and employers make over time under collective bargaining. Once the theoretical breakthrough is made, we can then again return to debates over the econometric specifications most appropriate for testing the theory. In the absence of a theoretical advance, even improvements in research design (such as more longitudinal analysis) are not likely to add much new insight into the existing body of evidence.

Employment and Training Policy

Barocci describes employment and training research in the 1970s as "an implosion," that is, a turning in on the major theoretical and policy problems by concentrating on the methodological issues relevant to evaluating the costs and benefits of different government programs. While progress has been made in clarifying what is *not* acceptable in evaluating these programs, consensus has yet to be achieved around either preferred methods of analysis or the effects of various programs. Thus, in a cost-benefit sense we are probably somewhat better off after spending millions of tax dollars for evaluation research in this area, but just how much better is hard to tell.

An unfortunate characteristic of the manpower research that developed out of the active manpower policy era of the 1960s and 1970s was its failure to link evaluation research with the theoretical work on labor market behavior. For example, about the only place that theory intrudes on the evaluation studies is in the specification of control variables in earnings equations. Human capital models have dominated the choice of these variables. Yet we seldom ask what difference it makes to the design of employment and training policies whether one sees the behavior of workers and firms through the eyes of neoclassical labor market theory, segmented labor market theory, or some alternative perspective. What assumptions about the behavior of the firm and about human resources management policies and strategies are needed to guide an effective labor market policy? How does our employment and training policy fit into macroeconomic policies? How do we link the regulatory policies discussed in Olivia Mitchell's chapter to these employment and training policies?

These issues will take on increased importance in the 1980s. Current political decisions to cut back drastically on federal expenditures and to revamp the design of the employment and training system will force academics and would-be policy advisers to reargue the basic question of whether or not the U.S. economy requires an active employment and training policy. Answers to this question depend heavily on both one's theory of how labor markets work and empirical evidence supporting one's theory. Thus, the 1980s will likely be a time when we return to very basic theoretical and empirical issues in this area.

Given the ambivalent conclusions reached in the evaluation research of the 1970s, it is unlikely that we will want to return to the same programs. Nor are policy-makers likely to be very tolerant of arguments for more experimentation in order to determine which program alternative offers the greatest net benefits. Indeed, given the "implosion" of the 1970s, it is not clear that researchers can realistically promise that answers would be forthcoming if such an "experimental society" were to be started up again in the 1980s. Future policy-makers will be no more tolerant of arguments for "true experiments" rather than "quasi experiments" than their counterparts were in the past. But they will once again, as in the early 1960s, be searching for new ideas and strategies for lowering unemployment, improving the functioning of the labor market, and improving the employment and earnings experiences of the most disadvantaged individuals and groups. The question is: Will we as researchers be able to draw on current and/or previous research to provide theoretically and empirically grounded policy prescriptions? Now may be the time to begin the debate so that, for once, researchers lead politicians in the search for answers.

The Labor Market Effects of Federal Regulation

Research on the effects of federal regulation of workplace practices followed the theoretical and methodological pattern established in other areas of labor economics research in the 1970s by adopting a neoclassical theoretical framework and relying heavily on econometric techniques. Olivia Mitchell reviews the results of a decade of this research. Policies arose out of a concern for workers affected by specific problems of discrimination, safety and health, and pension insecurity, and they followed a strategy of imposing specific restrictions on the behavior of employers. The evaluators of these policies, on the other hand, generally pressed beyond the specific problems to assess the effects of the policies on standard employment and earnings outcomes. The theoretical focus generally was one that asked: How would these policies play themselves out in a competitive labor market? How do they actually influence employment and earnings outcomes? Do they influence the specific labor market outcomes to which they were addressed? On balance, are their specific accomplishments of sufficient social benefit to balance any social and economic costs they may impose? Alongside these standard neoclassical evaluations were a number of studies that looked at legal questions and the response to the new regulations by employers, unions, and other labor market institutions. Unfortunately, there were few studies that integrated both approaches.

By the end of the decade, therefore, we find that we have two parallel sets of literature on most of these regulatory policies. One is based on economic theory and tends to focus on the cost side of the regulations, while the other is more legal and institutionally based and explores the benefits of these regulations and their consequences for due process.

Some encouraging signs of a movement toward a better mix of economic and institutional approaches are evident in those studies that attempt to use micro (organizational and/or individual) data sets.

Personnel/Human Resource Management

Personnel research did not disappear during the 1970s as George Strauss predicted a decade ago. Instead it reemerged under a modified name, "personnel/human resource management." Indeed, if the number of new scholars and job openings at major universities is any indication, this specialization is currently a growth sector within industrial relations. What accounts for the renewed interest? It probably has little to do with the theoretical or empirical advances in personnel research in the 1970s. Considerable progress was made during the decade in sharpening the conceptualization and measurement of standard personnel outcome variables and their correlates, as Dyer and Schwab point out. But personnel researchers tended to take a very micro (individual) and static approach to their topic despite the fact that its resurgence was stimulated primarily by changes in macro organizational and external forces.

Among these were increased pressures for productivity improvements and reduced labor costs, more and more rigorously enforced government regulations, the tightness of labor markets for executive, technical, and some highly skilled blue-collar workers, and the changing demographic characteristics of the labor force.

Thus, personnel/human resource management research lagged developments in management practice and public policy in the 1970s. While some research was done on the effects of regulatory policies such as OSHA, ERISA, and EEO, with few exceptions (most notably in the selection area), this work generally did not find its way into the journals most closely identified with the personnel field. In addition, while there is a good deal of discussion of the growing importance of human resource planning and policy development, especially within large firms, careful studies of the nature, extent, and effects of these planning activities and policies are only now beginning to appear (Foulkes 1980, Walker 1980, Dyer 1982). From all indications then, the 1980s should be an exciting time for personnel researchers *if* they can shift their attention away from analyses of purely individual behavior and simple relationships among two sets of well-worn variables, and out of the laboratory. What is needed is broader gauged research that examines the effects of external developments, organizational strategies and policies, and traditional personnel policies and relates them to important personnel/human resource management outcomes.

A challenge lies in making research on these broader issues theoretically well-grounded and empirically well-designed. The danger is that we will return to the prescriptive literature of the 1950s and 1960s and attempt to enumerate various "principles" of personnel/human resource management without a solid theoretical or empirical foundation. In the 1970s important strides were made in strengthening the quality of research on personnel issues. The next step is to build on this base while adopting a more macro perspective.

Labor economists are already moving in this direction. Examples of recent or current work of this nature include studies of the effects of seniority and ability on earnings and promotion probabilities within the firm (Medoff and Abraham 1981), studies of the effects of affirmative compliance activities on turnover rates (Osterman

1982), and studies of "internal labor markets" of white-collar and other professional occupations.

New legal developments should also be attracting the attention of personnel researchers. Until recently the American legal system has held that employees could be terminated "at will." Except for certain proscribed motivations, such as racial discrimination, employers were free to modify the terms of employment or sever the employee-employer relationship in the absence of a union contract. Nonunion employees, in short, had no remedies of due process if they felt they were mistreated. During the late 1970s and early 1980s, some courts began to find requirements of due process for nonunion workers implicit in various public policies or in the statements made by employers in personnel handbooks. There have also been periodic suggestions that European-style due process requirements should be imposed by law on employers. Such changes, whether made by statute or court interpretation, could have a profound impact on the nonunion sector and on the conduct of personnel management.

In short, the 1980s will see a challenge to the individual level, psychology-based foundation of personnel research by those addressing similar questions from an economic theory or organizational strategy base. If traditional personnel researchers do not take account of this other work, George Strauss's prediction, while a bit off in timing, may prove to be correct after all.

What is more likely to develop, however, is more diversity in the research and types of researchers working on personnel problems. Some will be psychologically based and will continue to focus on individual outcomes. Some will be labor economists who will look across firms using more aggregate data or existing demographic and other personnel data sets contained within the files of large firms. Still others will take a managerial strategy and policy point of view and will focus on personnel/human resource management planning and on outcomes that mix individual, subunit, and organizational data. The result could be a decade of exciting debate and ferment within the broad field of personnel/human resource management.

Organizational Behavior

The 1970s was a decade in which many people called for a

closer integration of labor-management relations and organizational behavior. Indeed, in the middle of the decade, the IRRA devoted an entire volume to reviewing the viability of such a linkage and the progress made up to that time (Strauss, Miles, Snow, and Tannenbaum 1974). Driving this work was the view that behavioral theories and methods could broaden the perspectives of industrial relations researchers and strengthen their empirical research methods. While behavioral theories and research methods had a long history of application in the personnel field, at the beginning of the 1970s it was still a rather unique (many at the time would have said misguided) piece of research that attempted to apply these theories and methods to research on collective bargaining and union-management relations. Brett and Hammer demonstrate in their chapter that this is no longer the case. We now have available a wide range of studies that cross the boundary between traditional industrial relations topics and organizational issues using a mixture of methodologies from both fields. Clearly, the call for researchers to span the boundary between organizational behavior and labor-management relations was answered during the 1970s.

The decade began with the expectation that the open systems theories of organization developed in the 1960s, which stress concepts such as the environment, technology, structure, decision-making, conflict, and innovation, would eventually be linked in a more clear-cut way to micro studies of group behavior, motivation, supervision, organizational change and development, etc. This, however, did not occur. Nor did the enthusiasm for quantitative analysis of organizations (also a product of the 1960s) continue to grow. By the mid-1970s a new school of qualitative analysis led by ethnographers was gaining popularity in organizational behavior.

Instead of building incrementally on the ideas of the 1960s, organizational behavior exploded in a rather scatter-shot fashion in the 1970s. It was a decade in which the leading theorists discovered metaphors and, it seemed, the more abstruse or arcane the metaphor the better. Weick, one of the advocates of the use of metaphors, provides a partial summary and illustration of these developments: "Metaphors are abundant in organizational theory; organizations have variously been portrayed as anarchies . . . , seesaws . . . , space stations . . . , marketplaces . . . , and data processing schedules"

(Weick 1979, p. 47). To this list could be added "loosely coupled systems," "garbage can models," "socially constructed realities," "ecological systems subject to natural selection processes," "political systems," "social networks," etc. Each metaphor implied a different view of the nature of organizations and, therefore, a different approach to building and testing organizational theories and deriving prescriptions for organizational actors or external agents interested in controlling the behavior of organizations. The result of all of this was that by the end of the decade the field of organizational behavior seemed to have lost its momentum and its sense of purpose.

Because of these developments, industrial relations researchers must now be more selective and informed consumers of and contributors to organizational behavior research. It is no longer fair to challenge students interested in both areas to achieve a more complete integration. Instead, researchers are now forced to choose from among the various schools of organizational behavior the one(s) that appears to make the most sense for gaining insights into industrial relations problems and concerns. For their chapter, Brett and Hammer chose macro theories that emphasize the political aspects of organizations and micro models that emphasize the social processing of information, as well as models of worker participation, decision-making, and bargaining. They also stress quantitative research while noting the power of qualitative case and ethnographic studies for generating new hypotheses or developing new theoretical insights.

Brett and Hammer point out that the theoretical integration of organization behavior and industrial relations that has occurred has been both quite selective and mutually beneficial. Organizational behaviorists who see organizations as political systems have drawn considerably on the views of conflict, bargaining, power, and formal systems of participation developed in industrial relations. In turn, industrial relations researchers have used the political perspective to round out their understanding of collective bargaining and various efforts to supplement bargaining with more direct forms of worker participation.

Unlike the chapters in this volume that are rooted in economic theory, those emphasizing the behavioral tradition focus less on public policy than on deriving implications for decision-makers within management and labor organizations. While this partly reflects a difference in levels of analysis, it also reflects differences in the traditions guiding research in these two areas. Yet there is some evidence that each group is trying to extend its reach to speak to the other's audience. Behavioral studies of conflict resolution and impasse procedures or of formal systems of participation are increasingly addressing issues of public policy as well as private practice. Economic analysis of implicit contracts between employees and employers, organizational responses to government regulations, and the effects of private and public training programs are increasingly reaching into organizations. Perhaps now is the time to examine the links between public policy, economic analysis, and organizational behavior research just as the 1970s was the time for linking organizational behavior and collective bargaining research.

Labor History

During the 1970s the industrial relations community was treated to a decade of debate over the appropriate research paradigm for the study of labor history. It will be remembered as the decade during which the Wisconsin School historians who sought to understand labor history by studying the behavior and evolution of the labor union were challenged, and some would say overtaken, by social historians who attempt to document and interpret the history of workers rather than the history of their unions. As in most intellectual debates, the early entrants into this fray emphasized differences in political views, theory and method, and disciplinary underpinnings. The social historians generally reflect a more radical point of view, are rooted in social rather than economic history, and are more strongly identified with history than with economics or industrial relations. Later in the decade representatives of the old and new schools joined the debate at professional meetings and in journal reviews. By the end of the 1970s the accomplishments of the new school were being reappraised and the potential for some type of synthesis was being explored. Interestingly, the synthesis appears to be occurring around the workplace as the meeting ground between the social environment of workers and management and union institutions and policies.

Grossman and Moye set high expectations against which the accomplishments of the social historians are to be judged. They conclude that these expectations have not yet been met and to meet them in the future will require both greater synthesis of the two approaches and some new directions as well. They point out that the next decade will require a number of choices as labor historians seek not only to determine the appropriate balance between the old and the new labor history, but also to address issues that have been given inadequate attention by both schools. In the balancing category, for example, historians will need to decide whether to bring economic history back into the field. Grossman and Moye argue that there is an inconsistency between the new school's intention to conceptualize the workers in their complete environment (not just the institutional environment) and the crowding out of detailed consideration of economic issues. If economic history makes a comeback, historians will also need to determine whether they wish to continue to draw on traditional research methods or embrace the cliometrics methodology that has gained popularity in other areas of economic history.

The authors offer two subject areas as examples of topics that have fallen between the cracks of the new and old schools and which, they believe, deserve greater attention in the years ahead. They particularly stress the need for careful historical studies of public policy issues. In a world where so much analysis of labor policy focuses on recent or current experiences, this type of historical work would surely serve as a useful complement. Indeed, a number of recent works are in this vein, such as the study of the development and evolution of the National Labor Relations Board (Gross 1981) and the ongoing work of Grossman (1973) in cataloging the history of policies and leadership at the U.S. Department of Labor. Jacoby's (1982) current work on the history of the law of employment contracts in the U.S. and Great Britain represents an even more direct example of the work that is being called for here.

Other areas that lie between the new and the old school involve the history of the organization of work, the effects of technology at the workplace, and the role of managerial practices as control devices and strategies. This work tends to take on a more radical perspective (Braverman 1974, Edwards 1979, Hill 1981, Sabel 1982) and therefore should find a comfortable niche within the new school of labor history. Yet it is also consistent with the early work of the Wisconsin School since Commons's own approach was to try to understand the interaction of changing markets, technology, and managerial practices and their effects on workers and their unions. Perhaps this work, along with the work on labor-management cooperation (Moye 1980, Jacoby 1981) will serve to put many of the current developments in industrial relations in a more informed historical perspective.

It might also be noted that while the Wisconsin School focused too narrowly on unions, the new historians tend to focus narrowly on the history of blue-collar production workers. This may have been acceptable given the nature of the labor force in the 19th and early 20th century; however, if the history of workers after 1950 is to be written, it is clear that scholars will have to come to grips with the experiences, aspirations, and organizational contexts of white-collar, professional, technical, and managerial workers (not to mention college professors). The blue-collar worker is a shrinking minority in the labor force and can no longer be used to characterize the "typical" American worker. To understand the history of contemporary workers, the diversity of occupations, status groups, and demographic characteristics of the labor force will need to be taken into account.

During the 1980s, labor historians might usefully consider lessons from the past as insights for the present. For example, the current interest in quality of working life and worker participation in management has earlier precedents. Although the labels used for these concepts were different in the past, the concepts themselves are not new. What can be learned about the economic and social conditions that cause revivals of these ideas? A number of nonunion employers have adopted notions of quality of working life and "Theory Z" as alternatives to unionization. To what extent can these management strategies be compared to the "employee representation plans" and "company unions" of the 1920s and 1930s?

While the social historians can be criticized for failing to produce a synthesis by the early 1980s, this criticism must be tempered by the fact that the field is still emerging. The criticism will be more telling if it is still valid in 1990. If the field is to mature to the point where a better synthesis of its basic ideas is evident, its early contributors will have to demonstrate the same loyalty and long-standing commitment to their ideas and points of view that was the hallmark of the generation of scholars they now so roundly criticize. Their ability to continue to advance their new paradigm will determine whether they have mounted a lasting challenge to the institutionalists or merely represent a passing fad. Put another way, we have a number of years to wait to see if any of these new scholars can make as clear and lasting an imprint on our thinking about labor history as did the best of their precursors, such as Commons, Perlman, and Taft.

Unions and Collective Bargaining

The 1970s are described by Roomkin and Juris as the decade in which researchers studying unions and collective bargaining searched for a stronger scientific and analytic base. Model-building and quantitative methods were applied to a broad array of the traditional issues in this field identified earlier by the institutionalists. As a result, significant advances were made in the study of such diverse issues as union growth, the propensity of individual workers to join unions, strikes, dispute-resolution procedures, and the outcomes and effects of collective bargaining. By the end of the decade, therefore, more precise and empirically grounded statements could be made about such things as why unions grew more rapidly in some periods than in others, how aggregate strike rates vary in relation to changes in economic conditions, and whether or how mediation, fact-finding, conventional arbitration, and final-offer arbitration affect strikes, dependence on third parties, and wage and compensation levels.

These empirical advances did not, however, provide answers to the "big picture" questions that have always been central to the study of unions and collective bargaining. Questions about the future of the American labor movement, the viability and social utility of the U.S. collective bargaining system, or the relevance and effectiveness of the National Labor Relations Act are as open to debate now as they were before the empirical revolutions of the 1970s. It is clear that addressing these and other "big picture" questions will require a blending of the model-building and empirical advances of the 1970s with a more thorough appreciation and use of the historical/institutional methods of the earlier generation.

Indeed, this type of blending may be the next logical development in the evolution of collective bargaining research. The model-building/empirical emphasis of the 1970s developed during what might have been the final stage in the incremental evolution and maturation of the post-World War II system of collective bargaining. Thus, it was appropriate for researchers to concentrate on explaining across-sectional variations in what appeared to be a relatively stable, or incrementally changing, system. By all indications, the 1980s appears to be a time of greater upheaval and potential change. A debate is already shaping up among practitioners and scholars over whether the visible changes in collective bargaining and the less visible changes occurring at the workplace and in the higher level cloisters where union and employer strategies are formulated are only new variations on old patterns or structural adjustments that will transform in some fundamental and lasting ways the roles played by unions and collective bargaining.

Roomkin and Juris suggest a viable way for researchers to address these questions without discarding the advances in research methodology. They argue for more systematic attention to the effects of time, age, and maturity in collective bargaining relationships. This in turn will require a mixing of quantitative longitudinal research with a well-informed historical perspective. The key questions for researchers will be whether the aging of the American collective bargaining system has gone beyond the stage of maturity to one of atrophy or whether the current readjustments will result in a renewal of collective bargaining and the labor movement in the 1980s. In short, the big picture is likely to reemerge as a central topic of interest to collective bargaining researchers, policy-makers, and practitioners alike in the years ahead.

Comparisons with Earlier Decades

Now that we have reviewed and commented on the points raised by the various authors, it might be well to consider a number of developments from earlier decades that did *not* appear to drive research in the 1970s.

There is no mention in any of the chapters of major contributions to a "grand" or "general" theory of industrial relations in the tradition of the work of Commons and his early generation of institutional economists or the more recent contributions of Dunlop (1958) and Kerr, Dunlop, Harbison, and Myers (1960). Similarly, there appeared little of the soul-searching over the scope of industrial relations as an academic discipline that occurred in the 1960s after the publication of the Dunlop and Kerr et al. books (although at the 1976 IRRA meetings there was some soul-searching *about* the Kerr et al. work). Indeed, the term "industrial relations theory" does not play an important role in research reviewed in any of the previous chapters. Instead, either the work was atheoretical or its theoretical focus shifted back to the basic disciplines closest to the problem areas covered.

Similarly, there were no major interdisciplinary research projects launched similar to the earlier contributions of the Illini City Study of the 1950s (Chalmers, Derber et al. 1954), the studies of *The Causes of Industrial Peace* (Golden and Parker 1955) sponsored by the National Planning Association, the encyclopedic Brookings Study of *The Impact of Collective Bargaining on Management* (Slichter, Healy, and Livernash 1960), or the original father of all mammoth research projects in industrial relations, *The Documentary History of American Labor* (Commons and Associates 1936).

No great intellectual debates will stick in the minds of students of the 1970s, such as the 1946 Machlup-Lester debate over the utility of marginal analysis, or the Ross-Dunlop debate of the 1940s and 1950s over whether trade union behavior can best be studied from a political or an economic perspective. Nor did the pressures of public events lead to the formation of any highly visible national study and/or research commission that approaches the stature of the Industrial Commissions of the early part of the century or, on a more limited scale, the various state-wide public-sector labor relations study committees of the 1960s such as the Taylor Committee in New York. The original National Manpower Policy Task Force continued under the sanitized name of the National Council on Employment Policy, and other employment policy commissions were active, such as the National Commission on Employment Policy, the National Commission on Unemployment Statistics, the Minimum Wage Study Commission, the President's Commission on Pension Policy, and the Select Commission on Immigration and Refugee Policy. None of these, however, had much visibility in the research community, nor did they affect public policy. Indeed, the major labor relations law debate of the 1970s—the Labor Law Reform Act of 1977–1978—took place devoid of any empirical or theoretical contributions (other than through expert testimony and personal lobbying). And, as Barocci noted, the major shifts in employment and training policy currently under consideration are evolving without significant input from the research community.

Even when we examine where industrial relations research, broadly defined, had its greatest impacts on practice, attention shifts from the work of the third-party neutrals trained in the days of the War Labor Board who worked on such projects as the Missile Sites Labor-Management Panel, the Armour Automation Commission, or various emergency boards set up under the Taft-Hartley or the Railway Labor Acts. While industrial relations researchers and practitioners did play prominent roles in administering incomes policies and in the various other tripartite committees that were activated in recent years, the professionals who may have been having the greatest long-term effect on practice were those trying to bring about new forms of labor-management relations through the applications of behavioral science theories and techniques. Some of these professionals were organizational development consultants attempting to introduce quality of working life programs in union and nonunion firms; others were the management consultants advising firms on how to remain nonunion or win representation election contests; still others were helping install and monitor equal employment opportunity and affirmative action compliance and upgrading personnel programs.

In summary, industrial relations research in the 1970s retreated from the national headlines, avoided the search for a grand theory, and instead sought refuge in the basic disciplines and concentrated on making more limited, but empirically better grounded, contributions to middle-range theories and public and managerial policies. Perhaps this reflected the decline of collective bargaining as an issue of national concern and visible importance. Where collective bargaining issues were important, they tended to be focused around the macroeconomic and incomes policies discussed in the Flanagan and Mitchell chapter. Perhaps it also reflected the relatively status quo, incremental adjustment pattern that characterized collective bargaining during the 1970s and up through the start of the 1980s (Freedman 1979, Kochan 1980, Mitchell 1981).

Will these trends continue, or are we likely to see major shifts in the patterns of the literature in the 1980s and a return to the broad theoretical issues and national level public policy debates? Clearly, no new paradigm or theory is likely to emerge in a social vacuum. Breakthroughs or major shifts in directions in industrial relations research have always been and will likely continue to be driven by the pressures of public events. If there appears to be renewed interest in the search for a new industrial relations paradigm or grand theory, it will be stimulated by a perception that the current environment and events are challenging the existing industrial relations system in some fundamental ways. If we see renewed national debate over industrial relations issues, it will be because the basic legal and institutional framework established in the New Deal legislation of the 1930s and elaborated upon with the regulations enacted since 1964 are now being reevaluated, modified in fundamental ways, or ignored. If we see the coming together of new versions of interdisciplinary coalitions such as the War Labor Board or the Slichter, Healy, Livernash team, it will be because practices have changed so fundamentally that our old descriptions (and therefore the prescriptions that followed them) are no longer accurate or relevant. This is one scenario for research in the 1980s.

On the other hand, we may see a continuation of the trends established in the 1970s: more efforts to improve research methods, more precise but limited theories, and retreat from industrial relations per se and back into the basic disciplines. If this occurs, the jurisdictional claim of industrial relations as the central depository of research on employment issues will be further eroded and its teaching and research bases within major universities will be further weakened.

The 1970s may well go down in the history of industrial relations research as the decade in which the baton was passed from that venerable generation of War Labor Board researchers and founders of the Industrial Relations Research Association to a younger group of researchers who have broadened the set of issues that fall into this field, applied different theories and methods, and in some cases challenged the established research paradigms. We leave it to the industrial relations researchers of the 1980s to determine the future course of the field and to the reviewers of the 1992 research volume to examine the record and render the next verdict.

References

Braverman, Harry. *Labor and Monopoly Capital.* New York: Monthly Review, 1974.

Chalmers, W. E., and others, Milton Derber, Coordinator. *Labor-Management Relations in Illini City,* 2 vols. Urbana: Institute of Labor and Industrial Relations, University of Illinois, 1954.

Commons, John R., and Associates. *History of Labor in the United States.* New York: Macmillan, 1936.

Dunlop, John T. *Industrial Relations Systems.* New York: Holt, Rinehart, and Winston, 1958.

Dyer, Lee. "Human Resource Planning." In *Personnel Management,* eds. K. Rowland and G. Ferris. Boston: Allyn and Bacon, 1982.

Edwards, Richard. *Contested Terrain.* New York: Basic Books, 1979.

Foulkes, Fred. *Personnel Policies in Large Non-Union Companies.* Englewood Cliffs, N.J.: Prentice-Hall, 1980.

Freedman, Audrey. *Managing Labor Relations.* New York: The Conference Board, 1979.

Golden, Clinton S., and Virginia D. Parker. *Causes of Industrial Peace Under Collective Bargaining.* New York: Harper & Bros., 1955.

Gross, James A. *The Reshaping of the National Labor Relations Board.* Albany: State University of New York Press, 1981.

Grossman, Jonathan. *The Department of Labor.* New York: Praeger, 1973.

Hill, Stephen. *Competition and Control at Work.* Cambridge, Mass.: MIT Press, 1981.

Jacoby, Sanford M. "The Origins of Internal Labor Markets in American Manufacturing Firms, 1910–1940." Ph.D. dissertation, University of California, Berkeley, 1981.

———. "The Duration of Indefinite Employment Contracts in the United States and England: An Historical Analysis." Working Paper, Institute of Industrial Relations, University of California, Los Angeles, January 1982.

Kerr, Clark, John T. Dunlop, Frederick Harbison, and Charles A. Myers. *Industrialism and Industrial Man.* Cambridge, Mass.: Harvard University Press, 1960.

Kochan, Thomas A. *Collective Bargaining and Industrial Relations: From Theory to Policy and Practice.* Homewood, Ill.: Irwin, 1980.

Medoff, James L., and Katharine G. Abraham. "Are Those Paid More Really More Productive? The Case of Experience." *Journal of Human Resources* 16 (Spring 1981): pp. 186–216.

Mitchell, Daniel J. B. "Collective Bargaining and the Economy." In *U.S. Industrial Relations 1950–1980: A Critical Assessment,* eds. Jack Stieber, Robert B. McKersie, and D. Quinn Mills. Madison, Wis.: Industrial Relations Research Association, 1981. Pp. 1–46.

Moye, William T. "Presidential Labor-Management Committees: Productive Failures." *Industrial nad Labor Relations Review* 34 (October 1980): pp. 51–66.

Osterman, Paul. "Affirmative Action and Equal Employment Opportunity: A Study of the Female Quit Rate." *Review of Economics and Statistics* (forthcoming 1982).

Sabel, Charles F. "The End of Fordism," Ch. 5 in *Work and Politics.* New York: Cambridge University Press, 1982.

Slichter, Sumner, James J. Healy, and E. Robert Livernash. *The Impact of Collective Bargaining on Management.* Washington: Brookings Institution, 1960.

Strauss, George, and Peter Feuille. "IR Research: A Critical Analysis." *Industrial Relations* 17 (October 1978): pp. 258–77.

Strauss, George, Raymond E. Miles, Charles C. Snow, and Arnold S. Tannenbaum, eds. *Organizational Behavior: Research and Issues.* Madison, Wis.: Industrial Relations Research Association, 1974.

Walker, James E. *Human Resource Planning.* New York: McGraw-Hill, 1980.

Weick, Karl E., Jr. *The Social Psychology of Organizing*, 2nd ed. Reading, Mass.: Addison-Wesley, 1979.